W9-DBD-389

FILM, TELEVISION, AND VIDEO PERIODICALS

GARLAND REFERENCE LIBRARY
OF THE HUMANITIES
(VOL. 1032)

FILM, TELEVISION, AND VIDEO PERIODICALS
A Comprehensive Annotated List

Katharine Loughney

GARLAND PUBLISHING, INC. • NEW YORK & LONDON
1991

Library of Congress Cataloging-in-Publication Data

Loughney, Katharine.
    Film, television, and video periodicals : a comprehensive
annotated list / Katharine Loughney.
        p. cm. — (Garland reference library of the humanities; vol.
1032)
    Includes indexes.
    ISBN 0–8240–0647–X (acid-free paper)
    1. Motion pictures—Periodicals—Bibliography. 2. Television—
Periodicals—Bibliography. 3. Video recordings—Periodicals—
Bibliography. I. Title. II. Series.
Z5784.M9L68   1991
[PN1993]
016.79143'.05—dc20   90–14071
                                                                    CIP

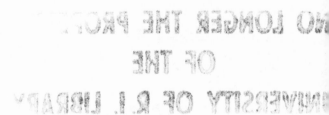

Printed on acid-free, 250-year-life paper
Manufactured in the United States of America

To Pat and Katie

CONTENTS

INTRODUCTION

Purpose

The purpose of this book is to help guide researchers through the large number of serial publications devoted to moving image materials. Thousands of periodicals covering motion pictures, television and video are being published worldwide each year. The magazines may focus on moving image materials as an art form, as popular entertainment or as a business venture. They may be concerned with film only, with broadcasting only, with home video, or a combination of the three. Each magazine has a different way of treating the entertainment industries and each has a different readership. It is important to know what information is being published and where it is available. This book is a comprehensive annotated listing of the film, television and video periodicals currently being published.

Scope

The scope of this directory is to list the most widely used and accessible film, television and video periodicals in the United States. The list is intended to be comprehensive, not selective. It is not judgmental; it contains scholarly journals as well as fan magazines. Coverage is predominantly English language, but foreign publications are included, selected on the basis of availability in the United States and longevity of publication. The scope is not intended to be historical. Emphasis is on periodicals in current distribution, although recently discontinued titles are included.

Use

The book is intended to be used as a reference source for librarians, teachers, film scholars, students, and audiovisual specialists. The information found in the entries will help the reader find out who the publisher is, where the magazine is published, and if it meets the reader's needs. People in the motion picture, television, and cable industries will find the book helpful for tracking down current information. Writers, educators, and cinema students can identify and locate the journals which will emphasize scholarship. Fans, collectors and home video enthusiasts will be able to find a network of like-minded people who share their interests.

Arrangement and Indexes

Main entries, arranged alphabetically by title, begin on page three. Special indexes comprise the second half of the book and begin on page 271 with the Geographical Index. The Geographical Index is a list of the magazine titles published in each country. It is arranged alphabetically by the name of the country. After each title is the span of dates delimiting the years of publication.

The genre indexes follow, beginning with the Film Index. This is a list of magazines that focuses primarily on film studies or motion picture entertainment. The Television Index is next, containing magazines which specialize in television, cable and broadcasting. The third index is the Video Index. It covers periodicals that deal with video for entertainment use at home, for instructional use in the classroom, and for training purposes in business and industry.

The genre indexes also include sections listing popular and fan magazines; scholarly and educational journals; and technical or professional magazines. The last index lists annual publications. Annuals include directories, yearbooks, cumulative indexes, and source books that are updated yearly.

Comments

The author would appreciate any comments or suggestions that would help make *Film, Television, and Video Periodicals: A Comprehensive Annotated List* more useful. Send any changes, updates, or new serial titles to:

Katharine Loughney
c/o Garland Publishing
136 Madison Avenue
New York, New York 10016

Acknowledgments

I would like to thank the many people who have helped me. Of those professionals who have aided me in the compilation of the manuscript, I would like to thank Vincent Aceto and his associate Deborah Jamison of the Film and Television Documentation Center at the State University of New York at Albany. I am indebted to their generosity in sharing with me their vast knowledge of film and television periodicals. Their publication, **Film Literature Index**, continues to be an invaluable reference source for all film scholars. Likewise, I would like to thank the International Federation of Film Archives and the editor of the **International Index to Film/Television Periodicals,** who sent me several hard-to-find European publications. I would like to acknowledge the scholarship of Anna Brady, Richard Wall and Carolynn Newitt Weiner who compiled another great film reference source, the **Union List of Film Periodicals**.

Because this manuscript was compiled at the Library of Congress, I want to thank the able staff of the Newspapers and Current Periodicals Reading Room, who aided my research. Thanks are in order to my former supervisor, Patrick J. Sheehan, Head of the Reference Section at the Motion Picture, Broadcasting and Recorded Sound Division, who never failed to alert me to new publications and title changes.

I would like to thank Sam Brylawski of the Recorded Sound Reference Center at the Library of Congress for his expertise with computer hardware; and also to Barbara Pruett of the U.S. International Trade Commission Library for her continued help and assistance with computer software.

Lastly, I would like acknowledge my gratitude to my husband, Patrick Loughney, whose encouragement and support continued to sustain me until the work was completed.

Main Entries

The main entry, in boldfaced print, is arranged alphabetically under the title of the magazine. After the title comes the country of publication. Most of the countries' names are spelled out, but for some countries, such as the United States and the United Kingdom, the names are abbreviated. A list of the countries and their abbreviations appears below. If any title changes have occurred in the publication's history, the former titles will be noted next. Similarly, any alternate or variant titles will appear following the country. If the publication is bilingual, it may have a parallel title which is linked to the main title by an equals sign (=).

The next items in the entry are the publisher's name, address and telephone number. Care was taken to include the most recent information. In cases where the subscription address and telephone number are different from the publisher's editorial address and telephone, both are provided.

The frequency is next and appears in parenthesis. This indicates how often a periodical is published and can be daily, weekly, biweekly, monthly, bimonthly, quarterly, or annually. After the frequency follows the ISSN number. ISSN stands for the International Standard Serial Number and is the unique number representing the magazine internationally. It indicates that the magazine has been officially cataloged using the Anglo-American Cataloging Rules II. It helps libraries identify the publication and is a shorthand way of accessing the catalog record containing all the pertinent bibliographic data describing the magazine. In some cases, ISSN numbers have not been assigned and, therefore, will not appear in the entry.

The note area follows next and contains the span of years that the magazine has been published. The note includes publication years for former titles as well as the current title. It includes the publication dates for periodicals which have been discontinued in the 1980s. A short description of the periodical's scope follows next. It is an uncritical content analysis of the publication, describing its literary emphasis, design qualities, the nature of its articles, intended audience, language (if other than English), and illustrations.

The last items in the entry are the Library of Congress and Dewey classification numbers. The classification scheme is a way of shelving a literary work according to its subject content. The L.C. and Dewey numbers will help the reader locate the publication in his/her public, state or university libraries. However, not all periodicals have been cataloged and therefore, some titles will not have a classification number. In this case, the periodicals will probably be shelved alphabetically under the title. In both cases, it is always best to check first with a librarian in order to locate the publication in a particular library.

Cross References

Cross references are provided to refer the reader to the main entry from a former title, alternate title, parallel title or subtitle. They appear in boldface type and are arranged alphabetically. The country of origin is included to help identify the entry.

Filing Rules

Arrangement is alphabetical by title. When a title begins with either an English or foreign language article, such as *a*, *an*, *the*, *les*, *das*, etc., it is ignored for filing purposes. Articles falling within the framework of the magazine title continue to be filed alphabetically. Titles are arranged alphabetically word-by-word, not letter-by-letter. Therefore, the entry for **Broadcast Investor** comes before **Broadcaster**.

Punctuation, such as hyphens or apostrophes, appearing within the title are ignored in filing. Therefore, **Audio-Visual Communications** is filed as **Audio Visual Communications** and not as **Audiovisual Communications**. Titles consisting of numbers are spelled out. **16MM Film User** is treated as **Sixteen Millimeter Film User**.

All titles beginning with acronyms are filed at the very beginning of the alphabetical listing under the letter. For example, titles beginning with **T.V.** are filed at the beginning of the letter "T" section, before titles beginning with "T" which are spelled out, e.g., **Take One**. Finally, titles that contain an ampersand (&) are filed as if the ampersand were spelled out, e.g., **Film & History** is filed as **Film and History**. However, for foreign titles such as **Film & Fakten** from West Germany, the ampersand is translated as *und* and filed accordingly.

Boldface

All magazine titles are in boldface print, including main entry, parallel titles, former and alternate titles, cross references, and titles appearing in the notes and contents areas.

Dates

Publication spans are expressed in dates, e.g., 1980-1985. Dates that are in doubt are designated by a lower case "u", meaning unknown. For example, 197u describes a magazine that began sometime in the 1970s. The decade is certain, but the exact year is unknown. For those entries that are designated 19uu, the century is certain, but both the year and decade are uncertain. Dates that end with a question mark (?) signify that the date is probable, but not verified. A date appearing as 1971? means that the magazine probably began in 1970, but could have begun in late 1970 or early 1972.

Brackets

Information enclosed in brackets ([]) indicates that it is supplied by the author. Brackets are used when volume and issue numbers are not established. Occasionally, the premiere issue of a magazine is not designated by either a volume or issue number. For some magazines, numbering is completely left off. When this happens, the author has supplied the information as accurately as can be verified and enclosed it in brackets.

Abbreviations

The following abbreviations are used to designate bibliographic data:

ed.	edition
ISSN	International Standard Serial Number
n.	number
v.	volume
yr.	year
=	parallel title

The following abbreviations are used to designate months of the year:

Jan	January	Jul	July
Feb	February	Aug	August
Mar	March	Sep	September
Apr	April	Oct	October
May	May	Nov	November
Jun	June	Dec	December

The following abbreviations are used to designate countries of the world. All other countries not included in the list below are spelled out:

E.Germany	East Germany
P.R.C.	People's Republic of China
S.Africa	South Africa
U.K.	United Kingdom
U.S.	United States
U.S.S.R.	The Union of Soviet Socialist Republics
W.Germany	West Germany

Film, Television, and
Video Periodicals

FILM, TELEVISION, AND VIDEO PERIODICALS

-A-

A. & E. Cable Network Program Guide (U.S.). Alternate title: **Arts & Entertainment Cable Network Program Guide**. A & E Cable Network, PO Box 729 Madison Square Station, New York, NY 10159; (monthly).
Note: [v.1], Feb 1, 1984 -.
Complete monthly program listings for the Arts & Entertainment Cable Network, 555 Fifth Ave., New York, NY 10017. Specializes in fine dramas, musical performances, dance, opera and documentaries on artists, composers and writers.

A.A.A.S. Science Books (U.S.). See: **Science Books & Films**.

A.A.A.S. Science Books & Films (U.S.). See: **Science Books & Films**.

A.B.C. News Index (U.S.). Alternate title: **American Broadcasting Corporation News Index**. Research Publications, Inc., 12 Lunar Dr., Woodbridge, CT 06525. Tel: 203/397-2600; 800/732-2477; (quarterly); ISSN: 0891-8775; OCLC 15049670.
Note: v.1,n.1 Jan-Mar 1986 -.
Provides subject analysis to the A.B.C. News transcripts available on microfiche from Research Publications. Indexes the following programs by subject, title, and names of personalities: *20/20, ABC News Special, Business World, Closeup, Nightline, Our World, This Week with David Brinkley, Viewpoint, The Weekend Report, World News Saturday, World News Sunday,* and *World News Tonight*.
Dewey: 070 11.

3

A.B.U. Technical Review (Japan). Alternate title: **Asia-Pacific Broadcasting Union Technical Review**. Asia-Pacific Broadcasting Union, NHK Broadcasting Centre, 2-2-1 Jinnan, Shibuya-ku, Tokyo 150 Japan; (bimonthly); ISSN: 0126-6209; OCLC 3348172.
Note: [n.1] 196u -.
The Asia-Pacific Broadcasting Union is a professional union of organizations in the Pacific rim that coordinates the development of radio and television in the region. This highly technical magazine covers equipment, engineering, construction, channel spacing, reception over long distances and transmission systems. Published in English.
TK6630.A1A84; Dewey: 621.38/05.

A.C.S.S. Newsletter (U.S.). See: **Asian Cinema Studies Society Newsletter.**

A.E.J.M.C. News (U.S.). Formerly: **The A.E.J.M.C. Newsletter**; alternate title: **Association for Education in Journalism and Mass Communication News.** Association for Education in Journalism and Mass Communication, University of South Carolina, College of Journalism, Columbia, SC 29208; (10 times/yr; Oct-Jul); ISSN: 0747-8909; OCLC 10179124.
Note: v.1-v.16,n.7, 1968?-July 1983 as **The A.E.J.M.C. Newsletter**; v.17,n.1 Oct 1983- as **A.E.J.M.C. News.**
Newsletter free to members of this academic community. Concerned with teaching journalism, broadcasting and mass communications on a college level.

The A.E.J.M.C. Newsletter (U.S.). See: **A.E.J.M.C. News.**

A.F.I. Close-up (U.S.). Alternate titles: **American Film Institute Close-up; Close-up**. The American Film Institute, John F. Kennedy Center for the Performing Arts, Washington, DC 20566; (quarterly); ISSN: 0742-2105; OCLC 9928874.
Note: v.1-v.5, Fall 1982-Spring 1987.
Newsletter free to members of the American Film Institute. Keeps members apprised of happenings and events of the A.F.I. Discontinued publication.

A.F.I. Education Newsletter (U.S.). Alternate title: **American Film Institute Education Newsletter**. American Film Institute, Education Services, 2021 N. Western Ave., PO Box 27999, Los

Angeles, CA 90027; (bimonthly); ISSN: 0883-6213; OCLC 4770038.
Note: v.1-v.6,n.1, Feb/Mar 1978-Sep/Oct 1982.
Designed to inform prospective film students about courses, seminars, and publications offered by the American Film Institute. Reports on schools and universities throughout the U.S. which offer film studies. Discontinued 1982.
Dewey: 791 11.

A.F.I. Preview (U.S.). See: **Preview.**

A.F.T. & T. (U.S.). Alternate title: **Arizona Film, Theatre & Television.** Arizona Film, Theatre & Television, PO Box 2234, Scottsdale, AZ 85252-2234; (monthly); ISSN: 0896-0364; OCLC 16893919.
Note: [v.1], 1985 -.
Newsletter keeping up on the latest film and television productions, location shooting, and theater presentations in Arizona. Interviews industry people producing or writing in Arizona.
Dewey: 791 11.

A.F.V.A. Bulletin / American Film and Video Association (U.S.). Alternate title: **American Film and Video Association Bulletin.** Formerly: **E.F.L.A. Bulletin; Educational Film Library Association. E.F.L.A. Bulletin.** Address: American Film and Video Association, 920 Barnsdale Rd., Suite 152, La Grange Park, IL 60525. Tel: 312/482-4000; (quarterly); ISSN: n/a; OCLC 17988051.
Note: v.1-v.10, Sep 1977-1987 as **E.F.L.A. Bulletin**; v.11,n.1, Spring 1988- as **A.F.V.A. Bulletin.**
Newsletter for librarians, educators and audiovisual specialists who buy or use films and videos for elementary, secondary and high schools. Contains reviews and recommendations for educational and instructional films and tapes. Acts as a clearinghouse for information on educational 16mm film and video.

A.I.T. Newsletter (U.S.). Alternate titles: **Agency for Instructional Technology Newsletter; Newsletter. Agency for Instructional Technology.** Address: Agency for Instructional Technology, Box A, Bloomington, IN 47402-0120. Tel: 812/339-2203; 800/457-4509; (bimonthly); ISSN: 0193-578X; OCLC

5232321.
Note: v.1, 1973 -.
Promotes the utilization of television and computers for
educational instruction. "Acquires and distributes a wide
variety of TV and related printed materials" to schools.
Dewey: 371 11.

A.M.C.B. (Singapore). See: **Asian Mass Communication Bulletin
(A.M.C.B.).**

A.P.E.C. Cinema: Revue Belge de Cinema (Belgium). See: **Revue
Belge du Cinema.**

A.R.D. Fernsehspiel (W.Germany); Rundfunkanstalten der
Bundesrepublik Deutschland (A.R.D.), Bertramstr. 8, 6000
Frankfurt Am Main, West Germany; (quarterly); ISSN: n/a.
Note: [v.1] 195u -
Articles on German television, describes new programs,
profiles popular TV performers. Contains the programming
schedule. Published in German.

**A.S.I.F.A. Bulletin de l'Association Internationale du Film
d'Animation, Canada** (Canada). Alternate titles: **A.S.I.F.A.
Association Internationale du Film d'Animation, Canada;
Association Internationale du Film d'Animation, Canada.**
Address:
ASIFA Canada, Bureau 3, 10707, rue Grande Allee, Montreal,
Que. H3L 2M8 Canada. Tel: 514/842-9763; (quarterly); ISSN:
0828-7511; OCLC 12227573.
Note: [n.1], 1974? -.
Newsletter of the Canadian chapter of the International
Association of Film Animation; published in French and
English. Focuses on Canadian film and video animation and
animators.
Dewey: 778.5/347.

A.S.I.F.A. News (Belgium). Alternate titles: **A.S.I.F.A.
Nouvelles; A.S.I.F.A. Novosti; L'Association Internationale
du Film d'Animation News.** Address: A.S.I.F.A. International,
Bureau de depot, Bruxelles X, Belgium; (quarterly); ISSN: n/a.
Note: [n.1], 1974? -.
Text published in French, English and Russian. International
newsletter for people working in film and video animation.

Keeps current on the latest independent creations, new graphic styles and studio works. Reports on the Zagreb Film Festival and other festivals devoted to animation.

A.S.I.F.A. Nouvelles (Belgium). See: **A.S.I.F.A. News**.

A.S.I.F.A. Novosti (Belgium). See: **A.S.I.F.A. News**.

A.V.M.P.: Audio Video Market Place (U.S.). See: **Audio Video Market Place: A.V.M.P.**

A.V.R.D. (U.S.). See: **AudioVideo Review Digest**.

A.V. Business Communications (Canada). Alternate title: **Audio Visual Business Communications**. Address: A.V. Business Communications, 777 Bay St., Toronto, Ont. M5W 1A7 Canada; (10 times/yr);
ISSN: 0827-763X; OCLC 15236237.
Note: v.1-v.9,n.7, 1977?-Aug 1986.
Articles covered business applications of audiovisual media. Discontinued in August 1986.
HD9999; Dewey: 651.7.

A.V. Praxis (W.Germany). Formerly: **Film, Bild, Ton** (0015-1130). Institute for Film und Bild in Wissenschaft und Interricht, Monatlich ein Heft, 1.70 DM, 8 Munchen 19, Nibelungenstr. 9a/VI West Germany.
Note: v.1-21, 1951-1971 as **Film, Bild, Ton**; v.22, 1972- as **A.V. Praxis**.
Scholarly journal covering film, television, photography and other arts. Interested in scientific applications of audiovisual materials, using film and video to record natural phenomena. Articles cover the use of television for classroom teaching, documentary filmmaking, underwater photography, restoration of nitrate film, and state of the art video technology.
PN1993.F43.

A.V. Video (U.S.). Formerly: **Audio Visual Product News** (0164-6834); **Audio Visual Directions** (0746-8989). Montage Publishing, Inc., 25550 Hawthorne Blvd., Suite 314, Torrance, CA 90505. Tel: 213/373-9993; (monthly; plus supplements in Jan, May & Sep); ISSN: 0747-1335; OCLC 10380646.

Note: v.1-v.2,n.9, Fall 1978-Sep/Oct 1980 as **Audio Visual Product News**; v.2,n.10-v.6,n.1, Nov/Dec 1980-Jan 1984 as **Audio Visual Directions**; v.6,n.2, Feb 1984- as **A.V. Video**. A guide for educators, librarians and business training officials involved with teaching through audiovisual presentation. Reviews multimedia equipment such as video recorders, playback machines, camcorders, overhead projectors, transparencies, special effects slides, audio accompaniment and multi-imaging products. Outlines use of AV for marketing sales and services. Presents innovative and artistic ways of training and educating by making use of audiovisual technology.

Aamplitude (U.S.); Asian American Arts and Media, Inc., 1851 Columbia Rd., NW. No. 501, Washington, DC 20009; (6 times/ yr); ISSN: 0889-9460; OCLC 14104845. Note: v.1,n.1, Spring 1985 -. Newsletter for members of Asian American Arts and Media. "Seeks to explore the cross-cultural interfaces of East and West, and to develop public awareness of the evolving Asian American Arts." Dewey: 700 11.

Academy Bulletin (U.S.). See: **The Bulletin of the Academy of Motion Picture Arts and Sciences.**

Academy of Canadian Cinema & Television (Canada). See: **Infocus: Academy of Canadian Cinema & Television.**

Academy of Motion Picture Arts and Sciences. Bulletin (U.S.). See: **The Bulletin of the Academy of Motion Picture Arts and Sciences.**

Academy Players Directory (U.S.); Academy of Motion Picture Arts and Sciences, 8949 Wilshire Blvd., Beverly Hills, CA 90211. Tel: 213/278-8990; (quarterly); ISSN: n/a; OCLC 8117752. Note: [v.1] 1937 -. List of working performers arranged alphabetically by name under categories: leading men, leading women, ingenues, juveniles, children. Each entry includes photograph and contact or agent. PN1999.A1.A3; Dewey: 791.43/028/02573.

Access (U.S.); Telecommunications Research & Action Center, National Citizens Committee for Broadcasting, PO Box 12038, Washington, DC 20005. Tel: 202/462-2520; (biweekly); ISSN: 0149-9262; OCLC 2250216.
Note: n.1, Jan 13, 1975 -. Three preliminary issues published in 1974.
Citizen's action group organized to reform TV access. Some of the concerns addressed by the newsletter are better representation of minorities and women, less stereotyping of characters, cutting back of excessive sex and violence on television, regulating commercial time and upgrading the quality of children's television. Reports on new rules and regulations from the F.C.C., censorship, the Fairness Doctrine and equal employment opportunities.

Action (Canada). Alternate title: **Action: Canadian Film & Television Association**. Address: Canadian Film & Television Association, 663 Yonge St., Suite 401, Toronto, Ont. M4Y 2A4 Canada; (quarterly); ISSN: 0845-227X; OCLC 19752022.
Note: v.1,n.1 Jun 1986 -.
"The voice of independent production." Incorporates the membership of the Canadian Association of Motion Picture Producers (C.F.T.A.). Newsletter informing members of new laws and regulations concerning film and television production in Canada and the United States. Acts as a clearinghouse for news and information for Canadian film and TV producers.
HE8693; Dewey: 791.4/06/071.

Action! (U.S.); Directors Guild of America, 7950 Sunset Blvd., Los Angeles, CA 90046; (bimonthly); ISSN: 0001-7361.
Note: v.1, Sep/Oct 1966 -.
Professional bulletin for the members of the Directors Guild. Lengthy interviews with members paralleling their latest successful releases. Contains biographical sketches of award winning members, analyzing their works and listing comprehensive filmographies. Members encouraged to write about experiences such as shooting on location, how to achieve special effects, how to avoid pitfalls, setting up a scene, maintaining order on the set, and the dangers of directing hazardous stunts.
PN1995.9.P7A25.

Action: Canadian Film & Television Association (Canada). See: **Action.**

L'Activite Cinematographique Francaise en C.N.C., Centre National de la Cinematographie (France); Centre National de la Cinematographie C.N.C., 12, rue de Lubeck, 75784 Paris Cedex 16, France. Tel: 505-14-40; (annual); ISSN: 0397-8435; OCLC 15547698.
Note: ed.1 1977? -.
Compiles statistical charts for the production of feature films and shorts in France, including financial reports. Lists theaters around France, showing the number of film programs, restrictions if any, and audience statistics. PN1993.5.F7A648; Dewey: 384.8/0944.

Actors Cues (U.S.). See: **Show Business.**

Adam Film World Directory of Adult Films (U.S.). See: **Adam Film World Guide. Adam Film World Directory of Adult Films.**

Adam Film World Guide. Adam Film World Directory of Adult Films (U.S.); Knight Publishing Corporation, 8060 Melrose Ave., Los Angeles, CA 90046. Tel: 213/653-8060; (monthly); ISSN: 0743-6335; OCLC 10621205.
Note: n.1, 1984 -.
Covers adult film and video entertainment. Reviews sexually explicit theatrical and home video motion pictures. Also publishes an annual directory indexing the film and video titles reviewed throughout the year.

Adult Cinema Review (U.S.); Adult Review Magazine, Subscription Dept., 300 W. 43rd. St., New York, NY 10036; (monthly); ISSN: 0277-2914; OCLC 7528740.
Note: v.1,n.1 Jul 1981 -.
Reviews adult films and home videos. Includes graphic presentations and explicit advertisements.

Adult Video Supplement (U.S.). See: **Bowker's Complete Video Directory.**

Adult Video News (U.S.); Adult Video News, Inc., 6003 Castor Ave., Philadelphia, PA 19149. Tel: 215/752-3387; (monthly); ISSN: 0883-7090; OCLC 12197226.

Note: n.1, 1985? -.
A publication containing reviews of the latest adult home
videocassettes. Graphic photos and advertisements are
displayed. Lists top selling titles, annual awards, new
starlets. Also has a section for gay reviews.
Dewey: 791 11.

Advertising in Movies (U.S.); Kaufman Astoria Studios, 34-31 35th
St., Astoria, New York 11106. Tel: 718/729-9288; (bimonthly);
ISSN: n/a.
Note: v.1,n.1 Mar/Apr 1985 -.
"The magazine for product placement." Newsletter designed to
promote product exposure in feature films, as a form of
subliminal advertising.

Afterimage (U.K.); Afterimage Publishing, 1 Birnam Rd., London,
England N4 3LJ; (irregular); ISSN: 0261-4472; OCLC 1685279.
Note: n.1, Apr 1970 -.
Each issue is devoted to a special theme with several well
written, insightful articles detailing different aspects of
it. Some of the subjects covered are: film and politics,
avant garde film, Third World cinema, new British cinema, and
independent filmmakers in Great Britain. Concentrates on
film and filmmakers, although does have an occasional article
on television. Also contains filmographies, interviews, and
script excerpts.
PN1993.A52; Dewey: 791.43/05.

Afterimage (U.S.); Visual Studies Workshop, 31 Prince St.,
Rochester, NY 14607; (10 times/yr, monthly except Jul & Aug);
ISSN: 0300-7472; OCLC 1335227.
Note: v.1, 1972 -.
Main focus is on independent, avant garde and experimental
photography, cinema, video and pictorial books. Features
thoughtful interviews with the artists. Contains essays on
photography, camerawork, ethics and aesthetics. Keeps
current with various film festivals, exhibitions and art
shows.
TR640.A2; Dewey: 770/.5.

Agency for Instructional Technology Newsletter (U.S.). See:
A.I.T. Newsletter.

Airwaves (U.K.). Formerly: **Independent Broadcasting / I.B.A.**
(0305-6104). Independent Broadcasting Authority, 70 Brompton
Rd., London, England SW3 1EY; (quarterly); ISSN: 0267-3789;
OCLC 12211436.
Note: v.1-v.11, 1974-1984 as **Independent Broadcasting /
I.B.A.**; renumbered v.1,n.1 Winter 1984/85 as **Airwaves**.
Well-presented industry magazine with extensive information
on radio and television broadcasting in Great Britain.
Examines new developments within the industry, reports on
products, such as high-definition TV, provides a forum for
independent comment on significant issues affecting the
industry and measures audience demographics. Predominantly
British, but talks about importing shows from the U.S. and
Europe.
HE8689.9.G71528; Dewey: 384.55/4/0941.

Aktery Zarubezhnogo Kino (U.S.S.R.); Izdatelstvo "Iskusstvo,"
Leningradskoe Odelenie, Nevskii Prospekt, 28, Leningrad
191186, U.S.S.R.; (annual); ISSN: 0568-7446.
Note: v.1, 1965 -.
Short biographical sketches of international performers,
including such people as Barbra Streisand and Peter O'Toole,
as well as Soviet screen stars. Includes portrait shots,
publicity stills from movies and an extensive filmography.
Published in the Russian language.
PN1998.A2A58.

Amateur Cine World (U.K.). See: **Making Better Movies.**

American Broadcasting Corporation News Index (U.S.). See: **A.B.C.
News Index.**

American Cinematheque Newsletter (U.S.). See: **The Cinegram.**

American Cinematographer (U.S.); ASC Holding Corp., 1782 N.
Orange Dr., Hollywood, CA 90028. Tel: 213/876-5080;
(monthly); ISSN: 0002-7928; ISSN: 0002-7938; OCLC 1479664.
Note: v.1, Jan 1920 -.
Publication of the American Society of Cinematographers.
Professional journal of film and video production techniques.
Concentrates on photography, camerawork, lighting, special
effects, aerial shots and optics. Looks behind the scenes to

show how the techniques are achieved.
TR845.A55.

American Cinemeditor (U.S.). Formerly: **Cinemeditor** (0069-4169).
C.E. Publications, PO Box 26082, Encino, CA 91426-2082. Tel:
818/907-7351; (quarterly); ISSN: 0044-7625; OCLC 2514565.
Note: v.1-v.21,n.2 Winter 1950-Summer 1971 as **Cinemeditor**;
v.21,n.3 Autumn 1971- as **American Cinemeditor**.
Publication of the American Cinema Editors, an honorary
professional society. Devoted to film editing plus film and
television post-production disciplines. Discusses
techniques, evaluates new trends, analyzes the art and
science of film editing.
TR899.A54; Dewey 778.5/35/05 19.

American Classic Screen (U.S.); American Classic Screen, PO Box
7150, Overland Park, KS 66207; (bimonthly); ISSN: 0195-8267;
OCLC 3334436.
Note: v.1-v.8,n.2, Sep/Oct 1976-Nov/Dec 1984.
Popular magazine which concentrated on personality stories of
American film stars and directors. Included articles about
film history and technique. Reprinted interviews and
biographies of famous, bygone film stars, such as Victor
Seastrom, Barbara La Marr, George M. Cohan. Ceased
publication in 1984.
PN1993.A615; Dewey: 791.43/05.

American Close-up (U.S.). See: **Hollywood Close-up**.

American Film (U.S.); Billboard Publications, Inc., 6671 Sunset
Blvd., Suite 1514, Hollywood, CA 90028, Subscriptions:
Membership Services, American Film, PO Box 2046, Marion, OH
43305. Tel: 213/856-5350; 800/347-6969; (monthly except Jan/
Feb & Jul/Aug); ISSN: 0361-4751; OCLC 2246336.
Note: v.1,n.1 Oct 1975 -.
Subscription is included with membership to the American Film
Institute. Popular magazine of film and television arts.
Interviews film and television personalities. Articles cover
retrospective film studies as well as current trends.
Reviews films, videos and cinema-related books.
PN1993.A617; Dewey: 791.43/05.

American Film and Video Association Bulletin (U.S.). See:
A.F.V.A. Bulletin / American Film and Video Association.

American Film Institute Close-up (U.S.). See: **A.F.I. Close-up.**

American Film Institute Education Newsletter (U.S.). See: **A.F.I. Education Newsletter.**

American Movie Classics Magazine (U.S.); The Crosby Vandenburgh Group, 420 Boylston St., Boston, MA 02116; Subscriptions: American Movie Classics, PO Box 2065, Marion, OH 43305; Tel: 800/535-7700; (monthly); ISSN: n/a.
Note: v.1,n.1 Jan 1988 -.
Programming guide to the American Movie Classics cable channel, specializing in American films from the 1930s-1950s. Spotlights the films being aired, giving background information on the cast, the director and the studio.

American Museum of the Moving Image Newsletter (U.S.); American Museum of the Moving Image, 35th Ave. at 36th St., Astoria, NY 11106. Tel: 718/784-4160; (quarterly); ISSN: n/a.
Note: [n.1] 1988? -.
Daily schedule for the programs and exhibits shown at the American Museum of the Moving Image, "the only museum in America dedicated exclusively to film, television and video."

American Premiere (U.S.). Continues: **Premiere** (Hollywood). American Premiere Publications, Inc., 8421 Wilshire Blvd., Penthouse, Beverly Hills, CA 90211; (irregular); ISSN: 0279-0041; OCLC 7420478.
Note: v.1,n.1-v.2,n.5, Sep 1980-Mar 1981 as **Premiere**; v.2, n.6, May 1981- as **American Premiere**.
"The magazine of the Film industry." Rather slick magazine focusing on the film and television industries in southern California. Most issues present a theme with several articles elaborating a different aspect of it: "Film Financing and the Independent Producer," " Women and Film," "Incorporating the Individual." Offers a section called "Close-ups," which is a selection of new talent with their profiles and filmographies.
PN1993.5.U6A877; Dewey: 384/.8/0973.

The American Screenwriter (U.S.); Grasshopper Productions, Box 67, Manchaca, TX 78652. Tel: 512/282-2749; (bimonthly).
Note: v.1,n.1-v.5,n.4, May 1984-Dec 1988.
Newsletter format featuring articles on how to break into screenwriting for the motion picture and television industries. Contains helpful hints, suggestions and ploys. Offers a "reading service" for aspiring screenwriters.
Ceased publication.

American Widescreener (U.S.); American Widescreen Association, PO Box 883, Farmington, MO 63640; (bimonthly).
Note: v.1, 1982 -.
Official newsletter of the American Widescreen Association. Articles cover widescreen systems such as cinemascope, cinerama and Imax; new technology; and reviews of widescreen films.

Andere Sinema (Belgium); De Andere Film, Ommeganckstraat 21, 2018 Antwerpen, Belgium. Tel: (03) 234 16 40; (6 times/yr); ISSN: 0773-5855; OCLC 7952519.
Note: n.1, 1978 -.
Multi-lingual publication covering television and cinema. Reviews international motion pictures, reports on various film festivals, keeps current on the future of television and cable in Europe. Contains a popular mix of articles from reviewing opera on video to HDTV.

Animafilm. The Journal of Animated Film (Italy); Centro Internazionale per il Cinema di Animazione, p.za San Carlo, 161-10123, Torino, Italia. Tel: (011) 54.04.16; (quarterly).
Note: n.1, 1984 -.
Newsletter for professional members of ASIFA, an international organization for film and video animation. Published in English, Italian and French. Devoted to the art of animation, articles consist of information on new techniques, schools, festivals and awards, plus interviews, biographical sketches and filmographies of creative animators.

Animation Magazine (U.S.); Animation Magazine, Harvey Deneroff, Editor, PO Box 25547, Los Angeles, CA 90025; (quarterly); ISSN: 1041-617X; OCLC 18794679.
Note: v.1,n.1 Aug 1987 -.
Nicely illustrated magazine focusing on film and video

animation. Articles cover the history of cartoons, early
techniques, character development, new graphics and the
latest technology. Knowledgeable contributors write about
all aspects of animation from the silent period to New Age
graphics.
NC1766.U5A48; Dewey: 741.5805.

Animato! (U.S.); Animato, PO Box 1240, Cambridge, MA 02238;
(quarterly); ISSN: 1042-539X; OCLC 19081197.
Note: n.1, 1983? -.
"The animation fan's magazine." Reviews new home videos
featuring official collections from the major studios, as well as
public domain fare released by independent producers.
Reviews new books on the subject.
Dewey: 741 11.

Animatographe (France); S.A.R.L. L'Autrerive, 30, rue Etienne-
Marcel 75002, Paris, France. Tel: 43.66.39.10; (bimonthly);
ISSN: n/a; OCLC 16948924.
Note: n.1, Mar/Apr 1987 -.
Focuses on French animation and animators. Reports on new
techniques and trends in film and video animation. Published
in French.

Animator (U.K.); Filmcraft Publications, 13 Ringway Rd., Park
St., St. Albans, Herts. AL2 2RE, England; (quarterly); ISSN:
n/a.
Note: n.1, 1983 -.
Serious journal dedicated to the art of animation and the
moving image. Covers the silent period, the history of
theatrical animation during the 1930s and 1940s, the rise of
minimalist art in the 1950s and 1960s, and the post-modern
and new age art of today. Writes about cartoon series on
television and computer animation.

The Animator (U.S.); Northwest Film Study Center, 1219 S.W. Park
Ave., Portland, OR 97205. Tel: 503/221-1156; (quarterly);
ISSN: 0889-5589; OCLC 3509080.
Note: v.1,n.1 Winter 1972 -.
Newsletter of the Northwest Film Study Center, a non-profit
institution serving Oregon, Washington, Idaho, Montana and
Alaska through film education, exhibition and publication.
Reports on animation festivals, film programs, seminars, courses,

competitions, national grants and local news.
Dewey: 791 11.

L'Annee du Cinema (France); Calmann-Levy, 1, rue Jules Simon,
Paris 75015 France; (annual); ISSN: n/a; ISBN: 2-7021-1583-7;
OCLC 4990637.
Note: v.1, 1977 -.
Slick overview of the year's motion pictures composed as a
photographic essay with a brief critique of the film.
Complete cast and credit information for each film appears at
the end in a separate index. Reviews foreign films as well
as French films. Contains section with boxoffice statistics;
also a list of international film festivals and an obituary.
PN1993.A627; Dewey: 791.43/05.

Annuaire de la Cinematographie Suisse (Switzerland). See:
**Schweizer Filmindex = Index Suisse du Cinema = Indice
Svizzero del Cinema.**

Annuaire du Cinema et Television (France). See: **Annuaire du
Cinema, Television, Video.**

Annuaire du Cinema Francais (France). See: **Annuaire du Cinema
Francais et de L'Audiovisuel.**

**Annuaire du Cinema Francais et de L'Audiovisuel = Directory of
the French Film and Audiovisual Industries** (France).
Formerly: **Annuaire du Cinema Francais.** Unifrance Film
International, 114, Champs-Elysees, 75008 Paris, France. Tel:
43.59.03.34; (annual); ISSN: n/a; OCLC 10106718.
Note: ed.1-ed.6, 1977-1982 as **Annuaire du Cinema Francais**; ed.7,
1983/84- as **Annuaire du Cinema Francais et de L'Audiovisuel.**
A directory of the French film and television industries.
Contains addresses and telephone numbers for companies
providing equipment and services, such as production
companies, distributors, trade associations, exporters and
government organizations. Lists film and video festivals.
Published in French with English translations for title
headings.
PN1993.5.F7A75; Dewey: 384.55/029/444.

Annuaire du Cinema, Television, Video (France). Formerly:
Annuaire du Cinema et Television. Editions Bellefaye, 38 rue

Etienne-Marcel, 75002 Paris, France; (annual); ISSN: n/a;
OCLC 6565954.
Note: [ed.1-ed.22] 1964-1985 as **Annuaire du Cinema et
Television**; [ed.1], 1986- as **Annuaire du Cinema, Television,
Video.**
A directory for French motion picture and television actors
and actresses. Gives name, photo and agent. Contains a list
of international feature films for the preceding year with
production-distribution information and synopsis. Includes
French addresses for television networks from around the
world. Published in French.
PN1993.3.A476; Dewey: 384.8/02544 20.

Annuaire du Film Belge = Jaarboek van de Belgische Film
(Belgium). Alternate title: **Jaarboek van de Belgische Film.**
Cinematheque Royale de Belgique, rue Ravenstein 23, 1000
Bruxelles, Belgium. Tel: 02.513.41.55; (annual); ISSN: n/a;
ISBN: 33-7-8510090265; OCLC 4880205.
Note: v.1, 1958 -.
Comprehensive directory of motion picture and television
production and distribution companies serving Belgium. Gives
addresses, telephone numbers and personnel. Also lists post-
production services, film labs, cinema clubs, cultural
organizations, government agencies and film schools. Charts
feature length and short films released throughout the world
by nation. Contains indexes of names and film titles.
Published in Flemish and French.
PN1993.A628; Dewey: 791.43/09493.

Annual Directory of Religious Broadcasting (U.S.). See: **The
Directory of Religious Broadcasting.**

Annual Index to Motion Picture Credits (U.S.). Formerly: **Screen
Achievement Records Bulletin** (0147-2313). Academy of Motion
Picture Arts and Sciences, 8949 Wilshire Blvd., Beverly
Hills, CA 90211. Tel: 213/278-8990; (annual); ISSN: 0163-
5123; OCLC 4402113.
Note: v.1-2, 1976-1977 as **Screen Achievement Records
Bulletin**; v.3, 1978- as **Annual Index to Motion Picture
Credits.**
List of films which the "Academy can establish from two or
more reliable sources the following information: title,
distributor, a credit from one of the major craft categories,

and the name of at least one actor, unless the film is animated or a documentary feature." Contains credit index containing names of actors, art directors, cinematographers, costume designers, directors, editors, makeup, music directors, sound editors and writers.
PN1993.A48a; Dewey: 791.43/05.

Annuario della Cinematografia Svizzera (Switzerland). See: **Schweizer Filmindex = Index Suisse du Cinema = Indice Svizzero del Cinema.**

Anthologie du Cinema (France); L'Avant-Scene Cinema, 6, rue Git-le-coeur, 75006 Paris, France; (irregular); ISSN: 0570-2917; OCLC 2160971.
Note: n.1, 1965 -.
Issued as a supplement to the magazine **L'Avant-Scene Cinema**, this publication presents a tribute to an internationally acclaimed film director. The articles include a biographical sketch, a comprehensive filmography, and a critical analysis of the director's work. Handsomely illustrated with photos and stills. Published in French.
PN1993.A63; Dewey: 791.43/05.

Anuario del Cine (Argentina); Ediciones Cooregidor, Corriente 1585, Buenos Aires, C 1042 Argentina; (annual); ISSN: n/a; OCLC 4856509.
Note: v.1, 1977 -.
Annual compilation of motion picture producers and distributors. Lists feature films produced throughout the preceding year, giving title, cast and credits, length and synopsis. Published in Spanish.
PN1993.C37; Dewey: 791.43/05.

Arbeitsgemeinschaft Cinema (Switzerland). See: **Cinema.**

Arbitron Television Audience Estimates (U.S.); Arbitron Ratings, Co, 142 West 57th St., New York, NY 10019. Tel: 212/887-1300; (daily); ISSN: n/a.
Note: May 1949-1958 as monthly; 1958- as daily.
Provides radio and television audience estimates for specific programs, as well as for any part of the 24 hour programming day. Divided into regional offices, data is collected for that part of the country which defines the audience by

gender, age, race, employment status, socio-economic status
and lifestyle. Used by broadcasters and advertisers to
measure the value of air time and audience size.

Archives (France); Institut Jean Vigo-Cinematheque De Toulouse,
Palais des Congres 66000 Perpignan, France. Tel: 68.34.13.13;
(bimonthly); ISSN: 0985-2395.
Note: n.1, Sep/Oct 1986 -.
Serious newsletter for archives holding primary research or
original documentation on the history of the cinema.
Emphasis is on French and European cinema.

Archives/Cahiers de la Cinematheque (France). See: **Les Cahiers de
la Cinematheque.**

Arizona Film, Theatre & Television (U.S.). See: **A.F.T. & T.**

Art & Cinema (U.S.). Alternate title: **Art and Cinema**. VRI Arts
Publishing, PO Box 1208, Imperial Beach, CA 92032. Tel: 619/
429-5533; (3 times/yr); ISSN: 0363-2911; OCLC 1781862.
Note: v.1,n.1 Jan 1973 -.
Devoted to the study and presentation of film and video as
works of art. Concentrates on avant garde, independent and
experimental film and video. Offers an extensive slide
library of artwork, dance, and photography for sale.
N72.M6A77; Dewey: 700.

Art and Cinema (U.S.). See: **Art & Cinema.**

Art Murphy's Box Office Register (U.S.); Art Murphy's Box Office
Register, PO Box 3786, Hollywood, CA 90078; (annual); ISSN:
n/a; OCLC 13980331.
Note: [ed.1], 1982 -. (Issues for 1982, 1983 and 1984 were
published in 1985.)
Publishes boxoffice receipts counting income earned by
feature films released in the United States during the
preceding year. Includes foreign and domestic motion
pictures.
PN1993.A74; Dewey: 384.83/05 19.

Artibus et Historiae (Italy); Libreria Commissionaria Sansoni,
LICOSA, via Lamamora 45, 50121 Firenze, Italy; (2 times/yr);
ISSN: 0391-9064; OCLC 7377675.

Note: n.1, 1980 -.
An international journal published in English, French, German
and Italian. Emphasis is on the visual arts, including
architecture and cinema. Creatively designed and beautifully
illustrated articles analyze the visual arts in terms of
cultural influence, historical perspective and artistic
composition.
NX1.A1A77; Dewey: 705.

Arts & Entertainment Cable Network Program Guide (U.S.). See: **A.
& E. Cable Network Program Guide.**

ArtsAmerica Fine Art Film and Video Source Book (U.S.). Alternate
title: **Fine Art Film and Video Source Book**. ArtsAmerica,
Inc., 125 Greenwich Ave., Greenwich, CT 06830. Tel: 203/637-
1454; (annual); ISSN: n/a; OCLC 14937066.
Note: v.1, 1987 -.
An exclusive listing of fine art film and video documentaries
by subject (prehistoric art to 20th century art), historical
perspective, museum collections, museum professionals, and
techniques. Includes indexes by name, title and distributor.
N369.A74A78; Dewey: 016.7.

Asia-Pacific Broadcasting Union Technical Review (Japan). See:
A.B.U. Technical Review.

Asian Cinema (U.S.). Formerly: **Asian Cinema Studies Society
Newsletter**. Alternate titles: **A.C.S.S. Newsletter;
Newsletter. Asian Cinema Studies Society**. ACSS Newsletter,
Quinnipiac College, Box 91, Hamden, CT 06518-0569; (2 times/
yr.); ISSN: n/a; OCLC 13418934.
Note: v.1,n.1-v.3,n.1, Spring 1985-Spring 1988 as **Asian
Cinema Studies Society Newsletter**; v.3,n.2, Fall 1988- as
Asian Cinema.
Promotes filmmaking by Asian-Americans; reviews films and
videos of interest to and involving Asian-Americans. Lists
publications, conferences, lectures, special events, film
exhibitions, traveling shows and distribution sources for
independent filmmakers.

Asian Cinema Studies Society Newsletter (U.S.). See: **Asian
Cinema.**

Asian Mass Communication Bulletin (A.M.C.B.) (Singapore).
Alternate title: **A.M.C.B.** Asian Mass Communication Research
& Information Centre (A.M.I.C.), 39 Newton Rd., Republic of
Singapore (1130). Tel: 2515106/7; (quarterly); ISSN: n/a.
Note: n.1, 1974 -.
A newsletter for members of the A.M.I.C. Reports on
educational courses, consultant services, bibliographies,
training courses, seminars and conferences of interest to
teachers and students of mass communications in Asia.
Published in English.

**Association for Education in Journalism and Mass Communication
News** (U.S.). See: **A.E.J.M.C. News.**

Association of Independent Video and Filmmakers Newsletter
(U.S.). See: **The Independent.**

Attualita Cinematografiche (Italy); Edizioni Letture, Piazza San
Fedele 4, 20121 Milan, Italy. Tel: (02)804441; (annual);
ISSN: n/a; ISBN: 88-85000 592; OCLC 3529713.
Note: v.1, 1963 -.
Comprehensive directory of international films shown in Italy
during the previous year. Arranged alphabetically by Italian
release title, each entry includes director, cast, credits
and a lengthy, signed review. Contains indexes by director
and alternate titles. Includes some television. Published
in Italian.
PN1993.3.A87.

Audience (U.S.). Alternate title: **Audience Entertainment Magazine.**
Concord Communications Corp., 13365 Ventura Blvd., Sherman
Oaks, CA 91423; (monthly); ISSN: 0737-8114; OCLC 9461280.
Note: v.1, 1982 -.
A magazine designed for the serious film buff. In depth reporting
about issues concerning the motion picture industry, such as
nitrate preservation and colorization. Articles cover film
history, theory, and criticism. Reviews films and television
shows.

Audience Entertainment Magazine (U.S.). See: **Audience.**

Audio & Video News (U.S.). See: **AudioVideo International.**

Audio Video (Sweden); Audio Video, Affarsforlaget,
  Datadivisionen, Box 3188, 103 63 Stockholm, Sweden. Tel: 08-
  749 0011; (quarterly); ISSN: 0282-6364; OCLC 13243913.
  Note: v.1, 1985? -.
  Handsome publication investigating home and business
  applications of sound and video systems. Conducts extensive
  tests of hi-fi and video equipment. A technical journal for
  professionals working in the music, television and video
  industries.
  TK7881.4.A95.

Audio Video Market Place: A.V.M.P. (U.S.). Alternate title:
  A.V.M.P.: Audio Video Market Place. R.R. Bowker Co., 245 W.
  17th St., New York, NY 10011; (annual); ISSN: 0067-0553; OCLC
  10929022.
  Note: ed.1, 1969 -.
  "A multimedia guide." A comprehensive directory of suppliers
  of audiovisual products and services in the United States.
  Contains names and addresses for companies specializing in
  motion picture, television and video equipment. Has separate
  sections for producers, post-production, editing, music and
  sound specialists.
  LB1043.A86; LB1042.5.A2; Dewey: 011 11.

Audio Video Review Digest (U.S.). See: **AudioVideo Review Digest**.

Audio/Video Interiors (U.S.); CurtCo Publishing, 4827 Sepulveda
  Blvd., Suite 220, Sherman Oaks, CA 91403, Subscriptions:
  Audio/Video Interiors, PO Box 51604, Boulder, CO 80321-1604.
  Tel: 818/784-0700; (bimonthly); ISSN: 1041-5378; OCLC
  18798036.
  Note: v.1,n.1 Feb/Mar 1989 -.
  "Style and technology in harmony." Sophisticated magazine
  describing media design and installation by professionals
  working with decorators and architects. Displays glossy
  layouts of home and office interiors featuring entertainment
  centers, video recorders and playback equipment, television
  monitors, stereo speakers, record and CD players blending into
  the overall design of the edifice without being intrusive. A
  professional magazine for interior decorators and designers.

Audio Visual (U.K.). Formerly: **16 MM Film User; Film User**.
  Absorbed: **Industrial Screen** (0446-0855). Maclarens, PO Box

109, Davis House, 66-77 High St., Croydon CR9 1QH Surrey, England; (monthly); ISSN: 0305-2249; OCLC 5073185.
Note: v.1,n.1-v.1,n.12, Nov 1946-Oct 1947 as **16 MM Film User**; v.2,n.1-v.25, Nov 1947-Nov 1971? as **Film User**. Renumbered v.1,n.1, Jan 1972- as **Audio Visual**. Absorbed **Industrial Screen**, Jan 1964.
Contains critical reviews of new educational and industrial films and videos. Each review contains full description of work, production and distribution information and a rating, from mediocre to exceptional based on artistic merit and production values. Provides a film booking service. Also reviews equipment.
TS2301.A7A78; Dewey: 384.

Audio-Visual Communications (U.S.). Formerly: **Film and Audio-Visual Communications**. Media Horizons, 50 West 23rd St., New York, NY 10010-5292. Tel: 212/645-1000; (monthly); ISSN: 0004-7562; OCLC 5140909.
Note: v.1,n.1 Feb 1967 -.
Trade journal designed for technical personnel involved in film and video production. Features articles on audiovisual graphics, hardware, management, production and technology. Profiles creative, innovative and successful people who are responsible for the special effects, graphic design and computer generated visuals used in the motion picture and television industries today.
TS2301.A7F472; Dewey: 621.38/044/05 19.

Audio Visual Directions (U.S.). See: **A.V. Video**.

The Audio-Visual Equipment Directory (U.S.). See: **Equipment Directory of Audio-Visual, Computer and Video Products**.

Audio-Visual Materials for Higher Education (U.K.). See: **B.U.F.V.C. Catalogue**.

Audio Visual Product News (U.S.). See: **A.V. Video**.

Audio-vizualis Kozlemenyek (Hungary); Orszagos Muszaki Informacios Kozpont es Konyvtar (OMIKK), Budapest VIII, Muzeum u.17, Hungary. Tel: 336-330; (bimonthly); ISSN: n/a.
Note: v.1, 1964 -.
A serious journal with articles studying the many uses of

audiovisual materials in education. Covers such topics as
computer-based searching in libraries, information retention
from video presentations, teaching the art of film at the
university level, use of computer imaging in speech pathology.
Published in Hungarian, with table of contents in Hungarian,
Cyrillic, German and English.
LB1043.A84.

AudioVideo (U.S.). See: **AudioVideo International.**

AudioVideo International (U.S.). Alternate titles: **AudioVideo;**
Audio & Video News. Dempa Publications, 400 Madison Ave.,
New York, NY 10017. Tel: 212/752-3003; (monthly); ISSN: 0093-
6499; OCLC 1792219.
Note: v.1,n.1, Jan 1973 -.
"An international review of the electronics world." Trade
journal reporting on electronic apparatus and appliances.
Reports on business trends and developments. Covers audio
and video equipment, personal computers and home entertainment
systems. Gives marketing advice, industry forecasts and
information on Japanese manufacturers.
TK7800.A83; Dewey: 621.38/05.

AudioVideo Review Digest (U.S.). Alternate titles: **A.V.R.D.;**
Audio Video Review Digest. Gale Research, Inc., Book Tower,
Dept. 77748, Detroit, MI 48277-0748; (3 times/yr; with annual
cumulations); ISSN: 1043-4038; OCLC 19451222.
Note: v.1,n.1 May 1989 -.
An index to reviews of non-print media: records, tapes, AV
kits, educational films and videos, filmstrips and feature
films from over 200 newspapers and periodicals. Entry gives
date, running time, audience level, review abstract, and subject
categories. Indexed by credits, media and subject.

Australian Films (Australia); National Library of Australia,
National Film Sound Archives, McCoy Circuit, Acton ACT 2601,
GPO Box 2002, Canberra, Australia. Tel: 062/671 711;
(annual); ISSN: 0045-0448.
Note: ed.1, 1959 -.
Seeks to present a comprehensive listing of Australian motion
picture production each year. Lists films produced in Australia,
or Australian productions produced overseas. Includes feature
films, telefeatures, documentaries, experimental films, animation

and significant television series. Each entry includes title, date, length, production company, distributors and short synopsis. Includes index by subject and distributor. PN1998.A87.

The Australian Journal of Screen Theory (Australia); University of New South Wales, Department of Drama, Box 1, Post Office Kensington, New South Wales 2033, Australia; (irregular); ISSN: n/a.
Note: n.1-n.15/16, 1976-1984.
Forum for students, scholars and professors to set forth new ideas or challenge established theories of cinema studies. Ceased publication.

Australian Motion Picture Yearbook (Australia). See: **The Cinema Papers Australian Production Yearbook: Film, Television, Video.**

Australian Video and Cinema (Australia). See: What's On Video and Cinema.

Australian Video and Communications (Australia). Merged with **Australian Video Review**; incorporated by **Australian Video and Cinema**, which later changed its name to **What's on Video and Cinema** (0185-628X). Video and Communications, PO Box 186, Glen Iris, Victoria 3146, Australia; (monthly); ISSN: 0706-6902; OCLC 11613294.
Note: v.1-v.3,n.34, 1982-Sep 1984 as **Australian Video and Communications**; Jul 1983, merged with **Australian Video Review**; Oct 1984, absorbed by **Australian Video and Cinema**. Popular magazine reviewing Australian feature films and new video releases; discontinued in October 1984.
PN1992.95.A9; Dewey: 791/43/75/0994.

Australian Video Review (Australia). See: **Australian Video and Communications.**

L'Avant-Scene Cinema (France). Alternate title: **L'Avant Scene du Cinema.** Address: L'Avant-Scene Cinema, 6, rue Git-le-coeur, 75006 Paris, France; (20 times/yr); ISSN: 0045-1150; OCLC 1518930.
Note: n.1, Feb 1961 -.
Each issue is devoted to one noteworthy, prize-winning film and contains a complete list of cast and credits, background

material on the film's production and verbatim transcripts of the dialogue. Useful for people interested in scriptwriting. Also contains short reviews of other films currently released. An annual index is published in the last issue of the year. Published in French.
PN1993.A93.

L'Avant-Scene du Cinema (France). See: **L'Avant-Scene Cinema.**

-B-

B. & N. (Italy). See: **Bianco e Nero.**

B.C.T.V.: Bibliography on Cable Television (U.S.). See:
Bibliography on Cable Television: B.C.T.V.

The B.F.I. Film and Television Yearbook (U.K.). See: Film and
Television Yearbook.

The B.K.S.T.S. Journal (U.K.). See: Image Technology.

B.M./E.: The Magazine of Broadcast Management/Engineering
(U.S.). See: B.M.E. for Technical and Engineering Management.

B.M.E. for Technical and Engineering Management (U.S.). Formerly:
B.M./E.: The Magazine of Broadcast Management/Engineering
(0005-3201), ACT III Publishing/Technical Division. 295
Madison Ave., New York, NY 10017; Tel: 212/679-0919;
(monthly); ISSN: 1043-7487; OCLC 18811451.
Note: v.1,n.1-v.24,n.7, Jan 1965-Jul 1988 as B.M./E.: The
Magazine of Broadcast Management/Engineering; v.24,n.8 Aug
1988- as B.M.E. for Technical and Engineering Management.
Highly technical magazine serving broadcast industry
executives and engineers. Contains interviews, articles on
production facilities and recording studios, information on
the latest equipment, technical advances and new
applications.
TK6630.A1B2; Dewey: 384.540/568.

B.U.F.C. Card Catalogue Index (U.K.). See: B.U.F.V.C. Catalogue.

B.U.F.V.C. Catalogue (U.K.). Formerly: B.U.F.C. Card Catalogue
Index; Catalogue of Films for Universities; Films for
Universities; Audio-Visual Materials for Higher Education;
alternate title: British Universities Film & Video Council
Catalogue. Address: British Universities Film & Video Council,
55 Greek St., London, W1V 5LR England; (annual); ISSN: 0268-

2443; ISBN: 0 901299 52 9.
Note: 1954-1959 as **B.U.F.C. Card Catalogue Index**; ed.1,
1960 as **Catalogue of Films for Universities**; revised ed.,
1968 as **Films for Universities**; renumbered ed.1-5, 1973-1981
as **Audio-Visual Materials for Higher Education**; renumbered
ed.1, 1983- as **B.U.F.V.C. Catalogue**.
Reference source for British librarians and teachers to help
them locate appropriate, advanced-level audiovisual works for
use in the classroom. Contains videocassettes, videodiscs,
films, tape-slide programs, slide sets, audio tapes and
computer software. Catalog of titles is on microfiche
accompanied by booklet of distributors. Includes genre list,
title index, and subject index.

B Westerns in Perspective (U.S.); B Westerns in Perspective, PO
Box 591, Stokesdale, NC 27357; (monthly).
Note: n.1, Jan 1983 -.
Fan magazine devoted to American westerns made in the 1930s
and 1940s.

Back Stage (U.S.). Alternate title: **Backstage**. Back Stage
Publications, Inc., 330 West 42nd St., New York, NY 10036.
Tel: 212/947-0020; (weekly); ISSN: 0005-3635; OCLC 1519001.
Note: v.1, Dec 2, 1960 -.
"The complete service weekly for the communications and
entertainment industry." Divided into two sections, the
first is a forum for industry news, agents, independent
filmmakers and people providing services to the entertainment
industry. The second section contains information about the
stage, film and TV casting, theatre reviews and New York
filming.
PN1560.B3; Dewey: 792.

Back Stage TV Film & Tape Production Directory (U.S.). Formerly:
**Backstage TV/Industrial Film Directory; Backstage Film/Tape &
Syndication Directory; Backstage: TV Film, Tape & Syndication
Directory** (0098-5481); alternate title: **Backstage: TV Film &
Tape Production Directory**. Address: Back Stage Publications,
Inc., 330 W. 42nd St., New York, NY 10036. Tel: 212/947-0020;
(annual); ISSN: 0734-9777; OCLC 8831506.
Note: 1974-1981 as **Backstage: TV Film, Tape & Syndication
Directory**; 1982-1984 as **Back Stage TV Film & Tape Directory**;
1985- as **Back Stage TV Film & Tape Production Directory**.

Comprehensive directory of companies, agents and services
catering to the entertainment industry. Each entry includes
names, addresses, telephone numbers, personnel and credits.
Services include production companies, ad agencies, music
facilities, animation studios, TV commercial producers,
engineering equipment outlets and post-production facilities.
PN1998.A1B23; Dewey: 384.8/029473.

Backstage (U.S.). See: **Back Stage**.

Backstage: TV Film, Tape & Syndication Directory (U.S.). See:
Back Stage TV Film & Tape Production Directory.

Backstage Film/Tape & Syndication Directory (U.S.). See: **Back
Stage TV Film & Tape Production Directory**.

Backstage TV Film & Tape Production Directory (U.S.). See: **Back
Stage TV Film & Tape Production Directory**.

Backstage TV/Industrial Film Directory (U.S.). See: **Back Stage TV
Film & Tape Production Directory**.

Beitrage zur Film- und Fernsehwissenschaft (E.Germany). Formerly:
Filmwissenschaftliche Beitrage. Hochschule fur Film und
Fernsehen der DDR, Direktorat Information/Dokumentation/
Publikation, 10 Konenstr. 10, 1086 Berlin, East Germany. Tel:
229-27-08; (6 times/yr); ISSN: 0232-718X; OCLC 9806972.
Note: v.1-v.22, 1960-1981 as **Filmwissenschaftliche Beitrage**;
v.23, 1982- as **Beitrage zur Film- und Fernsehwissenschaft**.
In-depth scholarly articles on film theory, history and
criticism, focusing on films, directors and performers in the
Eastern Bloc. However, also has issues on noted
international directors such as Truffaut, Visconti and
Fassbinder, as theorized from a Communist standpoint.
Critical of Capitalist film culture.
PN1993.F665; Dewey: 791.43/05 19.

Bertha Landers Film Reviews (U.S.). See: **Landers Film Reviews**.

Better Radio & Television (U.S.); National Association for Better
Broadcasting, 7918 Naylor Ave., Los Angeles, CA 90045. Tel:
213/641-4903; (quarterly); ISSN: 0006-0194; OCLC 9698284.
Note: v.1,n.1 Winter 1960 -.

Monitors the quality of broadcast television. Concerned with keeping the public knowledgeable about corporate decisions made by the industry about programming. Informs subscribers about laws and regulations made by the F.C.C. and Congress affecting broadcasters and the public.

Bianco e Nero (Italy). Alternate title: **B. & N.** Centro Sperimentale de Cinematografia, via Tuscolana 1524, 00173 Roma, Italy; (quarterly); ISSN: 0006-0577; OCLC 2810337.
Note: v.1,n.1 Jan 31, 1937 -.
A publication with very wide ranging scholarly topics, from film propaganda to costume design. Also covers technical matters such as use of Technicolor in the 1930s, film colorization and telecommunications satellites. Reviews the latest international features, publishes Italian boxoffice statistics and comments on the awards granted at various film festivals.
PN1993.B45; Dewey: 791.43/05.

Bibliographie: Publications des Membres de la F.I.A.F. (Canada). See: **Bibliography: F.I.A.F. Members Publications.**

Bibliography: F.I.A.F. Members Publications = Bibliographie: Publications des Membres de la F.I.A.F. (Canada); National Film, Television and Sound Archives, 395 Wellington St., Ottawa, Ontario, Canada K1A 0N3. Tel: 613/995-1311; (annual); ISSN: 0074-5944; OCLC 2443259.
Note: n.1, 1967? -.
Annotated bibliography of publications written or compiled by members of the International Federation of Film Archives (F.I.A.F.). Designed to keep members up to date with the latest creative efforts, findings and studies of fellow archives. Published in French and English.
Z5784; Dewey: 016.79143.

Bibliography on Cable Television: B.C.T.V. (U.S.). Alternate title: **B.C.T.V.: Bibliography on Cable Television.**
Communications Library, 1550 Bryant St., Lockbox 5891, San Francisco, CA 94101-5891. Tel: 415/626-5050; (annual); ISSN: 0742-4914; OCLC 4362309.
Note: [ed.1] 1975 -.
A comprehensive bibliography covering all aspects of the cable industry. Entries include works on access,

advertising, audience demographics, business, finance,
legislation, marketing, programming, regulations, satellites,
technology and equipment. Kept up-to-date by two loose leaf
supplements.

The Big Reel (U.S.); Empire Publishing, Inc., Route 3, Box 83,
Madison, NC 27025. Tel: 919/427-5850; (monthly); ISSN: 0744-
723X; OCLC 7757081.
Note: n.1, Jun? 1974 -.
Printed in a newspaper tabloid format, this periodical
publishes information and advertising for buying, selling and
trading 16mm films and videos. Also carries ads for movie
and TV memorabilia, autographs, posters and lobby cards.
Contains biographical sketches of popular performers.

The Big Trail (U.S.). Alternate title: **Newsletter of the Films of
John Wayne**. Tom Lilley, Editor, 540 Stanton Ave., Akron, OH
44301; (bimonthly).
Note: v.1,n.1 Aug 1984 -.
A fan magazine devoted to John Wayne.

Billboard (U.S.); Billboard Publications, Inc., One Astor Plaza,
1515 Broadway, 39th Floor, New York, NY 10036. Tel: 212/764-
7300; (weekly); ISSN: 0006-2510; OCLC 1532948.
Note: v.1, 1894 -.
Began as a theater, vaudeville and musical revue trade
publication. Today it is still predominantly music, but
covers home entertainment videocassettes, videodiscs and
computer software, focusing on the business activity of the
home entertainment industry. Contains home video release
charts.
PN2000.B5.

Billboard International Talent Directory (U.S.). See:
International Talent & Touring Directory.

Billboard's International Buyer's Guide (U.S.). See:
International Buyer's Guide.

Billboard's International Talent & Touring Directory (U.S.). See:
International Talent & Touring Directory.

Black Camera (U.S.); Indiana University. Department of African-
American Studies, Memorial Hall East, No. 37, Bloomington, IN
47405; (2 times/yr).
Note: v.1,n.1 Summer 1985 -.
Newsletter promoting independent filmmaking by African
Americans. Studies and reviews films and videos of interest
to and involving people of African descent.

Black Film Review (U.S.); Black Film Review, 110 S Street, NW,
Washington, DC 20001. Tel: 202/745-0455; (quarterly); ISSN:
0887-5723; OCLC 13323851.
Note: v.1,n.1 Winter 1984 -.
Affiliated with the University of the District of Columbia
Black Film Institute. For students and teachers, as well as
others interested in African American culture. Reviews new
films and videotapes of interest to blacks. Interviews
successful minority performers, producers and directors.
PN1995.9.N4B48; Dewey: 791.43/09/093520396073 19.

Black Oracle (U.S.). See: **Cinemacabre.**

The Black Video Guide (U.S.); Video Publications Ltd., 915 Olive
St., Suite 821, St. Louis, MO 63101. Tel: 314/534-8555;
(annual); ISSN: 0882-7532; 0892-7532; OCLC 11960720.
Note: ed.1, 1985/86 -.
Comprehensive list of motion picture, television and cable
productions available on video with casts, credits or subject
matter that is of interest to or concerns African Americans.
Includes educational, documentary and entertainment
productions from 1900 to the present. Each entry contains
title, date, length, synopsis, production company and
distributor.
PN1995.9.N4B52; Dewey: 016.79143/09.

Blimp. Zeitschrift fur Film (Austria); "Blimp," Griesplatz 36,
A-8020 Graz, Wien, Austria. Tel: (0316) 91 67 63;
(quarterly); ISSN: n/a.
Note: [n.1], 1986? -.
Popular magazine of motion picture study and appreciation.
Concentrates on film history from the silent period.
Publishes accolades to famous directors of the past. Covers
documentary and avant garde films as well as theatrical feature
films. Published in German.

Bob's Videomania (U.S.). See: **Videomania**.

Boletim Informativo S.I.P. (Brazil); Instituto Nacional do
Cinema. Setor do Ingresso Padronizado, Rua Mayrink Veiga 28-
70 Andar, Rio de Janeiro, Brazil; (annual); ISSN: n/a; ISBN
43-7-8803110686; OCLC 2405485.
Note: ed.1, 1974 -.
A motion picture yearbook for Brazil containing statistical
information about the entertainment industry. Includes
contacts and addresses for production and distribution
companies. Lists all feature films made throughout the
preceding year. Published in Portuguese.
PN1993.5B6I58a.

Bowker's Complete Video Directory (U.S.). Formerly: **Variety's
Complete Home Video Directory**; alternate title: **Complete Home
Video Directory**; R.R. Bowker Co. 245 West 17th St., New York,
NY 10011. Tel: 212/337-6934; (annual); ISSN: 0000-1015; OCLC
16418292.
Note: v.1-v.2, 1988-1989 as **Variety's Complete Home Video
Directory**; renumbered v.1, 1990- as **Bowker's Complete Video
Directory**.
A complete listing of all the home video productions available
for sale or rent in the United States. Each entry includes title,
year, MPAA rating, supplier, production information, video
distributor, cast, synopsis and price. Indexed by subject, personal
name and distributor. For the 1988 and 1989 editions, issued a
separate publication, **Variety's Complete Home Video Directory.
Adult Video Supplement**. The adult video supplement has been
discontinued.
Dewey: 011 11.

Box Office (U.S.). See: **Boxoffice**.

Boxoffice (U.S.). Alternate title: **Box Office**. R.L.D. Communications,
Inc., 1800 N. Highland Ave., Suite 710, Hollywood, CA 90028. Tel:
213/465-1186; (monthly); ISSN: 0006-8527; OCLC 5261926.
Note: v.1, Jan 21, 1932 -.
Began with regional editions covering boxoffice sales and
statistics throughout the United States. In 1978, absorbed
the Eastern, Southeast, Southwest and National Executive editions.
Contains articles on the latest feature films, as well as modern

movie theater technology, such as screens, projectors, multiplex and sound systems. Rates films according to boxoffice appeal with its best and worst awards.
PN1993.B6; Dewey: 791 11.

Bright Lights (U.S.); Bright Lights, Gary Morris, Editor, PO Box 26081, Los Angeles, CA 90026; (irregular); ISSN: 0147-4049; OCLC 3158214.
Note: v.1,n.1 Fall 1974 -.
"The magazine of American film." A literary fan magazine concentrating on Hollywood film stars from the 1930s through the 1950s. Many portrait and publicity stills illustrate nostalgia pieces on the golden age of Hollywood. Includes analytical critiques of award winning movies. Interviews stars and directors; contains biographical data and filmographies.

The British Federation of Film Societies Monthly Journal (U.K.). see: **Film** (U.K.).

British Film and Television Year Book (U.K.). See: **Screen International Film and Television Yearbook.**

British Film Institute. Monthly Film Bulletin (U.K.). See: **Monthly Film Bulletin.**

British Film Institute. National Film Theatre. Programmes (U.K.). See: **National Film Theatre. Programmes.**

British Film Institute Film and Television Yearbook (U.K.). See: **Film and Television Yearbook.**

British Kinematograph Society. The Journal (U.K.). See: **Image Technology.**

British Kinematograph Society. Proceedings (U.K.). See: **Image Technology.**

British Kinematograph, Sound and Television Society. The B.K.S.T.S. Journal (U.K.). See: **Image Technology.**

British Kinematography (U.K.). See: **Image Technology.**

British Kinematography, Sound and Television (U.K.). See: **Image Technology**.

British National Film & Video Catalogue (U.K.). Formerly: **British National Film Catalogue** (0007-1552). British Film Institute, 21 Stephen St., London, England W1P 1PL. Tel: 01-437-4355; (quarterly, with annual cumulations); ISSN: 0266-805X; OCLC 11008973.
Note: v.1-v.21, 1963-1983 as **British National Film Catalogue**; v.22,n.1 Spring 1984- as **British National Film & Video Catalog.**
Distribution catalog of latest film and video releases available from both commercial and governmental sources in Great Britain. Covers fiction and non-fiction films and videocassettes. Entries include title, distributor, year, production company, sponsor, physical description (running time, color, b&w, gauge or format), summary and audience. PN1998.A1B862; Dewey: 016.79143/75 19.

British National Film Catalogue (U.K.). See: **British National Film & Video Catalogue.**

British Universities Film & Video Council Catalog (U.K.). See: **B.U.F.V.C. Catalog.**

Broadcast (U.K.). Alternate title: **Broadcast Incorporating Television Weekly**. International Thomson Publishing, Ltd., 100 Avenue Rd., London, England NW3 3TP. Tel: 01-935-6611; (weekly); ISSN: n/a; OCLC 14589806.
Note: [n.1], 19uu -.
Weekly trade newspaper covering the radio and television industries in Great Britain. Contains market and programming analyses, profiles of executives, news about the British networks, ratings for the top 100 shows, and classified ads for employment. Includes a monthly supplement called **Invision**.

Broadcast + Technology (Canada). See: **Broadcast Technology**.

Broadcast Banker/Broker (U.S.). Formerly: **Broadcast Banking** (0749-677X). Paul Kagan Associates, Inc., 126 Clock Tower Place, Carmel, CA 93923-8734. Tel: 408/624-1536; (monthly); ISSN: 0889-2644; OCLC 13829133.
Note: n.1-n.25, Sep 11, 1984-Jun 1986 as **Broadcast Banking**;

n.26, Jun 25, 1986- as **Broadcast Banker/Broker.**
Newsletter analyzing interest rates and cash flow as they
apply to the radio, cable and television broadcasting
industries. Informs investors of equity and debt financing
for radio and TV.
Dewey: 384 11.

Broadcast Banking (U.S.). See: **Broadcast Banker/Broker.**

Broadcast Engineering (U.S.); Intertec Publishing, Box 12901,
9221 Quivira Rd., Overland Park, KS 66212. Tel: 913/888-4664;
(13 times/yr); ISSN: 0007-1994; OCLC 1537398.
Note: v.1,n.1 May 1959 -.
For broadcast industry executives and engineers. Technical
journal covering both commercial and educational broadcasting
facilities, such as radio and television stations, recording
studios, video production companies, closed-circuit
television, instructional TV, laboratories, engineering
studios, and government agencies. Beginning in 1981, volumes
include "Spec Book" as thirteenth issue.
TK6540.B8433.

Broadcast Investor (U.S.); Paul Kagan Associates, Inc., 126 Clock
Tower Place, Carmel, CA 93923-8734. Tel: 408/624-1536;
(monthly); ISSN: 0146-0110; OCLC 2827898.
Note: n.1, Mar 1977 -.
Newsletter evaluating the worth of radio and television
stations. An investment guide for stockholders trading in
privately owned radio and TV stations, plus public broadcast
companies.

Broadcast Investor Charts (U.S.); Paul Kagan Associates, Inc.,
126 Clock Tower Place, Carmel, CA 93923-8734. Tel: 408/624-
1536; (monthly); ISSN: 0736-9069; OCLC 9243216.
Note: n.1, Jan 21, 1983 -.
Charts stock price movements of over forty publicly held
broadcast companies covering a two year period.

Broadcast Pioneers Library Reports (U.S.); Broadcast Pioneers,
1771 N St., NW, Washington, DC 20036. Tel: 202/223-0088;
(quarterly); ISSN: n/a.
Note: v.1, Spring 1975 -.
Newsletter for members. Keeps members informed of meetings,

technical innovations, laws and legislation of interest to
people involved in the radio and television industries.
Contains profiles and interviews, as well as tributes to past
members.

Broadcast Plus Technology (Canada). See: **Broadcast Technology**.

Broadcast Programming & Production (U.S.); Gallay
Communications, Inc., 1850 N. Whitley Ave., Hollywood, CA
90028. Tel: 213/467-1111; (bimonthly); ISSN: 0191-4898; OCLC
2938326.
Note: v.1, 1975 -.
Trade publication for radio and television broadcast station
managers. Covers equipment, marketing, promotional efforts,
advertising and new technology. Lead articles discuss radio
and television history, as well as present-day innovations
and strategies.
PN1992.75.B75; Dewey: 384.54/05.

Broadcast Stats (U.S.); Paul Kagan Associates, Inc., 126 Clock
Tower Place, Carmel, CA 93923-1536. Tel: 408/624-1536;
(monthly); ISSN: 0749-2936; OCLC 11101064.
Note: n.1, Aug 17, 1984 -.
Newsletter containing statistics on the revenue, cash flow,
financial health and stock prices of radio and television
stations across the United States. Data garnered from the
Federal Communications Commission.

Broadcast Technology (Canada). Alternate titles: **Broadcast +
Technology; Broadcast Plus Technology.** Diversified
Publications, Ltd., 6 Farmers Lane, Box 420, Bolton, Ontario,
Canada L7E 5T3. Tel: 416/857-6076; (monthly; except Aug &
Dec); ISSN: 0709-9797; OCLC 17311668.
Note: v.1, 1975 -.
Trade journal for professionals working in the Canadian radio and
television broadcasting industries. Covers new equipment,
satellites, advertising, regulations, technology and related
interests.
TK6540; Dewey: 384.54/0971.

Broadcaster (Canada). Formerly: **The Canadian Broadcaster** (0319-
1389). Northern Miner Press, Ltd., 7 Labatt Ave., Toronto,
Ontario, Canada M5A 3P2. Tel: 416/363-6111; (monthly); ISSN:

0008-3038; OCLC 1743566.
Note: v.1-v.28,n.9, Jan 1942-Sep 1969 as **The Canadian Broadcaster**; v.28,n.10, Oct 1969- as **Broadcaster.**
Extensive coverage of the Canadian radio, television and cable industries. Reports on new applications of communications technology, government regulations, licenses granted, service in remote locations, use of satellites, and factors involved with serving a bilingual population.
HE8699.

Broadcasting (U.S.); Broadcasting Publications, Inc., 1705 DeSales St., Washington, DC 20036. Tel: 202/659-2340; (weekly); ISSN: 0007-2028; OCLC 6318655.
Note: [v.1], Oct 15, 1931 -.
Serious trade journal for the radio and television industries. Timely articles concerned with current trends in telecommunications, radio and television broadcasting. "The newsweekly of broadcasting and allied arts." Also available on microfilm.
TK6540.B85; Dewey: 621 11.

Broadcasting and the Law (U.S.). Formerly: **Perry's Broadcasting and the Law.** Broadcasting and the Law, Inc., 3050 Biscayne Blvd., Suite 501, Miami, FL 33137. Tel: 305/576-4743; (biweekly); ISSN: 0161-5823; OCLC 11641286.
Note: v.1-v.14, 1971-1984 as **Perry's Broadcasting and the Law**; v.14,n.24 Dec 15, 1984- as **Broadcasting and the Law.**
"Reports and interprets current court and F.C.C. rulings affecting broadcasting practice and operations." Keeps current with state and federal laws, legislation and regulations affecting the radio, television and cable industries.
KF2801.A3P47; Dewey: 343.73/09945.

Broadcasting/Cable Yearbook (U.S.). Alternate title: **Broadcasting/Cablecasting Yearbook** (0732-7196). Broadcasting Publications, Inc., 1705 DeSales St., NW, Washington, DC 20036. Tel: 202/659-2340; (annual); ISSN: 0277-3678; OCLC 6228239.
Note: 1980-1981 as **Broadcasting Cable Yearbook**, a merger of **Broadcasting Yearbook** (0068-2713) and **Broadcasting, Cable Sourcebook** (0097-8132); 1982-1988 as **Broadcasting/ Cablecasting Yearbook**; 1989- as **Broadcasting/Cable**

Yearbook.
Contains list of all cable and television stations in the
U.S., state by state, with their call letters, affiliates,
personnel, addresses and telephone numbers. Lists state and
federal regulatory agencies, engineering consultants, pay TV
networks, equipment manufacturers, markets, distributors, and
employment services.
HE8689.B77; Dewey: 384.54/0973.

Broadcasting/Cablecasting Yearbook (U.S.). See: **Broadcasting/
Cable Yearbook.**

Bulgarian Films (Bulgaria); Bulgarian Cinematography State Corp.,
135-A Rakovski St., Sofia, Bulgaria. Tel: 88-32-89; (8 times/
yr); ISSN: 0204-8884.
Note: v.1, 1959? -.
International forum for distribution of Bulgarian films.
Publishes a variety of material on contemporary Bulgarian
films and filmmakers. Includes information on the history
and background of Bulgarian cinema. Published in English,
French, Russian and Spanish.

Bullentin Finas (Malaysia); The Relations and Publications
Division, FINAS 198, Jalan Ampang, 50450 Kuala Lumpur,
Federal Territory, Peninsular Malaysia; (monthly); ISSN:
0127-9327.
Note: v.1, 1986 -.
Government publication published to disseminate information
on various aspects of the film industry such as film
festivals, new productions, and proposed laws and taxes
affecting the Malaysian film industry. Published in
Malaysian and English.

**Bulletin, Calendar of International Film and Television Events =
Bulletin, Calendrier des Evenements Internationaux du Cinema
et de la Television** (Italy). Alternate titles: **Calendar of
International Film and Television Events; Calendrier des
Evenments Internationaux du Cinema et de la Television.**
Address: International Film and Television Council, via Santa
Susanna 17, Rome 00187 Italy; (annual); ISSN: n/a; OCLC
5294645.
Note: ed.1, 1977/1978 -.
International directory published in French and English

describing all the film, television and video festivals worldwide. Gives name of festival, address, contact person, dates, summary of events, formats and themes judged, and prizes. Indexed by country.
PN1998.A1B78; Dewey: 791.4/025.

Bulletin, Calendrier des Evenements Internationaux du Cinema et de la Television (Italy). See: **Bulletin, Calendar of International Film and Television Events.**

Bulletin d'Information de L'A.C.P.Q. (Canada). See: **Cine Bulles.**

Bulletin d'Information du Centre National de la Cinematographie (France). See: **Informations C.N.C.**

Bulletin de L'Association Francaise de Recherche sur L'Histoire du Cinema (France). See: **1895: Bulletin de L'Association Francaise de Recherche sur L'Histoire du Cinema.**

Bulletin de la Cinematheque Suisse (Switzerland). See: **La Cinematheque Suisse.**

Bulletin for Film and Video Information (U.S.); Anthology Film Archives, 80 Wooster St., New York, NY 10012. Tel: 212/226-0010; (bimonthly); ISSN: n/a.
Note: v.1,n.1-v.2,n.6, Jan 1974-August 1976.
A guide to the resources and services of independent film and video. Listed workshops, distribution sources, stock film libraries, reference books, periodicals and complementary organizations which could aid the independent film and video producer. Discontinued publication in August 1976, although still maintains telephone reference service and acts as a clearinghouse for information.

Bulletin K.F.T.: Media Karyawan Film dan Televisi Indonesia (Indonesia); Pusat Perfilman H. Usman Ismail, J1. HR. Said Kuningan, Jakarta, Indonesia; (irregular); ISSN: 0216-3411; OCLC 11013843.
Note: n.1, 1980? -.
Magazine covering motion pictures and television broadcasting in Indonesia.
PN1993.5.I84B84.

Bulletin / MediaWatch. Evaluation-Medias (Canada). See:
MediaWatch Bulletin. Evaluation-Medias.

The Bulletin of the Academy of Motion Picture Arts and Sciences
(U.S.). Alternate titles: **Academy of Motion Picture Arts and
Sciences. Bulletin; Academy Bulletin.** Address: Academy of
Motion Picture Arts and Sciences, 8949 Wilshire Blvd., Beverly
Hills, CA 90211. Tel: 213/278-8990; (irregular); ISSN: n/a;
OCLC 9737223.
Note: Unnumbered, 1928-1946 as **Academy of Motion Picture Arts
and Sciences. Bulletin;** n.1-n.19, Mar/Apr 1973-Apr 1981 as **The
Bulletin of the Academy of Motion Picture Arts and Sciences.**
Newsletter providing "information on the full range of
Academy activities." Reports on the Oscars, fund raising
projects, educational activities, exhibits, student film
awards, new collections, materials donated, personnel changes
and library news. Publication suspended April 1981.

Bulletin of the Center for Soviet & East-European Studies (U.S.).
Formerly: **Bulletin of the Center for Soviet & East-European
Studies in the Performing Arts** (0008-9095). Herbert Marshall,
Southern Illinois University at Carbondale, 809 S. Forest,
Carbondale, IL 62901-6515. Tel: 618/453-5174; (quarterly);
ISSN: 0275-1658; OCLC 2262160.
Note: n.1-n.5, Spring 1969-Winter 1971 as **Bulletin of the
Center for Soviet & East-European Studies in the Performing
Arts;** n.6, Spring 1971- as **Bulletin of the Center for Soviet
& East-European Studies.**
Discusses the influence of film and television in East
Germany, Poland, Czechoslovakia, Hungary, Rumania,
Yugoslavia, Bulgaria, and the Soviet Union. Studies how film
and television is used in these countries, the role of
censorship, Western influences and state control of the media.
Dewey: 790 11.

**Bulletin of the Center for Soviet & East-European Studies in the
Performing Arts** (U.S.). See: **Bulletin of the Center for
Soviet & East-European Studies.**

Bulletin of the Czechoslovak Nationalized Film (Czechoslovakia).
See: **The Czechoslovak Film.**

Bulletin of the International Interchurch Film Centre
(Netherlands). See: **Interfilm Reports**.

Bulletin on Film (India); National Documentation Centre on Mass
Communication, Research and Reference Division, New Delhi,
India; (monthly); ISSN: n/a; OCLC 7685206.
Note: v.1, 1955? -.
A digest based on newspaper reviews of feature films in
distribution in India. A government publication meant
primarily for the use of the Ministry of Information and
Broadcasting. Published in English.

Burrelle's Media Directory. TV Clips (U.S.); Burrelle's, 75 East
Northfield Rd., Livingston, NJ 07039. Tel: 201/992-6600; 800/
631-1160; (weekly); ISSN: 0883-9778.
Note: Began 1978 -.
In addition to a clipping service for newspapers, Burrelle's
monitors television programs for subscribers located in the
Northeast corridor. It is a looseleaf service providing
news clips of TV programs which mention the subscriber's name.
Gives title of program, air date, time, network, Nielsen
audience, and quotes. Contains the following specific media
directories: Maryland, Delaware, and Washington, D.C.; New
England, New Jersey, New York State, and Pennsylvania; as well
as individual groups: Black, Hispanic, and Women's.
P88.8.B85.

Business Media Week (U.S.); Knowledge Industry Publications, 701
Westchester Ave., White Plains, NY 10604. Tel: 914/328-9157;
800/248-KIPI; (weekly); ISSN: 8756-9639; OCLC 11773448.
Note: v.1,n.1 Apr 15, 1985 -.
Professional magazine for media executives covering the
telecommunications and computer industries. Articles include
latest applications of computer software, interactive video,
cable and laserdisk technology in business and industry.
HF5001.B837; Dewey: 001.55/05.

Business T.V. (U.S.). Alternate titles: **Business Television; Telespan's
Business T.V.; Telespan's Business Television.** Circulation
Manager, Telespan's Business TV, c/o Telespan Publishing Corp.,
PO Box 6250, Altadena, CA 91001; (quarterly); ISSN: 0896-3142;
OCLC 17005404.
Note: [v.1], Fall 1986 -.

"The magazine of television for business use." Covers the
nearly 50 business television networks in operation around
the country. Articles identify select programs about
business management, manufacturing, finance, regulations and
law.
Dewey: 650 11.

Business Television (U.S.). See: **Business T.V.**

-C-

C.B.S. News Index (U.S.). Alternate title: **Columbia Broadcasting System News Index**. U.M.I., 300 N. Zeeb Rd., Ann Arbor, MI 48106; (annual); ISSN: 0362-3238; OCLC 2698451.
Note: v.1, 1975 -.
Provides comprehensive access to CBS News transcripts. Indexes the following programs by subject and personality: *CBS Morning News, CBS Evening News, Sunday Morning, CBS Sunday Night News, CBS News Special Report, CBS Reports, Face the Nation, 60 Minutes* and *West 57th*.
PN4888.T4C64; Dewey: 791.45/72.

C.D. Data Report (U.S.). Alternate title: **Compact Disk Data Report**. Langley Publications, PO Box 115-324, 1350 Beverly Rd., McLean, VA 22101. Tel: 703/241-2131; (monthly); ISSN: 8755-5727; OCLC 11347361.
Note: v.1,n.1 Nov 1984 -.
Focuses on the CD-ROM (compact disk random access memory) industry.
Dewey: 621 11.

C.D.-1 News. (U.S.); Link Resources Corporation, 79 Fifth Ave., New York, NY 10003. Tel: 212/627-1500; (monthly).
Note: v.1, 1987 -.
Devoted to the interactive compact disc (CD-1) system. "For the consumer electronics, entertainment, publishing, information and education industries."

C.D.-ROM Enduser (U.S.); DDRI, 6609 Rosecroft Place, Falls Church, VA 22043-1828. Tel: 703/237-0682; (monthly); ISSN: 1042-8623; OCLC 19231671.
Note: v.1,n.1 May 1989 -.
Designed for information specialists, teachers and librarians who use CD-ROMs in the workplace. Shows applications for school and library uses. Provides helpful instructions from distributors on how to run successful programs. Offers solutions for installation problems. Contains a directory of new releases on such subjects as agriculture, business, government statistics, dictionaries, law, engineering, and graphics.

C.D.-ROM Librarian (U.S.); Meckler Publishing, 11 Ferry Lane
West, Westport, CT 06880. Tel: 203/226-6967; (10 times/yr);
ISSN: 0893-9934; OCLC 15719667.
Note: v.1,n.1 Jan/Feb 1986 -.
"The optical media review for information professionals."
Latest information about compact disc technology for
educational and business applications.
Z681.3.067C3; Dewey 025 11.

C D T Notes (U.S.); C D T, PO Box 27573, Los Angeles, CA 90027;
(bimonthly).
Note: v.1, 1984 -.
Newsletter for people with disabilities in the media. Acts
as a clearinghouse for job opportunities. Keeps current with
the most recent audiovisual offerings on disabilities.

C.F.F.S. Newsletter (Canada). Alternate title: **Canadian
Federation of Film Societies Newsletter.** Canadian Federation
of Film Societies, James Quandt, Editor, 75 Markham St., Unit
6, Toronto, Ont. Canada M6J 2G4. Tel: 416/367-5927;
(irregular); ISSN: 0705-2162.
Note: [n.1]. 1980 -.
Provides information for all the film societies and cinema
clubs in Canada. Reports on film programs, events, exhibits,
festivals and news from the participating members. Published
in English.

C.F.S. Review (India). Alternate title: **Chennai Film Society
Review.** Chennai Film Society, 6, Madley Rd., Madras-17 India;
(annual); ISSN: n/a; OCLC 11320029.
Note: n.1, 1983 -.
Scholarly, well written publication documenting the views of
established Indian critics and filmmakers. Covers Indian
film history, censorship, literature and cinema, reality versus
idealized India, colonialism and British influences.
Published in English.
PN1993.5.I8C42; Dewey: 791.43/0954.

C.I.C.I.M.: Revue pour le Cinema Francais (W.Germany); Institut
Francais, Kaulbachstrasse 13, 8000 Munchen 22, West Germany.
Tel: (089) 28 53 11; (quarterly); ISSN: n/a.
Note: n.1, 1983? -.
Bilingual publication in French and German. Well illustrated

dossier concentrating on French cinema. Reviews new films, studies classic French productions, analyzes the works of notable directors and performers, tracks contemporary French filmmakers and their films.

C.O.M.S.A.T. Technical Review (U.S.). See: **COMSAT Technical Review**.

C.P.B. Report (U.S.). Alternate title: **Corporation for Public Broadcasting Report**. Corporation for Public Broadcasting (C.B.P.), 1111 16th St., NW, Washington, DC 20036. Tel: 202/ 955-5100; (biweekly); ISSN: n/a.
Note: [n.1] 1970 -.
Newsletter for public television stations, non-profit organizations, government agencies, independent filmmakers, and others interested in public TV.

C-SPAN Update (U.S.); C-SPAN Update, Subscription Service, PO Box 75298, Washington, DC 20013. Tel: 202/737-3220; (weekly); ISSN: 0746-3812; OCLC 10007954.
Note: v.1,n.1 Jun 1983 -.
For people subscribing to C-SPAN, the Cable Satellite Public Affairs Network. Newsletter describing the political events happening in Congress and around the nation; reports on the televised proceedings of the House of Representatives and Senate.

C.T.I.C. Cable Reports (U.S.). Alternate titles: **Cable Reports**; **Cable Television Information Center Cable Reports**; absorbed by **Cable Update**. Cable Television Information Center, 1500 N. Beauregard St., Suite 205, Alexandria, VA 22311. Tel: 708/ 941-1770; (monthly); ISSN: 0889-1877; OCLC 6122096.
Note: v.1,n.1-v.9,n.12 Oct 1979-Feb 1989 as **C.T.I.C. Reports**; Mar 1989- as **Cable Update**.
Monitored the cable industry.

C.T.V.D. Cinema, TV Digest (U.S.). Alternate title: **Cinema, TV Digest**. Hampton Books, Rt. 1, Box 76, Newberry, SC 29108. Tel: 803/276-6870; (irregular); ISSN: 0007-9219; OCLC 2058605.
Note: n.1, Winter 1961/62 -.
Reprints articles from foreign language publications covering mass media, broadcasting, film and television. Articles range from the serious to the sensational.
P87.C25; Dewey: 791.43/7.

Ca: Cinema (France); Editions Albatros, 14, rue de l'Armorique,
Paris 75015 France; (irregular); ISSN: n/a; OCLC 1788382.
Note: v.1, 1973 -.
Scholarly journal concerned with film history, theory and
criticism. Articles discuss semiotics, montage, film
narration and auteur theories. Includes textual analyses of
films on a frame-by-frame basis. Published in French.
PN1993.C2; Dewey: 791.43/05.

Cable Action Update (U.S.). Alternate title: **Weekly Cable Action
Update**. Warren Publishing, Inc., 2115 Ward Court, NW,
Washington, DC 20037. Tel: 202/872-9200; (weekly); ISSN: n/a;
OCLC 8903759.
Note: [n.1] Feb 1, 1982 -.
"Addenda to Television & Cable Factbook." Companion
newsletter to **Television Action Update**. Lists new cable
systems and franchises around the country with names, addresses,
telephone numbers, areas covered and basic services. Reports
on any changes to the operating cable systems in the United
States.
TK6675.W43; Dewey: 384.55/47/0973.

Cable Age (U.S.). See: **Cableage**.

Cable & Station Coverage Atlas (U.S.). See: **Cable and Station
Coverage Atlas and Zone Maps**.

Cable and Station Coverage Atlas and Zone Maps (U.S.). Alternate
titles: **Cable & Station Coverage Atlas; Television Digest's
Cable & Station Coverage Atlas**. Warren Publishing, Inc., 2115
Ward Court, NW, Washington, DC 20037. Tel: 202/872-9200;
(annual); ISSN: 0193-3639; OCLC 5060967.
Note: ed.1, 1967/1968 -.
A state-by-state guide to all the cable stations in the U.S.
Contains call letters, addresses, personnel and zone maps for
each station. Lists low power TV stations, pay TV and satellite
services, state regulatory agencies, and the FCC cable rules.
HE8700.7.C6C13; Dewey: 912/.13845547/05.

Cable Communications Magazine (Canada); Ter-Sat Media
Publications, Ltd., 4 Smetana Dr., Kitchener, Ontario N2B
3B8, Canada. Tel: 519/744-4111; (monthly); ISSN: 0318-0069;

OCLC 10615498.
Note: v.1, 193u -.
"The authoritative cable television publication covering news, views, issues and developments in North America and around the world." Journal of the television and cable broadcasting industries in Canada. Articles address equipment, laws, regulations, marketing forecasts, fiber optics, cable programming, management information, issues and developments affecting the Canadian cable industry. Published in English.
HE8700.7.C6C36; Dewey: 384.55/56/0971.

Cable Contacts Yearbook (U.S.); Larimi Communications associates, Ltd., 246 West 38th St., New York, NY 10018. Tel: 212/819-9310; (annual); ISSN: n/a; OCLC 9130594.
Note: ed.1, 1983 -.
An annual directory listing cable systems, news services, multiple systems operators, satellite networks and independent producers. Contains a list of cable programs with producer and network. Gives subscriber statistics, technical and visual support material requirements and program placement opportunities.

Cable File (U.S.). Alternate title: **Cablefile: The Standard Reference for the Cable Television Industry**. Titsch Publications, Inc., PO Box 5400, T.A., Denver, CO 80217; (annual); ISSN: 0363-1915; OCLC 8632575.
Note: ed.1, 1976 -.
Maintains a listing of all cable stations in the U.S. with call letters, addresses and personnel. Lists equipment manufacturers.
HE8700.7.C6C32; Dewey: 384.55/47/02573.

The Cable Guide (U.S.). Formerly: **Great TV Entertainment**; absorbed: **Cable Today**. T.V.S.M. Inc., 309 Lakeside Dr., Horsham, PA 19044. Tel: 215/443-9300; (monthly); ISSN: n/a.
Note: [v.1-3] 1980-1982 as **Great TV Entertainment;** renumbered v.1, 1982- as **The Cable Guide**; absorbed **Cable Today** in 1983?
"America's cable magazine." A programming guide to commercial, free and pay-TV networks. Publishes about 400 different editions for each cable franchise area around the United States. Contains information on new series and specials, editorial features on entertainers, interviews, and highlights movies and sporting events.

Cable Hotline (U.S.); Larimi Communications Associates, Ltd., 246
West 38th St., New York, NY 10018. Tel: 212/819-9310;
(monthly); ISSN: 0738-2782; OCLC 9551798.
Note: v.1, 1982 -.
Newsletter for cable operators providing information on guest
placements, commercials, programming and video equipment.
Articles cover data on local cable systems, new
telecommunications technology, and satellites.

Cable Libraries (U.S.); C.S. Tepfer Publishing Co., Inc., 607
Main St., Ridgefield, CT 06877; (monthly); ISSN: 0161-7605;
OCLC 1466550.
Note: v.1, May 1973 -.
Newsletter issued by the American Society for Information
Science, Washington, DC. Geared toward libraries which
operate a cable television production facility and their
municipal, county and city users. Gathers news from members
about successful installations and applications, long range
planning, and advice.
Z716.8.C32; Dewey: 021/.28.

Cable Marketing (U.S.); Associated Cable Enterprises, Inc., 352
Park Ave., South, New York, NY 10010. Tel: 212/685-4848;
(monthly); ISSN: 0279-8891; OCLC 7335110.
Note: v.1,n.1 Feb 1981 -.
Glossy, oversized trade journal for cable executives, station
owners, managers and advertisers. "Free (controlled)
subscriptions are limited to CATV system operators and their
corporate headquarters. All other subscriptions are
"controlled at the discretion of the publisher." Gives
strategies for boosting cable network ratings, financial
forecasts and sales management techniques. Covers advertising
on cable networks. Compiles an annual "Cable Marketing
Services Directory" in November, listing research firms,
consultants and public relations companies specializing in
the cable industry.
HE8700.7.C6C333; Dewey: 384.55/563/0973.

Cable Reports (U.S.). See: **C.T.I.C. Cable Reports**.

Cable T.V. Advertising (U.S.). Alternate title: **Cable Television
Advertising**. Paul Kagan Associates, Inc., 126 Clock Tower
Place, Carmel, CA 93923-8734. Tel: 408/624-1536; (monthly);

ISSN: 0270-885X; OCLC 6507764.
Note: [v.1] 1980 -.
Newsletter reporting on advertising sales of commercial time
for cable television. Covers both local and national ad
sales. Gives marketing projections for advertisers and
reports on case studies conducted by market-research firms.
Dewey: 659 11.

The Cable T.V. Financial Databook (U.S.). Alternate titles: **The
Kagan Cable T.V. Financial Databook; The Cable Television
Financial Databook.** Paul Kagan Associates, Inc., 126 Clock
Tower Place, Carmel, CA 93923-8734. Tel: 408/624-1536;
(annual); ISSN: 0736-8143; OCLC 16348427.
Note: ed.1, 1982 -.
A comprehensive directory of sources for capital for cable
enterprises. A financial source book listing brokers, lending
institutions, consultants, systems operators and equipment
suppliers catering to the cable industry. Includes operating
results and growth projections of the cable companies.
HE8700.7.C6C3335; Dewey: 384.55/47.

Cable T.V. Franchising (U.S.). Formerly: **Cable T.V. Regulation**;
alternate title: **Cable Television Franchising.** Paul Kagan
Associates, Inc., 126 Clock Tower Place, Carmel, CA 93923-
8734. Tel: 408/624-1536; (monthly); ISSN: 0731-0269; OCLC
8117803.
Note: [n.1]-n.147, 1975-Sep 10, 1981 as **Cable T.V.
Regulation**; n.148, Oct 1981- as **Cable T.V. Franchising**.
Legal in scope, this publication monitors federal, state and
city legislation directed toward the cable industry. Covers
lawsuits over regulations and legal battles between cities
and states over franchises. Lists cable TV rate increases.
Keeps current with cable franchise awards and renewals.
KF2844.A15C33; Dewey: 343.73/09946.

Cable T.V. Investor (U.S.). Alternate title: **Cable Television
Investor.** Paul Kagan Associates, Inc., 126 Clock Tower Place,
Carmel, CA 93923-8734. Tel: 408/624-1536; (monthly); ISSN:
0731-0250; OCLC 8117886.
Note: [n.1] 1969 -.
Investment newsletter analyzing stocks and bonds of private
and public cable television systems. Gives cash flow
multiples and value of franchiser.

Cable T.V. Investor Charts (U.S.). Alternate title: **Cable Television Investor Charts**. Paul Kagan Associates, Inc., 126 Clock Tower Place, Carmel, CA 93923-8734. Tel: 408/624-1536; (monthly); ISSN: 0732-7757; OCLC 8433468.
Note: n.1, Mar 1982 -.
Newsletter consisting of a chart service giving stock price movements of over forty publicly held cable companies. Each graph shows two years of stock price activity.

Cable T.V. Law & Finance (U.S.). Alternate titles: **Cable T.V. Law and Finance; Cable Television Law and Finance**. Leader Publications, Inc., 111 8th Ave., Suite 900, New York, NY 10011; (monthly); ISSN: 0736-489X; OCLC 9142582.
Note: v.1,n.1 Mar 1983 -.
Business journal for the cable television industry. Keeps readers apprised of new laws and legislation affecting the cable industry. Articles cover marketing techniques, predictions of future growth areas, new technology and statistical analyses.
KF2844.A15C28; Dewey: 343.73/09946.

Cable T.V. Law and Finance (U.S.). See: **Cable T.V. Law & Finance**.

Cable T.V. Law Reporter (U.S.). Alternate title: **Cable Television Law Reporter**. Paul Kagan Associates, Inc., 126 Clock Tower Place, Carmel CA 93923-8734. Tel: 408/624-1536; (monthly); ISSN: 0749-7652; OCLC 11189974.
Note: n.1, Sep 6, 1984 -.
Newsletter covering legal cases around the country, including those dealing with antitrust, copyright, first amendment, taxation, piracy, franchising, rate regulation, privacy and international law.
KF2844.A59C33; Dewey: 343.73/09946.

Cable T.V. Programming (U.S.). Alternate title: **Cable Television Programming**. Paul Kagan Associates, Inc., 126 Clock Tower Place, Carmel, CA 93923-1536. Tel: 408/624-1536; (biweekly); ISSN: 0278-503X; OCLC 7817522.
Note: n.1, Sep 25, 1981 -.
Charts programming lineups for cable networks. Covers both the basic package and pay-TV subscriptions. Surveys the cost breakdown and economics of the many cable TV systems and

networks.
Dewey: 384 11.

Cable T.V. Regulation (U.S.). See: **Cable T.V. Franchising.**

Cable T.V. Technology (U.S.). Alternate title: **Cable Television Technology.** Paul Kagan Associates, Inc., 126 Clock Tower Place, Carmel, CA 93923-8734. Tel: 408/624-1536; (monthly); ISSN: 0276-5713; OCLC 7382679.
Note: n.1, Apr 23, 1981 -.
Newsletter on construction of new cable systems and the rebuilding or updating of existing systems. Contains growth projections of cable systems.

Cable Television Advertising (U.S.). See: **Cable T.V. Advertising.**

Cable Television Business (U.S.). Formerly; **T.V.C.** (0164-8489). Cardiff Publishing Co., 6300 S. Syracuse Way, Suite 650, Englewood, CO 80111. Tel: 303/220-0600; (biweekly); ISSN: 0745-2802; OCLC 9013459.
Note: v.1-v.19, 1964-1982 as **T.V.C.**; v.19,n.22 Nov 15, 1982- as **Cable Television Business.**
One of the first publications devoted to the cable television industry. Covers the industry thoroughly, including financial reports, laws and legislation, regulation, politics, economic growth, and business potential. Articles discuss programming, advertising, competition, new technology, and systems management. Interviews successful leaders in the field.
TK6675.T2; Dewey: 384.55/56/05.

The Cable Television Financial Databook (U.S.). See: **The Cable T.V. Financial Databook.**

Cable Television Franchising (U.S.). See: **Cable T.V. Franchising.**

Cable Television Information Center Cable Reports (U.S.). See: **C.T.I.C. Cable Reports.**

Cable Television Investor (U.S.). See: **Cable T.V. Investor.**

Cable Television Investor Charts (U.S.). See: **Cable T.V. Investor Charts.**

Cable Television Law and Finance (U.S.). See: **Cable T.V. Law & Finance.**

Cable Television Law Reporter (U.S.). See: **Cable T.V. Law Reporter.**

Cable Television Magazine (U.S.). See: **Cable T.V. Magazine.**

Cable Television Programming (U.S.). See: **Cable T.V. Programming.**

Cable Television Technology (U.S.). See: **Cable T.V. Technology.**

Cable Today (U.S.). See: **The Cable Guide.**

Cable Update (U.S.). Absorbed: **C.T.I.C. Cable Reports** (0889-1877). Miller & Holbrooke Information Services, 1225 19th St., NW, Washington, DC 20036. Tel: 202/785-0600; (monthly); ISSN: n/a.
Note: v.1-10, Oct 1979-Feb 1989 as **C.T.I.C. Cable Reports**; renumbered v.1,n.1 Mar 1989- as **Cable Update.**
"Monthly reports, analyses and documents related to cable TV and telecommunications of interest to state and local franchising authorities, municipal cable officers, libraries and other interested persons." Reproduces legal briefs throughout the country regarding cable lawsuits; includes documents and photocopies with subscription.
Dewey: 384 11.

Cable Vision (U.S.). See: **CableVision.**

Cableage (U.S.). Alternate title: **Cable Age**; incorporated by **Television/Radio Age** (0040-277X). Television Editorial Corp., 1270 Ave. of the Americas, New York, NY 10020. Tel: 212/757-8400; (biweekly); ISSN: 0279-4004; OCLC 7820357.
Note: v.1,n.1-v.3,n.13, May 18, 1981-Nov 7, 1983 published separately; from Nov 21, 1983- published as section of **Television/Radio Age**, assuming the numbering of the latter.
Presents news and information on the cable industry. Designed for people working in the telecommunications industry, subjects include marketing, commercials, new technology, equipment, finance, law, regulations and programming.
HE8690.T42; Dewey: 384.54/05.

Cablefile: The Standard Reference for the Cable Television Industry (U.S.). See: **Cable File**.

Cablenet Cableguide (U.S.); Telegude Publishing Co., PO Box 334, Mt. Prospect, IL 60056; ISSN: 0743-2372; OCLC 10548519.
Note: 1982-1985.
Ceased publication in 1985.

Cabletime (U.S.). See: **T.V. Entertainment Monthly**.

The CableTV Guide (U.S.). See: **T.V. Entertainment Monthly**.

Cableview (U.S.). Cableview Publications, 111 8th Ave., New York, NY 10011; (monthly); ISSN: 0734-9726; OCLC 8839116.
Note: v.1, 1981 -.
Programming guide to various cable channels. Contains long movie reviews, sports coverage, cultural events and profiles of screen personalities.

CableVision (U.S.). Alternate title: **Cable Vision**. International Thomson Communications, 600 S. Cherry St., Suite 400, Denver, CO 80222. Tel: 303/393-7449; (biweekly); ISSN: 0361-8374; OCLC 2441475.
Note: v.1, 1976? -.
Professionally oriented publication for cable subscribers, station owners and operators. Gives information on new cable networks, packages, equipment installations, advertising, latest technology, government rules and regulations.
HE8700.7.C6C334; Dewey: 384.55/47.

Les Cahiers de la Cinematheque (France). Formerly: **Archives/ Cahiers de la Cinematheque** (OCLC 8350848). Palais des Congres, 66000 Perpignan, France. Tel: 68.34.13.13; (irregular); ISSN: n/a; OCLC 3825624.
Note: n.1-20, 1971-1976 as **Archives/Cahiers de la Cinematheque**; n.21, 1977?- as **Les Cahiers de la Cinematheque**.
A serious film journal, often devoting an entire issue to one major theme, such as the treatment of the Middle Ages in film, or science fiction films. Because it explores international cinema in the context of a particular theme or motif, each issue has a distinctive title. Published in French.

Cahiers du Cinema (France). Formerly: **La Revue du Cinema**. Revue
Mensuelle Editee par la s.a.r.l., Editions de l'Etoile, 9,
passage de la Boule-Blanche (50 rue du Fg Saint-Antoine)
75012 Paris, France. 43.43.92.20; (monthly); ISSN: 0008-011X;
OCLC 1538067.
Note: v.1,n.1 Apr 1951 -.
Scholarly international journal published in French.
Contains articles on film theory, history and criticism, as
well as in-depth reviews of latest feature films. A handsomely
illustrated magazine published in French.
PN1993.C25; Dewey: 791.43/05.

**Les Cahiers du Scenario = De Scenariogids = The Screenwriter's
Companion** (Belgium); Institut de Sociologie, Universite Libre
de Bruxelles, 44 av. Jeanne, C.P. 124, B-1050 Bruxelles,
Belgium. Tel: 322-642.34.52; (irregular); ISSN: n/a.
Note: n.1, 1986 -.
Scholarly journal published mostly in French, but can have
occasional articles published in Flemish and English, too.
Devoted to the study and analysis of the screenplay.
Articles cover how to create a motion picture or television
script, comparisons between successful scriptwriters,
cultural differences exhibited in the works of scriptwriters
from different countries, and themes and situations portrayed
in literature and in cinema. Some issues devoted to the
various works of one screenwriter. Contains excerpts of
screenplays.

Calendar of International Film and Television Events (Italy).
See: **Bulletin, Calendar of International Film and Television
Events**.

Calendar / University Art Museum (U.S.). Alternate title:
University Art Museum. Calendar. Pacific Film Archive.
University of California at Berkeley, 2625 Durant Ave., Berkeley,
CA 94720. Tel: 415/642-1207; (monthly); ISSN: 0890-8850; OCLC
9909465.
Note: [n.1], 1978? -.
A calendar of events at the University of California at
Berkeley. Includes film showings and extensive film notes
for the Pacific Film Archive.
Dewey: 700 11.

Calendrier des Evenements Internationaux du Cinema et de la Television (Italy). See: **Bulletin, Calendar of International Film and Television Events**.

Camera Obscura (U.S.); Camera Obscura Collective, PO Box 25899, Los Angeles, CA 90025; (3 times/yr); ISSN: 0270-5346; OCLC 4818143.
Note: n.1, Fall 1976 -.
"A journal of feminism and film theory." Long, scholarly articles analyze films in the context of feminist doctrines. Seeks to establish a more equal treatment of women in the motion picture industry.
PN1995.9.W6C28; Dewey: 791.43/088042.

Camera/Stylo (France); Jean Durancon, 18, rue des Fosses-Saint-Jacques, 75005 Paris, France. Tel: 43.25.32.53 (matin); (quarterly); ISSN: n/a.
Note: n.1, 1985 -.
Respected journal devoted to cinema studies. Each issue is devoted to one topic of discussion, usually the life and work of a famous director, with several articles examining the subject or personality from various viewpoints. Includes extensive filmographies. Published in French.

The Canadian Broadcaster (Canada). See: **Broadcaster**.

Canadian Cinematography (Canada). See: **Cinema Canada**.

Canadian Communications Network Letter (Canada); Evert Communications Ltd., 982 Wellington St., Ottawa, Ontario K1Y 2X8 Canada. Tel: 613/728-4621; (42 times/yr); ISSN: 0825-3021; OCLC 11868888.
Note: v.1, 1981 -.
Newsletter reporting on the motion picture and broadcasting industries in Canada. Covers news and information about print media, motion pictures, television, cable, radio and satellite systems. Published in English and French.
HE8689.9; Dewey: 380.3/0971.

Canadian Federation of Film Societies Newsletter (Canada). See: **C.F.F.S. Newsletter**.

Canadian Film Digest Yearbook (Canada). Incorporating: **Canadian Professional Film Directory** (0382-8603). Film Publications of Canada Limited, 175 Bloor St., East, Toronto, Ont. M4W 1E1 Canada; (annual); ISSN: 0316-5515; OCLC 9457056.
Note: 1973/74-1975/76 as **Canadian Professional Film Directory**; 1977-1985 as **Canadian Film Digest Yearbook**; ceased publication in 1985.
Contained box office statistics, demographics on Canadian audiences, film theaters and drive-ins. Listed production services, such as studios, equipment sales and rentals, labs, special effects, animation, videotape facilities, government agencies, unions, guilds, awards and festivals. Ceased publication. Similar data is continued in **Film Canada Yearbook**.
PN1993.5.C2C23; Dewey: 338.4/779143/029571.

Canadian Journal of Communication (Canada); University of Calgary Press, McGill University, 3465 Peel St., Montreal, PQ H3Y 3G9 Canada. Tel: 514/398-4932; (quarterly); ISSN: 0705-3657; OCLC 3900226.
Note: v.1, 1974 -.
"Research, analysis and comment on communication and mass media." Scholarly journal offering articles on the effect of mass communications on popular culture. Examines the influence of television on politics. Studies print and broadcast advertising, censorship, and the use of multimedia for classroom teaching. Covers print media, television, radio, motion pictures, audio, home video, and cable. Published in English.
P87; Dewey: 301.16/1/0971.

Canadian Professional Film Directory (Canada). See: **Canadian Film Digest Yearbook**.

Cantrill's Filmnotes (Australia); Arthur & Corinne Cantrill, Box 1295L, G.P.O. Melbourne, Vic. 3001, Australia; (irregular); ISSN: 0158-4154; OCLC 3011071.
Note: n.1, Mar 1971 -.
Examines avant-garde, experimental and independent film in Australia. Discusses latest works, interviews filmmakers and reviews cinema books. Index for issues 1-50 available in separate volume.
PN1993.C333; Dewey: 791.43/05.

Canyon Cinema News (U.S.). See: **Cinema News**.

Canyon Cinemanews (U.S.). See: **Cinema News**.

Captioned Films/Videos for the Deaf (U.S.). Formerly: **Catalog of Educational Captioned Films for the Deaf; Catalog of Educational Captioned Films/Videos for the Deaf**. Captioned Films for the Deaf, 5000 Park St., North, St. Petersburg, FL 33709; (annual); ISSN: n/a; OCLC 13519856.
Note: v.1-3, 1980/81-1984/85 as **Catalog of Educational Captioned Films for the Deaf**; v.4-5, 1985/86-1987/88 as **Catalog of Educational Captioned Films/Videos for the Deaf**; renumbered ed.1, 1988/1989 as **Captioned Films/Videos for the Deaf**.
A catalog of educational, training and entertainment films and videos that have been captioned for the deaf. Each entry includes title, length, synopsis, cast, MPAA rating, genre category and private distributor. Contains a subject index. All films and videos can be ordered from Captioned Films for the Deaf in St. Petersburg, Florida.
HV2503.C38; Dewey: 011/.37 19.

Carnegie Institute Travel Sheet (U.S.); Section of Film & Video, Museum of Art, Carnegie Institute, 4400 Forbes Ave., Pittsburgh, PA 15213; (monthly).
Note: v.1-v.14,n.3, 1974-Mar 1987.
Kept track of traveling exhibitions throughout the United States. Discontinued March 1987.

Casablanca (Spain); Casablanca, Joaquin Costa 14, 28002, Madrid, Spain; (monthly).
Note: n.1-n.41, 1981-1984.
Popular film journal, nicely illustrated, presenting the works of noted directors, screenwriters, actors and actresses. Published in Spanish. Discontinued publication.

Il Castoro Cinema (Italy); Fernaldo Di Giammatteo, Editrice Firenze, 2328 Firenze, Italy; (bimonthly); ISSN: n/a.
Note: n.1, 1974 -.
Academic journal covering film history, theory and criticism. Some issues devoted to a particular director with a close analysis of his work, a biographical sketch and an extensive filmography. Contains bibliographies; published in Italian.

Catalog of Educational Captioned Films for the Deaf (U.S.). See:
Captioned Films/Videos for the Deaf.

Catalog of Educational Captioned Films/Videos for the Deaf
(U.S.). See: Captioned Films/Videos for the Deaf.

Catalogue de la Production Cinematographique Francaise (France);
Service des Archives du Film du Centre National de la
Cinematographie, 78390 Bois d'Arcy, France; (annual); ISSN:
0224-7518; OCLC 11723611.
Note: v.1, 1975 -.
Editions cover feature length, short films and documentaries
registered with the Commission de Controle des Films.
Documents the following information: alternate titles, code
number registration (with the Registre Public de la Cinema),
production company, distributor, director, screenwriter,
photographer, editor, cast members and awards. Indexed by
personality, title and company. Published in French.
PN1998.C332; Dewey: 016.79143/75/0944.

Catalogue of Films for Universities (U.K.). See: **B.U.F.V.C.
Catalogue.**

Catalogue of Yugoslav Documentary and Short Films (Yugoslavia).
See: Katalog Jugoslovenskog Dokumentarnog I Kratkometraznog
Filma.

Catholic Film Newsletter (U.S.). See: **Film & Broadcasting Review.**

Celebrity Bulletin (International); United States address:
Celebrity Service International, 1780 Broadway, Suite 300,
New York, NY 10019. Tel: 212/757-7979; (daily; except Sat &
Sun); ISSN: 0045-6020.
Note: v.1, 1952 -.
Tradepaper which tracks the daily activities of international
celebrities with coverage for New York, London, Paris, Rome
and Hollywood. Helps locate performers. Keeps current with
changes in agents, business managers, and contacts.

Celebrity Directory (U.S.). See: **Star Guide.**

Celebrity Plus (U.S.). Formerly: **Celebrity Focus**. Globe
   Communications Corp., 441 Lexington Ave., New York, NY 10017.
   Tel: 212/949-4040; (monthly); ISSN: 0897-4381; OCLC 17503250.
   Note: v.1,n,1-v.2,n.2, Jan 1987-Feb 1988 as **Celebrity Focus**;
   v.2,n.3 Mar 1988- as **Celebrity Plus**.
   Photo-articles on famous actors and actresses. Focuses on
   Hollywood, past and present. Includes biographical sketches,
   filmographies, interviews, health and beauty tips, and diets.
   PN1993.C36; Dewey: 791.43/028/05.

Celuloide (Portugal); F.M. Antunes & Novais, Lda., Rua David
   Manuel da Fonseca, 70, 2040 Rio Maior, Portugal; (monthly);
   ISSN: 0008-8781; OCLC 4659544.
   Note: v.1,n.1-v.30,n.371, 1958?-Apr 1986.
   "Revista Portuguesa de Cinema." Popular magazine reviewing
   international feature films and books on the cinema. Reports
   on European film festivals. Published in Portuguese.
   Discontinued publication in 1986.

Ceskoslovensky Film. See: **The Czechoslovak Film**.

Channel Four Television. Press Information (U.K.); The Press
   Office, 60 Charlotte St., London W1P 2AX England. Tel: 01-927-
   8888; (weekly).
   Note: 19uu -.
   Weekly accounting of every program on the British independent
   station, Channel 4. Contains background information on new
   series, documentary and news programs and specials.

Channel Guide (U.S.); University Graphics, Inc., 7340 E. Caley
   Ave., Suite 320, Englewood, CO 80111. Tel: 303/779-7930;
   (weekly); ISSN: 0744-6462; OCLC 8466485.
   Note: Began 1978 -.
   A program guide for broadcasts on U.S. geosynchronous
   satellites. Provides information on legislation, new
   technology and changes in the industry.

Channels (U.S.). Formerly: **Channels of Communications** (0276-
   1572). Alternate title: **Channels: The Business of
   Communications**. Channels, 19 West 44th St., New York, NY
   10036, Subscription Services Dept., PO Box 6438, Duluth, MN
   55806. Tel: 212/302-2680; (11 times/yr; monthly except Aug);
   ISSN: 0895-642X; OCLC 14471504.

Note: v.1,n.1-v.6,n.4, Apr/May 1981-Jul/Aug 1986 as
Channels of Communications; v.6,n.5, Sep 1986- as **Channels**.
Designed for broadcasting industry personnel, focuses on the
business aspects of the television industry. Articles on
finance, commercials, programming, technology, personalities,
public policy and law. Publishes a "field guide" each
November which is a "complete annual report on the electronic
media." Maps trends in TV survival: the battle among the
major networks for ratings, the increasing strength of cable
and independent stations, and competition from abroad
complicate the war for audience shares.
PN1992.6.C514; Dewey: 384.55/4/0973.

Channels of Communications (U.S.). See: **Channels**.

Chaplin (Sweden); Chaplin, Svenska Filminstitutet, Box 27 126, S-
102 52, Stockholm, Sweden; (bimonthly); ISSN: 0045-6349; OCLC
5659626.
Note: n.1, Apr 1959 -.
Published in Swedish, this respected film magazine contains
information on the latest international releases, in-depth
reviews, interviews with famous directors and performers, and
articles on film history, theory and criticism.

Chennai Film Society Review (India). See: **C.F.S. Review**.

Chia Ho Tien Ying (Hong Kong). English parallel title: **Golden
Movie News**. The Four Seas Publication, Ltd., 122B, Argyle
St., 1/F. Kowloon, Hong Kong. Tel: 3-7139710; (monthly);
ISSN: n/a.
Note: n.1, 1972? -.
A fashionable and popular movie magazine featuring
biographical sketches of Chinese actors and actresses. Many
photographs illustrate the popular stars and their films.
Photo captions and tag lines are in English. Articles and
feature stories are in Chinese.
PN1993.C44.

Children's Video Report (U.S.); Children's Video Report,
Subscriptions, 145 West 96th St., Suite 76, New York, NY
10025-6403. Tel: 212/227-8347; (bimonthly); ISSN: 0883-6922;
OCLC 12229443.
Note: v.1,n.1 May 1985 -.

Reviews and evaluates children's video for parents, teachers and librarians. Entries include subjective analysis of themes presented and what positive ideas and values the video reinforces; comments on the acting and production qualities, measures how children have reacted while viewing and how "repeatable" the video is for viewing over and over.

Children's Video Review (U.S.). See: **Children's Video Review Newsletter**.

Children's Video Review Newsletter (U.S.). Alternate title: **Children's Video Review**. E. P. Carsman Publisher, 110 Lena Court, Grass Valley, CA 95949. Tel: 916/273-7471; (bimonthly); ISSN: 0895-2094; OCLC 16531110.
Note: v.1,n.1 Apr/May 1987 -.
Newsletter for librarians, teachers and parents reviewing children's videocassettes. Each entry contains title, synopsis, age group, distributor, date of production, length, cost, and recommendation or pan.
Dewey: 791 11.

China & Overseas Movie News (Hong Kong). See: **Chung Wai Ying Hua**.

China Screen (P.R.C.). Alternate title: **China's Screen**.
China Film Export and Import Corp., 25 Xin Wai St., Beijing, China; (quarterly); ISSN: 0577-893X; OCLC 4099833.
Note: v.1, 1964? -.
Glossy international periodical published in Chinese, English, French and Spanish editions. Promotes latest Chinese releases giving cast and credit information and synopses. Interviews popular Chinese film stars.
PN1993.5.C4C45; Dewey: 791.43/05 19.

China's Screen (P.R.C.). See: **China Screen**.

Chitrabikshan (India); Cine Central, Calcutta, 2, Chowringhee Rd., Calcutta-13 India; (monthly).
Note: v.1, 1968 -.
Published in Bengali, features scholarly articles on famous Indian directors, state of the motion picture arts in India, censorship, film theory, cinema studies and interviews.
Promotes film appreciation, praising better quality features

and disdaining "cut and slash" cinematic fare. Tries to be
a forum for free discussion on major trends and issues.
PN1993.C47; Dewey: 791.43/05.

Christian Film & Video (U.S.). Alternate titles: **Christian Film
and Video; Christian Film & Video: A Bimonthly Review &
Resource Guide**. Christian Film & Video, Box 3000, Dept. Y,
Denville, NJ 07834; (bimonthly); ISSN: 0890-3387; OCLC
14227741.
Note: v.1,n.1 Jan? 1984 -.
Compiled by the Wheaton College Graduate School of
Communications. Newsletter for Christian clergy, librarians
and teachers in parochial schools. Reviews latest films and
videos with religious themes. Contains articles on how to
program, how to use communication satellites, how to handle
technical problems, and where to rent religious videotapes.
Dewey: 200 11.

Christian Film and Video (U.S.). See: **Christian Film & Video**.

Christian Film & Video: A Bimonthly Review & Resource Guide
(U.S.). See: **Christian Film & Video**.

Chung-hua Nein Kuo Tien Ying Nien Chien (Republic of China).
English parallel title: **Cinema in the Republic of China
Yearbook**. Motion Picture Agency, Taipei, Taiwan, Republic of
China. Tel: (02) 392-4243; (annual); ISSN: n/a; OCLC
12288038.
Note: v.1, 1984 -.
A directory of Taiwanese feature films and shorts made during
the year. Gives title, production company, distributor, cast
and synopsis. Lists people involved in filmmaking in the
Republic of China with addresses and telephone numbers.
Reviews scholarly cinema books. Published in Chinese.
PN1993.5.T28C48; Dewey: 791.43/0951/249.

Chung-kuo Tien Ying Chia Hsieh Hui (P.R.C.). See: **Chung-kuo Tien
Ying Nien Chien**.

Chung-kuo Tien Ying Nien Chien (P.R.C.). Alternate title: **Chung-
kuo Tien Ying Chia Hsieh Hui**. Zhongguo Dianying Chubanshe,
No. 22 Beisanhuan Donglu, Beijing, P.R.C.; (annual); ISSN:
n/a; OCLC 9179105.

Note: [ed.1] 1981 -.
An insular and serious look at Chinese films from the
People's Republic. Gives a historical perspective, going
back in time to the first efforts of Chinese filmmakers.
Also lists the features, documentaries and shorts made during
the preceding year. Published in Chinese.
PN1993.5.C4.C537; Dewey: 791.43/0951.

Chung Wai Ying Hua (Hong Kong). English parallel titles: **Movie
News; China & Overseas Movie News.** Development Publishers,
12 Jupiter St., First Floor, Hong Kong; (monthly); ISSN: n/a;
OCLC 10740225.
Note: [n.1], 1979? -.
Photo magazine describing the latest Chinese and foreign
feature film releases. Favors English-speaking products over
other European and Asian motion pictures. Promotes Hong Kong
cinema and movie stars. Text is in Chinese but titles are
translated into English.
PN1993.C49; Dewey: 791.43/05.

Ciak (Italy). See: **Ciak si Gira.**

Ciak si Gira (Italy). Alternate title: **Ciak.** Ciak si Gira,
Casella Postale 1823, Coso Suropa 57, 20101 Milan, Italy;
(monthly); ISSN: n/a; OCLC 14995051.
Note: v.1,n.1 May 1985 -.
Popular magazine devoted to the Italian motion picture and
television industries. Many photographs illustrate the
careers and personalities of film and TV stars. Reviews the
latest features and television shows. Published in Italian.

Ciennepi (Italy); Edizioni l'Airone Fedic, Via Odoardo Beccari,
32-00154, Rome, Italy. Tel: 06/57.54.166; (3 times/yr); ISSN:
n/a.
Note: v.1, 1981? -.
Irreverent journal mixing film studies and politics.
Articles cover new Soviet cinema, third world filmmaking,
reflections of modern Italy in the works of Italian
directors. Reviews cinema books; published in Italian.

Cine (Colombia); Publicacion de la Compania de Fomento
Cinematografico (FOCINE), Calle 17, No. 7-35, Oficina 1405,
Bogota, Colombia. Tel: 2431403; (irregular); ISSN: n/a.

Note: [n.1] 1981? -.
Serious overview of Colombian and Latin American cinema.
Offers filmographies with title, producer, director, editor,
cinematographer, music, cast, length and synopsis of feature
films released in Colombia. Keeps current with the selected
motion pictures awarded prizes at various international film
festivals.

Cine al Dia (Venezuela); Sociedad Civil "Cine al Dia," Apartado
50, 446 Sabana Grande, Caracas, Venezuela; (monthly); ISSN:
0009-692X; OCLC 5111264.
Note: n.1, 1967 -.
Popular monthly magazine reviewing the latest features.
Articles report on the state of Latin American cinema,
boxoffice hits, and the latest international releases.
Conducts interviews with favorite directors,
actors and actresses. Published in Spanish.

Cine Argentino (Argentina); Editorial Legasa S.A., Rawson 17 "A",
1182, Buenos Aires, Argentina; (annual); ISSN: n/a; OCLC
6511701.
Note: [n.1] 1968 -.
A directory of Argentinean features done throughout the
preceding year. The title entry includes production company,
director, producer, music, editor, extensive cast list,
photographic still and synopsis. Contains overviews of
Argentinean and Latin American cinema, film festivals and
obituaries. Indexed by personal name, company and title.
Published in Spanish.
PN1993.5.A7A24; Dewey: 791.43/0982.

Cine Bulles (Canada). Alternate title: **Bulletin D'Information de
L'A.C.P.Q.** Association des Cinemas Paralleles du Quebec,
4545 ave. Pierre-de-Coubertin, CP 1000, Succursale M,
Montreal, Quebec H1V 3R2 Canada; (quarterly); ISSN: 0820-
8921; OCLC 9818972.
Note: v.1, 1980 -.
Serious film journal surveying the French-Canadian motion
picture industry. Reviews current releases; tries to promote
Canadian cinema; conducts interviews with filmmakers.
Published in French.
Dewey: 791.43/09714.

Cine Camera (U.K.). See: **Making Better Movies.**

Cine Cubano (Cuba); Redaccion Y Administracion, Calle 23 No.
1155, Vedado, Havana 4 Cuba; (irregular); ISSN: 0009-6946;
0009-0946; OCLC 2259400.
Note: v.1,n.1 Jul 1960 -.
Film history and criticism from a Socialist point of view.
An ideological organ for the Cuban film administration,
focusing on Third World cinema. Commentaries on outstanding
films are written by eminent Cuban and Latin American
scholars and filmmakers. Reviews international films,
including English-language features. Published in Spanish.
Dewey: 791.

Cine Para Leer (Spain); Ediciones Mensajero, Sancho de Azpeitia,
2-48014 Bilbao, Spain; (annual); ISSN: n/a; OCLC 1793305.
Note: v.1, 1972 -.
"Historia critica de un ano de cine." Overview of motion
picture events happening in Spain during the preceding year.
Reports on Spanish film festivals, awards, Spanish films
released during the year and laws and legislation affecting
the industry. Reviews international features, giving a long
critique and cast and credit information. Contains a monthly
listing of older films which were shown in Spanish theaters
and cineclubs. Published in Spanish.
PN1993.C5163.

Cine: Publicacion de la Compania de Fomento Cinematografico
(Colombia); FOCINE (Compania de Fomento Cinematografico)
Ministerio de Comunicacions, calle 17 no. 7-35, Oficina 1405,
Bogota, Colombia; (bimonthly); ISSN: n/a; OCLC 8546356.
Note: n.1, Oct 1980 -.
Popular magazine reflecting the interests of film aficionados.
Contains well researched retrospective articles on great
performers, such as Buster Keaton and Max Linder. Critiques
the work of famous directors, cameramen and screenwriters.
Comments on film techniques, special effects, and innovative
animation. International in scope, published in Spanish.
PN1993.C515; Dewey: 791.43/05.

Cine Qua Non (Togo); Universite du Benin, Lome, Togo;
(irregular); ISSN: n/a.
Note: n.1, Jan 1972 -.

Published in French, this journal presents an overview of
African cinema. Seeks to promote African and Third World
film production by popularizing cinema studies and student
filmmaking at the University of Benin. Critiques French
language cinema books and journals.
PN1993.C51635; Dewey: 791.43/05.

Cine-Revue (Belgium). See: **Cine-Tele-Revue.**

Cine 7 (Greece); Cine 7, Kaninos 9, 7 Opophos, 106 77 Athens,
Greece; (irregular); ISSN: n/a.
Note: [n.1] 198u -.
Interested in fantastic, horror and science fiction movies.
A fanzine, published in Greek, covering cult films and videos.

Cine-Tele-Revue (Belgium); 101, avenue Reine Marie-Henriette, 1190
Brussels, Belgium; (weekly); ISSN: 0045-6918.
Note: v.1-v.64,n.43 1919?-Oct 1984 as **Cine-Revue**; v.64,n.44
Nov 1984- as **Cine-Tele-Revue.**
Trendy photo magazine presenting international stars of
motion pictures and television. Contains several interviews
per issue. Interested in contemporary works, but does cover
earlier films and television programs when profiling a performer.
Published in French; some issues have different editions for
Paris and Brussels.

Cine-Tracks (Canada); Institute of Cinema Studies, 4227 Esplanade
Ave., Montreal, Que. H2W 1T1 Canada; (Quarterly); ISSN: 0704-
061X; OCLC 3956495.
Note: v.1-5, Spring 1977-Summer/Fall 1982.
"A journal of film, communications, culture and politics."
Discontinued publication.
TR845; Dewey: 778.5/05

Cineaction! (Canada); Cineaction Collective, 40 Alexander St.,
Apt. 705, Toronto, Ontario M4Y 1B5 Canada; (3 times/yr);
ISSN: 0826-9866; OCLC 12734662.
Note: n.1, Spring 1985 -.
"A magazine of radical film criticism & theory."
Counterculture magazine analyzing cinema from a political
standpoint. Emphasis is placed on provocative theories not
found in standard film review journals.
PN1994; Dewey: 791.43/05.

Cineaste (U.S.); Cineaste, Subscription Department, PO Box 2242,
New York, NY 10009. Tel: 212/982-1241; (quarterly); ISSN: 0009-
7004; OCLC 1780823.
Note: v.1, Summer 1967 -.
A forum for activist filmmaking. Articles concentrate on
"the art and politics of the cinema," covering controversial
subjects on an international scale. Acts as a cutting edge
for information about new age Third World cinemas.
Interviews noted independent filmmakers, reviews recent films
and books on cinema.
PN1993.C5177; Dewey: 791.

Cinefan (U.S.); Fandom Unlimited Enterprises, PO Box 70868,
Sunnyvale, CA 94086. 415/960-1151; (irregular); ISSN: 0095-
1447; OCLC 1796246.
Note: n.1, Jul 1974 -.
Main interests are horror, science fiction and fantasy films.
Emphasis is on cult movies made by independent, avant garde
and experimental filmmakers, although covers major and
international releases as well. Examines what makes an
effective horror film, both graphically and musically.
Prints outspoken reviews.
PN1995.9.F36C55; Dewey: 791.43/0909/15.

Cinefantastique (U.S.); Cinefantastique, PO Box 270, Oak Park, IL
60303. 312/366-5566; (5 times/yr: Jan, Mar, May, Jul, Sep);
ISSN: 0145-6032; OCLC 2757769.
Note: v.1, Fall 1970 -.
Articles show how special effects and complicated make-up
techniques are achieved. Specializes in fantasy, science
fiction and horror films and television. Reviews latest
films and rates them for their scare potential.
PN1995.9.H6C48.

Cinefex (U.S.); Cinefex, PO Box 20027, Riverside, CA 92516;
(quarterly); ISSN: 0198-1056; OCLC 6178827.
Note: n.1, Mar 1980 -.
Handsomely published magazine devoted to the study and
display of cinematic special effects. Serious, well written
articles analyze the life-like results achieved through video
effects technology, miniatures, models, computer graphics,
makeup and special photography.
TR858.C45; Dewey: 778.5/345/05.

Cineforum (Italy); Federazione Italiana Cineforum, via A
   Locatelli 62, 24100 Bergamo, Italy; (10 times/yr); ISSN:
   0009-7039; OCLC 2612559.
   Note: v.1,n.1 1961 -.
   "Revista di studi cinematografici." An overview of
   international cinema by country, listing the latest releases,
   mapping trends and giving special emphasis to new surges of
   creativity coming from various nations such as (lately)
   Australia and Brazil. Also prints articles on famous
   directors containing biographical information, an analysis of
   their filmmaking and their influence on later directors.
   Contains comprehensive filmographies and indexes to previous
   articles.
   PN1993.C457; Dewey: 791.43/05.

Cinegrafie (Italy); Editrice Compositori Bologna, via Galliere 8,
   40121 Bologna, Italy. Tel: 051/237088; (2 times/yr); ISSN: n/a.
   Note: v.1,n.1 Feb 1989 -.
   A scholarly journal concentrating on international film
   history, theory and criticism. Well documented articles
   cover cinema studies from the early silent period to current
   trends. Profiles directors. Analyzes pivotal films on a
   scene-by-scene basis. Published in Italian.

Cinegram (U.S.); Ann Arbor Film Cooperative, 512 S. Main St., Ann
   Arbor, MI 48103; (bimonthly); ISSN: 0145-3483; OCLC 2728513.
   Note: v.1, Mar/Apr 1976 -.
   "Geared to popular, non-technical, know-how and news of film
   and video." Articles cover such topics as censorship,
   bootlegged videos, movies on cable, women in cinema,
   technical innovations. Gives advice on how to break into the
   film industry; how to get a script accepted; how to become an
   independent video and filmmaker. Interviews successful
   directors, writers and performers.
   PN1993.C5178; Dewey: 791.43/05.

The Cinegram (U.S.). Formerly: **American Cinematheque Newsletter**.
   American Cinematheque, 1717 Highland Ave., Suite 814,
   Hollywood, CA 90028. Tel: 213/461-9622; (bimonthly); ISSN:
   n/a; OCLC 13680967.
   Note: v.1,n.1-v.6,n.2, Winter 1984-Spring 1989 as **American
   Cinematheque Newsletter**; v.6,n.3 Jun 1989- as **The Cinegram**.
   Program schedule for the American Cinematheque, a non-profit

organization established to create a moving image cultural
arts center in Beverly Hills. Newsletter covering events,
fund raising and projects of the Cinematheque.

Cinejournal (Brazil); Uma Publicacao da Empresa Brasileira de
Filmes S.A. (Embrafilme), Orgao do Ministerio da Cultura, Rua
Mayrink Veiga, 28, 40. Andar, CEP 20090, Rio de Janeiro. Tel:
(021) 223-2171; (irregular); ISSN: n/a.
Note: [n.1] 198u -.
Statistical and scholarly analyses of the motion picture,
television and video industries in Brazil. Each issue
centers around a theme, such as legislation of Brazilian
cinema, the video market in Brazil, financial and growth
dimensions. Lists a bibliography of new books and
periodicals pertaining to the topic. Published in
Portuguese.

Cinema (Canada); The Canadian Film Institute, 150 rue Rideau St.,
Ottawa, Ontario KIN 5X6 Canada. Tel: 613/232-6727;
(bimonthly).
Note: 19uu -.
Calendar of film programs at the Canadian Film Institute;
published in French and English.

Cinema (France); Federation Francais des Cine-Clubs, 49 rue du
Poissonniere, 75009 Paris, France; (weekly); ISSN: 0045-6926;
OCLC 1770717.
Note: n.1, Nov 1954 -.
Title includes year date; for example, **Cinema 90**. Popular
magazine for active filmgoers. Contains extensive reviews.
Reports on production news, works in progress, exciting new
directors. Published in French.

Cinema (Israel). See: **Kolnoa**.

Cinema (Italy); Giovanni Grazzini, Editori Laterza, Rome, Italy;
(annual); ISSN: n/a; OCLC 12986409.
Note: v.1, 1977 -.
A chronicle listing of international feature films released
in Italy throughout the previous year. Each entry includes
original title, Italian release title, complete cast and
credits, length and synopsis. Indexed by title.
PN1995.C4855; Dewey: 791.43/75/05.

Cinema (Korea). See: **Yeonghwa.**

Cinema (Portugal); Orgao da Federacao, Portuguesa de Cineclubes, Rua de Camoes, 777-40. Dto., 4000 Porto, Portugal. Tel: 496.002; (quarterly); ISSN: n/a; OCLC 10137717.
Note: n.1, Sep 1982 -.
Academic publication for cinephiles; reviews contemporary international films, encourages participation in film festivals and documents program schedules for cinema clubs in Portugal. Also publishes articles on film history, biographical sketches of famous directors and filmographies. PN1993.F3413; Dewey: 791.43/05.

Cinema (Romania). Alternate title: **Cinema: Rivista Lumara de Cultura Cinematografica**. Revista a Consiliului, Culturii si Educatiei Socialiste, Bucuresti, Romania; (monthly); ISSN: 0578-2910.
Note: v.1, 1963 -.
National forum for information about Romanian films and filmmakers. Popular film magazine promoting future stars and established performers. Many photographs illustrate the Romanian films being described. Carries very little information about Western cinema. Published in English, French, Russian and Spanish languages.

Cinema (Switzerland). Formerly: **Filmklub-Cineclub**; Alternate title: **Arbeitsgemeinschaft Cinema**. Cinema, Postfach 5252, CH-8022, Zurich, Switzerland; (annual, 1983-); ISSN: n/a; OCLC 2859779.
Note: v.1-7, 1955-1961 as **Filmklub-Cineclub**; v.8, 1961- as **Cinema**.
"Cinema Suisse d'hier et d'aujourd'hui." Keeps current with new Swiss films, detailing production, direction and performances. Reviews the features released in Switzerland throughout the year. Each publication has a central theme with several thoughtful articles addressing different aspects of it, such as new Bulgarian cinema, "autokino," i.e., American road movies, or Federico Fellini. Each issue is in French and German.
PN1993.C5193.

Cinema Canada (Canada). Formerly: **Canadian Cinematography** (0576- 4823). Absorbed: **Cinemag** (0709-5635); **Cinema Canada**

Trade News North; Trade News North (0705-8799). Cinema
Canada, P.0. Box 398, Outremont Station, Montreal H2V 4N3
Canada. Tel: 514/272-5354; (monthly); ISSN: 0009-7071; OCLC
2259401.
Note: n.1-31, 1961-May/Jun 1967 as **Canadian Cinematography**;
n.32, Sep/Oct 1967- as **Cinema Canada.**
Popular magazine focusing on the Canadian motion picture and
television industries. Articles on Canadian productions, the
National Film Board, and Canadian performers and industry
personnel.
PN1993.5.C2C5; Dewey: 791.43/05.

Cinema Canada Trade News North (Canada). See: **Cinema Canada;
Cinemag; Trade News North.**

Cinema Contemporain (Greece). See: **Synchronos Kinematografos
= Cinema Contemporain.**

Cinema D'Oggi (Italy); Cinema D'Oggi, Viale Regina Margherita
286, 00198 Rome, Italy. Tel: 841271; (weekly); ISSN: n/a.
Note: [n.1] 194u -.
Trade newsletter keeping current with reviews of latest
Italian features and motion picture industry news.
Interviews producers and directors. Published in Italian;
also prints an English language edition.

Cinema e Cinema (Italy); Caposile srl, Piazzale Ferdinando
Martini, 3, 20137 Milan, Italy. Tel: (02) 5451254;
(quarterly); ISSN: n/a; OCLC 4675441.
Note: v.1,n.1 Oct-Dec 1974 -.
"Materiali di studio e di intervento cinematografici."
Scholarly journal with articles about film history, theory
and criticism. Retrospective essays on silent film and
Hollywood's golden age, as well as critiques of recent
feature films. Interviews directors; includes filmographies.
Published in Italian.
PN1995.C487; Dewey: 809.2/3.

Cinema em Close-up (Brazil); MEK Editores Ltda., Caixa Postal
8804, Sao Paulo, Brazil; (irregular); ISSN: n/a; OCLC
5937624.
Note: v.1, 1977? -.
Exploitative magazine catering to cut/slash horror movies and

soft core pornography. Introduces new stars of the genre and
reviews films. Published in Portuguese.
PN1993.C527.

Cinema Francais (France); UniFrance Film, 114, avenue des
  Champs-Elysees, 75008 Paris, France. Tel: 359-03-34; (monthly);
  ISSN: 0397-2313.
  Note: n.1, May 1976 -.
  Press information for French film productions, used for
  promotional purposes. Contains interviews of motion picture
  personalities, profiles popular stars, reviews feature films.
  Published in French and English.

Le Cinema Francais (France). See: **Cinema Francais, Production**.

Cinema Francais, Production (France). Formerly: **Le Cinema
  Francais**. UniFrance Film, 114, avenue des Champs-Elysees,
  75008 Paris, France. Tel: 359.03.34; (annual); ISSN: n/a;
  OCLC 7289897.
  Note: [ed.1-ed.32] 1945-1976 as **Le Cinema Francais**;
  renumbered ed.1, 1977- as **Cinema Francais, Production**.
  Records all feature length French films. Arranged
  alphabetically by title, each citation contains two stills, a
  synopsis in French and one in English, credits, cast and an
  address for foreign sales. Indexed by producer, exporter,
  director, screenwriter, composer, cinematographer and
  performer. Printed mostly in French, but has an English
  language preface.
  PN1993.5.F7C48; Dewey: 791.43/0944.

Cinema In India (India); National Film Development Corporation,
  1 & 8 Dalamal Towers, 211 Nariman Point, Bombay 400 021
  India. Tel: 204 9883; (quarterly); ISSN: n/a; OCLC 15926676.
  Note: v.1,n.1 Jan 1987 -.
  Academic journal presenting in depth articles on Indian cinema.
  Reviews new films, reports on international film festivals and
  cinema productions overseas. Articles cover censorship, the social
  impact of film on culture, analyses of great films, and interviews
  with noted Indian directors. Published in English and Hindi.

Cinema in the Republic of China Yearbook (Republic of China).
  See: **Chung-hua Nein Kuo Tien Ying Nien Chien**.

Cinema India-International (India); Cinema India-International,
A-15 Anand Nagar, Juhu Tara Rd., Bombay 400 049 India. Tel:
612 6866; (quarterly); ISSN: n/a; OCLC 11177126.
Note: v.1,n.1 Jan-Mar 1984 -.
Serious international journal covering all aspects of cinema
in India; also emphasizes films produced in Asian and Pacific
Island nations. Covers American and European film festivals,
directors and latest releases. Published in English.
PN1993.5.I8C53; Dewey: 791.43/0954 19.

Cinema Journal (U.S.). Formerly: **Society of Cinematologists.
Journal** (0009-7101). University of Illinois Press, 54 E.
Gregory Dr., Champaign, IL 61820; (quarterly); ISSN: 0009-
7101; OCLC 2244743.
Note: v.1/2-v.4/5, 1961/62-1964/65 as **Society of
Cinematologists. Journal**; v.6, 1966/67- as **Cinema Journal**.
Serious journal containing in depth articles on film history,
theory and criticism. A forum for academicians who teach
cinema studies to present their viewpoints. Articles include
subjective dissections of notable films on a frame by frame
basis, comparisons of great films and directors, examinations
of "star quality" and the perpetuation of myth through film.
House organ for the Society for Cinema Studies. Annual index
to articles found in the summer issue.
PN1993.S62; Dewey: 791.43/05.

Cinema Librarians' Newsletter (U.S.); Cinema Librarians' Discussion
Group, Wayne State University, University Libraries, Office of
the Director, Detroit, Michigan 48202;
(quarterly).
Note: v.1,n.1-v.9,n.1? Fall 1977-Summer 1986.
Numbering irregular. Discontinued Summer 1986.

Cinema Massimo (Italy). See: **M.N.C. Museo Nazionale del Cinema.**

Cinema News (U.S.). Alternate titles: **Cinemanews; Canyon
Cinemanews.** Formerly: **Canyon Cinema News** (0008-5758).
Foundation for Art in Cinema, 1365 San Anselmo Ave., San
Anselmo, CA 94960; (irregular); ISSN: 0198-7305; OCLC
4157348.
Note: v.1, Jan 1963-n.5, Sep/Oct 1976 as **Canyon Cinema News**;
volume numbering discontinued after v.2; n.6, Nov/Dec 1976-
1980? as **Cinema News**; numbering irregular.

Ernest attempt at reviewing films on a local level.
Publication intended to inform denizens of Southern
California about worthwhile projects for the arts and
humanities.

Cinema Nuovo (Italy); Edizioni Dedalo, Casella postale 362, 70100
  Bari, Italy; (bimonthly); ISSN: 0009-711X; OCLC 2259402.
  Note: v.1,n.1 Dec 15, 1952 -.
  Cultural magazine analyzing film in artistic terms.
  Scholarly and academic, it contains controversial articles on
  film theory and criticism. Welcomes new approaches and
  insights into the field of cinema studies. Articles center
  around current films, rather than on film history.
  Dewey: 791.

Cinema Papers (Australia). Merged with **Filmviews**. Cinema Papers,
  Main Office, 644 Victoria St., North Melbourne, Victoria
  3051, Australia; (bimonthly); ISSN: 0311-3639; OCLC 8024821.
  Note: n.1, Jan 1974 -. Merged with **Filmviews** in 1989.
  Well illustrated, large format periodical focusing on the
  motion picture industry in Australia. Cover story is almost
  always about a well-received Australian feature film. Also
  reviews current international films. Contains statistics and
  surveys of Australian film attendance.
  PN1993.5.A8C56; Dewey: 791.13/05.

The Cinema Papers Australian Production Yearbook: Film,
  Television, Video (Australia). Formerly: **Australian Motion**
  Picture Yearbook (0158-698X). Cinema Papers and MTV
  Publishing, 644 Victoria St., North Melbourne, Victoria 3051
  Australia; (annual); ISSN: ISBN 3-7-8803310600; OCLC
  14950688.
  Note: ed.1-3, 1980-1983 as **Australian Motion Picture**
  Yearbook; ed.4, 1986- as **The Cinema Papers Australian**
  Production Yearbook: Film, Television, Video.
  A directory for the Australian motion picture and television
  industries. Contains listing of all production and
  distribution companies, television networks, guilds, trades,
  unions, support services and agents.
  PN1993.5.A8A96; Dewey: 791.13/0994.

Cinema: Revista Lumara de Cultura Cinematografica (Rumania).
  See: **Cinema**.

Cinema Societa (Italy); Cinema Societa, via Porta Maggiore 81, 00185 Rome, Italy. Tel: (06)731-4313; (quarterly); ISSN: 0009-7152.
Note: n.1, Jun 1966 -.
Long articles on film theory and cinema studies. Discusses the relationship between contemporary society and the performing arts. Interviews artists; contains biographical sketches and articles written by film directors. Reviews film and scholarly books. Published in Italian.
PN1993.C534.

Cinema Sud (Italy). See: **Cinemasud**.

Cinema, TV Digest (U.S.). See: **C.T.V.D. Cinema, TV Digest**.

Cinema Technology (U.K.); British Kinematograph, Sound and Television Society, 549 Victoria House, Vernon Pl., London EC1B 4DJ, England. Tel: 01-242 8400; (quarterly); ISSN: 0950-2114; OCLC 18535915.
Note: v.1,n.1 Oct 1987 -.
Part of a subscription to **Image Technology**, appearing as a supplement to the monthly periodical. Promotes better cinema presentation in theaters. Addressed to projectionists and theater managers. Gives news and information on new projection and sound systems, theater complexes, seating, video projection, screens, IMAX, and other technical concerns relating to quality projection in movie houses.
TR845.C54; Dewey: 778.5/3/05.

Cinema Texas Program Notes (U.S.); University of Texas at Austin, Department of Radio/Television/Film, Austin, TX; (6 times/ yr); ISSN: 0739-0378; OCLC 5965998.
Note: v.1, 1971? -.
Extensive program notes on films being shown at the University of Texas. Entry includes complete cast and credits, from major players to minor technicians. Contains background on how the film came to be made, quotes from the director, a critique of the film without revealing the plot or ending and the director's filmography. Originally offered complementary mailings, but began pay subscriptions in September 1979 because of publication costs.

Cinema the World Over (Pakistan); NAFDEC, The National Film
Development Corporation, State Life Building, 204-205, Hotel
Metropole, Karachi, Pakistan; (bimonthly); ISSN: n/s; OCLC
2378535.
Note: v.1,n.1 Jul 1975 -.
Tries to improve appreciation for quality filmmaking in
Pakistan. Focuses on Pakistani filmmaking, young performers
and directors. Covers a wide range of topics from Third
World cinema to Hollywood screenwriters. Published in
English.
PN1993.C535; Dewey: 791.43/05.

Cinema 2002 (Spain); Cinema 2002, Ardemans 64, Madrid 28, Spain;
(monthly); ISSN: n/a.
Note: n.1, Mar 1975 -.
"Revista de Cine." Many photographs illustrate this popular
film journal. Contains long reviews of international
releases. Articles cover the motion picture industry in
Spain, reports from film festivals, retrospective essays
analyzing the work of directors and performers, and
interviews of contemporary artists.

Cinema Vision India (India); 1 Geetika, Swami Vivekenanda Rd.,
Santacruz (West), Bombay 400 054; (quarterly); ISSN: 0250-
6998; OCLC 6159902.
Note: v.1,n.1 Jan 1980-v.2,n.2 Jan 1983.
Publishes controversial theories on Indian cinema.
Documentation is often original and contains non standard
analyses of international filmmaking. Ceased publication.
PN1993.5.I8C54; Dewey: 384.8/0954.

Cinemabook (U.S.); Cinemabook, 344 East 50th St., New York, NY
10022; (quarterly); ISSN: 0363-9665; OCLC 2567857.
Note: v.1-[v.2], Spring 1976-1977.
Slightly irreverent commentary on "au courant" film theories.
Compares directorial styles. Interviews directors and
independent filmmakers. Ceased publication.
PN1993.C542; Dewey: 791.43/05.

Cinemacabre (U.S.). Formerly: **Black Oracle**. George M. Stover,
Jr., PO Box 10005, Baltimore, MD 21204; (irregular); ISSN:
0198-1064; OCLC 6294300.
Note: n.1, Winter/Spring 1978/79 -.

Collectors' magazine specializing in horror, science fiction
and fantasy films, television programs and videos. Forum for
fans of these genres to buy, sell and trade items. Reviews
new films and television programs of interest to the reader.

CinemAction (France); Editions Corlet, Z.I. Route de Vire, 14110
Conde-sur-Noireau, France. Tel: (16) 31.69.05.92; (quarterly);
ISSN: 0243-4504; OCLC 13384706.
Note: n.1, 1978 -.
A thematic review: each issue is devoted to a central subject
which is then presented from several different standpoints.
Some of the topics covered are documentary filmmaking,
analyses of famous directors, minority images on film, third
world cinema and the influence of television on film. Back
issues can be ordered separately. Some issues published in
various other journals. Published in French.

Cinemag (Canada). Absorbed by **Cinema Canada** (0009-7071).
Alternate titles: **Cinema Canada Trade News North; Trade News
North** (0705-8799); ISSN: 0709-5635.
Note: n.1-57, Nov 1977-Mar 1981. Absorbed by **Cinema Canada**
in Mar 1981.

Cinemagic (U.S.); Cinemagic, c/o O'Quinn Studios, Inc., 475 Park
Ave. South, New York, NY 10016; (bimonthly); ISSN: 0090-
3000; OCLC 7695186.
Note: v.1, Winter 1972-1977, published in Baltimore, MD;
renumbered v.1,n.1 1979 -.
A network for amateurs producing fantasy films and videos.
Covers scriptwriting, set direction, lighting, and finance. Offers
career guidance. Advises on technical equipment used for making
miniatures and models.
TR858.C462; 778.5/345.

Cinemanews (U.S.). See: **Cinema News**.

Cinemas (U.K.); The Government Statistical Service, H.M.S.O.
Books (PC 13A/1), Publications Centre, PO Box 276, London
SW8 5DT, England. Tel: 01-211 0363; (annual); ISSN: n/a; OCLC
8197124.
Note: [n.1] 1978? -.
Contains compilations of theater statistics in England,
Scotland and Wales. Does not include Northern Ireland, the

Isle of Man or the Channel Islands. Gives number of employees, screens, admissions, seating capacity, boxoffice takings and average charge for admission. Helps to monitor business trends, identify new markets and pinpoint seasonal factors.
PN1993.5.G7C54; Dewey: 384/8/0941.

Cinemascore (U.S.); Fandom Unlimited Enterprises, Box 70868, Sunnyvale, CA 94086. Tel: 408/247-4289; (irregular); ISSN: 0277-9803; OCLC 7717216.
Note: v.1,n.1 Jan 1979 -.
"The film music journal." For collectors, fans, scholars and enthusiasts of film music scores. Interviews composers, music and sound editors working in the motion picture industry. Studies music scores from older sound films, as well as silent film scores. Reviews motion pictures, record albums, compact discs and books of interest.

Cinemasessanta (Italy). Alternate title: **Cinema Sessanta**. Piazza Caprettari 70, 00186, Rome, Italy. Tel: 6877597; (bimonthly); ISSN: n/a.
Note: v.1, 1960 -.
Popular magazine concentrating on recent international motion pictures. Articles cover film reviews, economics, importing and exporting of film and television programs, new Italian directors and general film criticism. Published in Italian.

Cinemasud (Italy). Alternate title: **Cinema Sud**. The Editor, Cinemasud, Via Calore 8, 83100 Avellino, Italy; (irregular); ISSN: 0009-7160.
Note: v.1, 1958? -.
"Rivista neo-realista di avanguardia." Interested in experimental, independent and avant garde cinema. Reviews controversial films, tracks innovative directors and new techniques of filmmaking.

Cinemateca (Colombia). Alternate title: **Cinemateca; Organo de la Cinemateca Distrital**. Cinemateca Distrital, Cra. 7a, No. 22-79, Bogota, Columbia. 283 7818 or 282 6361; (monthly).
Note: v.1,n.1 Jul 1977 -.
Publication for the Directora Instituto Distrital de Cultura Y Turismo. Promotes Colombian film and films from other Latin American countries. Published in Spanish.

Cinemateca (Uruguay). Alternate title: **Cinemateca Uruguaya.**
Casilla de Correo, Central 1170, Montevideo, Uruguay;
(monthly); ISSN: OCLC 3939586.
Note: n.1, Jul 1977 -.
A film review journal published in Spanish. Reviews all
types of films from classic international features to
contemporary Latin American cinema.
PN1993.C5427; Dewey 791.43/05.

Cinemateca (Uruguay). See also: **Cinemateca Revista.**

Cinemateca Revista (Uruguay). Alternate titles: **Cinemateca;
Cinemateca Revista de Cine y Video.** Casillo de Correo,
Central 1170, Montevideo, Uruguay. Tel: 49 57 95; (monthly);
ISSN: OCLC 6136538.
Note: n.1, Jul 1977 -.
Promotes the motion picture industry in Uruguay. Contains
articles and reviews of popular feature films in Latin
America. Published in Spanish.

Cinemateca Uruguaya (Uruguay). See: **Cinemateca.**

Cinematheek Journal (Netherlands); Netherlands Filmmuseum,
Vondelpark 3, 1071 AA Amsterdam, Netherlands. Tel: (020)
831646; (monthly); ISSN: 0016-2639.
Note: n.1, 1978? -.
Literary newsletter from the Netherlands Filmmuseum; lists
films being shown, giving synopsis, cast and credits for
each. Focuses on Dutch and Belgian film information.
Occasional articles on directors, Dutch filmmaking and film
history. Published in Dutch with English summaries.

Cinematheque (France); L'Avant-Scene Cinema, 6, rue Git-le-coeur,
75006 Paris, France; (irregular).
Note: [n.1] 196u- .
Issued as a supplement to the magazine **L'Avant-Scene Cinema,**
this publication offers scholarly treatments of respected
scriptwriters, film composers, editors, and other creative
talents who work in film production. Contains filmographies,
short biographies and dossiers on their work. Published in
French.
PN1993.A93.

Cinematheque (Jerusalem, Israel). Israel Film Archive, PO Box 8561, Jerusalem, Israel 91083. (bimonthly); ISSN: n/a.
Note: unnumbered; 198u -.
A calendar of film programs shown at the Israel Film Archive. Each entry includes title, director, date, and synopsis. Not to be confused with the periodical of the same title published by the Tel Aviv Cinematheque. Published in Hebrew with English headings.

Cinematheque (Tel Aviv, Israel). Alternate title: **Sinematek**.
Tel-Aviv Cinematheque Municipality Building, Tel-Aviv, Israel. Tel: 03-438131; (bimonthly); ISSN: n/a.
Note: n.1, 1981 -.
Popular journal containing long reviews of the latest international feature films. Studies the works of respected directors with biographical information, analytical essays and filmographies. Published in Hebrew with synopses in English.
PN1993.S5754.

La Cinematheque Suisse (Switzerland). Alternate title: **Bulletin de la Cinematheque Suisse**. Cinematheque Suisse, Case Postale 2512, CH-1000 Lausanne 2 Switzerland; (monthly except Jul/Aug).
Note: n.1, Sep-Oct 1954 -.
Schedule for films being shown at the Swiss Film Archive. Contains background notes on the overall program theme, such as "New Spanish Cinema," or "Dance on Film." Each entry includes title, country of origin, date, length, director, scenarist, cast, and critique. Published in French.
PN1993.5.S9L33.

Cinematograph (U.S.); Foundation for Art in Cinema, The San Francisco Cinematheque, 480 Potrero Ave., San Francisco, CA 94110; (annual); ISSN: 0886-6570; OCLC 12966160.
Note: v.1, 1985 -.
Academic journal analyzing motion pictures in artistic terms. Emphasizes independent, avant garde and experimental productions. Interviews filmmakers and video artists.
Dewey: 791 11.

Cinematographe (France); Cinematographe S.A.R.L., 14 rue du Cherche-midi, 75006 Paris, France; (monthly); ISSN: OCLC 8373816.

Note: n.1-n.126 Feb 1973-Jan 1987.
Popular magazine presenting French and international films,
performers, boxoffice hits and favorite directors. Contains
interviews with notable people in the French motion picture
industry. Reviews current features and contains articles on
the French television industry. Published in French. Ceased
publication.

**Cinematographers, Production Designers, Costume Designers &
Film Editors Guide** (U.S.); Lone Eagle Publishing Co., 9903 Santa
Monica Blvd., No. 204. Beverly Hills, CA 90212-9942;
(annual); ISSN: 0894-8674; OCLC 16270198.
Note: ed.1, 1988 -.
A directory to "below the line" talent currently working for
the American motion picture industry. Divided into separate
sections, first section lists cinematographers, second lists
production designers, next is of costume designers, followed
by film editors. Each section is arranged alphabetically by
name and includes credits with date of production. Where
possible, the agent or manager is also listed.
PN1998.A1C58; Dewey: 791.43/025/75.

Le Cinematographie Francaise (France). See: **Le Film Francais**.

Cinemaya (India); Cinemaya, B 90 Defence Colony, New Delhi, 110
024 India. Tel: (011)61-7127; (quarterly); ISSN: n/a; OCLC
19234070.
Note: v.1,n.1 Autumn 1988 -.
"The Asian film magazine." Designed as a pan-Asian film
periodical, reflecting the diverse cultures and different
cinematic styles represented in various Asian countries.
Each issue features an article written by a noted filmmaker.
Profiles the complete oeuvres of a single director, recognized
as a master in his/her country, but not known
internationally. Contains film reviews, information on
productions in progress, and reports on events and
personalities. Published in English.

Cinemonkey (U.S.). Formerly: **Scintillation** (0147-5789).
Cinemonkey, PO Box 8502, Portland, OR 97207; (quarterly);
ISSN: 0162-0126; OCLC 4082345.
Note: v.1, Winter 1975? -.
Features articles on film theory and criticism. Publishes in

depth analytical reviews of current films. Primarily
interested in recent feature films, but occasionally runs a
retrospective look at the early classics. Reviews cinema
books and music scores.
PN1993.C546; Dewey: 791.43/05.

CineMotion (France); CineMotion, "Journalistes en Herbe", 1, rue
   Massue, 94300 Vincennes, France; (irregular); ISSN: n/a.
   Note: [n.1], 1988 -.
   Popular journal for anyone with opinions on the cinema.
   Welcomes articles from people who want to write about certain
   films, actors, directors, cinematic styles, montage, film
   music, scriptwriting, film history, festivals and anything
   else pertaining to motion pictures. Published in French.

Cineteca Nacional (Mexico); Direccione General de Radio
   Television y Cinematografia, Av Mexico--Coyoacan 389, 03330
   Mexico D.F.; (monthly); ISSN: n/a.
   Note: n.1, 1979? -.
   House organ for the Mexican Film Archive; contains the
   program schedule for the month. Lists the film titles and
   gives cast, credits, photograph and synopsis. Features
   background articles on directors, screenwriters and
   performers. Published in Spanish.
   PN1993.M4.

Cineteca Nacional Mexico (Mexico); Cineteca Nacional, Direccione
   General de Radio Television y Cinematografia, Av Mexico--
   Coyoacan 389, 03330 Mexico D.F.; (annual); ISSN: n/a; OCLC
   8603068.
   Note: v.1, 1976 -.
   Annual report published by the Mexican Film Archive
   containing information on the films and television programs
   held by the archive. Gives statistical reports on the
   programs held throughout the year. Updates members on
   acquisitions, exhibitions and preservation activities.
   Published in Spanish.
   PN1993.5.M4C5; Dewey: 384.8/0972.

Cinethique (France); Cinethique, Boite Postale 65, 75722, Paris,
   Cedex 15, France; (irregular); ISSN: n/a; OCLC 3158204.
   Note: n.1-n.37, 1969-1985.
   "Contribution a une politique culturelle Marxiste-Leniniste."

Polemic journal studying cinema in the context of Socialism.
Ceased publication.
Dewey: 791.

CineVue (U.S.); Asian CineVision, 32 E. Broadway, New York, NY
10002. 212/925-8685; (5 times/yr); ISSN: 0895-805X; OCLC
14000688.
Note: v.1,n.1 Apr 1986 -.
Newsletter promoting Asian-Pacific film, video and music.
Presents interviews, reviews and commentary on Asian American
arts and artists. Concentrates on independent Asian American
filmmakers.
Dewey: 791 11.

Cinewave (India); Cinewave, Government Housing Estate "B" Ideal
Association, F-2, Calcutta-700 054, India; (quarterly); ISSN:
n/a; OCLC 11313564.
Note: n.1, Jan 1981 -.
Interested in the promotion of better motion pictures,
particularly those films with good scriptwriting and
dialogue. Proposes to be a forum for new filmmakers and
critics to help promote a "concerned cinema" capable of
reaching the average moviegoer. Published in English.

Classic Film Collector (U.S.). See: **Classic Images.**

Classic Film/Video Images (U.S.). See: **Classic Images.**

Classic Images (U.S.). Formerly: **8mm Collector; Classic Film
Collector** (0009-8329). Alternate title: **Classic Film/Video
Images.** Muscatine Journal, 301 E. Third St., Muscatine, IO
52761. Tel: 319/263-2331; (monthly); ISSN: 0164-5560.
Note: n.1-14, 1962-Spring 1966 as **8 MM Collector**; n.15-60,
Summer 1966-Fall 1978 as **Classic Film Collector**; n.61, Winter
1978- as **Classic Images.**
Magazine for the film and video collector; forum for buying,
selling and trading films and videocassettes. Contains
articles on popular performers and directors.
PN1995.9.C54.C55; Dewey: 791.43/05.

Classic T.V. (U.S.); Classic TV, 2980 College Ave, Suite 2, Box
25, Berkeley, CA 94705; (monthly); ISSN: n/a.
Note: v.1, 1989 -.

Provides detailed listings for vintage television programs on cable channels: Nickelodeon, CBN Family Channel, TNT, WTBS and WWOR. Entries include episode titles, original network air dates, synopses and list of guest stars.

Cliffhanger (U.S.); The World of Yesterday, Route 3, Box 263-H, Waynesville, NC 28786. Tel: 707/648-5647; (irregular); ISSN: n/a.
Note: n.1, 198u -.
Collectors' magazine for people interested in old theatrical serials, such as *Flash Gordon, Rocketman,* and *The Lone Ranger.* Lists episodes, profiles cast members, keeps up on memorabilia, festivals and collector's items.

Close-Up (India); Film Forum, 421, Hind Rajasthan Centre, Bombay-14DD India; (quarterly); ISSN: n/a; OCLC 3113780.
Note: v.1,n.1 Jul 1968 -.
Scholarly film journal treating motion pictures as an artform. Concentrates on intellectual, well made and beautifully photographed productions by internationally acclaimed directors, such as Ingmar Bergman, Federico Fellini and Satyajit Ray. Discusses the current state of Indian filmmaking, censorship in India, regional cinema and marketing Indian films abroad. Published in English. PN1993.C598; Dewey: 791.43/0954.

Close-Up (U.S.). See: **A.F.I. Close-Up.**

Columbia Broadcasting System News Index (U.S.). See: **C.B.S. News Index.**

Columbia Film View (U.S.); Film Division of the School of the Arts of Columbia University, 523 Dodge Hall, Broadway and 116th St., New York, NY 10027; (bimonthly except Jun, Jul & Aug); ISSN: n/a; OCLC 12727047.
Note: v.1, 1982 -.
Academic journal of film theory and criticism with an international flair. Surveys New York film culture. Publishes long interviews with important directors, both mainstream and independent. Reviews the latest films and cinema books.

Combroad (U.K.). Formerly: **Commonwealth Broadcasting Conference**. Commonwealth Broadcasting Association, Broadcasting House, London, England W1A 1AA; (quarterly); ISSN: 0951-0826; OCLC 3614956.
Note: Jan 1967-Apr/Jun 1974 as **Commonwealth Broadcasting Conference**; Jul/Sep 1974- as **Combroad.**
News and reports from members of the British Commonwealth Broadcasting Association: Australia, Ghana, Britain, New Zealand, Canada, Barbados, etc. Articles discuss topics of interest to international broadcasting personnel, such as copyrights, competition, new technology, research, training, programming, growth, planning and the future. HE8689.C6613; Dewey: 384.55/4/09171241.

Communications & the Law (U.S.). See: **Communications and the Law.**

Communications and the Law (U.S.). Alternate title: **Communications & the Law.** Meckler Corp., 11 Ferry Lane West, Westport, CT 06880. Tel: 203/226-6967; (bimonthly); ISSN: 0162-9093; OCLC 4252472.
Note: v.1, Winter 1979 -.
A legal resource for attorneys, media specialists and journalists. Keeps current on laws and legislation pertaining to print and electronic media. Covers censorship, fair use, libel, copyright infringement and piracy relating to radio and television broadcasting, cable, satellite communications and journalism. K3.O39; Dewey: 343.73/09905.

Communications Booknotes (U.S.). Alternate title: **Mass Media Book Notes** (0740-6479). Center for Advanced Study in Telecommunications, 210 Baker Systems, 1971 Neil Ave., Columbus, OH 43210. Tel: 614/292-6239; (bimonthly); ISSN: 0045-3188; 0748-657X; OCLC 8701864.
Note: v.1, 1970? -. From n.44-n.139, Sep 1973-Jan 1982 also known as **Mass Media Book Notes**.
Surveys new non-serial publications in telecommunications, advertising, popular culture, international communications, journalism, and cinema. The November-December issue concentrates on cinema. Includes contributors from Australia, Canada, France, Great Britain and West Germany.

Communications Daily (U.S.); Warren Publishing, Inc., 2115 Ward
Court, NW, Washington, DC 20037. Tel: 202/872-9200; (daily);
ISSN: n/a.
Note: v.1,n.1 Jan 19, 1981 -.
"The authoritative news service of electronic
communications." Newspaper reporting on all electronic
media, including: television, cable, satellite, home video,
mobile radio, telephone and data communications, E-mail and
electronic information distribution.

Communications Law and Policy in Australia (Australia);
Butterworths, PO Box 345, North Ryde, NSW, Australia 2113;
(monthly); ISSN: n/a.
Note: [v.1] 1988 -.
Covers present legal cases and courtroom decisions. Quotes
extracts from all the relevant broadcasting, radio and
telecommunications regulations mandated in Australia. Information is presented in a looseleaf binder format which
incorporates annual updates.

Communications Research (U.S.); Sage Publications, Inc., 2111
West Hillcrest Dr., Newbury Park, CA 91320; (6 times/yr);
ISSN: 0093-6502; OCLC 1792462.
Note: v.1,n.1 Jan 1974 -.
Conducts studies on the effect electronic and print media
have on the public, analyzes the findings and prints the
results. Topics examined include audience comprehension of
televised news, demographics of soap opera audiences, musical
genres and heterosexual attraction, effects of graphic
violence on adolescents and children.
P91.C56; Dewey: 001.5.

Communications Satellite Technical Review (U.S.). See: **COMSAT
Technical Review.**

Community Video Report (U.S.). See: **Televisions.**

Compact Disk Data Report (U.S.). See: **C.D. Data Report.**

Comparative Literature and Film Studies (U.S.); Peter Lang
Publishers, Inc., 62 W. 45th St., 4th Floor, New York, NY
10036; (annual); ISSN: 0899-9902; OCLC 18283509.
Note: v.1, 1989 -.

Scholarly presentation of cinema studies in relationship to
comparative literature. Articles analyze film theory,
history and criticism.

Complete Home Video Directory (U.S.). See: **Bowker's Complete
Video Directory**.

Complete Home Video Directory. Adult Video Supplement (U.S.).
See: **Bowker's Complete Video Directory**.

Computer Entertainment (U.S.). Formerly: **Electronic Games** (0730-
6687). Reese Communications, Inc., Retailer Program, 460 W.
34th St., New York, NY 10001; (monthly); ISSN: 0883-8089;
OCLC 11886788.
Note: v.1-v.3, 1982-Apr 1985 as **Electronic Games**; v.3,n.5-
v.3,n.8, May 1985-Aug 1985 as **Computer Entertainment**.
Published information about home computer video games.
Discontinued in 1985.
GV1469.15.E57; Dewey: 001 11.

Computer Games (U.S.). Formerly: **Video Games Player** (0748-4453).
Carnegie Publications Corp., 888 7th Ave., New York, NY
10106; (bimonthly); ISSN: 0748-4461; OCLC 10932403.
Note: v.1,n.1-v.2,n.2, Fall 1982-Oct/Nov 1983 as **Video Games
Player**; v.2,n.3 Dec/Jan 1984- as **Computer Games**.
Designed for youthful aficionados of home computer and arcade
video games. Reviews software, plots strategies for winning,
surveys computer hardware.

COMSAT Technical Review (U.S.). Alternate titles: **C.O.M.S.A.T.
Technical Review; Communications Satellite Technical Review**.
Communications Satellite Corp., 22300 Comsat Dr., Clarksburg,
MD 20871. Tel: 301/428-4494; (2 times/yr); ISSN: 0095-9669;
OCLC 1429664.
Note: v.1, Fall 1971 -.
Highly technical magazine discussing the scientific advances
made in the telecommunications industry because of artificial
satellites. Shows new applications for improved information
dispersal through communications satellites.
TK5104.C64; Dewey: 621.38/0422.

**Conseil International du Cinema de la Television et de la
Communication Audiovisuelle** (France). English title:

**International Council for Film, Television and Audiovisual
Communication**. Formerly: **I.F.T.C. Newsletter**. Unesco, 1 rue
Miollis, 75732 Paris Cedex 15, France. Tel: 1-45.68 2556;
(monthly).
Note: n.1-n.?, 1973-May 1979 as **I.F.T.C. Newsletter**; n.1, Jun
1979- as **Conseil International du Cinema de la Television et
de la Communication Audiovisuelle**.
Published in collaboration with Unesco, this newsletter
provides concise information on international film and video
activities. Discusses the development of satellite
telecommunications, the impact of television on developing
nations and the use of film and video for teaching. Keeps
current with international film festivals and awards,
archives' meetings and international copyright. Emphasis is
on intercultural exchange of film and television programs
among nations. Published in French and English.

Continuum: An Australian Journal of the Media (Australia);
Department of Media Studies, WA College of Advanced
Education, Mt. Lawley, Western Australia, 6050, Australia; (2
times/yr); ISSN: 1030-4312; OCLC 16998366.
Note: v.1, 1987/88 -.
Scholarly journal studying cinema, television and print
media. Each issue is devoted to a theme with several
articles exploring different points of view from each of the
media. Focus is on Australia and the Pacific rim nations.

Contracampo (Spain). Alternate title: **Contracampo. Revista de
Cine**. Contracampo, Apartado 17.048, Madrid, Spain;
(irregular); ISSN: n/a; OCLC 8187546.
Note: v.1,n.1 Apr 1979 -.
Well designed and written publication concentrating on
Spanish interests. Topics include famous Spanish filmmakers
and artists like Luis Bunuel, Salvador Dali and Jaime Camino.
Other subjects can be as diverse as Surrealism, American
musicals, Film Noir, comedy and music videos. Contains
lengthy reports on the San Sebastian Film Festival and other
Spanish-based festivals. Reviews films and books. Published
in Spanish.
PN1993.C68; Dewey: 791.43/05.

Contracampo. Revista de Cine (Spain). See: **Contracampo**.

Copie Zero (Canada). Formerly: **Nouveau Cinema Canadien** (0550-1318); absorbed **New Canadian Film** (0548-4162). Continued by **La Revue de la Cinematheque**. Cinematheque Quebecoise, 335 Boulevard de Maisonneuve est, Montreal, Quebec H2X 1K1 Canada. Tel: 514/842-9763; (quarterly); ISSN: 0709-0471; OCLC 12853415.
Note: v.1-v.7,n.2, Mar 1968-Oct 1975 as **Nouveau Cinema Canadien**; v.7,n.3-v.9,n.2, Feb/Mar 1976-Jun 1978 as **Nouveau Cinema Canadien/New Canadian Film**; n.1-n.?, 1979-1988 as **Copie Zero**; continued by **La Revue de la Cinematheque**. Scholarly journal concentrating on French and Canadian film productions and filmmakers. Contains in-depth articles, interviews and filmographies. On occasion, issued a supplement, **Ecrits Sur la Cinema**. Published in French and English; discontinued.
PN1993.5.C2C66; Dewey: 384.8/09714 19.

Copie Zero (Canada). See also: **Ecrits Sur le Cinema**; **La Revue de la Cinematheque**.

Corporate Television (U.S.). Formerly: **International Television** (0737-3929). P.S.N. Publications, Inc., 2 Park Ave., New York, NY 10016; (bimonthly); ISSN: 0889-4523; OCLC 13893300.
Note: v.1,n.1-v.4, Jun 1983-Jul 1986 as **International Television**; renumbered v.1,n.1 Sep 1986- as **Corporate Television**.
"The official magazine of the International Television Association; the news magazine for business and industrial television." Trade magazine for TV executives. Expresses corporate viewpoints and concerns, such as profit making, growth patterns, competition, international cooperation, and regulations.
TK6630.A1C67; Dewey: 384.55/05.

Corporate Video (U.K.). See: **Televisual**.

Corporate Video Decisions (U.S.); Act III Publishing, Corporate Video Decisions, 401 Park Ave. South, New York, NY 10016. Tel: 212/545-5100; (monthly).
Note: v.1,n.1 Sep 1988 -.
Covers the issues of corporate/institutional video from a manager's point of view. Articles include video production, video conference, interactive video disks and presentation graphics. Shows how to best use a video function for

training, communications and marketing a product or service.
Introduces new technology and rates new equipment.

La Cosa Vista (Italy); Centro Universitario Cinematografico,
Dipartimento di Scienza Politiche, Universita degli Studi di
Trieste - 34127 Trieste (Italia) - Piazzale Europa, 1. Tel:
(040) 5603281; (quarterly); ISSN: n/a; OCLC 17864601.
Note: n.1, 1985 -.
"Studi e richerche sul cinema & altri media." Scholarly
journal published in Italian. Each issue is devoted to one
topic with many articles analyzing different aspects of it.
Covers film festivals and reviews academic books on the
media.

Costume Designers Guild. Membership Directory (U.S.). See:
Membership Directory. Costume Designers Guild.

Critic (U.S.). Formerly: Film Society Newsletter; Film Society
Review (0015-1408). American Federation of Film Societies,
144 Bleecker St., New York, NY 10012; (bimonthly); ISSN:
0090-9831; OCLC 1785349.
Note: n.1-[n.?], 1955-May 1965 as Film Society Newsletter;
renumbered v.1-v.7, Sep 1965-May 1972 as Film Society Review;
renumbered v.1,n.1, Sep/Oct 1972- as Critic.
Reviews and commentaries on motion pictures and television.
Essays deal with cinema in the context of its social and political
influences; looks at the society in which the production was made.
Publishes reviews of "campus critics" from the different university
film societies. Critiques film books.
PN1993.C78; Dewey: 791.43/05.

Critical Arts (S.Africa); Contemporary Cultural Studies Unit,
University of Natal, King George V Ave., Durban 4001, South
Africa; (quarterly); ISSN: 0256-0046; OCLC 7936723.
Note: v.1,n.1 Mar 1980 -.
Seeks to "challenge the existing social structure and
relations which govern the status quo orientation of South
Africa's media institutions." Devoted to the study of the
relationship between society and the media. Includes
television, radio, cinema, theater, music and the press.
P92.S58C74; Dewey: 016.00151/0968.

The Cue Sheet (U.S.); Society for the Preservation of Film Music,
   10850 Wilshire Blvd., Suite 770, Los Angeles, CA 90024;
   (quarterly); ISSN: 0888-9015; OCLC 13769635.
   Note: v.1,n.1 Jan 1984 -.
   Newsletter for members of the Society. Devoted to the
   preservation and exhibition of film music. Interested in
   reconstructing the musical scores that were written to
   accompany silent movies.
   Dewey: 780 11.

Cult Movie (Italy); Edizioni SpazioUno, c/o Circolo Ricreativo
   ENEL, via del Sole, 10-50123, Firenze, Italy. Tel: (055)
   219286; (bimonthly); ISSN: n/a; OCLC 9735547.
   Note: v.1,n.1 Dec 1980 -.
   An academic fan magazine that devotes each issue to a "cult"
   personage, usually American, who has had a great impact on
   filmmaking: Humphrey Bogart, Woody Allen, Dashiell Hammett,
   John Ford, etc. It portrays the chosen artist in a loving
   homage, detailing his work, his influence on the cinema, his
   turning points and successes. Backing up the articles is
   solid research containing comprehensive filmographies,
   interviews, photographs, documentation and portions of
   scripts. Published in Italian.
   PN1993.C89; Dewey: 791.43/05.

**Culture Statistics. Film Industry = Statistiques de la Culture
   L'Industrie du Film** (Canada); Publication Sales & Services,
   Statistics Canada, Ottawa K1A OV7 Canada; (annual
   (irregular)); ISSN: 0227-4000; OCLC 9149788.
   Note: v.1, 1978/79 -.
   Contains detailed statistics on theaters in Canada, film
   distributors, and film/video production companies. A
   statistical breakdown of the motion picture theater industry,
   analyzing family expenditures, paid admissions, capacity of
   seating per theatre, attendance rates, number of employees,
   salaries, operating costs and average annual profits. Gives
   sales and rentals of film and video products, as well as
   royalties and commissions paid by distributors to producers.
   PN1993.5.C2C84; Dewey: 384.8/0971.

Current (U.S.). Formerly: **Public Telecommunications Letter**;
   Alternate title: **Current: For People in Public
   Telecommunications**. Current, 2311 18th St., NW, Washington,

D.C. 20009. Tel: 202/265-8310; (biweekly); ISSN: 0739-991X;
OCLC 6758682.
Note: v.1-47, [19uu]-1980 as **Public Telecommunications
Letter**; renumbered v.1,n.1 Mar 1980- as **Current**.
Geared toward the independent television and radio producer,
this magazine publishes news about programs and series on PBS
that use independent productions. Informs about decisions at
National Public Radio, the Public Broadcasting System and the
Corporation for Public Broadcasting that have an impact on
independents. Acts as an open circuit to public broadcasting
grant opportunities, awards and scholarships.

Current: For People in Public Telecommunications (U.S.). See:
Current.

Current Research in Film (U.S.); Ablex Publishing Corp., 355
Chestnut St., Norwood, NJ 07648; (annual); ISSN: 0748-8580;
OCLC 11018239.
Note: v.1, 1985 -.
Presents articles from respected scholars covering such
topics as marketing motion pictures, film exhibition,
contemporary censorship, audience demographics, and
international film distribution. Compiles audience
statistics reflecting the age, financial status, schooling,
preferences, personal values, and expectations of the
theater-going public. Contains boxoffice statistics and
other economic analyses of the motion picture industry.
Contains information on laws and legislation affecting the
industry.
PN1993.C93; Dewey: 384.8/05.

The Czechoslovak Film (Czechoslovakia). Alternate titles:
**Ceskoslovensky Film; Bulletin of the Czechoslovak
Nationalized Film**. Czechoslovak Filmexport, Press Dept., 111
45 Praha 1, Vaclavske Namesti 28, Czechoslovakia;
(quarterly); ISSN: 0011-4588; OCLC 2158358.
Note: v.1, June 1948 -.
An overview of the Czech film industry. Contains
descriptions with photos of the latest Czech productions
available for distribution abroad. Covers features, shorts
and animation. Published in French, English, German, Russian
and Spanish.
PN1993.5.C9C9.

-D-

D.T.V. Presents (U.S.). See: **Daytime T.V. Presents**.

D.T.V.'s Greatest Stories (U.S.). See: **Daytime T.V.'s Greatest Stories**.

Daily Variety (U.S.); Daily Variety, Ltd., 1400 N. Cahuenga Blvd., Hollywood, CA 90028. Tel: 213/469-1141; (daily except Sat., Sun. & holidays); ISSN: 0011-5509; OCLC 2536362.
Note: v.1, 1933 -.
Popular trade newspaper of the motion picture, theater and television industries. Keeps current with the professional world of the performing arts.
PN1993.D3.

Danish Films (Denmark); The Danish Film Institute, Store Sondervoldstraede 4, PO Box 2158, DK-1016 Copenhagen K, Denmark. Tel: 451-57 6500; (annual); ISSN: n/a; OCLC 2471800.
Note: v.1, 1966 -.
Yearbook listing Danish films produced each year. Entries contain title, production/distribution information, cast, length, photo and synopsis. Published in Danish, English, French and German.
PN1993.3.D33.

Daytime T.V. (U.S.). Alternate title: **Daytime Television**.
Sterling's Magazines, Inc., 355 Lexington Ave., New York, NY 10017. Tel: 212/391-1400; (monthly); ISSN: 0011-7129; OCLC 1786473.
Note: v.1, Winter 1970 -.
Popular magazine for soap opera fans. Contains gossip, information about romances on and off the set, biographies and interviews. Gives the storylines of all the daytime soaps: *All My Children, Another World, As The World Turns, Capitol, Days of Our Lives, General Hospital, One Life To Live, Ryan's Hope, Search for Tomorrow, Santa Barbara,* and *The Young and the Restless*. Maintains a "plotline hotline," detailed cast

lists and publishes the Nielsen ratings for the programs.
PN1992.8S4D39; Dewey: 051.

Daytime T.V. Presents (U.S.). Alternate titles: **D.T.V. Presents;
Daytime Television Presents**. Sterling's Magazines, Inc., 355
Lexington Ave., New York, NY 10017. Tel: 212/391-1400;
(5 times/yr.).
Note: v.1, 1982 -.
Interviews the stars of daytime soap operas. Includes many
photographs, trivia games, gossip, storyline predictions.

Daytime T.V.'s Greatest Stories (U.S.). Alternate titles:
**D.T.V.'s Greatest Stories; Daytime Television's Greatest
Stories**. Sterling's Magazines, Inc., 355 Lexington Ave., New
York, NY 10017. Tel: 212/391-1400; (quarterly); ISSN: n/a.
Note: n.1, Spring 1984 -.
Specialized editions pertaining to certain topics recurring
on the various soap operas, such as "Soap Opera Wedding Album
1965-89." Uses photographs, interviews and commentary to
illustrate topic.

Daytime Television (U.S.). See: **Daytime T.V.**

Daytime Television Presents (U.S.). See: **Daytime T.V. Presents**.

Daytime Television's Greatest Stories (U.S.). See: **Daytime T.V.'s
Greatest Stories**.

Deep Focus (U.S.); Tisch School of the Arts, Office of Student
Affairs, New York University, 721 Broadway, New York, NY
10003. Tel: 212/998-1900; (2 times/yr); ISSN: n/a.
Note: 1986 -.
A student film journal acting as a forum for new ideas,
theories and interpretations of cinema studies. Articles
cover film history from the silent period to current features
and documentaries.

Deep Red (U.S.); FantaCo., Thomas Skulan, Publisher, 21 Central
Ave., Albany, NY 12210-1391; (quarterly); ISSN: 0896-4513;
OCLC 17159851.
Note: n.1, Dec 1987 -. Preceded by a 20 page promotional
issue in 1986.
Fanzine specializing in low budget slasher movies. Displays

graphically the special effects and horror makeup that are
presented in the films.
Dewey: 791 11.

Denk Ajans (Turkey); Denk Ajans: Film ve Tanitim Hizmetleri,
G.M.K. Blv. No: 21/13 Demirtepe-Ankara, Turkey. Tel: (4) 229
84 30; (monthly); ISSN: n/a.
Note: v.1,n.1 Oct 1989 -.
A popular magazine reporting on motion pictures, television
and video in Turkey.

Deutsche Filmkunst (E.Germany). See: **Filmspiegel.**

Deutsche Kameramann (W.Germany). See: **Film & T.V.
Kameramann.**

**Deutschen Institut fur Filmkunde. Information aus dem Deutschen
Institut fur Filmkunde** (W.Germany). Alternate title:
Information aus dem Deutschen Institut fur Filmkunde.
Deutschen Institute fur Filmkunde, 6200 Wiesbaden-Biebrich,
Schloss, West Germany. Tel: 0-61 21/6 90 74; (quarterly);
ISSN: n/a; OCLC 4850459.
Note: [n.1] Jan-Apr 1973 -.
Schedule of films shown at the Deutschen Institut fur
Filmkunde. Keeps patrons informed about preservation
projects, new books acquired, and bibliographies compiled at
the archive. Published in German.
PN1993.5.G3D46; Dewey: 791.43/0943.

Les Deux Ecrans (Algeria); Les Deux Ecrans, 27 Bd Zirout Youssef,
Alger, Algeria; (monthly); ISSN: n/a.
Note: n.1-n.55/56, 1978-1983.
Popular journal reviewing international feature films.
Published in Arabic and French. Ceased publication in 1983.

Development Communication Report (U.S.); Clearinghouse on
Development Communication, 1255 23 St., NW, Suite 400,
Washington, DC 20037. Tel: 202/862-1900; (quarterly); ISSN:
0192-1312; OCLC 4964722.
Note: [n.1] Jan 1973? -.
Examines telecommunications and mass media in developing
countries. An international look at the effect of print,
radio, television and telephone communications on social and

national development in the third world. Reviews
periodicals, books, films, videos and slide sets.
Dewey: 307 11.

The Dial from K.C.E.T./28 (U.S.). See: **K.C.E.T. Magazine**.

The Dial from K.C.T.S./9 (U.S.). See: **K.C.T.S. Magazine**.

The Dial from W.E.T.A. (U.S.). See: **W.E.T.A. Magazine**.

The Dial from W.T.T.W./Eleven (U.S.). See: **The Eleven Magazine**.

Dial. W.N.E.T./Thirteen (U.S.). See: **13 Program Guide**.

Dial/W.G.B.H. (U.S.). See: **'G.B.H.**

Directors Guild of America. Directory of Members (U.S.). See:
  Directory of Members. Directors Guild of America.

Directory / I.D.A. (U.S.). See: **I.D.A. Directory**.

Directory / International Documentary Association (U.S.). See:
  I.D.A. Directory.

Directory of Experts, Authorities & Spokespersons (U.S.).
  Formerly: **The Talk Show Guest Directory; Talk Show Guest
  Directory of Experts, Authorities & Spokespersons.** Broadcast
  Interview Source, 2233 Wisconsin Ave., NW, Washington, DC
  20007-4104. Tel: 202/342-5411; (annual); ISSN: 1045-9537;
  OCLC 16464424.
  Note: ed.1-ed.2, 1985-1986 as **The Talk Show Guest Directory**;
  ed.3, 1986/87 as **Talk Show Guest Directory of Experts,
  Authorities & Spokespersons**; ed.4, 1987/88- as **Directory of
  Experts, Authorities & Spokespersons**.
  A source book profiling companies, authorities, organizations
  and people who are available for interviews and discussion
  groups on talk shows. Used by the broadcasting industry to
  help locate experts and company spokespersons.
  PN1991.8.T35B76; Dewey: 791.45/5.

Directory of International Broadcasting (U.K.); BSO Publications,
  Ltd., 3/5 St. John St., London EC1M 4AE England. Tel:
  01-253-7174; (annual); ISSN: 0262-9771; OCLC 10930871.

Note: ed.1, 1979 -.
A gazetteer of manufacturers, companies and distributors supplying the British television and radio industries.
Covers hardware, equipment and services. Lists international and British broadcasting authorities, organizations, and stations.
TK6560.Z5D57; Dewey: 621.38/029/4.

Directory of Members. Directors Guild of America (U.S.).
Alternate title: **Directors Guild of America. Directory of Members.** Directors Guild of America, 7950 Sunset Blvd., Los Angeles, CA 90046. Tel: 213/656-1220; (annual); ISSN: 0419-2052; OCLC 2251189.
Note: ed.1, 1967/68 -.
A comprehensive listing of motion picture and television directors working in the United States or for American companies. Contains names, addresses, telephone numbers and agents.
PN1998.A1D52; Dewey: 791.43/0922.

Directory of Members. The Publicists Guild of America (U.S.).
See: **The Publicists Guild Directory.**

The Directory of Religious Broadcasting (U.S.). Alternate title: **Annual Directory of Religious Broadcasting** (0160-029X).
National Religious Broadcasters, CN 1926, Morristown, NJ 07960. Tel: 201/428-5400; (annual); ISSN: 0731-0331; OCLC 8098075.
Note: Began 1974? -.
Source directory for religious radio and television stations, with full or partial format of programming. Contains call letters and key personnel for each station. Lists individual programs and their producers; covers international broadcasting, equipment, consultants, fund raising and donor management, and satellite program services.
BV655.D57; Dewey: 384.54/53/02573.

Directory of the French Film and Audiovisual Industries (France).
See: **Annuaire du Cinema Francais et de L'Audiovisuel.**

Dirigido Por... (Spain); Albert Turro, Editor, Rbla. de Catalunya, 108 3., 1. Barcelona 8, Spain; (monthly); ISSN: n/a.
Note: [n.1] 1973? -.

Main interest of this Spanish language periodical is to
present the work of internationally acclaimed motion picture
directors. Essays include biographical sketches,
filmographies and still photographs illustrating the director
and his/her work. Reports on film festivals. Includes a
section for critical reviews of current television and cinema
productions.

Disc Deals (U.S.); Disc Deals, PO Box 391, Pine Lake, GA 30072;
(monthly); ISSN: 0882-2794; OCLC 11803954.
Note: v.1,n.1 May 1985 -.
Newsletter for buying, selling and trading laser discs (LV),
CED video discs and CD audio discs. Prints articles on
state-of-the art laser video and audio disc equipment,
technology and applications.
Dewey: 384 11.

Discourse (U.S.). Subtitle: **Journal for Theoretical Studies in
Media and Culture**. Center for Twentieth Century Studies at
the University of Wisconsin-Milwaukee. Subscriptions:
Indiana University Press, 10th & Morton Sts., Bloomington, IN
47405. Tel: 812/885-9449; (2 times/yr); ISSN: 0730-1081; 0734-
063X; OCLC 7415086.
Note: n.1, 1978 -.
An interdisciplinary journal "devoted to the study of
contemporary culture, with an emphasis on critical and
cultural theory, literary studies, the experimental arts, and
mass culture." Cinema studies and its relationship to
contemporary life is an integral theme. Articles analyze
television and mass media as well as art, literature and
music.
P87.D57; Dewey: 302.2/34/05.

The Discovery Channel: T.D.C. (U.S.). Alternate title: **T.D.C.:
The Discovery Channel**. Cable Educational Network, Inc., 8201
Corporate Dr., Suite 1200, Landover, MD 20785. Tel: 301/577-
1999; (monthly); ISSN: 0890-8540; OCLC 14405192.
Note: v.1,n.1 Mar? 1985 -.
Programming guide to cable television's Discovery Channel.
This channel specializes in nature and science programs,
nonfiction adventure stories and documentaries. Also
publishes articles related to the series being aired.
Features updates on new video equipment, cable technology,

and antennas.
Dewey: 384 11.

Discovery In Focus (U.S.). Alternate title: **In Focus: The Discovery Channel**. The Discovery Channel, 8201 Corporate Dr., Suite 1200, Landover, MD 20785. Tel: 301/577-1999; (quarterly).
Note: v.1, 1987 -.
Newsletter for cable television's Discovery Channel, which began in 1985. Articles include background information on the science and technology, nature, history and world culture programs being aired. Includes articles written by the filmmakers themselves about filming their productions. Contains editorials on program development and introductions to the staff.

Diskurs Film (W.Germany); Verlegergemeinschaft Schaudig/Bauer/Ledig, Tristanstrasse 13, D-8000 Munchen 40, West Germany; (annual). ISSN: n/a.
Note: v.1, 1987 -.
"Munchner Beitrage zur Filmphilologie." Each volume contains a collection of scholarly essays centered around a particular theme, such as strategies of film analysis, the silent film, and the treatment of love in the cinema. Published in German.

The Disney Channel Magazine (U.S.); The Disney Channel, 4111 W. Alameda Ave., Burbank, CA 91505. Tel: 818/840-7768; (monthly); ISSN: 0747-4644; OCLC 10895644.
Note: v.1,n.1 Jan 1983 -.
Programming guide to the Disney cable network. Also contains articles on parenting and child development, as well as games and activities for children.

Domitor (Canada); Domitor, Etudes Cinematographiques, Departement des Litteratures, Universite Laval, Quebec G1K 7P4 Canada; (quarterly); ISSN: n/a.
Note: v.1, 1986? -.
The membership bulletin of the international organization "Domitor," which is open to film archivists, academics, librarians and anyone interested in the study of early cinema. Keeps track of festivals, symposia, exhibitions and publications dealing with film history from 1893-1929. Publishes news and views of the international organization. Editions available in French, Italian and English.

Editions available in French, Italian and English.

Downlink Directory (U.S.); Virginia A. Ostendorf, Inc., PO Box
2896, Littleton, CO 80161-2896. Tel: 303/797-3131; (annual);
ISSN: n/a; OCLC 13277183.
Note: ed.1 1986 -.
"A reference guide to satellite downlinking services." Lists
satellite receive sites in the U.S. and Canada which are available
for public use. Divided into two sections: C-Band and KU-Band,
which are further divided into separate sections: Permanent
Downlinks and Transportable Downlinks. Each section is
arranged alphabetically by state, listing the name of the site, the
address, telephone number, personnel, technical data (frequency,
audio-stereo, size, access, transponders, etc.), and viewing capacity.
HE7771.D68; Dewey: 384.5/1/02573

Dutch Film (Netherlands); The Information Service of the Ministry
of Welfare, Health and Cultural Affairs, Rijswijk,
Netherlands, Published by Government Publishing Office, The
Hague, Netherlands; (annual); ISSN: n/a; OCLC 4750613.
Note: ed.1, 1966/68 -.
A comprehensive list of Dutch features arranged
alphabetically by title. Each entry contains director,
producer, scriptwriter, cinematographer, editor, sound,
music, cast, release date, running time, format, language
versions, and address for foreign sales. Contains a section
for low budget features, documentary features, documentary
shorts, theatrical shorts and animation films. A promotional
directory, published in English, Dutch, French, German and
Spanish.
PN1993.3.D83; Dewey: 791.43/09492.

-E-

E.B.U. Review (Switzerland). Alternate title: **European Broadcasting Union Review**. E.B.U., Geneva, Ancienne Route 17A, Case postale 193, CH-1211 Geneva 20 Switzerland. Tel: 98 77 66; (monthly); ISSN: 0012-7493; OCLC 2110118.
Note: n.1, 1950? -.
Consists of two editions: the Geneva edition covering programs, administration and law, published January, March, May, July, September and November; and the Brussels edition, covering technical matters, published February, April, June, August, October and December. Reports from active members of the European broadcasting community, covering such topics as opera on television, new forms of dramatic musical work, educational radio for adults, and the impact of TV on political elections. Publishes separate English and French editions. May have ceased publication with v.33, 1982.
PN1991.3.E8E2; Dewey: 384.5/094.

E.F.L.A. Bulletin (U.S.). See: **A.F.V.A. Bulletin / American Film and Video Association**.

E.-I.T.V. Magazine (U.S.). Formerly: **Educational & Industrial Television**. Broadband Information Services, Inc., Educational-Industrial Television, PO Box 6018, Duluth, MN 55806; (monthly); ISSN: 0046-1466.
Note: v.1-v.15,n.5, 1969?-May 1983 as **Educational & Industrial Television**; v.15,n.6-v.20,n.2, Jun 1983-Feb/Mar 1988 as **E.-I.T.V.** Ceased with Feb/Mar 1988 issue.
A newsletter for schools and companies utilizing television for in-house educational and industrial purposes. Reviews educational television productions. Contains a directory of educational, instructional and training programs for students and workers on video, including adult education and company sponsored training programs.
LB1044.7.E364; Dewey: 371.3/358/05.

E.P.D. Film (W.Germany). Alternate title: **Film**. Gameinschaftswerk der Evangelischen Publizistik (GEP), Friedrichstrasse 2-6, 6000 Frankfurt 17, West Germany. Tel: 069/71 57 0; (monthly); ISSN: 0176-2044.
Note: v.1, 1984 -.
Church related publication reviewing international feature films released in Germany. Reviews contain original title, country of origin, year of production, director, screenwriter, music, production company, cast, length and photo. Published in German.

East-West Film Journal (U.S.); East-West Center, Journals Department, University of Hawaii Press, 2840 Kolowalu St., Honolulu, HI 96822; (2 times/yr); ISSN: 0891-6780; OCLC 14978918.
Note: v.1,n.1 Dec 1986 -.
Long, scholarly articles analyzing cinema and culture in the different countries comprising the Pacific rim. Tries to "foster better understanding and relations among peoples of the East and West through culture and communication." Topics covered include humor in Japanese film, the influence of Zen in cinema, Chinese film in the 1960s, new Australian cinema, Eastern motifs in American motion pictures.
PN1993.E25; Dewey: 791.43/05.

Ecran (France). Merged with **Image et Son/Revue du Cinema** to form **La Revue du Cinema/Image et Son/Ecran** (0019-2635).
Note: n.1-n.86, Jan 1972-Dec 1979; merged with **Image et Son/ Revue du Cinema**, Jan 1980.

L'Ecran Fantastique (France); 1, Media, 69 rue de la Tombe-Issoire 75014 Paris, France; (monthly); ISSN: n/a; OCLC 9001967.
Note: v.1, 1976? -.
Dedicated to science fiction, horror and fantasy filmmaking. Specializes in long treatises on big budget science fiction features, such as *Star Wars* and *Moonraker*. Describes the set designs, music, miniature work, photography and makeup; profiles cast members and directors. Occasional articles pay homage to the former great directors and stars of this genre. Reviews applicable feature and short films.
PN1995.9.F36E35.

Ecrits Sur le Cinema (Canada). Supplement to: **Copie Zero** (0709-0471). Cinematheque Quebecoise, Musee du Cinema, 335 est, boul. de Maisonneuve, Montreal, Quebec H2X 1K1 Canada; (irregular); ISSN: 0822-6350; OCLC 10199273.
Note: n.1, 1982 -.
An annotated bibliography of publications on Quebec cinema from 1911 to 1981. Published in French. Issued as a supplement to **Copie Zero**.
Dewey: 016.79143/09714.

Educational Film Library Association. E.F.L.A. Bulletin (U.S.). See: **A.F.V.A. Bulletin / American Film and Video Association**.

Educational-Industrial Television Magazine (U.S). See: **E.-I.T.V. Magazine**.

Educational Technology (U.S.). Formerly: **Teaching Aids News**. Educational Technology Publications, Inc., 720 Palisade Ave, Englewood Cliffs, NJ 07632. Tel: 201/871-4007; (monthly); ISSN: 0013-1962; OCLC 991536.
Note: v.1-v.5, 1961-1965 as **Teaching Aids News**; v.6, 1966- as **Educational Technology**.
Predominantly a publication on primary and secondary education for teachers, school librarians and media specialists. However, articles study the use of educational 16mm films, videocassettes and computer software as teaching aids in the classroom.
LB1043.E33; Dewey: 371.3/078.

Educators Guide to Free Audio and Video Materials (U.S.). Formerly: **Educators Guide to Free Tapes, Scripts and Transcriptions** (0070-9441). Educators Progress Service, Inc., 214 Center St., Dept. D8, Randolph, WI 53956. Tel: 414/326-3126; (annual); ISSN: 0160-1296; OCLC 3255077.
Note: ed.1, 1954 -.
A directory listing free audio tapes, videocassettes and phonorecords available to schools serving primary grades through college level. The materials are sponsored by nonprofit organizations, government agencies and private companies. Revised and updated during the summer months, each entry includes title, organizational sponsor, length, date, grade level and contents description.
LB1043.Z9E34; Dewey: 371.3/07/8.

Educators Guide to Free Films (U.S.); Educators Progress Service,
   Inc., Dept. D8, 214 Center St., Randolph, WI 53956. Tel: 414/326-
   3126; (annual); ISSN: 0070-9395; OCLC 1048582.
   Note: ed.1, 1941 -.
   Designed as a resource for teachers and librarians of primary
   through high school grades, this catalog compiles a list of
   free 16mm films available from nonprofit organizations,
   government agencies and private companies. Each edition is
   revised and updated annually during the summer months to
   coincide with the new school year. Each film entry includes
   title, sponsor, length, date, grade level and synopsis.
   LB1044.E3; Dewey: 371.335230838.

Educators Guide to Free Filmstrips (U.S.). See: **Educators Guide
   to Free Filmstrips and Slides.**

Educators Guide to Free Filmstrips and Slides (U.S.). Formerly:
   Educators Guide to Free Filmstrips. Educators Progress
   Service, Inc., 214 Center St., Dept. D8, Randolph, WI 53956.
   Tel: 414/326-3126; (annual); ISSN: n/a; OCLC 16221769.
   Note: ed.1, 1949 -.
   A bound directory covering free filmstrips and slides
   available to teachers and librarians serving primary grades
   through college level. Each entry includes title, sponsor,
   length, date, grade level and synopsis.
   LB1044.E3; Dewey: 371.335230838.

Educators Guide to Free Guidance Materials (U.S.); Educators
   Progress Service, Inc., 214 Center St., Dept. D8, Randolph,
   WI 53956. Tel: 414/326-3126; (annual).
   Note: ed.1, 1962 -.
   A directory which lists free films, filmstrips, slides,
   tapes, transcriptions, pamphlets and printed materials
   available to guidance counselors and teachers working with
   junior high and high school students. Each entry includes
   title of work, sponsor, length, date, grade level, subject
   matter and content.

Educators Guide to Free H.P.E.R. Materials. See: **Educators Guide
   to Free Health, Physical Educational and Recreation Materials.**

**Educators Guide to Free Health, Physical Educational and
Recreation Materials. (U.S.). Alternate title: Educators
Guide to Free H.P.E.R. Materials.** Educators Progress Service,
Inc., 214 Center St., Dept. D8, Randolph, WI 53956. Tel: 414/326-
3126; (annual); ISSN: n/a; OCLC 1064332.
Note: ed.1, 1968 -.
A directory which covers free films, filmstrips, slides,
tapes, transcriptions, pamphlets and printed materials on
health, physical education and recreation. The materials are
free to schools serving elementary through high school
grades. Each entry includes title, organizational sponsor,
length, date, grade level, suitability and contents
description. Includes indexes.
Z6121.E38; Dewey: 011.

Educators Guide to Free Home Economics Materials (U.S.);
Educators Progress Service, Inc., 214 Center St., Dept. D8,
Randolph, WI 53956. Tel: 414/326-3126; (annual); ISSN:
0883-2811; OCLC 11544824.
Note: ed.1, 1984 -.
A bound directory which covers free films, filmstrips,
slides, tapes, transcriptions, pamphlets and printed
materials on home economics. Designed for schools serving
junior and high school levels. Each entry under the various
formats includes title, sponsor, length, date, grade level,
appropriateness and contents description.
TX1.E66; OCLC 016.64/0208.

Educators Guide to Free Science Materials (U.S.); Educators
Progress Service, Inc., 214 Center St., Dept. D8, Randolph,
WI 53956. Tel: 414/326-3126; (annual); ISSN: 0070-9425; OCLC
1567641.
Note: ed.1, 1960 -.
A directory listing free films, filmstrips, slides, tapes,
transcriptions, pamphlets and printed materials on science.
Divided by format, each entry lists the title, organizational
sponsor, length, date, grade level and contents description.
The materials are free to primary and secondary schools.
Q181.A1E3; Dewey: 507.

Educators Guide to Free Social Studies Materials (U.S.);
Educators Progress Service, Inc., 214 Center St., Dept. D8,
Randolph, WI 53956. Tel: 414/326-3126; (annual).

Note: ed.1, 1961 -.
A directory which covers free films, filmstrips, slides,
tapes, transcriptions, pamphlets and printed materials on
social studies, civics, geography, public affairs and
political science. Available free to schools, colleges and
universities from nonprofit organizations, government
agencies and private companies. Each entry includes title,
source, length, date, grade level and content description.

Educators Guide to Free Tapes, Scripts and Transcriptions (U.S.).
See: **Educators Guide to Free Audio and Video Materials**.

Educators Guide to Media & Methods (U.S.). See: **Media &
Methods**.

Eiga Gijutsu (Japan). See: **Eiga Terebi Gijutsu**.

Eiga Mokuroku (Japan); Tokyo Toritsu Hibiya Toshokan, 1-ban 1-go,
Hibiya Koen, Chiyoda-ku, Tokyo 100, Japan; (annual); ISSN:
n/a; OCLC 8134764.
Note: [n.1] 1980? -.
Catalog of motion picture titles presented at the Tokyo
Metropolitan Hibiya Library. Gives title, year, production
company and synopsis. Published in Japanese.
PN1993.5.J3.

Eiga Terebi Gijutsu (Japan). English parallel title: **Motion
Picture and Television Engineering**. Formerly: **Eiga Gijutsu**;
English parallel title: **Motion Picture Engineering**. Motion
Picture and Television Engineering Society of Japan, Tokyo,
Japan; (monthly); ISSN: n/a.
Note: n.1-n.158, 1948-1965 as **Eiga Gijutsu**; n.159, 1965- as
Eiga Terebi Gijutsu.
Trade journal for motion picture and television engineers in
Japan. Covers film stock, cameras, lighting techniques,
printing equipment, laboratories and projectors. Published
in Japanese.

Eigakan Meibo (Japan); Jiji Eiga [Sushinsha], 8, Kayabacho 3,
Chuo-ku, Tokyo, Japan; (annual); ISSN: n/a; OCLC 4161115.
Note: [ed.1] 1978? -.
A directory of motion picture theaters in Japan. Covers
seating capacity, format and lens options, equipment.

Published in Japanese.
PN1998.A1E43.

Eigashi Kenkyu (Japan); Tadao Sato, 4-24-14 Matsubara, Setagaya-ku, Tokyo, Japan; (irregular); ISSN: n/a; OCLC 4944192.
Note: n.1, Spring 1973 -.
"The study of the history of the cinema." A personal tribute to the world of motion pictures. Contains articles on internationally famous directors, such as Sergei Eisenstein, Akira Kurosawa, John Ford. A scholarly and thoughtful analysis of great films. Published mostly in Japanese, with occasional articles in English.
PN1993.E45; Dewey: 791.43/0952.

8 MM Collector (U.S.). See: **Classic Images**.

8 MM Magazine (U.K.). See: **Film Making**.

8 MM Movie Maker and Cine Camera (U.K.). See: **Making Better Movies**.

1895: Bulletin de L'Association Francaise de Recherche sur L'Histoire du Cinema (France). Alternate title: **Bulletin de L'Association Francaise de Recherche sur L'Histoire du Cinema**. Jean-Pierre Jeancolas, Director, Palais de Tokyo 2, rue de la Manutention 75116 Paris, France; (quarterly); ISSN: 0769-0959.
Note: v.1,n.1 Spring 1987 -.
Learned journal concentrating on the beginnings of French cinema, covering the years 1895 to 1915.

Eikonos (Spain). Alternate title: **Revista de la Imagen y el Sonido: Eikonos**. Editorial ECO, S.A., Cruz, 44, Barcelona-17, Spain; (monthly?); ISSN: n/a; OCLC 3462455.
Note: n.1, 1976 -.
Popular photo-magazine published in Spanish. Lead articles usually describe the latest international release from a noted director. Analyzes the ten best Spanish television programs for the year. Covers film music, discotheques, phonodiscs and cassettes. Reviews books and periodicals on cinema and television.
TR1.R474.

Ekran (Yugoslavia). Alternate title: **Ekran; Revija za Film in Televizijo.** Ulica talcev 6/11, p.p. 14, 61104, Ljubljana, Yugoslavia. Tel: 061-318-353; (10 times/yr); ISSN: 0013-3302; OCLC 6456416.
Note: v.1,n.1 1963 -.
A popular culture magazine which concentrates on film rather than television. In-depth presentation of film theory and criticism; some issues devoted to one theme, such as a certain director. Reviews current international cinema, with particular emphasis on American features. Published in Yugoslavian.
PN1993.E49.

Ekran; Kino TV Video (Poland). Alternate title: **Ekran; Tygodniowy Magazyn Filmowo-Telewizyjny.** Ekran, ul. Kredytowa 5/7, 00-056 Warszawa, Poland; (biweekly); ISSN: 0013-3294.
Note: v.1,n.1, Mar 3, 1957 -.
A programming guide for Polish television. Gives background information on upcoming shows. Reviews films and home videocassettes, rates television sets and videotape players/ recorders. Publishes boxoffice statistics and TV ratings. Published in Polish.
PN1993.E5.

Ekran; Revija za Film in Televizijo (Yugoslavia). See: **Ekran.**

Electronic Fun with Computers & Games (U.S.); Fun & Games Publishing Inc., 350 E. 81st St., New York, NY 10028; (monthly); ISSN: 0746-0546; OCLC 9715337.
Note: v.1,n.1 Nov 1982 -.
Artistic graphics illustrate this magazine for youthful computer game wizards. Features a centerfold for "Game of the Month." Articles cover holography, modems, and software. Lengthy section critiques all the new electronic games, featuring a rating system and playing tips.

Electronic Games (U.S.). See: **Computer Entertainment.**

The Eleven Magazine (U.S.). Formerly: **The Dial from W.T.T.W./Eleven;** Chicago Educational Television Association, 5400 N. St. Louis Ave., Chicago, Il 60625. Tel: 312/583-5000; (monthly); ISSN: 0273-4079; OCLC 7055098.
Note: v.1-v.8, 1980-1987 as **The Dial from W.T.T.W./Eleven;**

renumbered v.1,n.1 May 1987- as **The Eleven Magazine**.
Programming guide for the PBS station WTTW in the Chicago
metropolitan area. Contains articles on new series, special
events, and current programs.
PN1992.8.P8D53; Dewey: 791.44/0973.

Emmy (U.S.); Academy of Television Arts and Sciences, 3500 W.
Olive Ave., Suite 700, Burbank, CA 91505; (bimonthly); ISSN:
0164-3495; OCLC 4629234.
Note: v.1, Winter 1979 -.
This popular magazine covers all aspects of television
production; contains background material on popular shows and
information about cable networks. Interviews successful TV
producers, scriptwriters, casting agents and network
personnel.
PN1992.3.U5E45; Dewey: 791.45/05.

Encore (Australia); Trade News Corporation Pty, Ltd, PO Box 1377,
Darlinghurst, NSW 2010, Australia. Tel: (02) 699 1344;
(biweekly); ISSN: n/a.
Note: [v.1], 198u -.
Trade journal reporting on the Australian entertainment
industry. Covers news about production companies, exhibition
and distribution, equipment, cinematography, commercial
television, corporate video, graphics and animation.

Enfoque (Chile); Cooperacion Chile-Canada, Antonia Lopez de Bello
075, Barrio Bellevista, Santiago, Chile. Tel: 375251;
(irregular); ISSN: n/a; OCLC 15140867.
Note: n.1, Spring 1984? -.
"Revista de cine." A review, in Spanish, of international feature
films released in Chile. Contains lengthy reviews, articles on film
music, interviews of Chilean filmmakers, editorials on the state
of Latin American cinema, and profiles of famous directors.
PN1993.E57; Dewey: 791.43/05.

The Entertainment and Sports Lawyer (U.S.); Forum Committee on
the Entertainment and Sports Industries of the American Bar
Association, 750 North Lake Shore Dr., Chicago, IL 60611;
(quarterly); ISSN: 0732-1880; OCLC 8320374.
Note: v.1,n.1 Spring 1982 -.
Presents overviews of litigation concerned with the motion
picture and television industries. Keeps members apprised of

courtroom strategies, methodologies, and rulings in latest
cases. Reviews new professional publications.
KF4290.A15E57; Dewey: 344.73/099.

Entertainment Law & Finance (U.S.). Formerly: **Entertainment
Legal News** (0747-8593). Leader Publications, 111 Eighth Ave.,
Suite 900, New York, NY 10011. Tel: 212/463-5709; (monthly);
ISSN: 0883-2455; OCLC 11939470.
Note: n.1-n.9 Nov 1983-Mar 1985 as **Entertainment Legal News**;
renumbered v.1,n.1 Apr 1985- as **Entertainment Law & Finance**.
Covers new laws pertaining to music, film, theater,
broadcasting and related arts. Information includes
management contracts, residuals, strategy workshops for
entertainment lawyers, profiles of practicing attorneys and
landmark court decisions.
KF4290.A15E575; Dewey: 344.73/099.

Entertainment Law Journal (U.S.). See: **Loyola Entertainment Law
Journal**.

Entertainment Law Reporter (U.S.); Entertainment Law Reporter
Publishing Co., 2210 Wilshire Blvd., No. 311, Santa Monica,
CA 90403; (monthly); ISSN: 0270-3831; OCLC 5108098.
Note: v.1,n.1 June 1979 - (Preceded by a number dated 1978,
called Preview edition).
Outlines recent court cases concerning motion pictures,
television, radio, music, theater, publishing and sports.
Contains articles on contractual law, royalties, copyright,
etc. Covers new legislation and regulations. Lists major
publications on law and the arts, plus recently published law
review and bar association articles of interest to
entertainment lawyers.
KF4290.A59E57; Dewey: 344.73/099.

Entertainment Legal News (U.S.). See: **Entertainment Law &
Finance**.

Entertainment Weekly. (U.S.); The Time, Inc. Magazine Co., 1675
Broadway, New York, NY 10019. Subscription address:
Entertainment Weekly, PO Box 61840, Tampa, FL 33661-1840;
(weekly); ISSN: 1044-0682.
Note: v.1,n.1 Feb 16, 1990 -.

Photomagazine covering movies, home video, television, music and literature. Contains biographical sketches of popular performers. Critical reviews describe what's worth watching, reading, and listening to.

The Equipment Directory of Audio-visual, Computer and Video Products (U.S.). Formerly: **The Audio-visual Equipment Directory** (0571-8759). NAVA, the International Communications Industries Association, 3150 Spring St., Fairfax, VA 22031. Tel: 703/273-7200; (annual); ISSN: 0884-2124; OCLC 10817326. Note: eds. 1-29, 1953-1983 as **The Audio-visual Equipment Directory**; ed. 30, 1984- as **The Equipment Directory of Audio-visual, Computer and Video Products**. Contains technical information on all audiovisual, computer and video equipment. Includes manufacturer, price, parts list and diagram for each item. TS2301.A7A8; Dewey: 621.38/044/0294 19.

Etudes Cinematographiques (France); Lettres Modernes: Minard, 73, rue du Cardinal Lemoine 75005 Paris, France. Tel (1) 354 46 09; (irregular); ISSN: 0014-1992. Note: n.1, Spring 1960 -. Serious journal exploring the relationship of cinema to culture. Long articles pay tribute to cinema as a major art integral to the culture of modern man. Also studies the sociology, psychology and aesthetics of film. PN1994.E8; Dewey: 791.43/09.

European Broadcasting Union Review (Switzerland). See: **E.B.U. Review.**

Evaluation-Medias. MediaWatch Bulletin (Canada). See: **MediaWatch Bulletin. Evaluation-Medias.**

Evangelischer Film-Beobachter (Frankfurt, W. Germany). See: **Medium.**

Eyepiece (U.K.). Alternate title: **Eyepiece: Journal of the Guild of British Camera Technicians.** The Guild of British Camera Technicians, Subscriptions Dept., 303/315 Cricklewood Broadway, London NW2 6PQ England. Tel: 01-450-0000 or 3821; (bimonthly); ISSN: n/a. Note: v.1,n.1 Jan/Feb 1980 -.

Professional journal for motion picture and television
cameramen. Contains articles on camera techniques, lighting,
filming on location, and achieving special effects.
Describes new camera equipment, lenses, filters and film
stock. Interviews successful cameramen, directors of
photography and lighting experts.

Eyepiece: Journal of the Guild of British Camera Technicians
(U.K.). See: **Eyepiece.**

-F-

F.I.A.F. Bulletin (Belgium). Alternate titles: **Federation Internationale des Archives du Film. Bulletin D'Information; International Federation of Film Archives. Bulletin.** Federation Internationale des Archives du Film, Coudenberg 70, 1000 Bruxelles, Belgium; (2 times/yr.); ISSN: 0443-9627. Note: n.1, 1971? -. Bulletin for members and official observers of the Federation. Contains annual reports and news from each participating archive. Published in English and French.

F.I.A.T./I.F.T.A. Bulletin (International). Alternate titles: **International Federation of Television Archives Bulletin; Federation Internationale des Archives de Television Bulletin.** International Federation of Television Archives, RAI Radiotelevisione Italiana, Dir Amministrativa GSA, via Cernaia 33, 10121 Torino, Italy. Tel: 11 8800, ext. 2626; (irregular); ISSN: n/a; OCLC: 16167045. Note: n.1, 1980? -. International in scope, this publication is printed by the organization of the current presiding officer; therefore, the address changes with the incoming president. Newsletter of events, conferences and reports from the various members of the International Federation of Television Archives. Contains articles on television history, preservation problems and solutions, changing technology and future needs. Available only to members, each issue is published in French, English and Spanish. TR886.3.F5; Dewey: 778.59/9 19

F.L.Q. Film Library Quarterly (U.S.). See: **Sightlines.**

F.M. (W.Germany). See: **Fotomagazin.**

F./T.A.A.C. Newsletter (U.S.). Alternate title: **Film/Television Archives Advisory Committee Newsletter.** National Center for Film & Video Preservation, The American Film Institute, 2021 N. Western Ave., Los Angeles, CA 90027; (quarterly). Note: v.1,n.1 Summer 1988 -.

Missive reporting on news and events from member film and
television archives. Informs about new acquisitions, paper
documentation, cataloging the collections, job opportunities
and general announcements.

Facets Features (U.S.); Facets Multimedia, Inc., 1517 W.
Fullerton Ave., Chicago, IL 60614. Tel: 312/281-9075; 800/
331-6197; (monthly); ISSN: 0362-0905; OCLC 2190964.
Note: [n.1] 1975 -.
Combines a media catalog with articles about film, video,
phonorecords and theater. Reviews cinema books, software,
motion pictures, home video, record albums and CDs.
PN1993.F26F6; Dewey: 791.43/05

Facts About Film Finland (Finland). Merged with **Finland-Filmland**
to form **Finland-Filmland: Facts About Film in Finland**. Suomen
Elokuvasaatio--The Finnish Film Foundation, Kaisaniemenkatu
3B 25, SF-0000 Helsinki 10, Finland; (3 times/yr); ISSN:
0355-1520.
Note: v.1,n.1-v.?,n.3 Mar 1971-Nov 1977 as **Facts About Film
Finland**; n.1, 1978- as **Finland-Filmland: Facts About Film in
Finland**.
Began as a glossy publication covering all aspects of the
motion picture industry in Finland: movie theaters,
festivals, history of Finnish film, statistics. Presently is
much smaller in scope and published annually.

Facts, Figures & Film (U.S.). See: **T.V. Facts, Figures & Film**.

Famous Monsters (U.S.). See: **Famous Monsters of Filmland**.

Famous Monsters of Filmland (U.S.). Alternate title: **Famous
Monsters** (0278-4203); incorporated: **Monster World**. Warren
Publishing Co., 2240 Galahad Dr., Indianapolis, IN 46208;
(monthly (except Feb & Dec)); ISSN: 0014-7443; OCLC 1775562.
Note: n.1, 1958 -.
Fan magazine for people who relish horror, science fiction
and fantasy films. Shows how the grisly effects are
achieved. Contains news of upcoming horror features.
Reviews and rates motion pictures and television programs.
Articles cover history of horror films and famous monsters of
the past.
PN1995.9.H6F27; Dewey: 791.43/09/0916

Fandom Directory (U.S.); Fandata Publications, 7761 Asterella
Court, Springfield, VA 22152-3133; (annual); ISSN: 8756-8349;
OCLC 7344904.
Note: n.1, 1979 -.
Directory listing names and addresses for fan clubs,
fanzines, conventions, dealers, memorabilia shops and
research libraries. Contains classified advertising and an
international fan location service. Covers films and
television, comic books, "fantastic fiction," science fiction
and cult art.

Fangoria (U.S.); Starlog Communications International, Inc., 475
Park Ave. South, New York, NY 10016; (monthly, except Jan &
Mar); ISSN: 0164-2111; OCLC 4618144.
Note: v.1,n.1 Oct 1979 -.
Specializes in reviewing with graphic photos, horror, fantasy
and science fiction movies. A behind-the-scenes depiction of
special effects and makeup techniques for current horror
films and videos. Interviews performers, special effects
technicians, and makeup artists.

Fantastic Films (U.S.); Fantastic Films Magazine, Inc., Box 1900,
Evanston, IL 60201. Tel: 312/883-4445; (bimonthly); ISSN:
0273-7043; OCLC 6871092.
Note: v.1-v.8?, 1977-1984?
A fan magazine for people who like science fiction, horror
and fantasy films, television programs, theater, games and
comic books. Reviews and rates films and television for
their special effects, plotline, "scare potential," and set
design. Ceased publication.

FantaZone (U.S.). Alternate title: **Tiger Beat Special,
FantaZone.** D.S. Magazines, Inc., 1086 Teaneck Road, Teaneck,
NJ 07666. Tel: 201/833-1800; (quarterly); ISSN: n/a.
Note: v.1,n.1 Summer 1989 -.
Fanzine for young enthusiasts of science fiction and fantasy
motion pictures, television series like "Star Trek," and
videos. Contains many publicity photographs. Interviews
scriptwriters, directors, performers. Goes behind the scenes
to show how special effects are achieved. Reviews current
releases and describes films that are in production.

Far East Film News (Japan). See: **Movie/TV Marketing.**

Favorite Westerns & Serials Plus (U.S.). See: **Favorite Westerns, Serial World.**

Favorite Westerns, Serial World (U.S.). Formed by a merger between **Serial World** and **Favorite Westerns.** Alternate title: **Favorite Westerns & Serials Plus** (8750-3166). Norman H. Kietzer, Editor and Publisher, 201 McConnell St., PO Box 3325, Mankato, MN 56001; (quarterly); ISSN: 0891-074X; OCLC 14562062.
Note: n.1-n.17, 1980?-1984 as **Favorite Westerns**; n.1-n.37, 1976?-1984 as **Serial World**; n.18 (n.38), Summer 1984- as **Favorite Westerns, Serial World.**
A fanzine for collectors of old theatrical serials: *Batman, Jack Armstrong, Superman,* etc., and westerns from the 1930s-1950s, starring: Roy Rogers, Gene Autry, Tim Holt, etc. Nicely illustrated biographical sketches of the stars, including filmographies.
PN1995.9.W4F36; Dewey: 791.43/09/093278

Federation Internationale des Archives de Television Bulletin (International). See: **F.I.A.T./I.F.T.A. Bulletin.**

Federation Internationale des Archives du Film. Bulletin D'Information (Belgium). See: **F.I.A.F. Bulletin.**

Federation News (Australia). See: **Filmviews. Fernseh- und Kino-Technik** (W.Germany). Formerly: **Kino-Technik: Schmalfilm, Fernsehen, Film-theater.** Deutsche Kinotechnische Gesellschaft fur Film und Fernsehen, Malvenstr. 12, 1000 Berlin 45, West Germany; (monthly); ISSN: 0015-0142; OCLC 5167600.
Note: v.5-v.22, 1951-1968 as **Kino-Technik: Schmalfilm, Fernsehen Film-theater**; v.23, 1969- as **Fernseh- und Kino-Technik.**
Official publication of the Deutsche Kinotechnische Gesellschaft fur Film und Fernsehen (West German Society for Television and Film Technique). Technical journal covering television, cinematography, equipment, new technology, electronics, computer-generated visual imagery, and video. Published in German.

Das Fernsehspiel im Z.D.F. (W.Germany). Alternate title: **Das Fernsehspiel im Zweites Deutsches Fernsehen.** Zweites Deutsches Fernsehen, Information und Presse, Verlag fur Wissenschaft und Forschung--AULA GmbH (2) Mainz, West

Germany; (quarterly); ISSN: n/a; OCLC 8912905.
Note: n.1, 1973? -.
Quarterly review of telefeatures and theatrical movies
broadcast on German television. Each critique contains
title, production company, director, music, cinematographer,
cast, synopsis and publicity stills. Published in German.
PN1992.8.F5F45; Dewey: 791.43/75/05

Das Fernsehspiel im Zweites Deutsches Fernsehen (W.Germany).
See: **Das Fernsehspiel im Z.D.F.**

Fiber Optics & Communications Weekly New Service (U.S.). See:
Fiber Optics Weekly Update.

Fiber Optics Weekly Update (U.S.). Formerly: **Fiber Optics &
Communications Weekly News Service.** Information Gatekeeper
Inc., 214 Harvard Ave., Boston, MA 02134. Tel: 617/232-3111;
(weekly); ISSN: 0732-9407; OCLC 8501522.
Note: v.1, 1981? -.
Professional newsletter reporting on the latest innovations,
applications and legislation affecting the fiber optics and
telecommunications industries.

Field of Vision (U.S.); Island Cinema Resources, 135 St. Paul's
Ave., Staten Island, NY 10301. Tel: 718/727-1135; (2 times/
yr); ISSN: 0193-9548; OCLC 5270063.
Note: n.1, 1977 -.
Began as a local effort from the Pittsburgh, Pennsylvania
Film-Makers league. Concerned with independent and
experimental filmmakers, video artists and still
photographers. Acts as a forum for distribution and
exhibition of independent visual works. Contains interviews
and profiles of working artists. Reviews books on cinema and
photography.
NX510.P4F53; Dewey: 700.5

Filament (U.S.); Motion Pictures Area of the Dept. of Theatre
Arts, Wright State University, Dayton, OH 45435; (annual).
Note: v.1, 1981 -.
"A journal of film and television history, theory,
criticism." All articles are written by Wright State
students, covering the fields of film, television and
photography.

Filipino Film Review (Philippines); Film Ratings Board,
Experimental Cinema of the Philippines, MFC, CCP Complex,
Roxas Blvd., Pasay City, Philippines. Tel: 833-2014;
(bimonthly); ISSN: n/a.
Note: v.1,n.1 Jan-Mar 1983 -.
Emphasis is placed on reviewing Filipino films. Articles
cover how to judge a film, censorship, quality of the local
film product, and what to look for when watching a film--the
narrative content, lighting, visual display and sound track.
Tries to encourage quality productions by educating the
public. Published in English.

Film (Korea). See: **Yeonghwa.**

Film (Poland). Alternate title: **Film; Magazyn Ilustrowany.** Film,
ul. Pulawska 61, 02-595 Warszawa, Poland. Tel: 45-40-41;
(weekly); ISSN: 0137-463X.
Note: v.1, 1946 -.
Oversized fan magazine with many photographs illustrating the
careers, films, and loves of international film stars. Focus
is on Polish actors and actresses of both stage and screen,
but contains gossip and photos of popular performing artists
from America and Europe as well. Reviews latest feature
films and television programs.
PN1993.F414

Film (U.K.). Subtitle: **The British Federation of Film Societies
Monthly Journal.** British Federation of Film Societies, 81
Dean St., London W1V 6AA England; (monthly); ISSN:
0015-1025; OCLC 6101893.
Note: series 1: n.1-n.67, Oct 1954-Sep 1972; series 2: n.1, Apr
1973 -.
Numbers for 1954-spring 1969 issued under the federation's
former name: Federation of Film Societies. Clearinghouse for
information about film programs, festivals and events
scheduled by British film societies. Contains short reviews
of recent releases. Reports on the Federation's activities,
such as film restoration projects, student festivals and
awards, lectures and "viewing sessions" at the various film
societies.
PN1993.F394

Film (U.S.); Northwest Film & Video Center, 1219 S.W. Park Ave., Portland, OR 97205. Tel: 503/221-1156; (bimonthly); ISSN: n/a.
Note: 197u -.
Newsletter for members; encourages the study, appreciation and utilization of the visual arts. Hosts the annual Northwest Film and Video Festival each Fall. Offers classes and workshops on filmmaking, music video production, screenwriting, sound production, editing and cinema studies. Presents film showings of older American and foreign classics, as well as hard to find films, foreign documentaries and animation.

Film (W.Germany). See: **E.P.D. Film**.

Film a Divadlo (Czechoslovakia); Film a Divadlo, Volgogradska 8, 815 85 Bratislava, Czechoslovakia; (biweekly); ISSN: 0426-1356.
Note: v.1, 1957 -.
Newspaper-like, oversized, popular film and television magazine with many photographs. Focuses on favorite international film stars, including many Americans whose films are currently being released in Czechoslovakia. Promotes Czech performing artists with photos, filmographies and biographical sketches.
PN1993.F4145.

Film A Doba; Mesicnik pro Filmovou Kulturu (Czechoslovakia); Film A Doba, Vaclavske nam 43, 11648 Praha 1, Czechoslovakia; (monthly); ISSN: 0015-1068; OCLC 5249564.
Note: v.1, 1955 -.
Academic international film periodical concentrates on Czech films and film industry, although covers films from other European countries, Latin America and the U.S. Articles on film history, criticism, animation, international directors, screenplays, interviews and film festivals. Annual index for preceding year found in the February issue. Published in Czech with English, French and Russian summaries.

Film and Audio-visual Communications (U.S.). See: **Audio-visual Communications**.

Film & Broadcasting Review (U.S.). Formerly: **Catholic Film Newsletter** (0008-8021). Office for Film and Broadcasting of the U.S. Catholic Conference, 1011 First Ave., New York, NY 10022; (biweekly); ISSN: 0362-0875; OCLC 2004802.
Note: v.1-v.40,n.24, 1935-Dec 1975 as **Catholic Film Newsletter**; v.41,n.1-v.45,n.17, Jan 15, 1976-Sep 1, 1980 as **Film & Broadcasting Review**.
Contains reviews of international features released in the United States and American television programs, rating them for moral suitability. Films are divided by categories based on maturity: adult, adolescent and child. Content is rated "A" for unobjectionable, "B" for somewhat objectionable and "C" for condemned. Publication suspended in 1980.
PN1995.F457; Dewey: 791.43/7.

Film & Fakten (W.Germany) arranged as **Film und Fakten**.

Film & History (U.S.). Alternate title: **Film and History**. The Historians Film Committee, c/o The History Faculty, New Jersey Institute of Technology, Newark, NJ 07102; (quarterly); ISSN: 0360-3695; 0885-1107; OCLC 2578168.
Note: v.1, 1971 -.
Combines the discipline of history with film studies, using documentary film and historical dramatizations to analyze, interpret and portray history. Reviews scholarly books pertaining to both studies.
PN1995.2.F54; Dewey: 791.43/09/09358.

Film and History (U.S.). See: **Film & History**.

Film & Kino (Norway). See: **Film og Kino**.

Film & T.V. Kameramann (W.Germany), arranged as **Film und T.V. Kameramann**.

Film & T.V. World (Canada). Formerly: **Filmworld** (0708-0956). Daisons Publications, 70 Snidercroft Rd., Concord, Ont. Canada L4K 1B1; (monthly); ISSN: 0712-5771; OCLC 8443628.
Note: v.1-6, Dec 1977-Mar 1983.
"Canada's only newspaper for the film, TV and cable industries." Published in English and French. Available on microfilm. Ceased publication in March 1983.
PN1993.F675; Dewey: 384.554/0971.

Film and Television (U.S.). See: **Review of the Arts: Film and Television**.

Film and Television Yearbook (U.K.). Alternate titles: **B.F.I. Film and Television Yearbook; British Film Institute Film and Television Yearbook**. British Film Institute, 21 Stephen St., London, England W1P 1PL; (annual); ISSN: n/a; ISBN 085-170-1981; OCLC 10249447.
Note: ed.1, 1983 -.
The annual report of the British Film Institute. Describes the various services offered by the B.F.I.: the National Film Theatre, film productions and financial statements. Lists the feature films released in Great Britain for the preceding year, both British and international, giving the original title, country, length, director, cast and Monthly Film Bulletin review citation. Contains a directory of companies, libraries, archives, services, studios, and trade organizations.
PN1993.5.G7; Dewey: 384.80941.

Film + Ton-Magazine (W.Germany). See: **Fotomagazine**.

Film & Video Finder (U.S.). Created by a merger of **N.I.C.E.M. Index to 16 MM Educational Films** and **N.I.C.E.M. Index to Educational Videotapes**; alternate title: **Film and Video Finder**. National Information Center for Educational Media, a division of Access Innovations, Inc., Albuquerque, NM 87196. Published by: Plexus Publishing, Inc., 143 Old Marlton Pike, Medford, NJ 08055; (annual); ISSN: 0898-1582; OCLC 15047373.
Note: ed.1-20, 1967-1986 as **N.I.C.E.M. Index to 16 MM Educational Films**; ed.1-2, 1985-1986 as **N.I.C.E.M. Index to Educational Videotapes**; renumbered ed.1, 1987- as **Film & Video Finder**.
Comprehensive listing of all educational 16mm films and videotapes in distribution in the United States. Contains two volumes of title entries, arranged alphabetically, with production company, distributor, year and short synopsis. Third volume is a subject index; it also lists names and addresses for distributors mentioned in the first two volumes.
LB1044.Z9F58; Dewey: 011 11.

Film and Video Finder (U.S.). See: **Film & Video Finder**.

Film & Video News (U.S.). Formerly: **Film News**. Gorez Goz
Publishing Company, 1058 Eighth St., La Salle, IL 61301,
Subscriptions: Films & Video News, 1016 Church St., Peru, IL
61354; (quarterly); ISSN: 0195-1017; OCLC 7000440.
Note: v.1-v.38,n.3, Dec 1939-Fall 1981 as **Film News**; v.38,n.4,
April 1984- as **Film & Video News**. Publication suspended for 3
years.
"The international review of AV materials and equipment."
Concentrating on documentary and educational motion pictures
and video, this publication is aimed at teachers, librarians
and other professionals who need to purchase audiovisual
materials and equipment. Reports on the results of
documentary film festivals. Gives advice on how to use
successfully film and video in the classroom. Prints well
researched articles on independent filmmakers; interviews
producers and directors.
PN1993.F62; Dewey: 791.43/53/05.

Film & Video Production (U.S.). Alternate title: **Opticmusic's
Film & Video Production**. Optic Music, Inc., 8170 Beverly
Blvd., Suite 208, Los Angeles, CA 90048. Tel: 213/653-8053;
(monthly); ISSN: 0894-4423; ISSN 0889-5651; OCLC 16102698.
Note: v.1, 1983 -.
Trade journal for motion picture and television producers,
directors and distributors. Covers all aspects of film and
video production: feature films, television programs, music
videos, commercials, special effects, animation and audio.
Interviews industry professionals.
Dewey: 791 11.

Film Arsboken (Sweden). See: **Filmarsboken**.

Film, Bild, Ton (W.Germany). See: **A.V. Praxis**.

Film Bulletin (U.S.). Subtitle: **America's Independent Motion
Picture Journal**. Wax Publications, 1239 Vine St.,
Philadelphia, PA 19107. Tel: 215/568-0950; (biweekly); ISSN:
0015-1165; OCLC 5089599.
Note: v.1, 1933 -.
"The industry magazine with the forward look." Designed for
industry personnel, theater operators and marketing
officials, this trade journal gives the latest information
about current and future releases, and works in progress.

Rates films for their boxoffice potential. Contains trade
news such as executive changes at the major studios,
financial reports, mergers, and takeovers.
PN1993.F435; Dewey: 792.9305.

Film Canada Yearbook (Canada). Continues: **Canadian Film Digest
  Yearbook** (0316-5515). Film Canada Yearbook, 1430 Yonge St.,
  Suite 214, Toronto, Ont., M4T 1Y6 Canada. Tel: 416/922-5772;
  (annual); ISSN: 0831-5175; OCLC 14633258.
  Note: 1977-1985 as **Canadian Film Digest Yearbook**; renumbered
  ed.1, 1986- as **Film Canada Yearbook**.
  Thorough analysis of Canadian theater statistics, audience
  demographics, boxoffice receipts, number of theaters and
  drive-ins, and people employed. Contains a directory of
  Canadian companies involved in the motion picture, television
  and video industries.
  PN1993.3.C3; Dewey: 338.4/779143/029571.

Film Canadiana (Canada). See: **Film/Video Canadiana**.

Film Collector's World (U.S.). See: **Movie Collector's World**.

Film Comment (U.S.). Formerly: **Vision. A Journal of Film
  Comment**. Film Society of Lincoln Center, 140 W. 65th St., New
  York, NY 10023; (bimonthly); ISSN: 0015-119X; 0015-120X;
  OCLC 2266507.
  Note: v.1,nos.1-2, Spring-Summer 1962 as **Vision**; v.1,n.3,
  Autumn 1962- as **Film Comment**.
  Slick film journal containing articles on the latest feature
  releases. Includes interviews of motion picture personnel
  and subjective pieces on film theory and criticism. Annual
  index appears in the following year's spring issue.
  PN1993.F438.

Film Criticism (U.S.); Film Criticism, Box D, Allegheny College,
  Meadville, PA 16335; (3 times/yr; Fall, Winter, Spring);
  ISSN: 0163-5069; OCLC 4021815.
  Note: v.1,n.1 Spring 1976 -.
  Scholarly publication containing articles on film theory and
  criticism. Special issues center on one particular theme
  with several well written, provocative articles discussing
  different aspects of it. Subjects chosen are such topics as
  film narration, Japanese cinema, Frank Capra, and the new

European cinema. Reviews scholarly film books. An index is
available to the published articles.
PN1993.F4183; Dewey: 791.43/75/05.

Film Culture (U.S.); Film Culture Non-Profit Inc., 32-43 Second
Ave., New York, NY 10003-8631. Tel: 212/226-0010;
(irregular); ISSN: 0015-1211; OCLC 1569194.
Note: v.1,n.1 Jan 1955 -.
Promotes avant-garde, experimental and independent films and
filmmakers. Keeps track of trends, new creative talents, and
new techniques. Concerned about how to get independent films
recognized and distributed.
PN1993.F44; Dewey: 791.4305.

Film Directions (Northern Ireland); Arts Council of Northern
Ireland, 8 Malone Rd., Belfast GT9 5BN, Northern Ireland.
Tel: Belfast 667 687; (quarterly); ISSN: n/a; OCLC 6885983.
Note: n.1, Autumn? 1977 -.
Cultural magazine of film, television and video; encompasses
academic, political and popular viewpoints. Well written
articles focus on the performing arts in Northern Ireland:
new creative talents in acting, writing and directing, the
latest Irish productions in film and theater, and the
emerging independence of local television. Analyzes American
and British influences on popular culture and discusses the
effects of politics on the arts.
PN1993.5.I85F54; Dewey: 791.43/05.

Film Dope (U.K.); Film Dope, 45 Lupton St., London NW5 2HS
England; (irregular); ISSN: 0305-1706; OCLC 6497960.
Note: n.1, Dec 1972 -.
Directory containing biographical sketches of international
film and TV personalities: stars, directors, writers, and
producers. Sketch includes filmography, photos, critique of
performances and short biography. Issues are arranged
alphabetically by last name; each issue is devoted to a major
personality, either living or dead. Lesser known
personalities with shorter records are included at end.

Film Echange (France). Alternate title: **Filmechange**. Societe
Auxiliaire pour le Cinema et la Television, 16, rue des
Quatre-Vents, 75006 Paris, France. Tel: 46 34 28 20;
(quarterly); ISSN: 0181-4141; OCLC 11980388.

Note: [n.1] 1978 -.
"Droit, Economie, sociologie de l'audiovisuel." Literary
journal devoted to the study, documentation and research of
film and television. Articles cover film history of the
silent period, as well as modern concerns over international
laws affecting television and cable, and box office receipts
from selected countries. Concerned with the economics of
film and television distribution in Europe, the U.S. and
Japan. Published in French.

Film-Echo (W.Germany). See: **Film-Echo/Filmwoche**.

Film-Echo/Filmwoche (W.Germany). Created by a merger between
Film-Echo and **Filmwoche**. Film-Echo/Filmwoche, Wilhelmstrasse
42, 62 Wiesbaden, West Germany; (weekly); ISSN: 0015-1149;
OCLC 13976618.
Note: v.1-v.16,n.8, 1947-Jan 1962 as **Film-Echo**; merged with
Filmwoche in Feb 1962 continuing the numbering of **Film-Echo**;
v.16,n.9/10, Feb 1962- as **Film-Echo/Filmwoche**.
Popular trade magazine containing many photos, small articles
and gossip about film stars. Publishes a film chart
categorizing the current features being released in the
different provinces of West Germany. Reviews and rates
films. Published in German.
PN1993.F46.

Film en Televisie + Video (Belgium). Formerly: **Film en
Televisie**. Film en Televisie, Haachtsesteenveg 35, 1030
Brussels, Belgium. Tel: 02/217.00.96; (10 times/yr); ISSN:
0015-1084.
Note: [n.1] 1956? -.
International film and television review published in
Flemish. Well laid out and nicely photographed, it covers
the European and American movie scene. Articles include
background material and critiques of recent controversial
feature films, reports from film and video festivals,
television criticism, and video release charts.

Film File: Media Referral Service (U.S.); Media Referral Service,
PO Box 3586, Minneapolis, MN 55403; (annual); ISSN: 0731-5716;
OCLC 8205606.
Note: ed.1-ed.4, 1981/1982-1984/1985. Discontinued in 1986.
For teachers and librarians, this publication is designed as

a subject index for educational and non-fiction films. Each
entry includes individual title, grade level, length, date,
format and distributor. Helpful for finding titles to
illustrate classroom topics and augment instruction. Ceased
publication.
PN1998.F53; Dewey: 011.37.

Le Film Francais (France). Title varies: **Le Film Francais/La
Cinematographie Francaise**; absorbed **La Cinematographie
Francaise** in 1966. Le Film Francais, 12, avenue George V,
75008 Paris, France; (weekly); ISSN: 0181-3528.
Note: v.1,n.1 Dec 1944 -.
"Organe de l'industrie cinematographique Francaise." Trade
journal for the motion picture and television industries in
France. Publishes boxoffice charts, audience ratings,
financial reports, economic forecasts and broadcasting
statistics. Keeps current with mergers, co-productions and
personnel changes within the industry. Lists the titles and
distributors of feature films and shorts in France. Reports
on the boxoffice appeal of American movies, using their
French-equivalent titles. Publishes editions in French and
English.
PN1993.F487.

Film Heritage (U.S.); University of Dayton, Department of
Information Services, Dayton, OH 45469; (quarterly); ISSN:
0015-1270; OCLC 1569199.
Note: v.1,n.1-v.12,n.3, Fall 1965-Spring 1977.
Academic film review. Discontinued publication.
PN1993.F55; Dewey: 791.43/05.

Film History (U.S.); American Museum of the Moving Image, 34-12
36th St., Astoria, NY 11106; (quarterly); ISSN: 0892-2160;
OCLC 15122313.
Note: v.1,n.1 Spring 1987 -.
Scholarly journal devoted to the historical development of
motion pictures. International in scope, publishes in-depth
articles which are the result of original research using
primary documentation. Surveys film and manuscript holdings
of motion picture archives and libraries from around the
world.
PN1993.F56; Dewey: 791.43/09 19.

Film in the Cities (U.S.); Film in the Cities. A Media Arts
Center, 2388 University Ave., St. Paul, MN 55114. Tel: 612/
646-6104; (bimonthly).
Note: 197u -.
Fosters "the creation and appreciation of film, photography,
video and audio as art forms for a public of diverse ages,
income levels and backgrounds" in the Twin Cities.

Film India (India). See: **Mother India**.

The Film Journal (U.S.). Formerly: **The Independent; The
Independent Film Journal** (0019-3712). Pubsun Corp., 244 West
49th St., Suite 305, New York, NY 10019. 212/246-6460;
(monthly); ISSN: 0199-7300; OCLC 6106518.
Note: v.1,n.1-v.16,n.13, Jan 16, 1937-Jan 19, 1946 as **The
Independent**; v.17,n.1-v.82,n.11, Feb 2, 1946-Oct 1979 as **The
Independent Film Journal**; v.82,n.12, Nov 1979- as **The Film
Journal**.
Designed for industry personnel, exhibitors, film booking
agents and theater owners. Articles cover productions in
progress, recent releases, and studio personnel changes.
Each issue contains pull-out section entitled "Buying and
Booking Guide" which reviews latest releases with emphasis on
boxoffice results.

Der Film Kreis (W.Germany). See: **Fotomagazin**.

Film Kultura (Hungary). See: **Filmkultura**.

Film-Kunst (Austria). See: **Filmkunst: Zeitschrift fur Filmkultur
und Filmwissenschaft**.

Film Library Quarterly (U.S.). Alternate title: **F.L.Q. Film
Library Quarterly**; absorbed by **Sightlines** (0037-4830);
(quarterly); ISSN: 0015-1327; 0160-7316; OCLC 1569203.
Note: v.1,n.1-v.17,nos.2-4, Winter 1967/68-1984; absorbed by
Sightlines, 1985.
Well written journal reviewing films appropriate for school
and public libraries. Articles reflected the combined
interest of using film and audiovisual materials in
libraries. See entry under **Sightlines**.
Z692.M9F5; Dewey: 791.43/05.

Film Literature Index (U.S.); Film and Television Documentation
Center, Richardson 390, State University of New York at
Albany, 1400 Washington Ave., Albany, NY 12222. Tel: 518/442-
5745; (quarterly with annual cumulations); ISSN: 0093-6758;
OCLC 1792681.
Note: v.1, 1973 -.
Comprehensive index to over 230 international film and
television magazines. Articles are indexed by author, title
and subject. Entries include film reviews from other popular
non-film magazines as well, such as **The Rolling Stone** and
The New Yorker. Essential for any kind of film research.
Z5784.M9F46; Dewey: 791.43/01/6.

Film Logbuch (Austria); Fritz Edlinger, Seilerstatte 13/25, 1010
Wien, Austria; (quarterly); ISSN: n/a.
Note: 198u-1989.
Popular film magazine covering international feature films;
published in German. Ceased publication in 1989.

Film; Magazyn Ilustrowany (Poland). See: **Film**.

Film Making (U.K.). Formerly: **8 MM Magazine**; alternate title:
Filmmaking; absorbed by **Making Better Movies**; ISSN: 0013-
2543; OCLC 3183178.
Note: v.1-v.8, 1962-1970 as **8 MM Magazine**; v.8,n.9-v.18,n.10,
Sep 1970-Oct 1980 as **Film Making**; absorbed by **Making Better
Movies** [Nov] 1980.
British magazine for amateur and independent filmmakers.
Ceased publication.
TR845.E5.

Film Monthly (U.S.). Formerly: **Films Illustrated**; **Photoplay
Movies & Video**. Film Monthly/M.A.P. Ltd., No. 1 Golden
Square, London, W1R 3AB England; (monthly); ISSN: n/a.
Note: v.1-v.11 (Nos. 1-124), Jul 1971-Dec 1981? as **Films
Illustrated**; numbering discrepancy: begins as v.33,n.1-v.40,
n.3, Jan 1982-Mar 1989 as **Photoplay Movies & Video**; v.40,n.4
Apr 1989- as **Film Monthly**.
"The magazine that loves movies." Comprehensive monthly film
review that critiques and rates films that are currently in
release in Great Britain, including those shown on
television. Publishes screen biographies of popular actors

and actresses and previews upcoming features.
PN1993.F64727; Dewey: 791.43/05.

Film News (U.S.). See: **Film & Video News.**

Film News-International (U.S.); V.P.A., Inc., 1800 Avenue of the
Stars, Los Angeles, CA 90067. Tel: 213/552-5315; (monthly);
ISSN: 0741-0492; OCLC 10067676.
Note: v.1,n.1 Oct 1982 -.
Newsletter reporting on the business aspects of the motion
picture and television industries. Topics covered are
commercial television, pay/cable television, home videos,
16mm films, military applications, novelization and TV
adaptations, new technologies and merchandising.

Film og Kino (Norway). Alternate title: **Film & Kino**; formerly:
Norsk Filmblad. Film og Kino, Stortingsgaten 16, 0161 Oslo 1,
Norway; (8 times/yr); ISSN: 0015-1351; OCLC 9880649.
Note: v.1-v.32, 1930-1964 as **Norsk Filmblad**; v.33, 1965- as
Film og Kino.
Magazine published by the Norwegian Cinematographers Guild.
Concentrates on Scandinavian cinematography, technical
matters, cameras and equipment. Covers other topics
pertinent to filmmaking, such as shooting on location,
professional cooperation, use of computers and graphic
design.
PN1993.F419.

Film Polski (Poland). See: **Polish Film. Film Polonais.**

Film Producers, Studios & Agents Guide (U.S.); Lone Eagle
Publishing Co., 9903 Santa Monica Blvd., No. 204, Beverly
Hills, CA 90212-9942; (annual); ISSN: 0894-8666; OCLC
16270193.
Note: ed.1, 1988 -.
A directory listing professionals in the motion picture
industry. Divided into three sections: film producers,
studios/production companies, and agents/agencies. The first
section lists producers, executive producers and
independents, but not associate producers. Gives the
business address, telephone number and list of film credits
with year of production. Second section comprises the major
studios, giving the address, telephone number and executive

personnel. Third section lists talent agencies and business
managers for the entertainment industry.
PN1998.A1F484; Dewey: 791.43/0232/02573.

Film Quarterly (U.S.). Formerly: **Hollywood Quarterly** (0987-990);
Quarterly of Film, Radio and Television. University of
California Press, 2120 Berkeley Way, Berkeley, CA 94720;
(quarterly); ISSN: 0015-1386; OCLC 1569205.
Note: v.1-v.5,n.4, Oct 1945-Summer 1951 as **Hollywood
Quarterly**; v.6,n.1-v.11,n.4, Fall 1951-Summer 1957 as
Quarterly of Film, Radio and Television; v.12,n.1, Fall 1958-
as **Film Quarterly**. (Temporarily suspended Fall 1957-Summer
1958.).
This scholarly journal began as a joint venture of the
University of California and the Hollywood Writers'
Mobilization. International in scope, it contains in-depth
film reviews and critical analyses of the latest books
published on film, broadcasting and television. Articles
cover a wide variety of viewpoints and theories on cinema
studies. Interviews directors, producers, actors and writers.
Compiles a yearly survey of scholarly English-language film
books.
PN1993.H457.

Film Reader (U.S.); Northwestern University, Film Division,
Evanston, IL 60201; (annual); ISSN: 0361-722X; OCLC 2247136.
Note: n.1, 1975 -.
"Dedicated to the application of current theories in film
scholarship." Provides a "proving ground for new theories
and an opportunity for reassessing older approaches; seeks to
stimulate controversy and encourage dialogue." Designed as a
publishing forum for film students.
PN1993.F623; Dewey: 791.43/05.

Film Review Annual (U.S.); Jerome S. Ozer, Publisher, 340 Tenafly
Rd., Englewood, NJ 07631; (annual); ISSN: 0737-9080; OCLC
9101779.
Note: v.1, 1981 -.
Full-length reviews of features released in the U.S. during the
course of the preceding year. Each entry lists title, production
information, cast, crew, running time, and MPAA rating. Reviews
taken from the following: **Christian Science Monitor, Cineaste,
Film Quarterly, Films in Review, Los Angeles Times, Monthly**

Film Bulletin, The New Leader, New Statesman, New York, New York Post, Newsday, Newsweek, Saturday Review, Sight and Sound, Time, The Village Voice, and Women's Wear Daily. PN1995.F465; Dewey: 791.43/75/0973.

Film Review Digest (U.S.). Currently: **Sightlines** (0037-4830); A.F.V.A., 920 Barnsdale Rd., LaGrange Park, IL 60525. ISSN: 0428-3708; OCLC 1714144.
Note: v.1,n.1-v.13,n.4, Oct 1953-Summer 1967; merged with **The Filmlist** and **E.F.L.A. Bulletin** to form **Sightlines** Sep/Oct 1967-
A review for 16mm educational films, as well as better feature films.

Film Rutan (Sweden). See: **Filmrutan.**

Film Society Newsletter (U.S.). See: **Critic.**

Film Society Review (U.S.). See: **Critic.**

Film Szinhaz Muzsika (Hungary); Film Szinhaz Muzsika, VII, Lenin krt. 9-11, 1906 Budapest Pf. 223, Hungary. Tel: 221-285; (weekly); ISSN: 0015-1416.
Note: v.1, May 17, 1957 -.
Cultural magazine covering film, theater, opera, music, dance and television. Glossy, oversized publication using many photographs to illustrate and critique current presentations in the performing arts. International film predominates with biographies and pictures of well-known film stars. Contains a schedule of movies, plays, and musical performances booked throughout Hungary. Published in Hungarian.
PN1993.F625.

Film Technology News (U.S.); Film Technology Co., Inc., 6900 Santa Monica Blvd., Los Angeles, CA 90038. Tel: 213/464-3456; (quarterly).
Note: [n.1] Spring 1986 -.
House publication for the company. Newsletter for technicians working in film preservation and archivists concerned with film restoration; contains useful hints on how to store and treat acetate film.

Film/Television Archives Advisory Committee Newsletter (U.S.). See: **F./T.A.A.C. Newsletter.**

Film Theory: Bibliographic Information and Newsletter
(W.Germany); U.S. subscription: Jan-Christopher Horak,
George Eastman House, 900 East Ave., Rochester, NY 14607.
Tel: 716/271-3361; (irregular); ISSN: 0724-0201; OCLC
11367288.
Note: n.1, Feb 1983 -.
Each issue contains an extensive bibliography of film theory.
Critiques film publications and reviews films. Lists conferences
and meetings held in the U.S. and Europe by film archives and
institutions. Published in English, French and German.
Z5784.M9F515; Dewey: 016.79143/75.

Film Threat (U.S.); Film Threat, PO Box 951, Royal Oak, MI 48068.
Tel: 313/571-9823; (6 times/yr); ISSN: 0896-6389; OCLC
17247866.
Note: n.1, Feb? 1985 -.
Irreverent magazine covering independent filmmakers, cult
movies, underground films and counterculture interests.
Issues are undated.
Dewey: 791 11.

Film Tutti i Film Della Stagione (Italy); Centro Studi
Cinematografici, Via Gregorio VIII, 6, 00165 Rome, Italy.
Tel: (06) 63.82.605; (bimonthly); ISSN: n/a.
Note: v.1,n.1 Jan/Feb 1983 -.
Each issue reviews comprehensively the latest international
feature film releases. Published in Italian, the magazine's
table of contents is an alphabetical index of the 45-50 films
that will be reviewed in the issue. The reviews that follow
contain a through listing of credits and cast, including the
production company, both the original and Italian
distributors, director, date, length, music, editor and
screenwriter.

Film & [i.e. und] Fakten (W.Germany). Alternate title: **Film und
Fakten**. SPIO/FSK Langenbeckstrasse 9, Postfach 5129, 6200
Wiesbaden, West Germany. Tel: 061 22/30 70 84; (bimonthly);
ISSN: n/a.
Note: v.1, 198u -.
Popular film and video magazine published in German,
reviewing contemporary international motion pictures. Covers
film history, with articles on the silent period, films of

the Third Reich, and Hollywood classics. Analyzes present day filmmaking in Germany and the effect video has on the market.

Film und Fakten (W.Germany). See: **Film & [i.e. und] Fakten.**

Film und Fernsehen (E.Germany). Formerly: **Rundfunk und Fernsehprogramm.** Henschelverlag, Oranienburger Strasse, 67-68, 1040 Berlin, East Germany; (monthly); ISSN: 0323-3227; ISSN 0014-5823; OCLC 7094962.
Note: v.1-5?, 1955-1959 as **Rundfunk und Fernsehprogramm;** renumbered v.1, 1959- as **Film und Fernsehen.** Numbering begins each year with Heft 1.
Edited by the Association of Film- and Television Makers in East Germany. Features articles and interviews with motion picture and television personalities and technicians. Includes statistics and surveys of film production and television programming in East Germany.
PN1993.F665; Dewey: 791.43/05.

Film & [i.e. und] T.V. Kameramann (W.Germany). Formerly: **Deutsche Kameramann;** alternate title: **Film und T.V. Kameramann.** Ingebord Weber, Rotbuchenstrasse 21, 8000 Munchen 90, West Germany. Tel: 089/ 690 4981; (monthly); ISSN: 0343-5571.
Note: v.1-v.26, 1952-1977 as **Deutsche Kameramann;** v.27, 1978- as **Film & T.V. Kameramann.**
Technical trade journal for professional film and television camera operators. Reviews and reports on the latest equipment, compares the products of the major film manufacturers and prints technical diagrams of new equipment. Articles cover filming techniques, news gathering in dangerous locations, such as Beirut, computer-generated imagery, satellite technology, and studies of high definition TV.

Film und T.V. Kameramann (W.Germany). See: **Film & [i.e. und] T.V. Kameramann.**

Film + [i.e. und] Ton-Magazin (W.Germany). See: **Fotomagazin.**

Film und Ton Magazin (W.Germany). See: **Fotomagazin.**

Film User (U.K.). See: **Audio Visual.**

Film/Video Canadiana (Canada). Formerly: **Film Canadiana** (0015-1173). Moving Image and Sound Archives, Documentation and Public Service, 395 Wellington St., Ottawa, Ontario K1A ON3, Canada. Tel: 613/995-1311; (quarterly 1969-1972; annual 1972/73-1983/84; biennial 1985/86); ISSN: 0836-1002; OCLC 18121299.
Note: v.1-v.10?, Fall 1969-1983/84 as **Film Canadiana**; v.11?, 1985/86- as **Film/Video Canadiana.**
Systematic and comprehensive bibliographic control of non-print materials in Canada. A combined effort of the Public Archives of Canada/National Film, Television and Sound Archives, the National Film Board of Canada, the National Library of Canada and the Cinematheque Quebecoise. Entries include the title, production company, distributor, length, format, credits, cast and summary. Published in English and French.
PN1993.5.C2; Dewey: 015.71/037.

Film World (India). See: **Filmworld.**

Film Writers Guide (U.S.); Lone Eagle Publishing Co., 9903 Santa Monica Blvd., No. 204, Beverly Hills, CA 90212-9942; (annual); ISSN: 0894-864X; OCLC 16270180.
Note: ed.1, 1988 -.
Alphabetical listing of English-language writers who received screen credit. Each entry includes the writer, his/her agent, the agent's address and telephone number, and a list of credits. Additional information such as "producer," "co-writer" and format classification, i.e, cable, mini-series, TV series and telefeature are listed with the credits. Indexed by film title and agent.
PN1996.F447; Dewey: 808.066791 20.

Filmarsboken (Sweden). Alternate title: **Film Arsboken.** Svenska Filminstitutet, Filmhuset Box 27126, S-102 52 Stockholm, Sweden. Tel: 08-665 11 00; (annual); ISSN: n/a; OCLC 2246436.
Note: v.1, 1961 -.
A yearbook containing statistics generated by the motion picture industry in Sweden. Lists the top grossing pictures in Sweden, including international boxoffice hits as well as popular Swedish movies. Compiles a complete bibliographic record for all of the films released in Sweden. Arranged by

title, the record includes production and distribution companies, cast, country of origin, length, date and synopsis. Contains indexes by personal names and titles. Includes television programs. Published in Swedish with English summaries.
PN1993.3.F54.

Filmbulletin (Switzerland); Filmbulletin, Postfach 6887, CH-8023 Zurich, Switzerland. Tel: 052-27 38 58; (bimonthly); ISSN: 0257-7852.
Note: [n.1] 1959? -.
Lavish publication concerned with international feature films. Contains detailed reviews, excellent articles, interviews with foremost directors and news about film festivals. Prints tributes to internationally acclaimed filmmakers who have recently died. Published in German.

Filmcritica (Italy); Licosa Libreria, via Lamarmora 45, 50121 Firenze, Italy; (10 times/yr); ISSN: 0015-1513.
Note: v.1, 1950 - . Absorbed **Spettatore Critico** in 1957.
Scholarly journal containing in depth critical analyses of film studies. Articles cover such topics as semiology, nouvelle vague, film noir and auteur theories. Emphasis is on film direction: interviews the great directors, publishes biographical sketches with comprehensive filmographies and contains dossiers on their careers. Comments on the European film festivals. Published in Italian.
PN1993.F6415.

Filme Cultura (Brazil). Alternate title: **Filme e Cultura.** Empresa Brasileira de Filmes-EMBRAFILME, Rua Mayrink Veiga, 28, 7o, Andar, Rio de Janeiro-RJ, Brazil; (bimonthly); ISSN: 0015-1521; OCLC 5229347.
Note: v.1,n.1 Oct 1966 -.
Popular journal modeled after **Cahiers du Cinema**, documenting current international cinema and famous directors. Contains information on Latin American films, directors, awards and festivals. Published in Portuguese.
PN1993.F6417.

Filme der Bundesrepublik Deutschland (W.Germany). See: **Kino: Filme der Bundesrepublik Deutschland.**

Filme e Cultura (Brazil). See: **Filme Cultura.**

Filmechange (France). See: **Film Echange.**

Filmfaust (W.Germany); Filmfaust Verlag, Furstenberger Strasse 175, D-6000 Frankfurt/M.1, West Germany. Tel: 069/598259; (bimonthly); ISSN: 0176-1110; OCLC 5594184.
Note: n.1, Apr/May 1977 -.
"Zeitschrift fur den internationalen film." Glossy, popular film magazine reviewing the latest international feature releases. Gives title, cast, credits, synopsis and critical analysis. Keeps current on German film production; promotes German performers; reveals the latest gossip. Carries news about television, but to a lesser extent. Occasionally publishes retrospective articles on film history and biographical sketches of silent film stars.
PN1993.F474.

Filmfax (U.S.); FILMFAX, PO Box 1900, Evanston, IL 60204; (bimonthly); ISSN: 0895-0393; OCLC 14292774.
Note: n.1, Jan/Feb 1986 -.
"The magazine of unusual film and television." A fan magazine devoted to fantasy, science fiction and cult films. Tries to capture the genre of "B" movies from the 1940s and 1950s. Articles compare the original films with the modern day remake--with such films as *The Fly, The Little Shop of Horrors,* and *Invasion of the Body Snatchers.* Conducts interviews, reviews new films, tracks video releases of older cult films, and publishes classified ads for movie memorabilia.

Filmhaftet (Sweden); Filmhaftet Uppsala, Postadress Box 16046, 750 16 Uppsala, Sweden. Tel: 018/46 2400; (quarterly); ISSN: 0345-3057.
Note: n.1, Summer 1973 -.
"Tidskrift om film och TV." Intelligent, well thought out articles analyzing contemporary motion pictures and television programs in the context of popular culture. Some of the topics covered include American film productions and the Vietnam War, children's television in Sweden, and an analysis of Danish TV. Published in Swedish.

Filmihullu (Finland); Annankatu 13 B 11, 00120 Helsinki 12, Finland; (8 times/yr); ISSN: n/a; OCLC 7500515.
Note: n.1, 1968 -.
Concerned with popular film and television in Finland. Contains critical reviews, some controversial articles on the substance of modern filmmaking, homages to Finnish actors and actresses, and descriptions of TV productions. Occasional issues unnumbered or incorrectly dated. Published in Finnish.

Filmindia (India). See: **Mother India**.

Filmklub-Cineclub (Switzerland). See: **Cinema**.

Filmkritik (W.Germany); Filmkritiker Kooperative, Kreittmaystr. 3, 8000 Munich 2, West Germany; (monthly); ISSN: 0015-1572; OCLC 2649122.
Note: v.1,n.1-v.28,n.11, Jan 1957-Nov 1984 (n.335).
Concerned with controversial and unpopular views of film theory and criticism. Ceased publication.
PN1995.F485.

Filmkultura (Hungary). Alternate title: **Film Kultura**. Magyar Filmtudomanyi Intezet es Filmarchivum, 1143 Budapest Nepstadion ut 97, Hungary; (bimonthly); ISSN: 0015-1580; OCLC 8039636.
Note: n.1, Jan/Feb 1970 -.
Scholarly film journal delving into the interaction between film and society. Articles cover theoretical as well as practical aspects of the cinema's influence on other arts, on culture and history. Analyzes the work of famous directors such as Dovzhenko and Griffith on a frame-by-frame basis.
PN1993.F647153.

Filmkunst: Zeitschrift fur Filmkultur und Filmwissenschaft (Austria). Alternate title: **Film-Kunst**. Filmkunst, 1010 Wien, Rauhensteingasse 5, Austria; (4 times/yr); ISSN: 0015-1599; OCLC 5258455.
Note: n.1, 1949/50 -.
Contains scholarly articles on film theory and history. Emphasizes German and Austrian films and directors, but includes other European and American efforts as well. Published in German.

The Filmlist (U.S.). Currently: **Sightlines** (0037-4830).
Educational Film Library Association, New York, NY;
(monthly); ISSN: n/a; OCLC 9570816.
Note: v.1,n.1-v.2,n.8, Sept 1965-Apr/May 1967. Absorbed by
Sightlines in Sep/Oct 1967.
Merged with **Film Review Digest** and **E.F.L.A. Bulletin** to form
Sightlines.

Filmmaking (U.K.). See: **Film Making**.

Filmmakers (U.S.). Formerly: **N.Y. Filmmakers' Newsletter** (0015-
1610); **Filmmakers Newsletter** (0015-1610); Alternate title:
Filmmakers Monthly. Filmmakers, Subscription Dept., PO Box
115, Ward Hill, MA 01830; (monthly); ISSN: 0194-4337; OCLC
4567259.
Note: v.1,n.1-5, Nov 1967-Mar 1968 as **N.Y. Filmmakers'**
Newsletter; v.1,n.6-v.11,n.11, Apr 1968-Sep 1978 as
Filmmakers Newsletter; v.11,n.12-v.15,n.3, Oct 1978-Jan 1982
as **Filmmakers**.
"Magazine for professionals and semi-professionals working in
film and videotape production in studios, independent
production houses, university film departments, television
stations and the military." Articles cover shooting on
location, camera equipment, economic forecasts and careers in
filmmaking. Ceased publication in 1982.
PN1993.F647154; Dewey: 384.8/05.

Filmmakers Monthly (U.S.). See: **Filmmakers**.

Filmmakers Newsletter (U.S.). See: **Filmmakers**.

Filmmuseet (Denmark); Danske Filmmuseum, Store Sondervoldstraede, 1419 Copenhagen, Denmark. Tel: (01)57 1003;
(bimonthly); ISSN: n/a.
Note: [n.1], Jan-Mar, 1969 -.
Elaborate film schedule for the Danish Film Archive. Entries
include review, still photo, cast, credits, year of release,
original title and Danish title.
PN1993.4.C64F54.

Filmmuveszeti Konyvtar (Hungary); Magyar Filmintezet, 1143
Nepstadion ut 97, Budapest, 10 Hungary; (annual); ISSN: 0428-
3805.

Note: n.1, 1961 -.
A performing arts annual containing scholarly treatises on
Hungarian filmmaking, theater and music compositions.
Original documentation, bibliographies, notes and graphics
are used to set forth new theories. Concentrates on film
music, technical aspects of synchronization, advances in
theatrical sound systems, as well as the artistic
applications of music on film.
PN1993.F647155.

Filmo-Bibliografischer Jahresbericht (E.Germany); Staatlichen
Filmarchiv der D.D.R., Hausvogteiplatz 3/4, 1800 Berlin, East
Germany; (annual); ISSN: 0015-1750; OCLC 6073024.
Note: v.1, 1965? -.
A yearly compilation of film and television programs produced
in East Germany with title, studio, length, cast, credits and
synopsis. Also lists foreign films released in East Germany
from other countries, most notably from the Eastern Bloc and
Third World nations such as Libya, Afghanistan, Nicaragua and
Vietnam. Contains information on international film
festivals. Indexed by title. Published in German.
PN1993.3.F55.

Filmoteca Espanola (Spain); Ctra. Dehesa de la Villa, s/n, 28040
Madrid, Spain. Tel: 449 00 11; (monthly).
Note: unnumbered.
Calendar for film programs at the Spanish Film Archive in
Madrid. Contains short articles on featured directors and
performers. Published in Spanish.

Fil'movi Novini (Bulgaria). Alternate title: **Filmovi Novini**.
Bulgarskite Filmovi Deitsi, Blvd. "Rusky" 8/a Sofia 100,
Bulgaria; (monthly); ISSN: 0204-8760.
Note: v.1, 1955 -.
"Organ na komiteta za kultura i na suiuza na Bulgarskite
filmovi deitsi." Popular culture magazine exhibiting a
Western influence. Contains biographical sketches of popular
American actors and actresses, as well as promotional pieces
on Bulgarian film and television stars. Many photographs
illustrate short articles. Published in Cyrillic.
PN1993.F64717

Filmovi Novini (Bulgaria). See: **Fil'movi Novini**.

Filmowy Serwis Prasowy (Poland); Redakcja Wydawnictw Filmowych
Centrali, Dystrybucji Filmow, ul. Mazowiecka 6/8, 00-950
Warszawa, Poland. Tel: 26-28-67; (bimonthly); ISSN: PL ISSN
0430-4519.
Note: v.1, 1955 -.
Comprehensively reviews international motion pictures. Each
review includes original release title, Polish title, date,
production company, distributor, director, producer,
scenario, music, cast members, synopsis and photograph.
Includes information about the Polish film industry.
Published in Polish.

Filmrutan (Sweden). Alternate title: **Film Rutan**. Filmrutan
Expedition, Box 82, 85102 Sundsvall, Sweden. Tel: 060-15 87
40; (quarterly); ISSN: 0015-1661; OCLC 5248429.
Note: v.1, 1958 -.
Journal of film criticism. Reviews international feature
films, giving the Swedish release title, original title,
country of origin, year of release, length, credits, cast,
publicity still, synopsis and critique. Reports on film
festivals. Published in Swedish.

Films and Filming (U.K.). Absorbed **Focus on Film** (0015-5128).
Films and Filming Subscriptions Dept., 8 Grove Ash,
Bletchley, Milton Keynes MK1 1BZ England. Tel: 0908-71981;
(monthly); ISSN: 0015-167X; OCLC 1569213.
Note: v.1, Oct 1954 -. Absorbed **Focus on Film**, n.38, Apr
1981 -.
Popular journal containing interviews of famous directors,
producers and performers; film and video reviews; and news of
international events and festivals. Glossy magazine
promoting latest features.
PN1993.F64725; Dewey: 791.43/05.

Films et Documents (France); Federation du Cinema Educatif, 27,
rue de Poissy, 75005 Paris, France; (bimonthly); ISSN: n/a.
Note: v.1, 1946 -.
"Revue des techniques audio-visuelles." Designed for
teachers and librarians, this publication examines
projectors, screens, video equipment, cameras and other
audiovisual products for use in schools. Reviews educational
films and videos. Recommends books for teaching filmmaking
and film studies. Also contains a music section for

reviewing new albums and books on music theory. Published in French.
PN1993.F475.

Films Finlandais (Finland). See: **Finnish Films = Films Finlandais.**

Films for Universities (U.K.). See: **B.U.F.V.C. Catalogue.**

Films Illustrated (U.K.). See: **Film Monthly.**

Films in Review (U.S.). Formerly: **National Board of Review Magazine; New Movies: The National Board of Review Magazine.** National Board of Review of Motion Pictures, Inc., Films in Review, PO Box 589, Lenox Hill Station, New York, NY 10021. Tel: 212/628-1594; (monthly; except bimonthly for Jun/Jul and Aug/Sep issues); ISSN: 0015-1688; OCLC 1569214.
Note: v.1-v.19,n.8, Mar/Apr 1926-Dec 1944 as **National Board of Review Magazine**; v.20,n.1-v.23,n.6 Jan/Feb 1945-Jan/Feb 1949 as **New Movies: The National Board of Review Magazine**; renumbered v.1,n.1 Feb 1950 - as **Films in Review**.
Focuses on classic American films made by the major studios. Nostalgic, but intelligent journal of film history and criticism. Publishes long biographical articles on film stars and directors, containing comprehensive filmographies. Reviews contemporary films and film books.
PN1993.F6473; Dewey: 791.43/7.

Films of Yesteryear (U.S.); The World of Yesterday, Route 3, Box 263-H, Waynesville, NC 28786. Tel: 704/648-5647; (irregular); ISSN: 0275-5718; OCLC 6783318.
Note: n.1, Jul 1977 -.
Fan magazine for people interested in Hollywood films of the 1930s-1950s. Articles comprise comparison studies of movie plots with the original literary work, biographical sketches of favorite performers, and extensive filmographies.
PN1993.F6474; Dewey: 791.43/75/05.

Films on Screen and Video (U.K.); Ocean Publications, 22-24 Buckingham Palace Rd., London SW1W 9SA England; (monthly); ISSN: n/a; OCLC 11021782.
Note: v.1,n.1, Jan 1981 -.
Gossipy, popular, brief articles describe the British film

industry. Contains a section reporting on the works-in-progress at the various studios and on location. "Soundtracks" section gives information on the availability of recordings of motion picture soundtracks. Contains long film reviews and critiques film books. PN1993.F6475; Dewey: 791.43/05.

Films Sonen, Dansk Filmfortegnelse (Denmark). See: **Filmsaesonen Dansk.**

Films Swedois (Sweden). See: **Swedish Films = Film Swedois.**

Filmsaesonen Dansk (Denmark). Alternate title: **Films Sonen, Dansk Filmfortegnelse.** Det Danske Filmmuseum, Store Sondervoldstraede, 1419 Kobenhavn K, Denmark. Tel: 01 57 6500; (annual); ISSN: 0107-1033; OCLC 7626287.
Note: v.1, 1979/80 -.
Published in Danish with English translations of preface and instructions. A yearbook listing all feature films and theatrical shorts released in theaters or on television during the year. Alphabetically arranged by Danish release title, each entry includes original title, country of production, date, length, Danish distributor, detailed cast and credits, a short synopsis and a still photograph. Indexed by director and film title. PN1997.8.F56.

Filmska Kultura (Yugoslavia). Alternate title: **Filmska Kultura; Jugoslavenski Casopis za Filmska Pitanja.** 41000 Zagreb, Ilica 21/1, Yugoslavia. Tel: 412-527; (monthly); ISSN: Yu 0015-170X.
Note: v.1,n.1, Jul 1957 -.
Scholarly articles discuss the latest film theories. Contains in-depth biographies of famous international performers and directors, such as Ingrid Bergman, Jacques Tati, Luis Bunuel. Also profiles Yugoslavians who are successful in the motion picture and television industries in Yugoslavia. Published in Yugoslavian. PN1993.F64765.

Filmska Kultura; Jugoslavenski Casopis za Filmska Pitanja (Yugoslavia). See: **Filmska Kultura.**

Filmske Sveske (Yugoslavia); Institut za Film, Cika Ljubina 15/
II, Beograd, Yugoslavia; (monthly; except Jul & Aug); ISSN:
0430-4527.
Note: v.1,n.1 Jan 1968 -.
Scholarly, learned journal with in depth articles on film
theory as applied to language studies. Interested in
literature and film, poetry and experimental film, and Slavic
film history. Includes notes on film festivals. Published
in Yugoslavian.
PN1993.F6478.

Filmski Svet (Yugoslavia); Beogradski Graficki Zavod, Vojvode
Misica 17, Beograd, Yugoslavia; (monthly); ISSN: 0015-1718.
Note: n.1, August 30, 1952 -.
A popular fan magazine filled with photos of favorite
international film and television stars. Covers the latest
releases, reviews films, interviews directors and performers.
Contains gossip columns and articles on the private lives of
actresses and models.
PN1993.F6479.

Filmspiegel (E.Germany). Formerly: **Deutsche Filmkunst** (0417-
1748); absorbed **Neue Filmvelt**. Filmspiegel, 1040 Berlin,
Oranienburger Strasse 67/68, Postfachnummer 220, East
Germany. Tel: 2 87 9253; (biweekly); ISSN: 0015-1734.
Note: v.1-v.10, 1953-Dec 1962 as **Deutsche Filmkunst**; absorbed
Neue Filmvelt in 1954; v.11, Jan 1963- as **Filmspiegel**.
Popular "photo-magazine" concentrating on contemporary cinema
and television productions. Keeps up with international
releases. Presents biographical sketches of performers,
including American and Western European. Reports on East
European film festivals and films from Communist countries
and the Third World.
PN1993.N3952.

Filmviews (Australia). Formerly: **Federation News** (0046-3582).
Merged with **Cinema Papers**. Australian Council of Film
Societies, 19 Warnes Rd., Mitcham, Victoria, 3132, Australia;
(quarterly); ISSN: 0158-3778; OCLC 16274424.
Note: v.1-v.24, 1956?-1979 as **Federation News**; v.25,n.1-v.32,
Mar 1980 (n.103)-1988 as **Filmviews**. Merged with **Cinema
Papers** in 1989.
The official magazine of the Australian Council of Film

Societies. Keeps the various film societies current with
events concerning the appreciation of film, such as
festivals, programs, lectures, symposia, classes. Reviews
films and publishes film schedules.

Filmvilag (Hungary). Alternate title: **Filmvilag: Filmmuveszcti
Folyoirat.** Berc u. 19-21, Budapest, 1. Hungary; (monthly);
ISSN: Hu 0428-3872.
Note: v.1, 1958 -.
International film journal containing thoughtful and
provocative articles on a broad range of film topics: Soviet
cinema, Indian directors, erotic film, cinema studies, Cuban
filmmaking. Publishes excerpts taken from books, such as
Norman Mailer's *Marilyn* and the correspondence between
Eisenstein and psychologist Wilhelm Reich. A regular feature
includes Hungarian film directors writing about their
favorite movies. Printed in Hungarian with short summaries
in English.
PN1993.F658.

Filmvilag: Filmmuveszcti Folyoirat (Hungary). See: **Filmvilag.**
Filmwarts (W.Germany); Filmwarts e.V., Offizin, Stiftstrasse 11,
3000 Hannover 1, West Germany. Tel: (0511) 17622; (monthly);
ISSN: n/a.
Note: n.1, 1988 -.
Scholarly journal concentrating on contemporary independent
filmmakers and recently released features and documentaries.
Interested in directors whose work is not in the mainstream.
Conducts lengthy interviews; reviews and analyzes avant
garde, experimental and modern works. Published in German.

Filmwissenschaftliche Beitrage (W.Germany). See: **Beitrage zur
Film- und Fernsehwissenschaft.**

Filmwoche (W.Germany). Merged with **Film-Echo** to form
Film-Echo/ Filmwoche.
Note: v.1-v.17,n.5, 1923-Jan 1962 as **Filmwoche**; merged
with **Film-Echo**, continuing the numbering of **Film-Echo**, v.16,
n.9/10, Feb 1962- as **Film-Echo/Filmwoche.**

Filmworld (Canada). See: **Film & T.V. World.**

Filmworld (India). Alternate title: **Film World.** Filmworld
International Publication, Ltd., 8 Harniman Circle, Rotawala
Bldg., Second Floor, Bombay 400023 India; (monthly); ISSN:
0015-1475; OCLC 7495198.
Note: v.1,n.1 Oct? 1964 -.
Fan magazine featuring favorite Indian movie stars. Many
photos illustrate the personality sketches and interviews.
Replete with on and off screen romances, conflicts and
jealousies. Contains gossip columns and trivia contests.
Surveys production activities.
PN1993.F635.

Fine Art Film and Video Source Book. See: **ArtsAmerica Fine Art
Film and Video Source Book.**

Finland-Filmland. See: **Finland-Filmland: Facts About Film in
Finland.**

Finland-Filmland: Facts About Film in Finland (Finland). Created
by merger between **Facts About Film Finland** (0355-1520) and
Finland-Filmland (0355-1539). Suomen Elokuvasaatio--The
Finnish Film Foundation, Kaisaniemenkatu 3B 25, SF-00100
Helsinki 10, Finland. Tel: 171 017; (3 times/yr. from 1978-
1981; annual from 1982).
Note: v.1,n.1-v.4?,n.3 1978-1981; continued as an annual,
1982 -.
Promotes Finnish cinema, both in Finland and abroad. Covers
international film festivals, statistics on the Finnish film
industry and boxoffice receipts. Contains articles on
Finnish film history. Publishes separate editions in English,
Finnish, French and German.

Finnish Films = Films Finlandais (Finland); Suomen Elokuvasaatio-
-The Finnish Film Foundation, Kaisaniemenkatu 3B 25, SF-00100
Helsinki 10, Finland. Tel: 171 017; (annual); ISSN: n/a; OCLC
10054130.
Note: ed.1, 1980 -.
Yearbook describing the films and television programs
produced in Finland. Contains names, addresses and telephone
numbers of production and distribution companies. Published
in Finnish, French and English.

Fischer Film Almanach (W.Germany); Fischer Taschenbuch Verlag, GmbH, Frankfurt am Main, West Germany; (annual); ISSN: n/a; OCLC 9289249.
Note: v.1, 1980 -.
Alphabetical listing of feature films released in West Germany. The entry includes original title, German release title, country of origin, date, length, director, cinematographer, writer, music composer, sound engineer, costume designer, cast and synopsis. Reports on European film festivals; contains an obituary of famous film people who have died during the year. Published in German. PN1997.8.F59; Dewey: 791.43/05.

Flicker Film Journal (U.S.); Flicker, PO Box 578309, Chicago, IL 60657; (irregular); ISSN: n/a.
Note: v.1, 198u -.
A film journal "featuring camp and exploitation." A cult magazine concentrating on independent, avant garde and experimental filmmaking. Interviews film and videomakers.

Focus! (U.S.); Documentary Film Group, University of Chicago, 1212 E. 59th St., Chicago, IL 60637; (2 times/yr (Spring/ Summer and Fall/Winter)); ISSN: 0015-4989.
Note: n.1-n.15, Mar 1967-1977?; [n.1], Jan 1990 -.
Scholarly journal documenting film history, theory and criticism. Subjects vary widely from nostalgia pieces on Hollywood silent classics to analytical treatments of documentaries. Contains biographical articles on great directors, such as Alfred Hitchcock, Frank Borzage and Joseph L. Mankiewicz. Includes academic analyses of great films on a frame-by-frame basis and interviews people working in film today. After a long hiatus, started publishing again.

Focus on Film. See: **Films and Filming.**

Formato Dieciseis (Panama); Universidad de Panama, Apartado 6-1775, Estafeta el Dorado, Panama. Tel: 23-9324; (irregular); ISSN: n/a; OCLC 12207722.
Note: [n.1], 1977? -.
Popular journal containing several lengthy film reviews of international feature films plus shorter reviews describing additional films released in Panama. Articles cover Latin American cinema, biographical sketches of popular actors and

actresses, and reports from various film festivals. Published in Spanish.

Foto Magazin. See: **Fotomagazin.**

Fotomagazin (W.Germany). Formerly: **Film + [i.e. und] Ton-Magazin** (0015-1114); continues **Der Film Kreis**; absorbed **Ton Magazin** (0495-8446); Alternate titles: **Foto Magazin; F.M.** Heering-Verlag GmbH, Ortlerstrasse 8, 8000 Munchen 70 West Germany; (monthly); ISSN: 0340-6660; OCLC 818152.
Note: v.1-v.11, Jan/Feb 1955-Dec 1965 as **Der Film Kreis**; absorbed **Ton Magazin** in Jan 1966; v.12-v.27,n.12, Jan 1966-Dec 1981 as **Film + Ton Magazin**; v.28,n.1, Jan 1982- as **Fotomagazin**.
Centers on the technical aspects of filmmaking. Advises on camera and sound equipment, projectors, lenses, lighting and video technology. Contains a separate section on music which talks about high fidelity sound, compact disks, sound systems, etc. Advises on the best equipment for amateur film and video making. Reports on the Berlin Film Festival.
TR1.F756; Dewey: 770.5 19.

Framework (U.K.); Framework, Turnaround, 27 Horsell Rd., London N51 XL England; (irregular); ISSN: 0306-7661; OCLC 5257024.
Note: v.1,n.1 Spring 1975 -.
Academic journal for advanced film students, teachers and film scholars. Contains substantial articles on film theory, criticism and history. Reviews current cinema and video; reviews film books and magazine articles.
PN1993.F75; Dewey: 791.43/05.

Frauen und Film (W.Germany); Stroemfeld/Roter Stern, Postfach 180 147, D-6000, Frankfurt am Main, West Germany; (irregular); ISSN: n/a; OCLC 4421946.
Note: n.1, 1974 -.
Long scholarly articles on the treatment of women in the cinema. Feminist viewpoints analyze the works of international directors, such as Alfred Hitchcock, Kenneth Anger, Woody Allen, Rainer Werner Fassbinder. Interviews women directors; keeps current with the latest independent films and videos made by women.
PN1995.9.W6F69; Dewey: 791.43/088042.

-G-

G.B.C. Radio and TV Times (Ghana). Formerly: **Ghana Radio Review and TV Times; Ghana Radio & Television Times**. Ghana Broadcasting Corp., Subscriptions, Graphic Rd., PO Box 742, Accra, Ghana; (weekly); ISSN: n/a.
Note: v.1-v.6,n.19, 1960-Jul 2, 1965 as **Ghana Radio Review and TV Times**; v.6,n.20-v.16,n.51, Jul 9, 1965-Feb 6, 1976 as **Ghana Radio & Television Times**; v.16,n.52, Feb 13, 1976- as **G.B.C. Radio and TV Times**.
Programming journal of the Ghana Broadcasting Corporation published in English. Contains articles on news and politics, such as "Soviet-Cuban Roles in Africa" and "Adult Education Through Radio and TV." Covers radio schedules as well as television.
PN1991.3.G5G48.

'G.B.H. (U.S.). Formerly: **Dial/W.G.B.H.** WGBH-TV, Box 200, Boston, MA 02134. Tel: 617/492-2777; (monthly); ISSN: n/a.
Note: v.1-v.7 1980-1986 as **Dial/W.G.B.H.**; renumbered v.1,n.1 Jan 1987- as **'G.B.H.**
Programming guide to the public broadcasting channel in the Boston metropolitan area. Magazine is part of the membership subscription. Background articles cover new series and specials.
PN1992.8.P8; Dewey: 791.44/0973.

G.P.Newsletter (U.S.). See: **G.P.N. Newsletter**.

G.P.N. Newsletter (U.S.). Alternate titles: **G.P.Newsletter; Great Plains National Newsletter**. Great Plains National Instructional Television Library, PO Box 80669, Lincoln, NB 68501-0669. Tel: 800/228-4630; 402/472-2007; (4 times/yr; between Sep and Apr); ISSN: 0738-7555; OCLC 5091726.
Note: v.1, Sep 1974 -.
Newsletter for educators, librarians and school audiovisual specialists listing videocassettes available from the GPN instructional television library. Grade levels of programs are predominantly elementary through high school, but also has titles for college and adult education. Includes vocational guides, tutorials and instructional/training tapes

for teachers and school administrators. No copying
restrictions apply to GPN items.

Galaxy One Magazine (U.S.); University Graphics, Inc., 7340 East
Caley Ave., Suite 320, Englewood, CO 80111; (monthly); ISSN:
0884-7614; OCLC 12428784.
Note: 198u- .
Programming guide for owners of the smaller four-six foot
television receive only (TVRO) satellite-to-earth station
antennas.

Gambit (U.S.). See: **K.C.E.T. Magazine**.

Game Player's (U.S.); Signal Research, Inc., PO Box 29364,
Greensboro, NC 27429. Tel: 800/222-9631; (monthly); ISSN:
1042-3133; OCLC 19005472.
Note: v.1,n.1 Jun 1989 -.
"The leading magazine of video and computer entertainment."
Contains gaming news from around the world, the latest in
Japanese innovations, hi-tech joysticks and previews of next
generation machines. Reviews the latest hit games for
Nintendo, Sega, Atari, P.C., Commodore 64, Amiga and
Macintosh. In-depth examinations of games with maps,
strategy hints, tips and screen shots.
Dewey: 793 11.

Gamepro (U.S.); IDG Communications/Peterborough, Inc., 80 Elm
St., Peterborough, NH 03468, Ed. & Production Offices: 2421
Broadway, Suite 200, Redwood City, CA 94063. Tel: 800/288-
4776; (bimonthly); ISSN: 1042-8658; OCLC 19231826.
Note: v.1,n.1 May/Jun 1989 -.
For video game enthusiasts, gives pre-release reviews of new
games, tips and tactics for winning, news of developments in
the industry. Holds contests for readers, interviews
programmers, critiques new gaming machines, gives strategies
and secret moves.
Dewey: 794 11.

George Eastman House Newsletter (U.S.). See: **International
Museum of Photography at George Eastman House Newsletter**.

Get Animated! Review (U.S.); Get Animated!, PO Box 1458, Burbank
CA 91507; (quarterly); ISSN: 1045-8204; OCLC 20290074.

Note: v.1,n.1 Aug 1989 -.
"Reviews of record on the art and industry of animation."
Reviews animation in all moving image media: 16mm,
television, cable, home video, theatrical feature length
motion pictures and shorts. Reviews books and periodicals on
the art of animation. Includes information on fan clubs.
Dewey: 741 11.

Get Animated! Update (U.S.); Get Animated!, PO Box 1582,
   Burbank, CA 91507; (monthly); ISSN: 0892-5968.
   Note: Began 1986?
   Newsletter for film and video animators and industry
   personnel. Contains latest information about new releases of
   animated feature films, Saturday morning TV, video releases
   and TV commercials using animation techniques. Covers
   international animation festivals and news about noteworthy
   animators and studios such as Disney and Hanna-Barbera.

Ghana Radio & Television Times (Ghana). See: **G.B.C. Radio and
   TV Times**.

Ghana Radio Review and TV Times (Ghana). See: **G.B.C. Radio and
   TV Times**.

Giornale Dello Spettacolo (Italy); Via di Villa Patrizi 10,
   00161, Rome, Italy. Tel: 841481; (weekly); ISSN: n/a.
   Note: v.1, 19uu -.
   Trade paper for motion picture executives and theater owners
   in Italy, giving boxoffice statistics, theater revenues,
   audience data. Publishes articles on motion picture
   technology: cameras, projection equipment, video imagery,
   special effects, etc. Informs about copyrights, legal
   restrictions, international piracy and federal regulations.
   Published in Italian.

Golden Movie News (Hong Kong). See: **Chia Ho Tien Ying**.

The Golden Years of Radio & T.V. (U.S.); World of Yesterday
   Publishing, Route 3, Box 263-H, Waynesville, NC 28786. Tel:
   704/648-5647; (irregular); ISSN: n/a.
   Note: [n.1] 1987? -.
   Fanzine for collectors of old television and radio serials,
   such as *Ozzie & Harriet*, *Ellery Queen*, and *Fibber Magee*

and Molly. Forum for buying, selling and trading. Includes mediagraphies.

Gore Zone (U.S.). See: **GoreZone.**

GoreZone (U.S.). Alternate title: **Gore Zone.** Starlog Communications, Inc., 475 Park Ave. South, New York, NY 10016; (bimonthly); ISSN: 0896-8802; OCLC 17313713. Note: n.1, May 1988 -.
Specializes in reviewing "cut and slash" movies and unrated videos. Contains many graphic photographs, including a pull-out poster-sized centerfold. Shows how the gory special effects are achieved. Includes fiction of the same genre: supernatural, macabre, violent and bloody.
Dewey: 791 11.

Graffiti (U.S.). Alternate title: **Graffiti: The Newsletter of ASIFA / Hollywood.** International Animated Film Society, ASIFA Hollywood, 5301 Laurel Canyon Blvd., no. 219, North Hollywood, CA 91607. Tel: 818/508-5224; (bimonthly); ISSN: 0748-6324; OCLC 10241831.
Note: Began Oct 1979 -. Issues for Oct 1979-Jun 1981 lack volume numbering.
Subscription is part of membership in the International Animated Film Society (ASIFA-Hollywood). Articles cover latest techniques and technologies for film and video animators and graphics designers.
Dewey: 791 11.

Grand Angle (Belgium); Circulation, Grand Angle, rue d'Arschot, 29, 6370 Mariembourg, Belgium. Tel: 060/31.21.68; (monthly; except Aug); ISSN: n/a.
Note: n.1, Dec 1978? -.
Reviews comprehensively international feature film releases. Each entry includes French release title, original language title, date, production and distribution information, director, scriptwriter, editor, cast, synopsis, photograph and rating. Also publishes biographical sketches of contemporary directors with an analysis of their work and an extensive filmography. Published in French.

Grand Maghreb (France); Centre d'Information sur le Grand Maghreb, Institut d'Etudes Politiques de Grenoble II, B.P.

45, 38402 Saint-Martin-d'Heres Cedex France. Tel:
76.82.60.00; (9 times/yr.); ISSN: 0249-6879; OCLC 12954304.
Note: n.1, 1981 -.
French language publication interested in studying North
African cinema. Articles address the image of North Africa
in motion pictures and television. Devoted to the culture,
study, research and politics of the area as defined in moving
image materials.
DT181.G73.

Great Plains National Newsletter (U.S.). See: **G.P.N. Newsletter**.

Great TV Entertainment (U.S.). See: **The Cable Guide**.

Greater Amusements (U.S.). See: **Greater Amusements and
International Projectionist**.

**Greater Amusements; America's Foremost Motion Picture Regional
Trade Journal** (U.S.). See: **Greater Amusements and
International Projectionist**.

Greater Amusements and International Projectionist (U.S.).
Alternate title: **Greater Amusements**; formerly: **Greater
Amusements; America's Foremost Motion Picture Regional Trade
Journal**; absorbed **International Projectionist**. Gallo
Publishing Corp., 1 East 42nd St., Suite 805, New York, NY
10017. Tel: 212/786-7966; (bimonthly); ISSN: 0017-3703.
Note: v.1-[v.90,n.6], 1914-1965 as **Greater Amusements;
America's Foremost Motion Picture Regional Trade Journal**;
v.90,n.7, Jul 1965- as **Greater Amusements and International
Projectionist**; absorbed **International Projectionist** in Jul
1965.
A trade journal incorporating the technical aspects of
projection with theater maintenance and equipment
information. Keeps current with productions in progress,
studio buyouts, and financial reports of the different studios.
Quarterly sections include: Refreshments and Concessionaires,
Drive-in Operations and Theater Equipment Buyer.
PN1993.G73.

Griffithiana (Italy); Cineteca D.W. Griffith, Salita Santa Maria
della Sanita 43-45, 16122 Genova, Italia; (irregular); ISSN:
OCLC 12125035.

Note: v.1,n.1 Nov 1978 -.
Publication of the organizers of the Pordenone Silent Film
Festival in Italy. Each issue is devoted to a theme
pertaining to silent film, such as early film producer
Thomas Ince, the Vitagraph Studio or slapstick comedy. The
scholarly articles capture a different aspect of the central
theme. Articles may be submitted in any language, but they
are also published in Italian.
PN1993.G74; Dewey: 791.43/05.

Guide to Free Computer Materials (U.S.); Educators Progress
Service, Inc., 214 Center St., Dept. D8, Randolph, WI 53956.
Tel: 414/326-3126; (annual); ISSN: 0748-6235; OCLC 9914291.
Note: ed.1, 1983 -.
A bound directory listing free films, videotapes, pamphlets,
charts, programs and disks in the computer field. Products
are offered free to schools, colleges and universities
offering computer courses or wishing to set up a curriculum
of computer studies. Each entry includes title,
organizational sponsor, scope, date, grade level and contents
description.
QA76.16.G84; Dewey: 001.64/029/4.

Guide to Wildlife, Science and Research Film-makers (U.K.);
British Universities Film and Video Council Publications, 55
Greek St., London W1V 5LR England. Tel: 01-734-3687;
(quarterly).
Note: v.1,n.1 Autumn 1986 -.
Published in cooperation with the Scientific Film Association
and the British Kinematograph, Sound and Television Society.
Promotes the work of independent filmmakers who specialize in
nature, wildlife and science films. Lists their productions
and how to contact them for stock footage or new assignments.
Contains index of subject specialties.

-H-

H.D.T.V. Review (U.S.). Alternate title: **High Definition Television Review**. Meckler Corporation, 11 Ferry Lane West, Westport, CT 06880. Tel: 203/226-6967; (quarterly); ISSN: 1044-9507; OCLC 19957294.
Note: v.1, 1990 -.
Presents information on high definition television, such as standards, methodology, applications and the latest equipment available. Covers the Japanese and European markets.

Hard Rock Video (U.S.). Formerly: **Rock Video; Rock Video Idols Magazine**; alternate title: **Rock Video Magazine**. Comics World Corporation, 475 Park Ave. South, New York, NY 10016. Tel: 212/689-2830; (monthly); ISSN: 0883-9190; 0742-5163; OCLC 12252376.
Note: n.1-n.11, Apr 1984-Mar 1985 as **Rock Video**; [n.12-n.15], Apr 1985-Sep 1985 as **Rock Video Idols Magazine**; [n.16], Oct 1985- as **Hard Rock Video**.
"The magazine of superstars." Covers mostly music, but includes reviews and descriptions of music videos.
Interviews the media stars about their videos and record albums.
Dewey: 780 11.

The Health Science Video Directory (U.S.); Esselte Video, 600 Madison Ave., New York, NY 10022; (quarterly); ISSN: 0363-0781; OCLC 2997033.
Note: v.1, 1977 -.
Index listing all the videotapes available for rent or sale in the U.S. concerned with medicine and health. Each entry gives title, date, production company, length, synopsis and distributor.
R835.H4; Dewey: 016.61.

High Definition Television Review (U.S.). See: **H.D.T.V. Review**.

Historical Journal of Film, Radio and Television (U.K.); Carfax Publication Co., PO Box 25, Abingdon, Oxfordshire OX14 3UE

England; (3 times/yr; Oct, Mar & Jun); ISSN: 0143-9685; OCLC
7522224.
Note: v.1,n.1 Mar 1981 -.
Scholarly interdisciplinary journal concerned with
encouraging the use of mass media for teaching history,
political science, popular culture and social studies.
Stresses the impact of mass communications on the political
and social history of the Twentieth Century.
PN1993.5.A1H54; Dewey: 791.4/05.

Hollywood Close-up (U.S.). Alternate title: **American Close-up.**
J. Rosenstein, Hollywood, CA; (weekly); ISSN: 0737-2442;
OCLC 7227269.
Note: v.1, 1958 -. (Aug 12, 1971-Jan 13, 1972 as **American
Close-up**).
Trade paper covering news and events concerning Hollywood and
its environs. Designed for show people, professionals, and
technicians working in the motion picture and television
industries in Los Angeles. Keeps current with new productions,
casting calls, employment opportunities.

Hollywood Close-up (U.S.). See also: **S.A.G. Hollywood Close-up.**

The Hollywood Reporter (U.S.). Special monthly issue has title:
The Hollywood Reporter Magazine. Hollywood Reporter, 6715
Sunset Blvd., Hollywood, CA 90028. Tel: 213/464-7411; (daily
except Saturday, Sunday & holidays); ISSN: 0018-3660; OCLC
1752197.
Note: v.1, 1930 -.
A publication devoted to the latest news, developments and
events affecting the entertainment industry. This trade
newspaper charts boxoffice receipts and television ratings.
Contains marketing and financial information; executive changes
and mergers; productions-in-progress and their tentative release
dates. Reports on international motion picture and television
events.
Dewey: 791 11.

The Hollywood Reporter Magazine (U.S.). See: **Hollywood Reporter.**

Hollywood Reporter Studio Blu-Book Directory (U.S.); The
Hollywood Reporter, 6715 Sunset Blvd., Hollywood, CA 90028;
(annual); ISSN: 0278-419X; OCLC 7789567.

Note: ed.1, 1978 -.
A directory of celebrity contacts, guilds, trades and unions pertaining to the motion picture industry in the Los Angeles area. Contains a comprehensive listing of all production and post-production companies with names, addresses and telephone numbers. Lists all service occupations needed by the industry such as food caterers, animal trainers, stunt people, subtitling contractors and voice instructors.
PN1998.A1H6; Dewey: 384.8/025794.

Hollywood Script Writer (U.S.). See: **Hollywood Scriptwriter**.

Hollywood Scriptwriter (U.S.). Alternate title: **Hollywood Script Writer**. Hollywood Scriptwriter, 1625 Wilcox Ave., no. 385, Hollywood, CA 90028. Tel: 818/991-3096; (monthly); ISSN: n/a; OCLC 13441838.
Note: n.1, Jun? 1980 -.
Provides helpful guidance on how to write scripts for movies and television, plus advice on how to get them accepted. Includes contact people and script agents.

Hollywood Studio Magazine (U.S.). Alternate title: **Hollywood Studio Magazine: Then and Now**. Hollywood Studio Magazine, 3960 Laurel Canyon Blvd., Suite 450, Studio City, CA 91604-3791; (10 times/yr); ISSN: 0894-2188; OCLC 5314947.
Note: v.1, 1966 -.
Nostalgia magazine containing articles about the major studios and famous stars from Hollywood's golden age. Many photographs illustrate biographical sketches of the performers. Contains classified advertising for movie memorabilia.
PN1993.H54; Dewey: 791.43/0973.

Hollywood Studio Magazine: Then and Now (U.S.). See: **Hollywood Studio Magazine**.

Home Satellite T.V. (U.S.). Alternate title: **Home Satellite Television**. Miller Magazines, Inc., 2660 E. Main St., Ventura, CA 93003. Tel: 805/643-3664; (bimonthly); ISSN: 0890-3549; OCLC 14206746.
Note: v.1, Jul? 1985 -.
Trade journal intended for owners of private earth stations. Explains the technology, installation, trouble-shooting,

systems maintenance, legal aspects and new products.
Contains classified advertisements for equipment and services.
Dewey: 384 11.

Home Satellite Television (U.S.). See: **Home Satellite T.V.**

Home Shopping Investor (U.S.); Paul Kagan Associates, Inc., 126
Clock Tower Place, Carmel, CA 93923-8734. Tel: 408/624-1536;
(monthly); ISSN: 0890-1155; OCLC 14197246.
Note: n.1, Aug 18, 1986 -.
Newsletter tracking televised home shopping on the cable
networks. Charts profit margins, revenues and stocks for
these companies.
Dewey: 332 11.

Home Video Publisher: H.V.P. (U.S.); Knowledge Industry
Publications, Inc., 701 Westchester Ave., White Plains, NY
10604. Tel: 914/328-9157; (weekly); ISSN: 0748-0822; OCLC
10881004.
Note: v.1,n.1 Jul 16, 1984 -.
Newsletter for executives and retailers concerned with the
home video market. Covers video production, distribution,
promotion, sales, marketing and advertising.
Dewey: 381 11.

Home Viewer. The Monthly Video Program Guide (U.S.); Home
Viewer Publications, 11 N. 2nd St., Philadelphia, PA 19106. Tel:
215/629-1588; (monthly); ISSN: n/a; OCLC 14257125.
Note: v.1,n.1 Dec 1981 -.
Popular magazine for the home video market. Interviews stars;
reviews and rates the latest videocassettes. Lists all
new tapes by category and title. Contains many photographs
and advertisements.

Home Viewer Business Extra (U.S.). See: **Video Extra.**

Home Viewer's Official Video Software Directory Annual (U.S.).
Alternate title: **Official Video Software Directory Annual.**
Home Viewer Publications, 11 N. 2nd St., Philadelphia, PA
19106. Tel: 215/629-1588; (annual); ISSN: n/a; OCLC 15994803.
Note: ed.1 1985 -.
A trade directory listing over 750 video industry
organizations; entry contains address, telephone number, year

established, number of employees, branches, annual sales,
retail locations, lines carried, formats, terms, and key
personnel. Also contains one section devoted to vital
statistics: number of VCRs per household, number of
videocassettes rented each year, number bought, key market
indicators, rate of growth of the industry, etc. Lists
forthcoming trade shows and conventions.
HD9697.V543U5427; Dewey: 338.7/621388332.

Hope Reports Briefing (U.S.); Hope Reports, Inc., 1600 Lyell
Ave., Rochester, NY 14606. Tel: 716/458-4250; (quarterly);
ISSN: 0748-5433; OCLC 10988419.
Note: v.1,n.1 Sep 1986 -.
Concerned with future media developments in the interactive
video, photo-optical and computer fields. Reports sales,
revenues, net profits and GNP of the audiovisual industry.
Comments on the findings and results of the research
analyzed.
Dewey: 338 11.

Hope Reports Industry Quarterly (U.S.). Alternate title: **Hope
Reports Quarterly**. Hope Reports, Inc., 1600 Lyell Ave.,
Rochester, NY 14606. Tel: 716/458-4250; (quarterly); ISSN:
0147-7242; OCLC 3233764.
Note: v.1, 1972 -.
Combines four periodicals: **Manufacturer/Import/Export
Quarterly, AV Software Quarterly, Production Quarterly**,
and **Dealer Quarterly**. Contains national and regional
statistics on TV product sales and services. Covers audio,
video, computer and photo-optical projection equipment and
products.
Dewey: 338 11.

Horfunk und Fernsehen (W.Germany); Westdeutscher Rundfunk,
Bibliothek, Koln, West Germany; (annual); ISSN: n/a; OCLC
3566578.
Note: v.1, 1975/76 -.
A directory to West Germany radio and television programs,
companies, performers and stations. Gives names, addresses,
telephone numbers and top personnel. Published in German.
PN1991.3.G4Z44a.

Hors Cadre (France); L'Universite de Paris VIII, Service de la
 Recherche, 2, rue de la Liberte, 93526 Saint-Denis Cedex 02
 Paris, France; (annual); ISSN: 0755-0863; OCLC 10654101.
 Note: v.1, Spring 1983 -.
 "Le cinema a travers champs disciplinaires." Long scholarly
 articles focusing on film theory and criticism. Espouses
 unpopular or untried hypotheses relating to cinema studies.
 Acts as a forum for denouncing or arguing against popular or
 currently held theories. Published in French.
 PN1993.H63; Dewey: 791.43/75.

Hosogaku Kenkyu (Japan). See: **Studies in Broadcasting**.

How-to Video (U.S.); Publications and Communications, Inc., 12416
 Hymeadow Dr., Austin, TX 78750-1896. Tel: 512/250-9023;
 (monthly); ISSN: 0892-2306; OCLC 15124648.
 Note: v.1,n.1 Jun 1987 - v.1,n.5 Oct 1987.
 Publication listing non-theatrical videos of interest to
 librarians, educators, trainers, and business personnel, as
 well as the home enthusiast. Acted as a clearinghouse for hard
 to find "how-to" videos. Temporarily discontinued in Oct 1987.
 Dewey: 338 11.

Hungarofilm Bulletin (Hungary); Bathori U., 10, H-1054 Budapest,
 Hungary; (5 times/yr); ISSN: 0018-7798; OCLC 5977776.
 Note: 1965?-Dec 1988.
 An export catalog for Hungarian films. Lists latest
 releases, giving production information, cast, credits and
 synopsis for each film. Contains articles on "personalities
 of the Hungarian cinema," statistics, filmographies and film
 festivals. The annual index for the preceding year is
 included with the January issue. Published in English. Ceased
 publication under this title; intends to begin publishing again,
 possibly in 1990, under new title.

-I-

I.A.M.H.I.S.T. Newsletter (Netherlands); International
Association for Audio-visual Media in Historical Research and
Education, History Department, Postbox 1738, 3000 DR
Rotterdam, Netherlands; (irregular); ISSN: n/a.
Note: n.1, 1977? -.
For members of the International Association for Audio-visual
Media in Historical Research and Education, an association of
educators, historians and film scholars. International in
scope, the newsletter presents latest events, conferences,
projects, audiovisual works and news from members. Published
in English.

I.C.I.A. Membership Directory (U.S.). See: **International
Communications Industries Association. Membership Directory**.

I.D.A. Directory. (U.S.). Alternate titles: **Directory / International
Documentary Association; Directory / I.D.A.** International
Documentary Association, 1551 S. Robertson Blvd., Los
Angeles, CA 90035. Tel: 213/284-8422; (annual); ISSN: 8755-8947;
OCLC 11465135.
Note: v.1, 1984 -.
Directory of members of the International Documentary
Association, an organization promoting quality non fiction
film and video. Members can include writers, editors, camera
operators, musicians, researchers, technicians, journalists,
broadcast and cable programmers and academics, as well as
independent film and videomakers. Member biographies
include name, address, phone, profession, biographical
sketch and filmography.
PN1995.9.D6I52a; Dewey: 070 11.

I.E.E.E. Journal on Selected Areas in Communications (U.S.).
Alternate title: **Institute of Electrical & Electronics
Engineers Journal on Selected Areas in Communications**.
Institute of Electrical & Electronics Engineers, 345 E. 47th
St., New York, NY 10017-2394, Mailing address: 445 Hoes

Lane, Box 1331, Piscataway, NJ 08855-1331. Tel: 212/705-7900; (9 times/yr); ISSN: 0733-8716; OCLC 9450566.
Note: v.1,n.1 Jan 1983 -.
Professional trade journal covering scientific theories and reports on telecommunication engineering. Examines the technical aspect of the television and radio broadcasting industries.

I.E.E.E. Transactions on Broadcasting (U.S.). Alternate title: **Institute of Electrical & Electronics Engineers Transactions on Broadcasting**. Institute of Electrical & Electronics Engineers, 345 E. 47th St., New York, NY 10017-2394, Mailing address: 445 Hoes Lane, Box 1331, Piscataway, NJ 08855-1331. Tel: 212/705-7900; (quarterly); ISSN: 0018-9316; OCLC 1642875.
Note: [v.1] 1955 -.
Professional journal for electrical engineers working with broadcast transmission systems. Studies the design, performance, use, signal quality of transmitters, antennas and broadcast equipment.
Dewey: 384 11.

I.E.E.E. Transactions on Communications (U.S.). Alternate title: **Institute of Electrical & Electronics Engineers Transactions on Communications**. Institute of Electrical & Electronics Engineers, 345 E. 47th S., New York, NY 10017-2394, Mailing address: 445 Hoes Lane, Box 1331, Piscataway, NJ 08855-1331. Tel: 212/705-7900; (monthly); ISSN: 0090-6778; OCLC 9365835.
Note: [v.1], 1953 -.
Highly technical journal for electrical engineers working in telecommunications and broadcasting.

I.F.C. (India). See: **Indian Film Culture**.

I.F.P. Newsletter (U.S.). Alternate title: **Independent Feature Project Newsletter**. Independent Feature Project, 21 West 86 St., New York, NY 10024. Tel: 212/496-0909; (4 times/yr).
Note: [n.1] 1979? -.
For independent filmmakers and producers who are making documentaries and feature films outside the Hollywood studio system. Articles are concerned with financing, scriptwriting, casting, marketing and distribution. Contains advertisements for employment and positions wanted.

I.F.P.A. Communicator (U.S.). Formerly: **I.F.P.A. Newsletter**
(0579-6393); Alternate title: **Information Film Producers of**
America Communicator. Information Film Producers of America,
Box 1470, Hollywood, CA 90028; (bimonthly); ISSN: 0099-1090;
OCLC 2239934.
Note: v.1-v.72, 19uu-Dec 1972 as **I.F.P.A. Newsletter**; v.1,
n.1, Jan 1973- as **I.F.P.A. Communicator**.
Publication for members; reports on the news from the
regional chapters: Boston, Inland Empire, Los Angeles,
Midwest (Chicago), San Diego, Washington, D.C., etc. Covers
special assignments, projects, new products or services,
interesting films in production or release, awards given or
received, helpful tips, trade show information, promotions
and personnel changes. Offers help and professional advice
to audiovisual departments in schools, government agencies
and private companies. Publishes biographical sketches and
filmographies of members.
PN1993.I624A23; Dewey: 791.43.

I.F.P.A. Newsletter (U.S.). See: **I.F.P.A. Communicator**.

I.F.T.C. Newsletter (France). See: **Conseil International du**
Cinema de la Television et de la Communication Audiovisuelle.

I.N.T.V. Journal (U.S.). Formerly: **I.N.T.V. Quarterly**. Alternate
title: **Independent Television Journal**. View Communications
Corp., 46 East 21st St., New York, NY 10010-6213. Tel: 212/
673-7000; (7 times/yr: Jan, Feb/Mar, Apr/May, Jun/Jul, Aug/
Sep, Oct/Nov, Dec); ISSN: 0882-2271; ISSN 0899-787X; OCLC:
18216980.
Note: v.1,n.1-v.2,n.4, Spring 1985-Winter 1986 as **I.N.T.V.**
Quarterly; v.3,n.1, Jan 1987- as **I.N.T.V. Journal**.
"The magazine of independent television." A trade journal
designed for independent television stations. Compiles
statistics on growth and popularity of the independents,
reviews new programs, offers promotional techniques, advises
on new legislation, rules and regulations.
Dewey: 384 11.

I.N.T.V. Quarterly (U.S.). See: **I.N.T.V. Journal**.

Ikon: Ricerche Sulla Comunicazione (Italy). Alternate titles:
**Ikon; Cinema, Television, Iconografia; Ikon: Revista
dell'Istituto A. Gemelli.** Formerly: **Revue Internationale de
Filmologie.** Merged with **Ricerche Sulla Comunicazione**
continuing the numbering of the latter. Instituto Augostino
Gemelli, via le Monza 106, Milan, Italy. Tel: 282 7651;
(irregular); ISSN: 0019-1744; OCLC 5663307.
Note: v.1-v.11, 1947-1961 as **Revue Internationale de
Filmologie;** v.12-v.27, 1962-1977 as **Ikon; Cinema, Television,
Iconografia.** Renumbered v.1, 1978- as **Ikon: Ricerche Sulla
Comunicazione.**
Scholarly journal analyzing the mass media in a scientific,
historical or social context. Explores new methods of
teaching communications by studying film and television.
Forum for new theories concerning the media. Published in
Italian and French with English summaries.
PN1795.I5.

Illusions (New Zealand); Illusions c/o Drama Studies, Victoria
University of Wellington, PO Box 600, Wellington, New
Zealand; (3 times/yr); ISSN: 0112-9341; OCLC 16349844.
Note: v.1,n.1 Summer 1986.
"A New Zealand magazine of film, television and theatre
criticism." Focuses on New Zealand productions. Interviews
New Zealand filmmakers; profiles people involved in drama
studies, cinema and theater productions. Emphasis is on
independent, documentary and ethnographic filmmaking.

Iluzjon (Poland); Filmoteca Polska, ul. Pulawska 61, 02-595
Warsaw, Poland. Tel: 45 50 74; (quarterly); ISSN: 0209-3537.
Note: n.1, 1981 -.
Scholarly film journal containing biographical sketches and
filmographies of people working in the motion picture
industry from the silent period to the present. Publishes
articles on film history, theory, analysis and criticism.
Written in Polish.

Image (U.S.). Alternate title: **Image: Journal of Photography and
Motion Pictures of the International Museum of Photography.**
International Museum of Photography at George Eastman House,
900 East Ave., Rochester, NY 14607; (quarterly); ISSN: 0536-
5465; OCLC 1752688.
Note: v.1, Jan 1952 -.

Beautifully illustrated with photographs and frame enlargements
taken from the collections at the George Eastman House, this
magazine analyzes the art and science of film and photography.
Covers the scientific and technical aspects of photography as well
as the artistic.
TR1.I47; Dewey: 770.974789.

Image et Son/Revue du Cinema (France). Formerly: **U.F.O.C.E.L.
Informations**; merged with **Ecran** to form **La Revue du Cinema/
Image et Son/Ecran**; ISSN: 0536-5481.
Note: n.1-n.45?, 1947?-1951? as **U.F.O.C.E.L. Informations**;
n.46?-n.352, 1951?-Aug 1980 as **Image et Son/Revue du Cinema**;
merged with **Ecran** in Jan 1980.
See entry under **La Revue du Cinema/Image et Son** for current
information.

Image Technology (U.K.). Alternate title: **Image Technology;
Journal of the B.K.S.T.S.** Formerly: **British Kinematograph
Society. Proceedings; British Kinematograph Society. The
Journal; British Kinematography** (0373-109X); **British
Kinematography, Sound and Television** (0007-135X); **British
Kinematograph, Sound and Television Society. The B.K.S.T.S.
Journal** (0305-6996). Address: British Kinematograph, Sound and
Television Society, 547-549 Victoria House, Vernon Pl.,
London WC1B 4DJ England. Tel: 01-242 8400; (monthly); ISSN:
0950-2114; ISSN 0305-6996; OCLC 14257070.
Note: v.1-v.19, 1919?-1937? as **British Kinematograph Society.
Proceedings**; v.20-v.29, Dec 1937-Jun 1947 as **British
Kinematograph Society. The Journal**; v.29-v.47, Jul 1947-Dec
1965 as **British Kinematography**; v.48-v.55, Jan 1966-Dec 1973 as
British Kinematography, Sound and Television; v.56-v.68,n.6
Jan 1974-Jun 1986 as **British Kinematograph, Sound and
Television Society. The B.K.S.T.S. Journal**; v.68,n.7, July 1986- as
Image Technology.
Professional journal for members of the B.K.S.T.S. Contains
information on British products and services in the motion picture,
sound, television, and video industries. Keeps current with
technological and engineering innovations; reviews new products
and equipment.
TR845.B75; Dewey: 778.5/05.

Image Technology; Journal of the B.K.S.T.S. See: **Image
Technology**.

Imagenes (Puerto Rico); Universidad Interamericana de Puerto
Rico, Recinto Metropolitano, Decanato de Estudiantes,
Apartado 1293, Hato Rey, Puerto Rico 00919; (2 times/yr);
ISSN: n/a; OCLC 14137774.
Note: v.1,n.1 Segundo Semestre 1985 -.
Serious journal with wide ranging interests. Covers
filmmaking in Puerto Rico, briefings on colorization,
biographies of directors, reports from film festivals,
studies of new Latin American cinema and a variety of other
subjects related to cinema studies and popular culture.
Published in Spanish.

Immagine (Italy); Associazione Italiana per le Ricerche di Storia
del Cinema, Via Tuscolana, 1522 - 00173 Rome, Italy;
(quarterly); ISSN: n/a; OCLC 17303832.
Note: v.1, 1985 -.
Scholarly journal focusing on Italian film history, theory
and criticism. Contains long articles with original research
and documentation, usually concentrating on the silent
period. Published in Italian.
PN1993.I58; Dewey: 791.43/05.

In Cinema (U.S.); In Cinema, Ltd., 919 3rd. Ave., New York, NY
10022. Tel: 212/758-5580; (10 times/yr); ISSN: 0271-261X; OCLC
6592749.
Note: v.1,n.1 Jun 1980 -.
Patterned after a theater handbill, this magazine promotes
popular features in current release. A guide for New York
City moviegoers, it reviews the latest films, gossips about
the stars, interviews favorite performers and informs about
the New York and American Film Festivals held in New York.

In Focus (U.S.); Interdepartmental Program in Film Studies, Center
for Studies in Contemporary Culture, 101 S. College, University
of Massachusetts, Amherst, MA 01003. Tel: 413/545-3659;
(quarterly); ISSN: n/a.
Note: v.1,n.1 Summer 1989 -.
Newsletter reporting on film courses offered by the University
of Massachusetts. Contains a calendar of events for related
interests. Reviews new books on cinema studies.

In Focus: The Discovery Channel (U.S.). See: **Discovery In Focus.**

In Motion (U.S.); In Motion, 421 Fourth St., Annapolis, MD 21403.
  Tel: 301/269-0605; (monthly); ISSN: 0889-6208; OCLC 13997219.
  Note: v.1,n.1, Jan/Feb 1982 -.
  Specifically geared toward media professionals in the Mid-
  Atlantic region working on film and video production and
  related imaging techniques. Contains articles on handling three
  dimensional graphics, software for scriptwriting, and state of
  the art equipment.
  Dewey: 778.11.

In Plant (U.S.). Alternate title: **In Plant: Video/AV
  Communicator**. P.T.N. Publishing Corp., 210 Crossways Park Dr.,
  Woodbury, NY 11797. Tel: 516/496-8000; (bimonthly); ISSN:
  0040-0971; OCLC 1767216 (for **Technical Photography**).
  Note: 198u- .
  Supplement to **Technical Photography** magazine. Designed for
  technical photographers and producers of technical
  videotapes. Details newest products and services, such as
  computer graphics, cameras, lenses and recorders.
  TR1.T38; Dewey: 770.5.

In Vision (U.K.). See: **Invision**.

The Independent (U.S.). Formerly: **Association of Independent
  Video and Filmmakers Newsletter**. Foundation for Independent
  Video and Film, 625 Broadway, 9th Floor, New York City, NY
  10012. Tel: 212/473-3400; (10 times/yr); ISSN: 0731-5198;
  OCLC 8228619.
  Note: v.1,n.1-v.2?, Jul 1976-Fall 1978 as **Association of
  Independent Video and Filmmakers Newsletter**; renumbered v.1,
  n.1, Jan/Feb 1979- as **The Independent**.
  Forum for independent video and filmmakers concerned with
  making documentaries, non-fiction television specials and
  experimental cinema. Gives information on new trends in
  filmmaking and broadcast production, contacts, help wanted,
  and employment.
  PN1993.I617; Dewey: 791.43/0973.

The Independent (U.S.). See also: **The Film Journal**.

Independent Broadcasting / I.B.A. (U.K.). See: **Airwaves**.

The Independent Feature Project (U.S.); Independent Feature Project, 1776 Broadway, New York, NY 10019. Tel: 212/245-1622; (quarterly); ISSN: n/a.
Note: v.1,n.1 Winter 1981 -.
A newsletter for members of I.F.P. Helps to promote the production and distribution of independent 35mm feature films in the United States. A forum for independent filmmakers, reporting on new projects, opportunities and activities. Lists recent productions which have won critical acclaim and international distribution. Articles tell about American filmmakers working outside the Hollywood-New York axis.

The Independent Film Journal (U.S.). See: **The Film Journal.**

Index Suisse du Cinema (Switzerland). See: **Schweizer Filmindex = Index Suisse du Cinema = Indice Svizzero del Cinema.**

Indian Cinema (India); Directorate of Film Festivals, India in association with National Film Development Corp., Ltd., Vikas Publishing House, Lok Nayak Bhawan (Fourth floor) Khan Market, New Delhi 110 003 India; (annual); ISSN: n/a; OCLC 6676950.
Note: v.1, 1965? -.
Contains information on features and shorts selected for showing at the Indian Panorama, Directorate of Film Festivals. Divided into two sections, the first part is devoted to articles about Indian cinema, direction, music, editing, costume design, etc. The second section is the list of chosen films with title, distributor, credits, cast, synopsis and photograph. Each entry also has a short profile on the director of the film. Published in English.
PN1993.5.I8A3; Dewey: 791.43/0954.

Indian Film Culture (India). Alternate title: **I.F.C.** Federation of Film Societies of India, C-7 Bharat Bhawan, 3 Chittaranjan Ave., Calcutta 700072 India; (irregular); ISSN: n/a; OCLC 10048679.
Note: 1979? -.
Forum for Indian filmmakers and producers to air views, analyze the status of film in India and the attitudes that run through it. Some of the articles address interactions between theater and cinema, the role of women in Indian film, films made for children and the use of dance and music in

Indian cinema. The magazine's advisory board is composed of acclaimed Indian directors. Published in English. PN1993.5.I8I498; Dewey: 791.43/0954.

Indice Svizzero del Cinema (Switzerland). See: **Schweizer Filmindex = Index Suisse du Cinema = Indice Svizzero del Cinema.**

Industrial Photography (U.S.). Formerly: **Technical Photography** (0040-0971); **Tech Photo Pro Imaging Systems** (1040-0141). P.T.N. Publishing Corp, 210 Crossways Park Dr., Woodbury, NY 11797. Tel: 516/496-8000; (monthly). Note: v.1,n.1-v.20,n.5, Dec 1968/Jan 1969-May 1988 as **Technical Photography**; v.20,n.6-8, Jun-Aug 1988 as **Tech Photo Pro Imaging Systems**; v.20,n.9, Sep 1988- as **Industrial Photography**. Technical, professional journal for still and moving image photographers and cameramen. Covers industrial, military and government applications. Critiques new equipment, tests new products, gives information about film and video labs. TR1.T38; Dewey: 770/.5.

Industrial Screen (U.K.); ISSN: 0446-0855. Note: v.1-v.7, Mar/Apr 1957-Dec 1963. Absorbed by **Film User** in Jan 1964. **Film User** incorporated by **Audio Visual** in Jan 1972. Discontinued publication.

Infocus: Academy of Canadian Cinema & Television (Canada). Alternate title: **Newsletter. Academy of Canadian Cinema & Television** (0834-3179). Academy of Canadian Cinema & Television, 653 Yonge St., 2nd Floor, Toronto, Ont. M4Y 1Z9 Canada; (quarterly); ISSN: 0834-3187; OCLC 16440075. Note: v.1,n.1 Spring 1982 -. Newsletter for members, keeping them current with the latest happenings in the Canadian motion picture and television industries. This academy determines the Genie Awards, the Canadian equivalent of the Oscar. Text in English and French. PN1993.4; Dewey: 791.43/06/0971.

Information aus dem Deutschen Institut fur Filmkunde (W.Germany). See: **Deutschen Institut fur Filmkunde. Information aus dem Deutschen Institut fur Filmkunde.**

Information Film Producers of America Communicator (U.S.). See: **I.F.P.A. Communicator.**

Informations C.N.C. (France). Alternate title: **Bulletin d'Information du Centre National de la Cinematographie.** Center National de la Cinematographie, 12, rue de Lubeck, 75784 Paris, France. Tel: 1 45.05.14.40; (bimonthly); ISSN: 0397-8435; OCLC 2710578.
Note: n.1, Jul 1947 -.
Compiles statistical analyses of film productions in France. Reviews film books. Contains international information about film and video production.
PN1993.5.F7A3; Dewey: 338.4/7/791430944.

The Informer (U.S.); Seattle Film Society, 4245B Greenwood Ave. North, Seattle, WA 98103; (monthly); ISSN: n/a.
Note: unnumbered, [198u]-Feb 1986.
A fan magazine offering articles on favorite films, reviews of recent feature film releases, opinions, and essays for ardent moviegoers. A newsletter of the Seattle Film Society. Discontinued publication.

Initiatives (U.K.); Society for Education in Film and Television (SEFT), Crystal Management Liaison Ltd., 46 Theobalds Rd., London WC1X 8NW, U.K.; (3 times/yr).
Note: [n.1] 1969? -.
Newsletter for members of SEFT. An education bulletin for teachers and students of cinema studies.

Institute of Electrical & Electronics Engineers Journal on Selected Areas in Communications (U.S.). See: **I.E.E.E. Journal on Selected Areas in Communications.**

Institute of Electrical & Electronics Engineers Transactions on Broadcasting (U.S.). See: **I.E.E.E. Transactions on Broadcasting.**

Institute of Electrical & Electronics Engineers Transactions on Communications (U.S.). See: **I.E.E.E. Transactions on Communications.**

Inter Media (U.K.). See: **InterMedia.**

Interfilm. Bulletin of the International Interchurch Film Center
(Netherlands). See: **Interfilm Reports**.

Interfilm Reports (Netherlands). Alternate title: **Interfilm.**
Bulletin of the International Interchurch Film Centre.
International Interchurch Film Centre, PO Box 515, Hilversum,
Netherlands; (annual); ISSN: OCLC 4161019.
Note: ed.1, 1976 -.
Ecumenical journal concerned with the religious aspects of
motion pictures, video and television. Compiles a list of
film festivals and gatherings with religious themes.
PN1993.3.I537a; Dewey: 791.43/05.

InterMedia (U.K.). Alternate title: **Inter Media**. International
Institute of Communications, Tavistock House South, Tavistock
Square, London, England WC1H 9LF; (irregular); ISSN: 0309-
118X; OCLC 3049412.
Note: [v.1], Mar/Apr 1973 -.
Broadcasting magazine with an international scope;
contributors report from a worldwide constituency: Malaysia,
Korea, Canada, Britain, Australia, Japan, Ireland, and
others. Articles cover the development of broadcasting
standards, popular culture and the economics of global
television, international copyrights, HDTV, growth and
planning.
HE8689.I55; 384.54/05.

International Buyer's Guide (U.S.). Alternate title: **Billboard's**
International Buyer's Guide. Billboard, Dept. EB, 1515
Broadway, New York, NY 10036; (annual); ISSN: n/a; OCLC
11732817.
Note: ed.1, 1970/71 -.
International business directory for the music and video
industries. Predominantly music and recordings, but also
lists manufacturers and wholesalers of hardware, software and
accessories for compact disc, videodisc, videocassettes and
video games.

International Communications Industries Association. Membership
Directory (U.S.). Alternate title: **I.C.I.A. Membership**
Directory. International Communications Industries
Association, 3150 Spring St., Fairfax, VA 22031-2399. Tel:
703/272-7200; (annual); ISSN: n/a; OCLC 10708917.

Note: ed.1 1984 -.
A directory to audiovisual dealers, media consultants, rental
companies, distributors, manufacturers and producers.
Entries include names, addresses, telephone numbers and codes
for products, sales and services offered.
HD9697.A843U66; Dewey: 338.7/61001553.

**International Documentary: The Newsletter of the International
Documentary Association** (U.S.); International Documentary
Association, 1551 S. Robertson Blvd., Los Angeles, CA 90035.
Tel: 213/284-8422; (quarterly); ISSN: 0742-5333; OCLC
10378920.
Note: v.1,n.1, Spring 1982 -.
"Formed to promote non fiction film and video, to encourage
and celebrate the documentary arts and sciences, and to
support the efforts of non fiction film and videomakers
throughout the world." Newsletter reporting on distribution
outlets for documentaries, marketing advice, festival
listings, information on public and cable television, and the
latest video equipment. Membership can include anyone
sympathetic to the documentary cause, e.g. academics, musicians,
film editors, TV programmers, scriptwriters, as well as people
working in the field.
PN1995.9.D6I52.

International Federation of Film Archives. Bulletin (Belgium).
See: **F.I.A.F. Bulletin.**

International Federation of Television Archives Bulletin
(International). See: **F.I.A.T./I.F.T.A. Bulletin.**

International Film and T.V. Yearbook (U.K.). See: **Screen
International Film and Television Yearbook.**

International Film and Television Yearbook (U.K.). See: **Screen
International Film and Television Yearbook.**

International Film Guide (U.K.); Tantivy Press, Ltd., 2 Bedford
Gardens, London, England W8 7EH. Tel: (01) 661 215; (annual);
ISSN: n/a; ISBN: 0-900730-25-0.
Note: v.1, 1964 -.
A world survey of films by country, including Third World and
developing nations. A good source for information on hard to

find foreign films. Each edition includes biographical
sketches of several noted directors.
PN1993.3.I544.

International Index to Film Periodicals (U.K.); F.I.A.F.
(International Federation of Film Archives), 113 Canalot
Studios, 222 Kensal Rd., London, England W10 5BN; (annual);
ISSN: 0000-0388; OCLC 1783618.
Note: v.1, 1972 -.
This publication indexes articles on film and the
entertainment industry in many of the world's most important
film magazines. The articles are accessed by subject, title and
personal name. Available in printed form and on microfiche.
Z5784.M9I49; Dewey: 016.79143.

International Index to Television Periodicals (U.K.); F.I.A.F.
(International Federation of Film Archives), 113 Canalot
Studios, 222 Kensal Rd., London, England W10 5BN; (irregular);
ISSN: 0143-5663; ISBN 23-7-8806060212; OCLC 9721641.
Note: ed.1, 1979/1980 -.
This companion to the **International Index to Film Periodicals**
indexes many important television magazines from around
the world by subject, title and personal name. Most of the
periodicals are indexed by individuals working in member
archives in the countries where the magazines are published.
Periodicals indexed are chosen according to their social,
economic, political, critical or aesthetic viewpoints. Also
available on microfiche.
Z5784.M9I49.

International Journal of Instructional Media (U.S.); Westwood
Press, Inc., 251 Park Ave. South, 14th Floor, New York, NY
10010. Tel: 212/420-8008; (quarterly); ISSN: 0092-1815; OCLC
1789161.
Note: v.1, Fall 1973 -.
Professional journal for teachers and librarians examining
the application and use of educational media in the
classroom. Articles analyze how to achieve the best
instructional value when using film, video, close circuit
television, and other media as an adjunct to teaching.
LB1043.I574; Dewey: 371.3/078.

International Journal of Micrographics and Video Technology
(U.K.). Merger of: **Microdoc** (0026-2684) and **Micropublishing
of Current Periodicals** (0364-3999). Pergamon Press, Inc.,
Fairview Park, Elmsford, NY 10523; (quarterly); ISSN: 0743-
9636; OCLC 7932883.
Note: v.1-v.20,n.3, 1962-1982 as **Microdoc**; renumbered v.1,n.1,
1982- as **International Journal of Micrographics and Video
Technology.**
Concerned with micrographic preservation and technology for
information storage and retrieval. Includes microfilm,
microfiche, videodisc, laser disk, CD-ROM.
Z265.I565; Dewey: 686.4/3/05.

International Motion Picture Almanac (U.S.). Formerly: **Motion
Picture Almanac; Motion Picture and Television Almanac.**
Quigley Publishing Company, Inc., 159 West 53rd St., New
York, NY 10019. Tel: 212/247-3100; (annual); ISSN: 0074-7084;
OCLC 1624233.
Note: ed.1-ed.6, 1929-1935/36 as **Motion Picture Almanac**;
ed.7-ed.21, 1936/37-1951/52 as **International Motion Picture
Almanac**; ed.22-ed.24, 1952/53-1955 as **Motion Picture and
Television Almanac**; ed.25, 1956- as **International Motion Picture
Almanac.**
A directory of people involved in the industry. Arranged
alphabetically by last name, the entry includes
profession(s), birth date, address and credits. Contains a
directory of motion picture services, such as film labs,
storage facilities, talent agencies, production companies, and
theater circuits. Includes listing of motion picture corporations
with address, telephone numbers and corporate personnel.
PN1993.3.I55; Dewey: 791.43/05.

**International Museum of Photography at George Eastman House
Newsletter** (U.S.). Alternate title: **George Eastman House
Newsletter.** International Museum of Photography at George
Eastman House, 900 East Ave., Rochester, NY 14607. Tel: 716/
271-3361; (quarterly); ISSN: n/a; OCLC 5518234.
Note: v.1,n.1 Summer 1979 -.
A newsletter for members, contributors and volunteers.
Contains information about the museum and film archive at the
International Museum of Photography, such as new exhibits,
film programs, lectures, visiting scholars and other
scheduled events.

International Projectionist (U.S.). See: **Greater Amusements and International Projectionist**.

International T.V. & Video Guide (U.K.); Tantivy Press c/o New York Zoetrope, 80 East 11th St., New York, NY 10003; (annual); ISSN: n/a; ISBN 0900730-28-5; OCLC 9376481.
Note: ed.1-ed.5, 1983-1987.
Directory concentrating on English language television series, serials, and specials. Ceased publication in 1987.
PN1992.I57; Dewey: 384.55/4/05.

International Talent & Touring Directory (U.S.). Formerly: **Billboard International Talent Directory** (0190-9649); Alternate titles: **Billboard International Talent & Touring Directory**; **Billboard's International Talent & Touring Directory**. Billboard Publications, Dept. EB, 1515 Broadway, NY 10036. Tel: 800/223-7524; (annual); ISSN: 0732-0124; OCLC 13910485.
Note: ed.1-ed.2, 1979/80-1980/81 as **Billboard International Talent Directory**; ed.3, 1981/82- as **International Talent & Touring Directory**.
A comprehensive list of U.S. and international contacts for talent, booking agencies, facilities, services and products. For promoters and managers of entertainment tours featuring performing artists.
ML1.B51355; Dewey: 780.42/025.

International Television (U.S.). See: **Corporate Television**.

International Television Almanac (U.S.). See: **International Television & Video Almanac**.

International Television & Video Almanac (U.S.). Formerly: **International Television Almanac**. Quigley Publishing Co., Inc., 159 West 53rd St., New York, NY 10019. Tel: 212/247-3100; (annual); ISSN: 0539-0761; OCLC 1642171.
Note: ed.1-ed.31, 1956-1986 as **International Television Almanac**; ed.32, 1987- as **International Television & Video Almanac**.
Directory of professionals working in the broadcasting and video industries. Arranged alphabetically by name, each entry lists profession, date of birth, education and credits. Separate section contains a directory of services, such as

studio suppliers, talent agents, laboratories, equipment manufacturers, advertising agencies.
HE8700.I57.

Invision (U.K.). Alternate title: **In Vision.** International Thomson Publishing, Ltd., 100 Avenue Rd., London, NW3 3TP England. Tel: 01-935-6611; (monthly); ISSN: n/a; OCLC 14589813. Note: n.1, 1986 -.
Issued as a monthly supplement to **Broadcast.** Contains information about the latest technical equipment and products for the television and radio industries.

Iris (France); IRIS c/o Marc Vernet, 17, rue Vitruve, 75020 Paris, France; (2 times/yr); ISSN: 0751-7033; OCLC 9425440. Note: v.1,n.1 Spring 1983 -.
Serious journal for film scholars; contains studies of film theory, history and criticism. One issue presents several articles written on a certain topic. Each article published in French or English and abstracted in the other language.
PN1995.I75; Dewey: 791.43/05.

Iskusstvo Kino (U.S.S.R.). Formerly: **Proletarskoe Kino; Sovetskoe Kino.** State Committee of Cinematography and the Union of Cinematographers of the USSR, Ulitsa usievicha 9, 125319 Moscow A-319, U.S.S.R.; (monthly); ISSN: 0130-6405; OCLC 9170194.
Note: v.1-v.2, 1931-1932 as **Proletarskoe Kino**; v.3-v.5, 1933-1935 as **Sovetskoe Kino**; v.6, 1936- as **Iskusstvo Kino**.
Presents information about Soviet filmmaking from the cameraman's point of view. Articles contain opinions on colorization, cinerama, cinematography and East-West relations. Published in Cyrillic.
PN1993.K477.

-J-

J.P.F.& T. (U.S.). See: **Journal of Popular Film and Television.**

Jaarboek van de Belgische Film (Belgium). See: **Annuaire du Film Belge = Jaarboek van de Belgische Film.**

Jahrbuch der Schweizer Filmindustrie (Switzerland). See: **Schweizer Filmindex = Index Suisse du Cinema = Indice Svizzero del Cinema.**

Jeune Cinema (France); Federation Jean Vigo des Cine Clubs des Jeunes, 8 rue Lamarck, Paris 18e, France; (9 times/yr). Note: n.1, Sep/Oct 1964 -.
Organized as a forum for young people with an interest in cinema and video. Keeps current with contemporary feature film production. Specializes in films popular with younger audiences. Published in French.

Jeune Cinema & Theatre (Czechoslovakia). See: **Young/Jeune Cinema & Theatre.**

Jewish Media Roundup (U.S.); Jewish Media Service, 15 E. 26th St., New York, NY 10010-1579. Tel: 212/532-4949; (quarterly). Note: [v.1-10] 1977-1987; discontinued, June 1987.
"National clearinghouse for the creative use and evaluation of media in Jewish programming and teaching." Provided a source of information about Jewish-related films and TV distributed in the United States. Kept current with the latest film and television productions from Israel. Ceased publication.

Journal of Broadcasting & Electronic Media (U.S.); Broadcast Education Association, University of Massachusetts, Dept. of Communication, Amherst, MA 01003. Tel: 413/545-2795; (quarterly); ISSN: 0883-8151; ISSN 0021-938X; OCLC 11850577. Note: v.1,n.1 Winter 1956/1957 -.
Scholarly journal containing long articles on broadcasting, telecommunications and mass media. Examines the influence of the electronic media on popular culture, news gathering, public affairs, lifestyles and societal behavior. Reviews

textbooks, software and videotapes.
PN1991.J6; Dewey: 384.54/05.

Journal of Communication (U.S.); University of Pennsylvania, 3620
Walnut St., Philadelphia, PA 19104-6220; (quarterly); ISSN:
0021-9916; OCLC 1754508.
Note: v.1,n.1 May 1951 -.
Academic journal with articles on the theory, practice
and policy of communications and the media. Includes
research and policy developments in the communications field.
Focuses on TV and broadcasting, although also includes
articles on printed media. Analyzes the impact of mass
communications on culture. Reviews books.
P87.J6; Dewey: 001.5/05.

Journal of Educational Technology Systems (U.S.); Baywood
Publishing Co., Inc., Box 337, Amityville, NY 11701. Tel:
516/691-1270; (quarterly); ISSN: 0047-2395; OCLC 1785037.
Note: v.1,n.1 Summer 1972 -.
Publication designed for educators, audiovisual specialists
and librarians. Analyzes the impact of the new instructional
media on education. Reviews audiovisual equipment, VCRs,
videotapes, videodiscs, computers and software.
LB1028.3.J68; Dewey: 371.3/05.

The Journal of Fiber Optics (U.S.). See: **Lightwave: The Journal
of Fiber Optics.**

Journal of Film and Video (U.S.). Formerly: **Journal of the
University Film Producers Association; Journal of the
University Film Association** (0041-9311); **Journal of the
University Film and Video Association** (0734-919X). University
Film and Video Association, Rosary College, 79 E. Division
St., River Forest, IL 60305; (quarterly); ISSN: 0742-4671;
OCLC 8392102.
Note: v.1-v.19, 1949-1967 as **Journal of the University Film
Producers Association**; v.20-v.33, 1968-1981 as **Journal of
the University Film Association**; v.34-v.35, 1982-1983 as
Journal of the University Film and Video Association; v.36,
1984- as **Journal of Film and Video.**
Learned publication focusing on methodologies for teaching
film and video history, criticism, and production on a college
level. Well researched and documented articles written by

professors and graduate students. Reviews books on video and cinema studies.
PN1993.U63; Dewey: 791.43/09.

Journal of Mass Media Ethics (U.S.); Department of Communications, Brigham Young University, Provo, UT 84602. Tel: 801/378-3250; (2 times/yr); ISSN: 0890-0523; OCLC 13338929.
Note: v.1,n.1 Fall/Winter 1985/1986 -.
"Devoted to issues in mass media ethics." Academic journal surveying the field of mass communications in terms of moral values. Studies how journalists and broadcasters cover controversial and political topics. Looks at how information is presented by the media: the treatment of background material and off-the-record reports, the use of video simulation, computer imaging, file footage and montage. Reviews scholarly texts on communication theory.
P94.J68; Dewey: 175.1/05.

Journal of Photography and Motion Pictures of the International Museum of Photography (U.S.). See: **Image.**

Journal of Popular Film (U.S.). See: **Journal of Popular Film and Television.**

Journal of Popular Film and Television (U.S.). Formerly: **Journal of Popular Film** (0047-2719); alternate title: **J.P.F.& T.**
Heldref Publications, 4000 Albemarle St., NW, Washington, DC 20016; (quarterly); ISSN: 0195-6051; OCLC 4652347.
Note: v.1,n.1-v.6,n.4, Winter 1972-1978 as **Journal of Popular Film**; v.7,n.1, 1978- as **Journal of Popular Film and Television.**
Concentrates on commercial cinema and television: the stars, directors, producers, studios, networks, audience, and ratings, and examines them in the context of popular culture. Annual index published in the Winter issue.
PN1993.J66; Dewey: 791.43/05.

The Journal of the Producers Guild of America (U.S.). Formerly: **The Journal of the Screen Producers Guild.** Alternate titles: **Producers Guild of America. Journal; Screen Producers Guild. Journal.** The Producers Guild of America, 8201 Beverly Blvd., Los Angeles, CA 90048. Tel: 213/651-0084; (quarterly); ISSN:

0032-9703; OCLC 2266498.
Note: v.1,n.1-v.8,n.4, Apr 1952-Dec 1966 as **The Journal of the Screen Producers Guild**; v.9,n.1, Mar 1967- as **The Journal of the Producers Guild of America.**
"A magazine of opinion sponsored and published by the Producers Guild of America." Thoughtful articles analyzing motion picture and television production. Covers such topics as violence in the movies, TV criticism, creative scriptwriting and foreign film appeal in the U.S. Studies the current film market and ventures financial predictions. Reprints older writings by famous Hollywood producers from the 1930s and 1940s. Reviews film and television books.

Journal of the S.M.P.T.E. (U.S.). See: **S.M.P.T.E. Journal.**

The Journal of the Screen Producers Guild (U.S.). See: **The Journal of the Producers Guild of America.**

The Journal of the Society for Education in Film and Television (U.K.). See: **Screen Incorporating Screen Education.**

Journal of the University Film and Video Association (U.S.). See: **Journal of Film and Video.**

Journal of the University Film Association (U.S.). See: **Journal of Film and Video.**

Journal of the University Film Producers Association (U.S.). See: **Journal of Film and Video.**

Joven Cine & Teatro (Czechoslovakia). See: **Young/Jeune Cinema & Theatre.**

JoyStik (U.S.); Publications International, Ltd., 7373 N. Cicero, Lincolnwood, IL 60646. Tel: 708/676-3470; (bimonthly); ISSN: n/a; OCLC 8778077.
Note: v.1-v.7, 1982-1988.
Programed for winning at video arcade games. Each issue contains a detailed analysis and breakdown of several games. Provides information on hardware and software, techniques and strategies for winning, and new products. Ceased publication.

Jugend, Film, Fernsehen (W.Germany). See: **Medien und Erziehung.**

Jugoslavenski Casopis za Filmska Pitanja. See: **Filmska Kultura.**

Jugoslavija Film News (Yugoslavia). Formerly: **The Yugoslav Film** (0512-9877). Import-Export Motion Picture, 1000 Belgrade, Knez Mihailova, No.19 Post Box 243, Yugoslavia; (irregular); ISSN: 0448-021X.
Note: v.1,n.1-v.3,n.6/7, Summer 1961-Winter/Spring 1963 as **The Yugoslav Film**; v.3, Summer? 1963 [n.20]- as **Jugoslavija Film News.**
Promotes Yugoslavian films for export to the West. Contains descriptions of the films with still photos, cast and credits. Interviews performers and directors. Published in English and French.

Jump Cut (U.S.); Jump Cut Associates, PO Box 865, Berkeley, CA 94701. Tel: 415/658-4482; (irregular); ISSN: 0146-5546; OCLC 2971578.
Note: n.1, May/Jun 1974 -.
Populist film magazine concerned with film theory and criticism. Commentaries are political and social interpretations of cinema studies. Keeps current with the latest new cinema from Latin America and Africa. Reviews films. Available on microfilm.

-K-

K.C.E.T. Magazine (U.S.). Formerly: **Gambit** (0009-1480); **The Dial from KCET/28.** KCET-TV, Viewer Services, 4401 Sunset Blvd., Los Angeles, CA 90027. Tel: 213/666-6500; (monthly); ISSN: 0273-4060; OCLC 7055120.
Note: May 1970-Aug 1980 as **Gambit**; v.1-v.8, 1980-1987 as **The Dial from KCET/28**; renumbered v.1,n.1 Jan 1988- as **K.C.E.T. Magazine.**
Programming guide to the PBS television station for the Los Angeles area. Contains background information on current programs and upcoming series and specials.
PN1992.8D53; Dewey: 791.44/0973.

K.C.T.S. Magazine (U.S.). Formerly: **The Dial from K.C.T.S./9** (0733-6055). KCTS-TV, Viewer Services, 401 Mercer, Seattle, WA 98109. Tel: 206/728-6463; (monthly); ISSN: 0273-4079; OCLC 7910527.
Note: v.1,n.1-v.7,n.4 Sep 1980-Dec 1986 as **The Dial from K.C.T.S./9**; renumbered v.1,n.1 Jan 1987- as **K.C.T.S. Magazine.**
Programming guide for the PBS station KCTS in Seattle, Washington.
PN1992.8.P8D53; Dewey: 791.44/0973.

Kabel & Satellit (W.Germany). Alternate title: **Kabel und Satellit.** Neue Mediengesellschaft Ulm mbH, 111, Karlstr. 41, 7900 Ulm, West Germany. Tel: 0731 152001; (bimonthly); ISSN: n/a.
Note: v.1,n.1 1988 -.
Technical magazine published in German covering the independent broadcasting industries in Europe. Focuses on cable and satellite transmission technology. Articles on growth potential, programming, regulations and censorship.

Kabel und Satellit (W.Germany). See: **Kabel & Satellit.**

The Kagan Cable T.V. Financial Databook (U.S.). See: **The Cable T.V. Financial Databook.**

The Kagan Media Index (U.S.); Paul Kagan Associates, Inc., 126
    Clock Tower Place, Carmel, CA 93923-8734. Tel: 408/624-1536;
    (monthly); ISSN: 0893-2700; OCLC 15481089.
    Note: n.1, Mar 10, 1987 -.
    An encapsulation of the 24 other Paul Kagan Associates'
    newsletters tracking the economic health of the cable
    broadcasting industry. Includes charts, graphs, statistics
    and stock exchange data.
    Dewey: 338 11.

Kaitafilmi (Finland); Finnish Society of Amateur Film Makers,
    Foreign Relations Secretary, Norotie 12 B 13, SF-01600,
    Vantaa 60 Finland; (5 times/yr.).
    Note: n.1, 1954 -.
    Newsletter for members. Forum for amateur film and
    videomakers in Finland.

Katalog Jugoslovenskog Dokumentarnog I Kratkometraznog Filma
    (Yugoslavia). English translation title: **Catalogue of
    Yugoslav Documentary and Short Films**. Jugoslavija Film,
    Beograd, Knez Mihajlova 19/V, Yugoslavia; (annual); ISSN:
    n/a; OCLC 13247738.
    Note: [v.1] 1960 -.
    A compilation of Yugoslav documentary and short films
    produced each year. Published in Serbo-Croatian, English,
    French, German and Russian. Entry includes title in five
    languages, production company, format, length, director,
    scriptwriter, studio and short synopsis.
    PN1995.9.D6K34; PN1998.A1F44.

Kemp's Film and Television Yearbook (International) (U.K.). See:
    Kemp's International Film & Television Year Book.

Kemp's International Film & Television Directory (U.K.). See:
    Kemp's International Film & Television Year Book.

Kemp's International Film & Television Year Book (U.K.).
    Formerly: **Kemp's International Film & Television Directory**
    (0453-493X); **Kemp's Film and Television Yearbook
    (International)** (0075-5427). The Kemps Group, 1-5 Bath St.,
    London, EC1V 92A England. Tel: 01-253 4761; (annual); ISSN:
    8665-1563; OCLC 4423012.

Note: v.1-v.14, 1956-1969 as **Kemp's International Film & Television Directory**; v.15-v.22, 1970-1977/78 as **Kemp's Film and Television Yearbook (International)**; v.23, 1978/1979- as **Kemp's International Film & Television Year Book**. Divided into two parts: the first section covers British motion picture and television industry sales, products and services; the second part, which is arranged alphabetically by country, lists international film and television companies. The detailed British section gives names and addresses for organizations connected with the industry: agents, audiovisual equipment, cameras, costumes, distributors, festivals, insurance services, labs, makeup, music, production companies, properties, scenery, sound equipment, special effects, TV stations and video products. PN1998.A1K39; Dewey: 338.4/7/7914305.

Kine Weekly (U.K.). See: **Screen International**.

Kinematograph (W.Germany); Deutsches Filmmuseum, Schumainkai 41, D 6000 Frankfurt am Main, West Germany; (irregular); ISSN: n/a.
Note: [n.1] 1984? -.
Scholarly journal concentrating on silent film history before 1920. Studies include the influence of theater on film, the development of art and set design, the beginnings of feature film production, the use of melodrama, the popularity of silent comedy, and production techniques. Offers new theories on cinema studies for pre-1920 filmmaking.
Published in German.

Kinematograph and Lantern Weekly (U.K.). See: **Screen International**.

Kinematograph Weekly (U.K.). See: **Screen International**.

Kino (Poland). Alternate title: **Kino; Miesiecznik Poswiecony Tworczosci i Kulturze Filmowej**. Kino, 00-056 Warszawa, ul. Kredytowa 5/7, Poland. Tel: 26-67-85; 26-83-80; (monthly); ISSN: 0023-1673.
Note: v.1, 1966 -.
A Polish-language photo-magazine concentrating on Polish films, television shows, and performers. Exhibits an interest in American and Western European cinema through reviews, photos

and interviews. Reports on film festivals. A panorama of popular culture.
PN1993.K475.

Kino (U.S.S.R.). Kino, 5 Schmerlya St., Box 226037, Riga, Latvia, U.S.S.R. Tel: 520 140; 520 668; (monthly); ISSN: n/a.
Note: n.1, 194u -.
Magazine containing articles on popular film culture in the Soviet Union. Publishes biographical sketches of actors and actresses; keeps current with film festivals and awards; published in Russian and Latvian.

Kino: Filme der Bundesrepublik Deutschland (W.Germany); Export-Union des Deutschen Films e.V., Tuerkenstrasse 93, D-8000 Munich 40, West Germany. Tel: 089-390095/96; (quarterly).
Note: v.1, 1973 -.
A guide to export offices for German films, designed for booking agents and film programmers. Lists all West German features made throughout the year, with synopses, cast, credits and distributors.

Kino; German Film (W.Germany); Dorothea & Ronald Holloway, Helgolander Ufer 6, D-1000 Berlin 21, West Germany. Tel: 030 391 6167; (quarterly).
Note: v.1, 1968 -.
Promotes West German films in English-speaking nations. Contains latest information about German features, filmmakers and productions-in-progress. Includes interviews, filmographies and reviews.

Kino; Miesiecznik Poswiecony Tworczosci i Kulturze Filmowej (Poland); See: **Kino.**

Kino; Obrazkovy Filmovy Crtnactidenik (Czechoslovakia). Subtitle varies: **Kino; Zve do Kina.** Kino, Redakce 11648, Praha 1, Vaclavske nam 43 Czechoslovakia. Tel: 229051; (biweekly); ISSN: n/a; OCLC 6181475.
Note: v.1, 1946? -.
Popular fan magazine devoted to international film and television stars. Many photographs illustrate gossip pieces; includes American and West European performers as well as favorite Czech actors and actresses. Includes information on film clubs, latest releases, news about animation and a

calendar of film showings around the country.
PN1993.K48.

Kino; Zve do Kina (Czechoslovakia). See: **Kino; Obrazkovy Filmovy Crtnactidenik.**

Kino i Vreme (Bulgaria); Bulgarska Nacionalna Filmoteka, 1000 Sofia, 36 Gurko Str., Bulgaria. Tel: 87 02 96; (annual).
Note: v.1, 1972 -.
Published in Cyrillic with contents summaries in English and French. Prints long scholarly studies on film history relating to Socialism and Bulgarian society, such as "the influence of silent Soviet cinema on the film activities of German artists," "cinema and the New Deal," and "a view of Bulgarian documentary from its beginning to the end of World War II." Profiles famous directors, concentrating on Bulgarian and East European talents; includes Western directors to a lesser extent. Contains obituaries for cinematic artists who have died during the past year.
PN1993.5.B8K55.

Kino i Vremia (U.S.S.R.); Iskusstvo, 103009 Moscow, Sobinovsky per. 3, U.S.S.R. Tel: (095)203-58-72; (annual); ISSN: n/a; OCLC 5140527.
Note: v.1, 1977 -.
Published in Cyrillic, no translations, no illustrations.
Long articles analyze the cinematic arts in the Soviet Union. Covers Russian film history, theory and criticism.
PN1993.K477.

Kino Izkustvo (Bulgaria). See: **Kinoizkustvo.**

Kino TV Video (Poland). See: **Ekran; Kino TV Video**

Kino-Technik (W.Germany). See: **Fernseh- und Kino-Technik.**

Kino-und Fernseh-Almanach (E.Germany). See: **Prisma; Kino-und Fernseh-Almanach.**

Kinoizkustvo (Bulgaria). Alternate title: **Kino Izkustvo.** Komitet za Kultura, pl. Slaveikov 11, 4. etazh, Sofia, Bulgaria; (monthly); ISSN: 0323-9993; OCLC 17372186.
Note: v.1, 1935 -.

Scholarly journal with lengthy articles on film theory, such as an analysis of the portrayal of political struggle in the motion pictures of Eisenstein. Some of the articles include an examination of scriptwriting, documentary filmmaking, reminiscences of John Ford and the impact of video on film production. Critiques Soviet and Eastern Bloc films. In Cyrillic, but has summaries of contents in English. PN1993.K54.

Kinorabotnik (Bulgaria); Tsentur za Filmova Informatsiia, Propaganda i Reklama kum DP, "Razprostranenie na Filmi," ul. G. Genov, 23, Sofia, Bulgaria. Tel: 87-61-85; (monthly); ISSN: 0204-8388; 0453-8935; OCLC 6227913.
Note: [n.1] 1968 -.
Popular magazine published in Cyrillic. Reviews features, mostly those produced in the Soviet Union and Eastern bloc. However, does pick up some Western titles. Includes articles on performers, essays on film history, and reports on international film festivals.
PN1993.5.B8K57.

Kolnoa (Israel). English translation title: **Cinema**. Tel Aviv Cinematheque, Municipality Building, Tel Aviv, Israel; (quarterly); OCLC 8205952.
Note: v.1-v.8, 1974-1981?
Articles and essays on contemporary film culture: women in the cinema, politics and film, Third World cinema. Ceased publication?
PN1993.5.I86K64

Korea Cinema (Korea); Motion Picture Promotion Corporation, 34-5, 3-ka, Namsan-dong, Chung-ku, Seoul 100, Republic of Korea; (annual); ISSN: n/a.
Note: [v.1], 1967 -.
A directory to Korean films made during the past year. Each entry includes production company, director, screenwriter, cinematographer, cast, running time, synopsis and still. Includes theater-going statistics; gross receipts, attendance figures, number of theaters, and foreign imports.

Kosmorama (Denmark); Danske Film Museum, Store Sondervoldestraede, DK-1419 Copenhagen K, Denmark. Tel: (01) 57 6500; (quarterly); ISSN: 0023-4222; OCLC 5162166.

Note: v.1,n.1 Oct 1954 -.
Artistically designed film journal reviewing the latest
international feature releases. Contains articles on film
personalities with extensive filmographies. Publishes
obituaries/homages to the famous dead, such as Orson Welles
and John Huston. Reports on new cinematic developments in
various countries. Published in Danish.
PN1993.K63.

Kritisch Filmforum (Netherlands). See: **Skoop/Kritisch Filmforum.**

Kultur Chronik (W.Germany); Inter Nationes e.V. (IN),
    Kennedyallee 91-103, D-5300 Bonn 2 (Bad Godesberg) West
    Germany; (bimonthly); ISSN: 0724-343X; OCLC 11363811.
    Note: v.1, 1983 -.
"News and views from the Federal Republic of Germany." This
handsome and artistic publication surveys the cultural scene
in West Germany including architecture, literature, film,
television, music and photography. Publishes separate
editions in German, English, French and Spanish.
DD260.3.K84; Dewey: 943.005.

-L-

The **L.P.T.V. Report** (U.S.); Kompas/Biel & Associates, Inc., PO
  Box 25510, Milwaukee, WI 53225-0510. Tel: 414/781-0188;
  (monthly); ISSN: 0892-5585; OCLC 15246929.
  Note: v.1,n.1 Sep 1986 -.
  Newsletter for low power television stations, including "news
  and features for the community television industry." Covers
  products, services, legal and technical advice, antennas and
  other equipment, licenses, permits, and programming.

Lamp (U.S.); Light Audio Media Programs, Dept. of Art Media
  Studies, College of Visual and Performing Arts, Syracuse
  University, Syracuse, NY 13244; (annual); ISSN: n/a; OCLC
  15598149.
  Note: v.1-v.3, 1984-1986.
  Academic publication with articles on film history, theory
  and criticism. Ceased publication.

Landers Film Reviews (U.S.). Formerly: **Bertha Landers Film
  Reviews**. Landers Associates, PO Box 27309, Escondido, CA
  92027; (quarterly); ISSN: 0023-785X; OCLC 5063065.
  Note: v.1-v.4, 1956-1959 as **Bertha Landers Film Reviews**; v.5,
  1960- as **Landers Film Reviews**.
  A valuable information guide designed for librarians,
  teachers, audiovisual specialists, and anyone who buys films
  and multimedia for schools and public libraries. Reviews
  educational, non-theatrical, independent films, giving title,
  distributor, grade level, subject matter, synopsis and
  suitability. Each issue has a useful subject index. Also
  publishes an annual index with subject and title access.
  PN1995.L27; Dewey: 791.11.

The **Laser Disc Newsletter** (U.S.); Laser Disc Newsletter, 496A
  Hudson St., Suite 428, New York, NY 10014. Tel: 212/242-3324;
  (monthly); ISSN: 0749-5250; OCLC 11136006.
  Note: n.1, Sep 1984 -.
  Newsletter for laser disc buyers and collectors. Reviews

motion picture releases on laser disc. Accepts advertising for buying, selling and trading discs. Gives latest information on new laser disc technology and rates equipment.

Latest Composite Feature Release Schedule (U.S.); Exhibitor Relations. Co., 116 N. Robertson Blvd., Suite 708, Los Angeles, CA 90048. Tel: 213/657-2005; (monthly); ISSN: 0889-4566; OCLC 14073142.
Note: [v.1], 1974 -.
Oversized chart listing features in release or scheduled release by American distributors. Companies include: Buena Vista, Columbia, MGM/UA, Orion, Paramount, Tri-Star, Twentieth Century-Fox, Universal, Warner Bros. and Weintraub. Also charts pictures from smaller companies: Atlantic, New World, Vestron, Cannon and Concorde. Designed for theater owners, booking agents and film programmers who need to schedule programs in advance. Charts releases by date: Summer, Fall, Christmas, Jan/Feb, etc. Exhibitor Relations also publish "Exhibitor Twice-Weekly Service" and "Distributor Twice-Weekly Service" for the industry.
Dewey: 791 11.

Legal Video Review (U.S.); Lawrence R. Cohen Media Library, Social Law Library, 1200 Courthouse, Boston, MA 02108. Tel: 617/495-4840; (quarterly); ISSN: 0898-9427; OCLC 12257128.
Note: v.1,n.1 May 1985 -.
Contains reviews and appraisals of legal videotapes available to law schools, professors, librarians and students. Goal is "to bridge the preview gap and to reduce the number of unworthwhile presentations." Entries give distribution information and pass or fail grades for the law tapes.
Dewey: 340 11.

Levende Billeder (Denmark); Forlaget Levende Billeder, ApS, Skt. Peders Straede 28 B 4, 1453 Copenhagen K, Denmark. Tel: 33 15 30 33; (monthly); ISSN: 0108-5697; OCLC 11980612.
Note: v.1, 1975 -.
Popular photo magazine keeping current with the latest international feature film releases. Articles cover film festivals, favorite directors, actors, stage performers and musical entertainers. Prints obituaries for famous movie personalities. Published in Danish.

Librarian's Video Review (U.S.); Clearview Media Corp., Rt.1, Box
25, Bowling Green, VA 22427. Tel: 800/624-0894; (quarterly);
ISSN: 0893-8393; OCLC 15749205.
Note: v.1,n.1 Winter 1986/87 -.
Designed for teachers, librarians and audiovisual
specialists, this publication provides a guide to current
non-fiction, educational and documentary videocassettes.
Rates and reviews videos for school, library and home use.
Also helpful for parents selecting videos for their children.
Z692.A93L53; Dewey: 025.2/87.

Light Wave (U.S.). See: **Lightwave: The Journal of Fiber Optics**.

Lighting Dimensions (U.S.); Lighting Dimensions Associates, 135
Fifth Ave., New York, NY 10010-7193. Tel: 212/677-5997; (8
times/yr); ISSN: 0191-541X; OCLC 3662625.
Note: v.1, Jan 1977 -.
"The magazine for the lighting professional." Articles
written by professionals about how certain effects are
achieved through lighting; shows how to create a mood, a
look, a time period. Covers theatrical lighting, television,
cinema, and video as well as architectural lighting and neon
signs.
PN2091.E4L54; Dewey: 792.025/05.

Lightwave (U.S.). See: **Lightwave: The Journal of Fiber Optics**.

Lightwave: The Journal of Fiber Optics (U.S.). Alternate titles:
Light Wave; Lightwave. Howard Rausch Associates Inc., 235
Bear Hill Rd., Waltham, MA 02154. Tel: 617/890-2700;
(monthly); ISSN: 0741-5834; OCLC 10179779.
Note: Preview issue: Oct 1983; [v.1] 1984 -.
Serious technical journal concerned with all applications of
fiber optics, from photography to telecommunications.
TA1800.L55; Dewey: 621.36/92/05.

The Listener (U.K.); British Broadcasting Corporation, 35
Marylebone High St., London W1M 4AA England. Tel: 01 927-
4950; (weekly); ISSN: 0024-4392; OCLC 5313717.
Note: v.1, Jan 16, 1929 -.
Multi-disciplinary, fine arts magazine for viewers and
listeners of B.B.C. television and radio. Features a
"listeners' guide" which describes upcoming presentations,

such as feature films, documentaries and plays on TV; jazz, classical music and talk shows on radio. Contains articles about broadcasting; reviews books, radio and television programs.
AP4.L4165.

Literature/Film Quarterly (U.S.); Salisbury State College, Salisbury, MD 21801; (quarterly); ISSN: 0090-4260; OCLC 1784960.
Note: v.1,n.1 Winter 1973 -.
Scholarly film journal focusing on the relationship between film and literature. Analyzes successful adaptations of literary works into film, screenwriting techniques, and interviews with writers and screenwriters. Reviews relevant academic books.
PN1995.3.L57; Dewey: 791.43/05.

Lo Spettacolo (Italy). See: **Spettacolo, Lo.**

Loyola Entertainment Law Journal (U.S.). Formerly: **Entertainment Law Journal** (0740-9370). Business Manager, Loyola Entertainment Law Journal, 1441 West Olympic Blvd., Los Angeles, CA 90015; (2 times/yr); ISSN: 0273-4249; OCLC 10024788.
Note: v.1, 1981 as **Entertainment Law Journal**; v.2, 1982- as **Loyola Entertainment Law Journal**.
Acts as a "dialogue between the legal community and the entertainment industry." Analyzes laws, legislation and case histories pertaining to the performing arts. Topics covered include child labor laws applied to the motion picture industry, international implications of film distribution, docu-drama defamation standards and regulations of artist representation.
K5.N8; Dewey: 344.73/099 or 344.30499.

-M-

M.B. News (U.S.). Alternate title: **Museum of Broadcasting News.**
Museum of Broadcasting, 1 East 53rd St., New York, NY 10022.
Tel: 212/752-4690; (quarterly).
Note: n.1, 1977 -.
Newsletter for the members of the Museum of Broadcasting.
Contains schedule of events, new exhibitions, programs and
retrospectives at the Museum. Writes about popular TV shows
and performers. Hosts the Critic's Choice Awards for the
most important shows. Contains news about fund raising and
receptions. Seeks to promote the best in television writing,
performances and productions.

M.E.R.Z.: Medien und Erziehung (W.Germany). See: **Medien und
Erziehung.**

M.M.R.I. (U.S.). See: **Media Review Index.**

M.N.C. Museo Nazionale del Cinema (Italy). Alternate title:
Cinema Massimo. Edito dall'Associazione, Museo Nazionale del
Cinema, Piazza S. Giovanni n.2, 10122 Torino, Italy. Tel:
(011) 5661148; (bimonthly); ISSN: n/a.
Note: v.1,n.1 Apr/May 1989 -.
The programming schedule of the Museo Nazionale in Turin,
Italy. Contains articles on Italian film history. Profiles
the directors and performers whose work is being shown at the
Museo. Includes filmographies. Published in Italian.
PN1993.4.T87.

Macguffin (Denmark); Filmtidsskriftet Macguffin, Paradisgade 7-9,
8000 Arhus C. Denmark; (irregular); ISSN: 0108-5719.
Note: n.1-n.58, 1973-1987.
Nostalgia magazine covering film history, favorite directors
and stars. Published in Danish; ceased publication.

Mad World Update (U.S.); Mad World Campaign, 2630 Adams Mill
Rd., NW 202, Washington, DC 20009-2153. Tel: 202/265-5746;
(irregular).
Note: n.1, 1985 -.

Newsletter for fans devoted to the complete restoration of
Stanley Kramer's "It's a Mad, Mad, Mad, Mad World."
Campaigns for fundraising by exhibiting the film in theaters
around the country.

Magill's Cinema Annual (U.S.); Salem Press, Inc., PO Box 50062,
Pasadena, CA 91105; (annual); ISSN: 0739-2141; OCLC 9315435.
Note: v.1, 1982 -.
Reviews significant foreign and domestic feature films from
the preceding year. Each entry includes cast and credit
information, as well as a lengthy "essay-review" on the film.
Includes notes on retrospective films, cites award
presentations and publishes obituaries. Beginning with volume
six (1987), the annual contains indexes by title, director,
screenwriter, cast members, and subject headings. For the first
five volumes, covering the years 1982-1986, there is a separately
published guidebook which indexes all the films listed in those
volumes.
PN1993.3.M34; Dewey: 791.43/75/05.

Magyar Radio (Hungary). See: **Radio-es Televizio-Ujsag.**

Making Better Movies (U.K.). Formerly: **Movie Maker** (0027-2701);
created by a merger of **Amateur Cine World, Cine Camera**, and
Film Making. Henry Greenwood & Co., Ltd., 28 Great James St.,
London, WC1N 3HL. Tel: 01-404-4202; (monthly); ISSN: 0268-
0750; OCLC 13047345.
Note: v.1-v.19,n.10, Mar 1967-Oct 1984 as **Movie Maker**;
renumbered v.1,n.1 [Mar] 1985- as **Making Better Movies**;
absorbed **Film Making,** Nov 1980;.
British based magazine for the independent filmmaker working
in 16mm, Super 8mm and video formats. Covers production
techniques, equipment, shooting, mixing sound and editing.
Gives tips about how to best use a camcorder and making home
movies. Reviews cameras and other equipment. Contains a
classified section for buying and selling goods and services.
TR845.M33; Dewey: 778.5/05.

Mannheim Analytiques (W.Germany). See: **Mannheimer Analytika
= Mannheim Analytiques.**

Mannheimer Analytika = Mannheim Analytiques (W.Germany);
University of Mannheim, Department of French Literature,

Romanistik I, Universitat Mannheim, Schloss, 6800 Mannheim I,
West Germany /RFA; (2 times/yr); ISSN: 0176-1226; OCLC
15080033.
Note: [n.1], 1983 -.
Scholarly journal analyzing all aspects of communication
studies. Discusses mass media, audiovisual advertising,
televised sport, photography and journalism, book covers,
painting and cinema, literature into film, and radio
adaptations of plays. Articles are published in German,
French and English.

Marketing New Media (U.S.); Paul Kagan Associates, Inc., 126
Clock Tower Place, Carmel, CA 93923-8734. Tel: 408/624-1536;
(biweekly); ISSN: 0743-2178; OCLC 10568843.
Note: n.1, Mar 7, 1984 -.
Newsletter concerned with tracking the sales and promotion of
cable TV, pay-TV, Satellite Master Antenna TV and Multipoint
Distribution Service. Explains how to market the competitive
new telecommunications systems.

Marquee. The Journal of the Theatre Historical Society (U.S.);
Theatre Historical Society, Chicago Center & Archives, 2215
W. North Ave., Chicago, IL 60647. Tel: 312/252-7200; (quarterly);
ISSN: 0025-3928; OCLC 1756706.
Note: v.1,n.1 Feb 1969 -.
Publishes well documented articles on historical and
architecturally significant theaters and movie palaces in the
United States. Includes many photographs illustrating both
the interiors and exteriors of the buildings, many of which
are no longer in existence. Keeps active with theater
renovation projects and reports on successes and failures at
historical preservation. Since July 1979, includes
supplement: **T.H.S. Newsletter.**

The Mass Communication Bibliographers' Newsletter (U.S.);
Association for Education in Journalism and Mass
Communication, 1621 College St., University of South
Carolina, Columbia, SC 29208-0251; (3 times/yr); ISSN: n/a.
Note: v.1,n.1 Nov 1986 -.
Newsletter for members of the Association for Education in
Journalism and Mass Communication (AEJMC). Reports on
bibliographic control of literary and data resources in the
field of mass communications. Keeps current on new studies,

evaluates collections and disseminates information. Acts as
a forum for the exchange of ideas.

Mass Media Book Notes (U.S.). See: **Communications Booknotes**.

Matrix (U.S.). See: **The Professional Communicator**.

The Mayberry Gazette (U.S.); Andy Griffith Show Appreciation
Society, 403 College Ave., Clemson, SC 29633. Tel: 803/654-
5148; (bimonthly); ISSN: 1043-2639; OCLC 19453404.
Note: v.1,n.1 Mar 1985 -.
Fan magazine for people devoted to Andy Griffith's television
series: *The Andy Griffith Show, Mayberry, R.F.D.* and
subsequent reincarnations in syndication.
Dewey: 791 11.

Media Active (U.S.). See: **Mediactive**.

Media & Methods (U.S.). Formerly: **Educators Guide to Media &
Methods** (0013-2063); alternate title: **Media and Methods**.
American Society of Media Specialists & Librarians, 1429
Walnut St., Philadelphia, PA 19102. Tel: 215/563-3501; 800/
523-4540; (5 times/yr); ISSN: 0025-6897; OCLC 817432.
Note: v.1,n.1-v.5,n.9, Sep 1964-May 1969 as **Educators Guide
to Media & Methods**; v.6,n.1 Sep 1969- as **Media & Methods**.
Designed for educators and school librarians, this journal
critiques new audiovisual products and programs for schools
and universities. Publishes an annual "Buyer's Guide and
Reference Directory" on AV equipment, computer technology,
reference books and software. Reviews films and videos,
books, MTV, databases and records and audio cassettes.
LB1043.M357; Dewey: 371.33/5.

Media and Methods (U.S.). See: **Media & Methods**.

Media & Values (U.S.). Alternate title: **Media and Values**. Media
Action Research Center, Business Office, 1962 S. Shenandoah,
Los Angeles, CA 90034. Tel: 213/559-2944; (quarterly); ISSN:
0149-6980; OCLC 4027720.
Note: n.1, 1977 -.
"A resource for media awareness." A publication printed by
an interdenominational group interested in researching the
impact of television on viewers and the media's influence on

society. Each issue centers around a timely theme, such as
the Summer/Fall 1988 issue discussing the Presidential
campaign, "Elections: Image or Issues?" Articles are written
by eminent authors experienced in their fields: Daniel
Schorr, Cokie Roberts, Senator Ted Stevens, Norman Cousins.
P94.M35; Dewey: 302.2/34/05.

Media and Values (U.S.). See: **Media & Values.**

Media Arts (U.S.). Alternate title: **N.A.M.A.C. News.** National
Alliance of Media Arts Centers c/o Robert Haller, 135 St.
Paul's Ave., Staten Island, NY 10301. Tel: 718/727-5593;
(quarterly); ISSN: 0889-8928; OCLC 14155849.
Note: v.1, 1982? -.
Scholarly newsletter for people involved in the production,
exhibition, preservation and distribution of video, film,
audio and intermedia arts. Reports from the different regions
throughout the U.S. about local media artists, conferences,
seminars and exhibitions. Tries to increase the public's
understanding of and support for the field of media arts.
Dewey: 791 11.

Media Asia (Singapore); Asian Mass Communication Research &
Information Center (A.M.I.C.), 39 Newton Rd., Republic of
Singapore (1130). Tel: 2515106/7; (quarterly); ISSN: 0129-
6612; OCLC 2240297.
Note: v.1, 1974 -.
"An Asian mass communication quarterly." Well written essays
on the impact of broadcasting, cinema, and the print media on
the cultures of Asia. Promotes dissemination of information
and ideas pertaining to mass communications. Tries to raise
the standards of teaching, research and training Asian
students and educators by convening seminars, conferences and
workshops. Published in English.
P92.A7M43; Dewey: 301.16.

Media Business News (U.S.); Summit Media International, Inc., 603
Park Point Dr., Suite 275, Golden, CO 80401. Tel: 800/426-
8190; (weekly); ISSN: 0898-283X; OCLC 17778570.
Note: v.1, 1987 -.
Newsletter for the broadcasting industry, covering
television, cable, radio, publishing and satellite
communications. Contains updates on new laws, technology,

advertising and international opportunities. Included in subscription to **Media Business Review**.
Dewey: 380 11.

Media Business Review (U.S.); Summit Media International, 603 Park Point Dr., Suite 275, Golden CO 80401. Tel: 800/426-8190; (quarterly); ISSN: n/a.
Note: v.1,n.1 [Jan-Mar] 1987 -.
Designed for media executives and investors. An analysis of company performance ratings for the entire broadcast media: newspapers, advertising, publishing, radio, television, cable and syndication firms. Lists companies with investment charts divided into price of stock, dividends, profits, revenues, assets, value of shares, and cash.

Media, Culture & Society (U.K.). Alternate title: **Media, Culture and Society**. SAGE Publications, Ltd., 28 Banner St., London, EC1Y 8QE England; (quarterly); ISSN: 0163-4437; OCLC 4393549.
Note: v.1,n.1 Jan 1979 -.
Serious journal examining the impact of mass media on British society and culture. Covers the full range of media from the printed word to electronic communications. Reviews scholarly books in the field.
HM258.M373; Dewey: 302.2/34/05.

Media, Culture and Society (U.K.). See: **Media, Culture & Society**.

Media Digest (U.S.). Formerly: **Sneak Preview; The Media Digest**. National Film & Video Center, 4321 Sykesville Rd., Finksburg, MD 21048; (quarterly); ISSN: 0146-2091; OCLC 2880992.
Note: v.1-v.14?, 1972-1985?
Lead articles examined the status of film, television, and video in American society. Ceased publication.

Media Ethics Update (U.S.); Media Ethics Update, c/o Mass Communication, Emerson College, 100 Beacon St., Boston, MA 02116; (semiannual; Spring & Fall); ISSN: n/a.
Note: n.1, Fall 1988 -.
Scholarly newsletter covering ethics and the mass media. Prints new reports, events, classes, publications, seminars and studies concerned with moral choices within the field of communications.

Media Forum (Canada). See: **Media Magazine.**

Media History Digest (U.S.); Media History Digest Corp., c/o
    Editor & Publisher, 11 West 19th St., New York, NY 10011.
    Tel: 212/675-4380; (2 times/yr); ISSN: 0195-6779; OCLC
    5585069.
    Note: v.1,n.1 Fall 1980 -.
    Academic journal covering all aspects of mass communications:
    the press, television, motion pictures, advertising, books
    and radio. Studies media from a historical perspective,
    going back throughout American history to understand how the
    media affected our society, influenced policy and changed
    thinking.
    P87.M36; Dewey: 001.51/0973.

Media in Education and Development (U.K.); Taylor & Francis,
    Ltd., 4 John St., London, WC1N 2ET England, U.S.
    Subscription: Media in Education and Development,
    Publications Expediting, Inc., 200 Meacham Ave., Elmont, NY
    11003; (quarterly); ISSN: 0262-0251; 0013-1970; OCLC 8210710.
    Note: v.1, 1968? -.
    Focuses on the use of contemporary communications media in
    education and community development. Examines the
    interaction of new technologies and the British school
    system. Analyzes advertising, public service announcements,
    radio and close circuit television, as well as print media
    and broadcasting.
    LB1044.7.A2E4; Dewey: 371.3/358.

Media Information Australia (Australia); Australian Film
    Television & Radio School, cnr Balaclava and Epping Rds.,
    North Ryde, N.S.W. 2113. Tel: (02) 805 6611; (quarterly);
    ISSN: 0312-9616; OCLC 3782005.
    Note: v.1,n.1 Jul 1976 -.
    Academic journal covering both print and electronic media.
    Concentrates on Australia and the South Pacific. Analyzes
    the effect of television on culture; studies the presentation
    of the news, comparing print with television; examines
    patterns of advertising in the various media. Reviews
    scholarly books.

Media Magazine (Belgium); Media Magazine, 846, Chaussee
    d'Alsemberg, 1180 Brussels, Belgium. Tel: 02/378 3660;

(monthly); ISSN: n/a.
Note: n.1, Apr? 1985 -.
"Le mensuel Belge de la communication." Slick trade magazine
published in French with commentary on all broadcast media:
newspapers, periodicals, cinema, radio, television and
advertising. Profiles successful business men and women.
Reports on new technology, different television systems and
the latest equipment.

Media Magazine (Canada). Formerly: **Media Forum** (0228-2925).
Crailer Communications, Suite 7C, 40 Pleasant Blvd., Toronto,
Ont. M4T 1J9 Canada; (bimonthly?); ISSN: 0821-5715; OCLC
9666934.
Note: v.1-v.3,n.8, May 1980-Sep 1982 as **Media Forum**;
renumbered v.1,n.1-v.5,n.7, Nov 14, 1982-Jul/Aug 1986 as
Media Magazine.
Trade journal for media executives, analyzing the
broadcasting industry in Canada. Discontinued publication.
P87; HF5718.2; Dewey: 302.2/34/0971.

Media Matters (U.S.); Media Dynamics, Inc., 322 East 50th St.,
New York, NY 10022. Tel: 212/753-2674; (monthly); ISSN: n/a.
Note: n.1, 1984? -.
Covers the demographics of television viewing for the
broadcasting and advertising industries. Compiles
statistics, charts trends, tracks sales, and compares ratings
for the major networks, the independents, cable and public
broadcasting. Addresses marketing ploys and strategies for TV
commercials.

Media Mergers & Acquisitions (U.S.); Paul Kagan Associates, Inc.,
126 Clock Tower Place, Carmel, CA 93923-8734. Tel: 408/624-
1536; (monthly); ISSN: 0895-4550; OCLC 16688460.
Note: n.1, Aug 26, 1987 -.
Newsletter giving the status and value of major buyouts,
takeovers, mergers, and sales of companies in the entertainment
and publishing industries. Includes market predictions and
evaluations of the companies.
Dewey: 336 11.

Media Monitor (India); Living Media Research Foundation, 304
Competent House, F-14 Connaught Place, New Delhi, 11000
India; (monthly); ISSN: n/a; OCLC 14245624.

Note: v.1,n.1 Apr 1986 -.
Interested in monitoring both the print and electronic media
for professionalism and accountability to the public.
Emphasis is on being a critical journal which reviews and
discusses the performance of the news and information media.
Published in English.
P96.C762I425; Dewey: 001.51/0954.

The Media Network Newsletter (U.S.). See: **Mediactive**.

Media Perspektiven (W.Germany); Arbeitsgemeinschaft
  Rundfunkwerbung, Am Steinermem Stock 1, 6000 Frankfurt am
  Main 1, West Germany. Tel: (069) 155-2664; (monthly); ISSN:
  0170-1754; OCLC 17064982.
  Note: [v.1] 198u -.
  Scholarly journal analyzing the electronic and print media in
  West Germany. Covers motion pictures, television, radio,
  newspapers, books, magazines, and video. Gives statistical
  comparisons for the various media, charts growth patterns,
  popularity, market saturation. Published in German.

Media Relations/Video Monitor (U.S.). Formerly: **Video Monitor**;
  absorbed by **Social Science Monitor** (not in this list).
  Communications Research Associates, Inc., 10606 Mantz Rd.,
  Silver Spring, MD 20903-1228. Tel: 301/445-3230; (monthly);
  ISSN: 0888-9538; OCLC 13754425.
  Note: v.1-v.6, 1983-1988 as **Video Monitor**; v.7,n.1-v.7,n.6,
  Jan 1989-Jun 1989 as **Media Relations/Video Monitor**; absorbed
  by **Social Science Monitor** in Jul 1989 taking on the numbering
  of the latter.
  Newsletter providing public communicators with "research,
  training, and information services." **Video Monitor** is part
  of the package which includes **Social Science Monitor**,
  Media Relations/Video Monitor, and **Hi-Tech/Computer
  Alert**. Newsletter covers demographics of the viewing
  public, statistical analyses of the networks' news coverage,
  notes on corporate video, effective commercials for target
  audiences and cable growth.
  Dewey: 384 11.

Media Review Digest (U.S.). Formerly: **Multi Media Reviews Index**;
  alternate title: **M.M.R.I.** (0091-5858). The Pierian Press, PO
  Box 1808, Ann Arbor, MI 48106; (annual); ISSN: 0363-7778;

OCLC 988629.

Note: v.1-v.3, 1970-1972 as **Multi Media Reviews Index**; v.4, 1973/74- as **Media Review Digest**.

"The only complete guide to reviews of non-book media." An annual published primarily for educators, librarians and audiovisual specialists who are responsible for collections development and media selection policies for their school, library or university. Reviews, evaluates and describes the following media: motion pictures, video, filmstrips, audio and miscellaneous audiovisual materials.

LB1043.Z9M4 or Z5814.V8M961; Dewey: 011.

Media Sports Business (U.S.). Formerly: **Pay TV Sports** (0734-8533). Paul Kagan Associates Inc., 126 Clock Tower Place, Carmel, CA 93923. Tel: 408/624-1536; (monthly); ISSN: 0889-0951; 0734-8533; OCLC 13842835.

Note: n.1, Sep 22, 1982 -.

Business oriented newsletter covering the growth, popularity and future development of sports telecasting on cable and pay TV. Reports on the sports industry in general and on network programming. Analyzes the value of sports broadcasting and the economic factors that influence sports media rights. Dewey: 384 11.

Media Watch (Australia); Gerard Henderson, Institute of Public Affairs, 56 Young St., Sydney, N.S.W. 2000 Australia; (bimonthly); ISSN: 1031-1211.

Note: n.1, Apr 1988 -.

"Promotes debate and discussion on all areas of the Australian media." Examines how the news media, both print and broadcast, are reporting the issues of the day.

Media Watch (U.S.). See: **MediaWatch**.

Media Watch Bulletin. Evaluation-Medias (Canada). See: **MediaWatch Bulletin. Evaluation-Medias**.

Mediactive (U.S.). Alternate titles: **Mediactive: The Media Network Newsletter**; **Media Active**. The Media Network Newsletter, Box N, 121 Fulton St., 5th Floor, New York, NY 10038. Tel: 213/619-3455; (quarterly); ISSN: 0896-2375; OCLC 16975965.

Note: v.1,n.1 Spring 1986 -.

A newsletter containing "alternative media information." For
activists and organizers who are interested in independent
documentaries concerned with neighborhood and community
awareness, toxic waste, the Third World, homelessness, and
other topics not readily available on television or film.
Dewey: 384 11.

Mediactive: The Media Network Newsletter (U.S.). See: **Mediactive**.

Mediafilm (Belgium); Mediafilm, Cornet de Grezstraat 14, 1030
Brussels, Belgium. Tel: 02/217.24.98; (quarterly); ISSN: n/a.
Note: [n.1] 19uu -.
A serious journal studying film and television in artistic
and cultural terms. Divided into three sections, section
one, "Mediafilmstudie," contains long reviews of selected
international feature films. Section two,
"Mediafilmdocumentatie," is a dossier on the work and art of
a selected filmmaker. Section three, "Mediafimrubriek," is a
lengthy analysis of a certain motion picture or television
program. Published in Flemish.

Medias Visuels (Canada). See: **Visual Media = Medias Visuels**.

MediaWatch (U.S.). Alternate title: **Media Watch**. Media Research
Center, 111 S. Columbus St., Alexandria, VA 22314. Tel: 703/
683-9733; (monthly); ISSN: n/a.
Note: v.1,n.1 Jan 1987 -.
Newsletter from a conservative thinktank which monitors
American news reporting. Covers both newspapers and
television. Cites individual reporters who expound liberal
viewpoints. Observes politics and the media from a conservative
viewpoint.

MediaWatch Bulletin. Evaluation-Medias (Canada). Alternate
titles: **Bulletin / MediaWatch. Evaluation-Medias**;
Evaluation-Medias. MediaWatch Bulletin. MediaWatch, 250-1820
Fir St., Vancouver, B.C. V6J 3B1 Canada; (3 times/yr); ISSN:
0842-8379; OCLC 19272271.
Note: v.1,n.1 Mar 1987 -.
Monitors the portrayal of women in film and television.
Evaluates the roles given to women in the mass media.
Published in English and French.
HQ1233; Dewey: 305.4/2.

Medien Bulletin (W.Germany); Kellerer & Partner GmbH, Eschersheimer Landstrasse 69, D-6000 Frankfurt Am Main, West Germany. Tel: 069 590835-37; (biweekly); ISSN: 0723-2128.
Note: v.1,n.1 Feb 1982 -.
"Das info-magazine fur Funk, Fernsehen, neue medien." Covers the West German broadcasting stations: ARD, ZDF, ORF, SRG and RTL. Popular magazine reporting on television, cable, satellite and radio communications. "Das Medium fur die mediem." Published in German.

Medien und Erziehung (W.Germany). Formerly: **Jugend, Film, Fernsehen** (0022-5886); alternate title: **M.E.R.Z.: Medien und Erziehung**. Brieffach 150 607, 8000 Munich, West Germany; (quarterly); ISSN: 0341-6860; OCLC 7985950.
Note: n.1, 1957-1975? as **Jugend, Film, Fernsehen**; n.1, Jan 1976- as **Medien und Erziehung**.
Scholarly journal for educators interested in using moving image materials in the school environment. Reports on international documentary films. Contains thoughtful articles on film history based on primary documentation. Reviews motion pictures, videos, books, and music. Published in German.
P87.M375; Dewey: 302.2/34/05.

Medien-Wissenschaft: Rezensionen (W.Germany). Alternate title: **Medienwissenschaft**. Joachim Schmitt-Sasse, Institut fur Neuere Deutsche Literatur der Philipps-Universitat Marburg, Wilhelm-Ropke-Strasse 6A, 3550 Marburg, West Germany. Tel: (06421) 284644-34; (quarterly); ISSN: 0176-4241; OCLC 13310994.
Note: n.1, 1984 -.
Scholarly journal covering print and non-print media and their effect on culture. Publication is an annotated bibliography of the latest books arranged by genre: books, cinema, television, theater, video and the press. Indexed by author; published in German.

Medienforschung, Kommunikationspolitik und Kommunikationswissenschaft (W.Germany); Ernst Arnold, Buchdruckerei und Verlag GmBH, 4600 Dortmund 15, West Germany; (quarterly); ISSN: 0720-7425; OCLC 7856422.
Note: v.1, 1959 -.
"Documentation fur Presse, Rundfunk und Film." A periodical

index to over 125 German publications dealing with mass
communications, the press, radio, television, video and film.
Z5630.D63; Dewey: 016.3022/34.

Medienwissenschaft (W.Germany). See: **Medien-Wissenschaft:
Rezensionen.**

Medium (Frankfurt, W.Germany). Created by a merger of
Evangelischer Film-Beobachter and **Medium** (Witten). Medium,
Friedrichstr. 2-6, Postfach 170361, 6000 Frankfurt am Main
17, West Germany; (monthly); ISSN: 0025-8350; OCLC 5330335.
Note: v.1-v.8, 1964-1971 as **Medium** (Witten); merged with
Evangelischer Film-Beobachter and renumbered n.1, 1971 -.
"Zeitschrift fur Horfunk, Fernsehen, Film, Presse." General
film and television magazine reporting on new motion
pictures, film festivals, television programs. Contains
interviews with famous media personalities. Slanted towards
German and European audiences. Published in German.

Medium (Witten). See: **Medium** (Frankfurt).

Medium. Jewish Uses of the Media (U.S.); Jewish Media Service, 15
East 26th St., New York, NY 10019-1579; (irregular).
Note: n.1-n.35, Sep 1974-Fall 1986.
Contained listing of latest motion pictures, videos, and
television programs concerned with Judaism, or of interest
to Jews. Ceased publication.

Membership Directory. Costume Designers Guild (U.S.). Alternate
title: **Costume Designers Guild. Membership Directory.**
Costume Designers Guild, 14724 Ventura St., Building
Penthouse, Sherman Oaks, Ca 91403. Tel: 818/905-1557;
(annual); ISSN: n/a.
Note: ed.1, 1984 -.
A directory listing members of the Costume Designers Guild,
an organization for stage, motion picture and television
costume designers. Each entry gives name, address, agent,
telephone number and list of credits.

Memories (U.S.); Diamandis Communications, Inc, 1515 Broadway,
New York, NY 10036. Tel: 212/719-6202; (bimonthly); ISSN:
0898-9184; OCLC 17947860.
Note: v.1,n.1 Spring 1988 -.

Not entirely a film periodical; contains nostalgic pieces on
American popular culture from the 1920s-1960s. Usually
features a lead story on a popular Hollywood screen idol.
Celebrates anniversaries of outstanding films, such as *Gone
with the Wind* and *My Fair Lady*.
Dewey: 973 11.

Metro (Australia). See: **Metro: Media and Education Magazine.**

Metro: Media and Education Magazine (Australia). Alternate
title: **Metro.** Australian Teachers of Media, Inc. (A.T.O.M.),
PO Box 222, Carlton South, Victoria, 3053 Australia. Tel:
(03)482 2393; (quarterly); ISSN: 0312-2654; OCLC 11977681.
Note: [v.1] 1960? -.
Concerned with educational films and videos for use in the
classroom. Reviews appropriate media. Conducts interviews
with independent film and video makers. Sponsors a yearly
festival and presents the ATOM Award for outstanding
educational and documentary media.

Midnight Marquee (U.S.); Gary Svehla, 4000 Glenarm Ave.,
Baltimore, MD 21206; (annual, published every Oct); ISSN:
0886-8719; OCLC 13041675.
Note: n.1, 1964? -.
Fanzine devoted to fantasy, horror and science fiction motion
pictures made prior to 1965. Also includes critiques and
articles on some of the more recent horror movies like
Cronenberg's *The Fly*, Hooper's *Texas Chainsaw Massacre, Part 2*
and Cameron's *Aliens*.
Dewey: 791 11.

Millennium Film Journal (U.S.); Millennium Film Workshop, 66
East 4th St., New York, NY 10003; (3 times/yr); ISSN: n/a;
OCLC 3765443.
Note: n.1, Winter 1977/78 -.
Scholarly journal hosting discussions on new film theories.
A forum for the critical analysis of independent filmmaking;
particularly interested in experimental, avant garde and
independent films portraying contemporary society and urban
lifestyles. Reviews films and new cinema books.

Millimeter (U.S.); Penton Publishing, Millimeter Magazine, Inc.
Subscription Dept., 826 Broadway, New York, NY 10003. Tel:

212/477-4700; (monthly); ISSN: 0164-9655; OCLC 2254737.
Note: v.1,n.1 Nov 1973 -.
"The magazine of the motion picture and television production
industries." Designed for film and video professionals, this
magazine contains articles on improving production values,
utilizing state-of-the art technology and updating equipment.
Issues devoted to certain themes, such as animation,
teleproduction, TV commercials, special effects applications
and technology, and marketing. Publishes "production guides"
by state with information on location shooting, local
services, and equipment outlets. Features in depth
interviews with successful directors and producers.
TR845.M54; Dewey: 778.5/05.

Mitteilungen des Osterreichischen Filmmuseums (Austria);
Osterreichisches Filmmuseum, Augustinerstrasse 1, 1010 Wien,
Austria; (monthly).
Note: n.1, 1962? -.
Program schedule of events and film showings at the Austrian
film archive.

**Mitteilungen: Osterreichische Gesellschaft fur Filmwissenschaft
Kommunikations- Und Medienforschung** (Austria). Formerly:
**Osterreichische Gesellschaft fur Filmwissenschaft
Mitteilungen**. Osterreichische Gesellschaft fur
Filwissenschaft Kommunikations- Und Medienforschung, A-1010
Wien, Rauhensteingassse 5, Postfach 253, Austria; (quarterly);
ISSN: n/a.
Note: n.1, 1952 -.
Newsletter describing events at the Austrian film archive.
Reports on restoration projects, film festivals, new
acquisitions and personnel. Articles include information on
film history. Published in German.

Mnenya (U.S.S.R). English translation title: **Opinion**. Mnenya c/o
"Soyusinformkino" Goskino, SSSR, 109017 Moscow, B Ordynka 43,
U.S.S.R. Tel: 231-1133; (quarterly); ISSN: n/a.
Note: n.1, Jan-Apr 1989 -.
Intellectual journal covering independent or parallel cinema
productions as well as the films made by the state controlled
studios. Contains long articles analyzing and reviewing individual
motion pictures. Published in Cyrillic.

Modern Screen (U.S.). Alternate title: **Modern Screen Magazine**; absorbed **Radio Stars**. Sterling's Magazines, Inc., 355 Lexington Ave., New York, NY 10017. Tel: 212/391-1400; (bimonthly); ISSN: 0026-8429; OCLC 4055651.
Note: v.1,n.1 Nov 1930 -. Absorbed **Radio Stars** in 1939.
Fan magazine which chronicled the life and loves of motion picture stars during the Golden Age of Hollywood. Today the magazine has added television performers and daytime soap opera stars. Many photographs illustrate the personal lives and romances of popular actors and actresses.
PN1993.M334.

Modern Screen Magazine (U.S.). See: **Modern Screen**.

Le Moniteur du Film (Belgium). Alternate title: **Le Moniteur du Film en Belgique**. Le Centre d'Information sur l'Audio-Visuel (C.I.A.V.), Rue du Framboisier 35, 1180 Bruxelles, Belgium. Tel: 02/374/77.18; (11 times/yr); ISSN: 0771-4874.
Note: [n.] 1981? -.
"Revue mensuelle d'Information professionnelle sur l'Audio-Visuel." Trade magazine giving boxoffice statistics for motion pictures shown in Belgium. Gives television ratings and home video release charts. Keeps current on production and distribution information affecting Belgium. Published in French.

Le Moniteur du Film en Belgique (Belgium). See: **Le Moniteur du Film**.

Monthly Film Bulletin (U.K.). Alternate title: **British Film Institute. Monthly Film Bulletin**; absorbed: **Monthly Film Strip Review**. British Film Institute, 21 Stephen St., London, W1P 1PL England; (monthly); ISSN: 0027-0407; OCLC 2594020.
Note: v.1,n.1 Feb 1934 -. Absorbed **Monthly Film Strip Review** in 1950.
Contains long reviews and synopses of the latest international features released in Great Britain. Each entry contains citations for practically all the members of the cast and crew--from director to best boy. Includes detailed music credits, citing original works as well as older pieces used in the context of the film. For every review, the journal features a long synopsis describing the film and a critical analysis of it. Usually publishes one or two

biographical sketches of contemporary film directors per
issue.
LB1044.B66; Dewey: 371.335230838.

Monthly Film Strip Review (U.K.). See: **Monthly Film Bulletin.**

Mother India (India). Formerly: **Filmindia**; alternate title:
Film India. Sumati Publications Private Ltd., 55, Sir
Phirozeshan Mehta Rd., Fort, Bombay, India; (monthly); ISSN:
n/a.
Note: v.1,n.1-v.26,n.9, May 1935-Sep 1960 as **Filmindia**; v.26,
n.10 Oct 1960- as **Mother India.**
Pictorial fan magazine depicting the lives and romances of
India's popular film and television stars. Reviews films.
Contains gossip and astrology columns, plus articles on
health, beauty and makeup techniques. Published in English.
PN1993.5.I8M6.

Motion Picture (U.S.); Collective for Living Cinema, 41 White
St., New York, NY 10013; (3 times/yr); ISSN: 0892-4929; OCLC
14525901.
Note: v.1, Spring/Summer 1986 -.
Acts as a forum for the members of the Collective for Living
Cinema, a cooperative organization for independent
filmmakers. An intellectual journal analyzing film theory
and criticism, with an emphasis on avant garde and
experimental filmmaking. Articles cover feature films and
documentaries as well.
Dewey: 791 11.

Motion Picture (U.S.); Macfadden Women's Media, Inc., 205 E. 42nd
St., New York, NY 10017; ISSN: 0027-1624; OCLC 1640980.
Note: v.1-v.66,n.801, 1911-Nov 1977.
"America's first movie magazine--1910." Ceased publication
November 1977.
PN1993.M5.

Motion Picture Almanac (U.S.). See: **International Motion Picture
Almanac.**

Motion Picture and Television Almanac (U.S.). See: **International
Motion Picture Almanac.**

Motion Picture and Television Engineering (Japan). See: **Eiga Terebi Gijutsu.**

Motion Picture Engineering (Japan). See: **Eiga Terebi Gijutsu.**

The Motion Picture Guide Annual (U.S.); Cinebooks, Inc., 990 Grove St., Evanston, IL 60201. Tel: 312/475-8400; (annual); ISSN: n/a; OCLC 18261569.
Note: ed.1, 1986 -.
A comprehensive guide to American films released during the preceding year. Includes extensive cast and credit citations, ratings and long synopses. Indexes annual awards for the major film festivals: Berlin, Cannes, Venice, the British Academy, the New York Critics Circle Awards and the Oscars. Contains obituaries for performers and industry personnel.
PN1993.M4334.

Motion Picture Investor (U.S.); Paul Kagan Associates Inc., 126 Clock Tower Place, Carmel, CA 93923-8734. Tel: 408/624-1536; (biweekly); ISSN: 0742-8839; OCLC 10510574.
Note: n.1, Feb 10, 1984 -.
Newsletter documenting the financial status and stock movements of motion picture companies. Tracks buyouts, takeovers, changes in executive personnel, evaluation of profit and loss statements, and investment possibilities of the major corporations in the entertainment industry.

Motion Picture Product Digest (U.S.); Quigley Publishing, 159 W. 53 St., New York, NY 10019; (biweekly); ISSN: 0093-2132; OCLC 1790000.
Note: v.1-v.12,n.13, 1973-Dec 28, 1984.
Contained a release chart and review index by title of feature film. Had a "Film buyers rating guide" for theater operators, indicating how popular a title will be.
Discontinued in 1984.
PN1993.P765; Dewey: 791.43/7.

Motion Picture, TV and Theatre Directory (U.S.); Motion Picture Enterprises Publications, Inc., Box 276, Tarrytown, NY 10591. Tel: 212/245-0969; (semi-annual); ISSN: n/a; OCLC 6194071.
Note: [n.1], 1960? -.
Pocket-sized address book and telephone directory listing

companies serving the motion picture and television
industries in the New York metropolitan area. An advertising
guide to film labs, costume designers, camera stores,
restaurants, equipment rental outlets, talent agencies, and
any other services of interest to the film and video trades.
TR847.5.M68; Dewey: 778.5/025/73 19.

Movement (India); The Circulation Manager, Movement, 29 Rani
Jhansi Rd., New Delhi, 55 India; (quarterly); ISSN: n/a; OCLC
2453846.
Note: n.1, Jun 1968 -.
A scholarly film review, published in English. Examines
cinematic theories, Indian film history, musicology, the
influence of television and videos on Indian cinema,
censorship, the state of Indian film in comparison to foreign
motion picture production.
PN1993.M434; Dewey: 791.43/05.

Movie (U.K.); Movie, 2A Roman Way, London N7 BX6. Tel: 01-609
4019/4010; (irregular); ISSN: 0027-268X; OCLC 2361518.
Note: v.1,n.1 Jun 1962 -.
Publishes scholarly articles on film theory, analyzing
important features on a scene-by-scene basis. Concentrates
on recent film history, usually from the 1960s forward.
Contains interviews and biographical portraits of successful
directors. Emphasis is on English language features,
although accepts an occasional article on European or
Japanese efforts.
PN1993.M74516.

Movie & Film Collector's World (U.S.). See: **Movie Collector's
World**.

Movie Collector's World (U.S.). Formerly: **Film Collector's World**
(0745-5097), **Movie & Film Collector's World** (0746-0325);
absorbed **Video Shopper**. Movie Collector's World, PO Box 309,
Fraser, MI 48026. Tel: 313/774-4311; (biweekly); ISSN: 8750-5401;
OCLC 11489736.
Note: n.1-n.163?, 1978-Jul 1983 as **Film Collector's World**;
n.164?-199, Jul 15, 1983-Nov 1984 as **Movie & Film Collector's
World**; n.200, Nov 30, 1984- as **Movie Collector's World**.
Absorbed **Video Shopper** Oct 1988.
Tabloid format collector's magazine; profiles out of the

mainstream performers, cult personalities, obscure film and
television actors and actresses, as well as the better known
performers. Publishes nostalgia pieces. Acts as a forum for
buying, selling, collecting, trading videotapes of old movies
and TV shows. Previews and rates the new shows on
television.
Dewey: 791 11.

Movie Goer (U.S.). See: **Moviegoer**.

Movie Life (U.S.). Alternate title: **Toni Holt's Movie Life** (0199-
199X). Ideal Publishing Corp., 2 Park Ave, New York, NY
10016; (monthly); ISSN: 0027-2698; OCLC 4059544.
Note: v.1, 1937 -.
Fan magazine profiling current popular movie and television
stars. Well illustrated with many photographs. Focuses on
romance on and off the screen. Previews new films and
television shows.
PN1993.M746; Dewey: 791.4.

Movie Maker (U.K.). Formed by a union of: **Amateur Cine World**
and **8 MM Movie Maker and Cine Camera**; continued by **Making
Better Movies** (0268-0750). Daily News Ltd., London, England;
ISSN: 0027-2701; OCLC 2254347.
Note: v.1-v.19,n.10, Mar 1967-Oct 1985 as **Movie Maker**;
renumbered v.1, Nov 1985- as **Making Better Movies**.
TR845.M6.

Movie Marketing (Japan). See: **Movie/TV Marketing**.

Movie Mirror (U.S.); Sterling's Magazines, 355 Lexington Ave.,
New York, NY 10017. 212/391-1400; (bimonthly); ISSN: 0027-
271X; OCLC 4059566.
Note: v.1, 1956 -.
Devoted to cinema and television personalities. Photo essays
describe the lives and loves of popular stars. Magazine also
informs on fashion, make-up, self-improvement, health and
beauty aids for female readers.

Movie Mirror (U.S.). Merged with **Photoplay** to become: **Photoplay
Combined with Movie Mirror** (0733-2734); **Photoplay With TV
Mirror**. Futura Publications, New York, NY; (bimonthly);
ISSN: 0733-2734.

Note: v.1,n.1-v.18,n.1, Nov 1931-Dec 1940 as **Movie Mirror**;
v.18,n.2-v.91,n.8, Jan 1941-Aug 1977 as **Photoplay Combined
with Movie Mirror**; v.91,n.9-v.92,n.6, Sep 1977-Jun 1978 as
Photoplay With TV Mirror.
Fan magazine reporting on the personal lives and romances of
motion picture actors and actresses. Ceased publication.
PN1993.P5.

Movie News (Hong Kong). See: **Chung Wai Ying Hua**.

Movie/TV Marketing (Japan). Formerly: **Far East Film News** (0425-
7111); **Movie Marketing**. Alternate title: **Movie/Television
Marketing**. Movie/TV Marketing, Box 30, Central P.O., Tokyo,
100-91 Japan, U.S. address: P.O. Box 7159, Northridge, CA
91327. Tel: 818/368-0786; (monthly); ISSN: 0047-8388; OCLC
6166375.
Note: v.1-v.15, 1953-1961 as **Far East Film News**; v.16-v.20,n.7,
1961-Jan 1966 as **Movie Marketing**; v.20,n.8 Feb 1966- as
Movie/TV Marketing.
This trade journal is designed for film and TV industry
personnel throughout the world. Each year publishes two
annual issues: one devoted to the motion picture market,
entitled "The Motion Picture Year Book," and the other for
the television market, entitled "Worldwide TV Survey." These
two issues are the most comprehensive sources for names,
addresses and telephone numbers of production companies,
exporters, distributors and government agencies in 142
countries. Other issues include articles on sales and rental
statistics, trends, audiovisual piracy, new technology and
productions in progress. Published in English.
PN1993.M749.

Movie/Television Marketing (Japan). See: **Movie/TV Marketing**.

Moviegoer (U.S.). Alternate title: **Movie Goer**. Moviegoer, Inc.,
13-30 Corporation, 505 Market St., Knoxville, TN 37902;
(monthly); ISSN: n/a.
Note: v.1, 1982 -.
Keeps current with the latest feature film releases. Reviews
motion pictures, accompanying the critique with photographs
from the movie and a profile of the star.

Movieline (U.S.); Movieline, Inc., 1141 S. Beverly Dr., Los Angeles, CA 90035-1155. Tel: 213/282-0711; (monthly); ISSN: n/a.
Note: v.1,n.1 Sep 1989 -.
"Movies as a way of life." Published as an inside to the Hollywood movie colony. Slick, popular and gossipy, specializing in L.A. stories, industry news, behind-the-scenes reporting and glossy bio-layouts of the stars. Covers fashion, premieres and some reviews.

Movies U.S.A. (U.S.); Movies U.S.A., a Division of Entertex Industries, Inc., 8010 Roswell Rd., Atlanta, GA 30350. Tel: 404/668-0111; (monthly); ISSN: 1044-1336; OCLC 19691994.
Note: v.1, 1988? -. (v.2,n.5 Mar 1989, also called Premiere issue.).
"Official magazine of the Movietime Network." Popular movie fan magazine for cable subscribers, promoting the most recent productions. Cover story features the latest blockbuster movie of the month. Contains Hollywood gossip and movie trivia.
Dewey: 791 11.

Moving Image Review (U.S.); Northeast Historic Film, Blue Hill Falls, ME 04615. Tel: 207/374-2736; (semiannual); ISSN: 0897-0769; OCLC 17392285.
Note: v.1,n.1 Winter 1988 -.
Newsletter describing the events of Northeast Historic Film, a nonprofit organization whose mission is to "preserve and make available for the public, historic film/video of the northern New England region." Instrumental in surveying the motion picture resources and collections of the United States of particular interest to the Northeast.
Dewey: 791 11.

Moviola (Brazil); Clube de Cinema de Porto Alegre, Av. Borges de Medeiros, 915/70 Andar, Brazil; (irregular); ISSN: n/a.
Note: v.1, 1984 -.
Popular film magazine reviewing the latest international releases. Publication is part of the membership to the cinema club. Contains many photographs; published in Portuguese.

Multi Media Reviews Index (U.S.). See: **Media Review Index.**

Multicast (U.S.); Paul Kagan Associates Inc., 126 Clock Tower
   Place, Carmel, CA 93923. Tel: 408/624-1536; (monthly); ISSN:
   0146-0099; OCLC 2827987.
   Note: [n.1], Apr 3, 1981 -.
   Newsletter on the "Multipoint Distribution Service" (MDS),
   the FCC-regulated common carrier for pay TV and broadcasting
   data services. Review and analysis of the cable and pay TV
   industries.

Multichannel News (U.S.); Fairchild Publications, 300 S. Jackson
   St., Denver, CO 80209. Tel: 303/393-6397; (weekly); ISSN:
   0276-8593; OCLC 7398798.
   Note: v.1,n.1 Sep 15, 1980 -.
   Newsletter reporting on the cable and pay TV industries.
   Covers multipoint distribution service (MDS), investment
   possibilities, economic analysis of the cable industry,
   consulting firms, and contractors. Reviews programs.

-N-

N.A.M.A.C. News (U.S.). See: **Media Arts**.

N.B.C. Television Network Advance Program Schedule & Supplement
(U.S.). Alternate title: **National Broadcasting Company
Television Network Advance Program Schedule & Supplement**.
National Broadcasting Company, Media Relations, 30
Rockefeller Plaza, New York, NY 10112. Tel: 212/664-4444;
(weekly); ISSN: n/a.
Note: 196u -.
Loose leaf guide to prime time programs being aired on the
NBC network on a weekly basis. Carries the title, date and
time, regular cast and program description. Notes any
changes, pre-emptions, reruns. Mostly for internal consultation
by the corporation.

N.F.M. Programma (Netherlands); Netherlands Filmmuseum,
Vondelpark 3, 1071 AA, Amsterdam, The Netherlands. Tel: 020-
831646; (monthly); ISSN: n/a.
Note: n.1, 19uu -.
The film schedule for the Dutch Film Archive. Also contains
articles on film production in Holland. Published in Dutch.

N.F.S.A. Newsletter. See: **National Film & Sound Archive
Newsletter**.

N.F.T. National Film Theatre (U.K.). Alternate title: **National
Film Theatre. N.F.T.** British Film Institute, 21 Stephen St.,
London W1P 1PL, England; (monthly); ISSN: n/a.
Note: [n.1] May/Jun 1956 -.
The film schedule for members of the British Film Institute,
film fans and moviegoers. Elaborate newsletter presenting
the schedule for the National Film Theatre. Each title entry
includes photograph, cast, credits and critique. Contains
biographical sketches of motion picture directors and reports
on the London Film Festival.

N.I.C.E.M. Index to Educational Videotapes (U.S.). See: **Film & Video Finder**.

N.I.C.E.M. Index to 16mm Educational Films (U.S.). See: **Film & Video Finder**.

N.Y. Film Bulletin (U.S.). Alternate title: **New York Film Bulletin**. Abbey Film Society of Fordham College, N.Y. Film Bulletin, 116 E. 60th St., New York, NY 10022; (irregular); ISSN: 0548-8796.
Note: v.1, Jan 8, 1960 -.
Insular magazine for New York audiences. Concentrates on foreign films. Each issue is devoted to a central theme, usually a homage to a popular foreign director or controversial movie. Contains interviews, photographs and filmographies.
PN1991.N2.

N.Y. Filmmakers' Newsletter (U.S.). See: **Filmmakers**.

Na Ekranakh Mira (U.S.S.R.); Iskusstvo, 103051, Moscow, K-51 Tsvetnoi bul'var, 25, izd. Iskusstvo, U.S.S.R.; (annual); ISSN: n/a; OCLC 1783286.
Note: v.1, 1966 -.
Wide-ranging film review; publishes lengthy analyses of international feature films released throughout the preceding year. Covers motion pictures from the United States and Europe as well as Soviet and Eastern bloc countries. Each review contains title in Cyrillic, credits, cast, still photograph and synopsis. Printed in Cyrillic.
PN1993.N28.

National Board of Review Magazine (U.S.). See: **Films in Review**.

National Broadcasting Company Television Network Advance Program Schedule & Supplement (U.S.). See: **N.B.C. Television Network Advance Program Schedule & Supplement**.

National Film & Sound Archive Newsletter (Australia). Alternate title: **N.F.S.A. Newsletter**. National Film & Sound Archive, McCoy Circuit, Acton ACT 2000, Canberra, Australia. Tel: (062) 671 711; (irregular); ISSN: 0814-6888.
Note: n.1, 1985 -.

House organ for the Australian National Film & Sound Archive. Reports on the operations of the archive: acquisitions, donations, film titles preserved, new collections purchased, film cataloging and reference. Outlines fundraising events, publicity, seminars and conferences.

The National Film and Videotape Production Directory (U.S.). See: **On Location. The National Film and Videotape Production Directory.**

National Film Theatre. N.F.T. (U.K.). See: **N.F.T. National Film Theatre.**

National Gallery of Art Film Calendar (U.S.); National Gallery of Art, Washington, D.C. 20565; (quarterly); ISSN: n/a.
Note: 197u -.
Documents the free film showings at the National Gallery of Art in Washington, D.C. Gives title, director, date, length and synopsis. Exhibits art films, documentaries, hard to find foreign films and shorts.

National Nielsen T.V. Ratings (U.S.). See: **Nielsen National T.V. Ratings.**

National T.V. Nielsen Ratings (U.S.). See: **Nielsen National T.V. Ratings.**

Neue Filmwelt (E.Germany). See: **Filmspiegel.**

Neue Medien (W.Germany); Frankfurter Fachverlag Michael Kohl GmbH and Co., NeueMedien-Leserservice, Milchstrasse 1, D-2000 Hamburg 13, West Germany. Tel: 069 778410; (monthly); ISSN: n/a.
Note: v.1,n.1 1982 -.
Trade magazine devoted to information about German radio, television, cable and satellite. Interviews people in the industry. Covers new developments in satellite technology, the international marketplace for broadcasting, and the impact of cable and satellite on Europe.

New Canadian Film (Canada). See: **Copie Zero.**

The New Magic Lantern Journal (U.K.). Alternate title: **The Optical Magic Lantern Journal and Photographic Enlarger.** Magic Lantern Society of Great Britain, 36 Meon Rd., London W3 8AN, England; (irregular); ISSN: 0143-036X; OCLC 18512792. Note: [v.1], Apr 1978 -.
Title is a homage to original magazine, **The Optical Magic Lantern Journal and Photographic Enlarger, Incorporating The Lantern World,** published from 1889-1903. Main interest is in the history of visual imagery, beginning with magic lanterns, zoetropes, mutoscopes, nickelodeons and peep shows, the precursors of the motion picture. Provides background and insights on the history of silent cinema through original research and documentation.
TR505.O68; Dewey: 778.2 19.

New Media Markets (U.K.). Financial Times Business Information Limited: Second Floor, Tower House, Southampton St., London WC2E 7HA, England, Tel: 01-240 9391; (biweekly); ISSN: n/a. Note: v.1, 1983 -.
Business newsletter detailing the latest information on cable and satellite television, terrestrial broadcasting and home video marketing. Focuses on the industry in Great Britain, but contains news reports on the broadcasting industries in Europe and America. Gives statistics on viewing audiences, new cable subscribers and franchises.

New Movies: The National Board of Review Magazine (U.S.). See: **Films in Review.**

The New York Center for Visual History Newsletter (U.S.); The New York Center for Visual History, 625 Broadway, 12th Floor, New York, NY 10012. Tel: 212/777-6900; (quarterly); ISSN: n/a. Note: v.1,n.1 Winter 1987/1988 -.
Newsletter for members, covering events at the Center, the main goal of which is "to produce innovative documentary films on American culture not explored on television." Reports on new award winning motion pictures, productions in progress, and future projects funded by the Center. Plans new films to accompany exhibitions at New York City's museums and galleries.

New York Film Bulletin (U.S.). See: **N.Y. Film Bulletin.**

New York Production Manual (U.S.). See: **The Producer's Masterguide.**

New Zealand Film (New Zealand); New Zealand Film Commission, PO Box 11-546, Wellington, New Zealand. Tel: (4) 859-754; (bimonthly); ISSN: n/a.
Note: n.1, 1982 -.
Promotional device by government agency for motion pictures made in New Zealand. Keeps current with the latest releases, new documentaries made in New Zealand and showings of New Zealand productions at international film festivals.
Announces film courses, seminars and conferences presented by the New Zealand Film Commission.

New Zealand Film & Television Directory (New Zealand). Formerly: **Report of the New Zealand Film Commission for the Year.** New Zealand Film Commission, c/o Marlyn Publishing, 126 Vincent St., PO Box 7085, Auckland, New Zealand; (annual); ISSN: 0112-188X; OCLC 13441984.
Note: ed.1, 1983 as **Report of the New Zealand Film Commission for the Year**; ed.2, 1984- as **New Zealand Film & Television Directory**.
Compilation of the motion pictures and television programs produced in New Zealand for the year. Contains addresses, telephone numbers and personnel listings for New Zealand production and distribution companies.
PN1993.5.N43N48a; Dewey: 384.8/09931.

New Zealand Film Archive Newsletter (New Zealand); The New Zealand Film Archive, Box 9544, Wellington, New Zealand. Tel: (4) 847-647; (irregular); ISSN: 0113-1710.
Note: n.1, 1982 -.
House organ for the New Zealand Film Archive. Covers recent acquisitions, preservation work, staff development, exhibitions and screenings at the Archive. Also reports on new projects planned by the New Zealand motion picture and television industries.

News From Women Make Movies (U.S.); Women Make Movies, Inc., 225 Lafayette St., Suite 211, New York, NY 10012. Tel: 212/925-0606; (quarterly); ISSN: n/a.
Note: n.1, 198u -.
Newsletter free to members of Women Make Movies. Carries

news and events of interest to women film and video makers.
Lists new releases, giving title, director, date, length,
format, cost and synopsis. Acts as a distribution center for
more than 150 independent documentary, narrative and animated
films and videos made by women; a catalog is available.

Newsbank. Film and Television (U.S.). See: **Review of the Arts:
Film and Television.**

Newsletter. Academy of Canadian Cinema & Television (Canada).
See: **Infocus: Academy of Canadian Cinema & Television.**

Newsletter. Agency for Instructional Technology (U.S.). See:
A.I.T. Newsletter.

Newsletter. Asian Cinema Studies Society (U.S.). See: **Asian
Cinema Studies Society Newsletter.**

A Newsletter Called Fred (Canada). See: **Visual Media = Medias
Visuels.**

The Newsletter of A.S.I.F.A. / Hollywood (U.S.). See: **Graffiti:
The Newsletter of A.S.I.F.A / Hollywood.**

Newsletter of the Films of John Wayne (U.S.). See: **The Big Trail.**

The Newsletter of the International Documentary Association
(U.S.). See: **International Documentary.**

Nielsen National T.V. Ratings (U.S.). Formerly: **National T.V.
Nielsen Ratings**; **National Nielsen T.V. Ratings.** Media
Research Group, A.C. Nielsen Company, Nielsen Plaza,
Northbrook, IL 60062. Tel: 312/498-6300; (Biweekly); ISSN:
0737-7819; OCLC 9445450.
Note: June 9, 1956-Aug 1959 as **National T.V. Nielsen Ratings**;
Aug 1959-Oct 1982 as **National Nielsen T.V. Ratings**; Oct 11,
1982- as **Nielsen National T.V. Ratings.**
Subscription includes daily television ratings and market reports
for network television and cable shows. Also available is the
Nielsen Television Index (N.T.I.) which provides estimates of T.V.
viewing and nationally sponsored network program audiences for
52 weeks per year. Offers an online time sharing computer system
linked to clients for direct access to special analyses. Subscription

also includes the **Nielsen Station Index (N.S.I.)** measuring T.V. station audiences in local markets. Reports on season-to-season viewing habits by time periods and programs. Measures the designated market area ratings and estimates viewing over a wide range of demographic categories.
HE8700.66.U6N53; HE8697.A8N34; Dewey: 384.55/43 19.

Nielsen Newscast (U.S.); Media Research Group, A.C. Nielsen Company, Nielsen Plaza, Northbrook, IL 60062. Tel: 312/498-6300; (quarterly); ISSN: 0468-1835; OCLC 1760344.
Note: v.1, 1961? -.
Newsletter giving overview of findings from the Nielsen National T.V. Ratings. Data is "derived from Nielsen media audience measurements and are estimates of audience viewing." Contains information about the popularity of series, specials, mini-series and telefeatures. Gives statistics on home video usage and "cable churn," the changes of viewing habits as a result of pay television.

Nielsen Report on Television (U.S.); Nielsen Media Research, A.C. Nielsen Company, Nielsen Plaza, Northbrook, IL 60063. Tel: 312/498-6300; (annual); ISSN: n/a; OCLC 5395472.
Note: ed.1, 1956 -.
Annual summary of characteristics and trends of the American television audience. Charts the viewing patterns, statistics and demographics as measured by the **Nielsen National T.V. Ratings**.

Nihon Eiga Kaigai Fukyu Kyokai (Japan). English translation title: **UniJapan Film Quarterly**. UniJapan Film, Association for the Diffusion of Japanese Films Abroad, 9-13 Ginze 5-chome, Chuo-ku Tokyo, 104 Japan. Tel: (572) 5106-7; (quarterly); ISSN: n/a.
Note: v.1,n.1 Jul 1958 -.
List of selected Japanese feature and short films for export. Each entry under title gives production company, distributor, director, screenwriter, photographer, art director, music director, cast, synopsis and publicity still. Primarily a business directory containing names and international addresses for Japanese distribution companies. Published in English.
PN1993.N54.

Nihon No Yushu Eiga (Japan). English translation titles: **Selected Japanese Feature Films; Outstanding Japanese Films**. UniJapan Film, Association for the Diffusion of Japanese Film Abroad, 9-13 Ginze 5-chome, Chuo-ku, Tokyo 104, Japan. Tel: (572) 5106-7; (annual); ISSN: n/a; OCLC 2243435; OCLC 8436211. Note: v.1, 1974 -.
A selection of premiere Japanese features available for export. Each citation includes Japanese and English release titles, production company, distributor, director, extensive lists for cast and crew members, critique and photographic stills. Contains indexes for distribution companies and directors. Editions published in English and Japanese. PN1993.5.J3N55; Dewey: 791.43/75/0952.

Norsk Filmblad (Norway). See: **Film og Kino.**

Nosotros Reporter (U.S.); Nosotros Reporter, Inc., 1314 N. Wilton Pl., Hollywood, CA 90028. 213/465-4167; (monthly); ISSN: n/a. Note: n.1, 1970 -.
Newsletter for Hispanic American performers, administrators and technicians in the entertainment industry. Acts as a clearinghouse for career opportunities, job training, and employment in Hollywood and Southern California. Published in English.

Nouveau Cinema Canadien (Canada). See: **Copie Zero.**

Novyny Kino Ekrana (U.S.S.R.). See: **Novyny Kinoekrana.**

Novyny Kino Ekranu (U.S.S.R.). See: **Novyny Kinoekrana.**

Novyny Kinoekrana (U.S.S.R.). Formerly: **Novyny Kinoekranu** (0550-2896); alternate titles: **Novyny Kino Ekranu; Novyny Kino Ekrana.** Spilka Kinematohrafistiv Ukrainy, 252033 Kiev-33, ul. Saksaganskogo, 6 Novyny, U.S.S.R.; (monthly); ISSN: 0134-5613; OCLC 14689099.
Note: n.1-n.269, 1961?-Dec 1983 as **Novyny Kinoekranu**; n.270, Jan 1983- as **Novyny Kinoekrana.**
Ukrainian-based popular motion picture magazine. Oversized, with many illustrations and photographs, this magazine contains long reviews, occasional interviews with Slavic directors, and descriptions of recent Russian releases. Concentrates on Ukrainian and Russian filmmaking, but also has

some information about western films and celebrities.
Published in Cyrillic.
PN1993.N69.

Novyny Kinoekranu (U.S.S.R.). See: **Novyny Kinoekrana.**

Number Six (U.K.). Formerly: **Six of One.** Six of One, The
Prisoner Appreciation Society, PO Box 66, Ipswich, IP2 9TZ
England; (quarterly); ISSN: n/a.
Note: [v.1-v.18], Winter 1967/68-Summer 1985 as **Six of One;**
renumbered n.1, Fall 1985- as **Number Six.**
Fan magazine for people devoted to *The Prisoner* television
series, starring Patrick McGoohan. Editorials and articles
on the different episodes. Interviews people involved with
the production.

-O-

Obrazkovy Filmovy Crtnactidenik (Czechoslovakia). See: **Kino; Obrazkovy Filmovy Crtnactidenik.**

The Off-Hollywood Report (U.S.); The Independent Feature Project, 21 W. 86th St., New York, NY 10024. Tel: 212/494-0909; (10 times/yr); ISSN: n/a.
Note: v.1, 1986 -.
"Dedicated to supporting and promoting quality independent films." Gives advice on casting, financing, entertainment law, taxes, insurance, movie music and marketing for independent feature producers. Reports on appropriate film festivals for indies. Contains classified advertisements for employment opportunities, buying and selling film equipment.

Official Video Directory & Buyers Guide (U.S.); Palm Springs Media, Inc., PO Box 2740, Palm Springs, CA 92263. Tel: 619/ 322-3050; (annual); ISSN: 0890-782X; OCLC 14439679.
Note: ed.1, 1987 -.
A directory of manufacturers for video equipment and accessories, such as cleaning kits, decoders, filters, rewinders, tapes, etc. Includes names and addresses of companies providing satellite installation equipment and services.
HD9696.V533U546; Dewey: 338.7/621388332.

Official Video Software Directory Annual (U.S.). See: **Home Viewer's Official Video Software Directory Annual.**

On Cable (U.S.); On Cable Publications, Inc., 25 Van Zant St., Norwalk, CT 06855. Tel: 202/866-6256; (monthly); ISSN: 0273-5636; OCLC 7079441.
Note: v.1,n.1, Oct 1980 -.
Detailed coverage of programs on cable television tailored for specific regions throughout the United States. Publishes 54 different editions. Gives background reports on filming, personality profiles, coming attractions.

On Film (New Zealand). See: **OnFilm.**

On Film (U.S.); College of Fine Arts, U.C.L.A., 405 Hilgard Ave.,
   Los Angeles, CA 90024. Tel: 213/661-0944; (quarterly); ISSN:
   0161-1585; ISSN: 0160-1585; OCLC 3861406.
   Note: n.1, 1976 -.
   Scholarly and academic, this student publication combines
   cinema studies with politics. Offers articles on Third World
   cinema, film and propaganda, women's studies. Contains book
   reviews, bibliographies and filmographies.

On Line at the Movies (U.S.). Alternate title: **On Line.** "On
   Line", 1040 First Ave., Suite 357, New York, NY 10022;
   (monthly); ISSN: n/a.
   Note: v.1,n.1 Mar 1989 -.
   Playbill for the movies, free with admission. Short articles
   on the stars and their latest feature films.

On Location (U.S.); On Location Publishing Inc., 6777 Hollywood
   Blvd., Suite 600, Hollywood, CA 90028; (monthly); ISSN: 0149-
   7014; OCLC 3758217.
   Note: v.1-v.11, Oct 1977-May 1987.
   Covered production information for "film, video, audio,
   cable, special effects, animation, commercials, equipment,
   post-production and music video industries." Special
   features included television commercial production, filming
   on location with mobile units, and the latest on special
   effects. Ceased publication.
   PN1993.5.U605; Dewey: 791.43/0973.

On Location. The National Film & Videotape Production Directory
   (U.S.). Alternate title: **The National Film & Videotape
   Production Directory**. On Location, 6777 Hollywood Blvd.,
   Suite 501, Hollywood, CA 90028; (annual); ISSN: 0160-5933;
   OCLC 3673598.
   Note: v.1-v.8, 1977-1986/87.
   Comprehensive directory listing film and tape studio
   facilities, production and post-production centers, mobile
   equipment labs, technical facilities, and service suppliers
   in a state-by-state and city-by-city format. Gives a
   complete run down of film commissions and state licensing
   bureaus, location sites, unique places and climatological

statistics for each state. Ceased publication.
PN1998.A1O5; Dewey: 338.4/025/73.

OnFilm (New Zealand). Alternate title: **On Film**. OnFilm Magazine
    Ltd., PO Box 6374, Wellington, New Zealand. Tel: (04) 850-
    681; (bimonthly); ISSN: 0112-2789; OCLC 14152176.
    Note: v.1,n.1 Dec 1983 -.
    "New Zealand's film, television, video, photography and
    theatre magazine." Popular journal covering the media arts
    in New Zealand. Interviews New Zealand filmmakers, theater
    directors, playwrights, photographers. Reviews productions
    and exhibitions.

Opinion (U.S.S.R.). See: **Mnenya**.

Opsis (Canada); Canadian Society for the Advancement of Critical
    Cinema, 1616 W. 3rd. Ave., Vancouver, B.C. V6J 1K2 Canada; (3
    times/yr).
    Note: v.1,n.1 Spring 1984 -.
    "The Canadian journal of avant garde and political cinema."
    Seeks to promote politically oriented cinema through public
    screenings, seminars and film information networks. Articles
    cover censorship in Canada, new film theories, experimental
    filmmaking, lengthy interviews and spirited debates on
    controversial topics.

Optical Information Systems (U.S.). Formerly: **Videodisc,
    Videotex** (0278-9183); **Videodisc and Optical Disk** (0742-5740).
    Meckler Corporation, 11 Ferry Lane West, Westport, CT 06880.
    Tel: 203/226-6967; (bimonthly); ISSN: 0886-5809; OCLC
    12930983.
    Note: v.1,n.1-v.4,n.1, 1981-Jan/Feb 1984 as **Videodisc,
    Videotex**; v.4,n.2-v.5,n.6, Mar/Apr 1984-Nov/Dec 1985 as
    Videodisc and Optical Disk; v.6,n.1 Jan/Feb 1986- as **Optical
    Information Systems**.
    Technical journal concerned with the practical and scientific
    applications of optical disk technology. Covers software,
    new products, equipment, vendors, computers, utilization and
    training. The November/December issue is a special "Buyer's
    Guide and Consultant Directory," listing names and numbers
    for production companies, suppliers and consultants.
    TK5105.V52; Dewey: 001 11.

Optical Information Systems Update (U.S.). Formerly: **Videodisc
Update** (0733-0421); **Videodisc and Optical Disk Update** (0742-
5732). Meckler Corporation, 11 Ferry Lane West, Westport, CT
06880. Tel: 203/226-6967; (monthly); ISSN: 0887-5162.
Note: v.1,n.1-v.3, Jul 1982-1984 as **Videodisc Update**; v.3-
v.5,n.6, 1984-Mar 1986 as **Videodisc and Optical Disk Update**;
v.5,n.7, Apr 1986- as **Optical Information Systems Update.**
Companion newsletter to **Optical Information Systems**. Reports
on latest developments occurring in CD-ROM technology,
interactive videodisc and optical information storage.
Dewey: 004 11.

Optical Magic Lantern Journal and Photographic Enlarger (U.K.).
See: **The New Magic Lantern Journal.**

Opticmusic's Film & Video Production (U.S.). See: **Film & Video
Production.**

Orbit Video (U.S.); Orbit Publishing, a Division of CommTek
Communications Corp., 88330 Boone Blvd., Suite 600, Vienna,
VA 22180. Tel: 703/827-0511; (monthly); ISSN: 1042-1149; OCLC
18944872.
Note: v.1,n.1 Jan 1989 -.
Designed to be sold in video stores to aid consumers' selections.
The magazine is divided into three sections: new releases, current
hits, and classics. Reviews and rates home video selections, giving
title, year, length, MPAA rating, director, cast, short synopsis,
video distributor and format. Articles on "video lifestyles"
comment on furniture, food and environment for optimum video
watching.
Dewey: 791 11.

Organo de la Cinemateca Distrital (Colombia). See: **Cinemateca.**

Osterreichische Gesellschaft fur Filmwissenschaft Mitteilungen
(Austria). See: **Mitteilungen: Osterreichische Gesellschaft
fur Filmwissenschaft Kommunikations- Und Medienforschung.**

Oxford Review of Film and Theatre (U.K.). See: **Stills.**

-P-

P.B.S. Video News (U.S.). Alternate title: **Public Broadcasting System Video News**. Public Broadcasting System, 1320 Braddock Pl., Alexandria, VA 22314-1698. Tel: 703/739-5380; (bimonthly). Note: n.1, 1986 -.
Newsletter for teachers, librarians and audiovisual specialists describing the latest releases on video available from P.B.S. Gives pre-broadcast news on upcoming TV programs, Fall preview information, and description of new series.

P.R.C. News (U.S.). Alternate title: **Pre Recorded Cassette News**. Corbell Publishing, 12335 Santa Monica Blvd., Ste. 129, Los Angeles, CA 90025. Tel: 213/837-9420; (weekly); ISSN: 0898-302X; OCLC 17782034.
Note: v.1,n.1 July 29, 1988 -.
A weekly news brief for the home video industry. Gives the latest information about video marketing, such as colorization and VSDA convention news. Contains checklist of the cassettes to be released by the major studios: CBS/Fox, MCA Home Video, MGM/UA, Nelson Entertainment, Orion Home Video, Paramount, RCA/Columbia, Touchstone and Warner Home Video with prices and release dates.
Dewey: 338 11.

Pacific Coast Studio Directory (U.S.). Alternate title: **S.D.** **Pacific Coast Studio Directory**, 6313 Yucca St., Hollywood, CA 90028-5093. Tel: 213/467-2920; (quarterly); ISSN: 0731-2059; OCLC 7938827.
Note: v.1, 1920 -.
A comprehensive listing of all types of trade and service industries of interest to motion picture and television production companies on the West Coast. Gives names, addresses and telephone numbers for almost every supplier from animal trainers to wind machines.

Panorama (Czechoslovakia); PNS-UED, Odd. Vyvozu Tisku, Jindrisska 14, 125 05 Praha, Czechoslovakia; (quarterly); ISSN: 0031- 8059; OCLC 5913078.
Note: v.1, 1960 -.
"A miscellany of theoretical articles about the cinema." A serious journal devoted to the critical analysis of cinematic theories prevalent today, such as "Blind Alleys of Psychoanalytic Structuralism" or "Problems of Selection and the Practice Established in Czech Archives." Articles cover film as art, film as propaganda, film as entertainment. Published in Czech with synopses in English, French and Russian. PN1993.P24.

Panorama (U.S.); Triangle Communications, Inc., 850 3rd Ave., New York, NY 10022; (monthly); ISSN: 0191-8591; OCLC 4965436.
Note: v.1,n.1 Feb 1980 -. Preceded by an unnumbered prototype issue dated July 1979.
"Television today and tomorrow." An upscale counterpart to **TV Guide**. Focuses on the television and cable industries. Evaluates pay TV and cable networks: what you get for your money. Compares the major networks for news, documentaries and sports coverage. Contains background information on filming miniseries and telefeatures. Editorials cover such topics as the mission of public TV, sex on cable, and deregulation.
PN1992.P36; Dewey: 384.55/0973.

Patalogo (Italy). See: **Patalogo. Cinema + Televisione + Video.**

Patalogo. Cinema + Televisione + Video (Italy). Continues: **Patalogo.** Ubulibri, via Ramazzini 8, 20129 Milan, Italy; (annual); ISSN: n/a; OCLC 17205737.
Note: v.1-v.7, 1978-1984 as **Patalogo**; v.8-v.9, 1985-1986 as **Patalogo. Cinema + Televisione**; v.10, 1987- as **Patalogo. Cinema + Televisione + Video.** Continues to publish: **Patalogo. Teatro + Musica** which became a separate publication in 1985.
Originally intended to cover all the performing arts, "annuario dello spettacolo: cinema, teatro, musica, televisione." Later divided into two editions, one for film, television, and video; the other for theater and music. Annual listing of all the feature films, television programs, and video recordings released in Italy during

the preceding year. Entries contain title, cast, credits and brief
synopsis. Published in Italian.
PN1560.P37.

The Pay TV Movie Log (U.S.); Paul Kagan Associates Inc., 126
Clock Tower Place, Carmel, CA 93923. Tel: 408/624-1536;
(monthly). ISSN: n/a.
Note: [n.1], 198u -.
Reviews the feature films playing on eight premium cable
networks each month.

The Pay TV Newsletter (U.S.); Paul Kagan Associates Inc., 126
Clock Tower Place, Carmel, CA 93923. Tel: 408/624-1536;
(monthly); ISSN: 0146-0072; OCLC 2828077.
Note: [n.1], 1971 -.
Newsletter covering pay TV: cable, direct and over the air
satellite broadcasting. Analyzes the demographics of the
subscribers. Advises investors on the industry's revenues
and profits.

Pay TV Sports (U.S.). See: **Media Sports Business**.

The Perfect Vision (U.S.); Pearson Publishing Empire, 2 Glen
Ave., Box 357, Sea Cliff, NY 11579. Tel: 516/671-6342; 800/222-
3201; (quarterly); ISSN: 0895-4143; OCLC 16644742.
Note: v.1,n.1 Winter 1986 -.
Seeks to transcend the usual home video fare by offering
insights and information about quality film, television and
video products. Combines art and technology when reviewing
hardware and software, showing how to achieve the best
picture and sound for the performing arts: classic films,
opera, ballet and music.
Dewey: 384 11.

Perforations (Canada); National Film Board of Canada, PO Box
6100, Station A, Montreal, Quebec, Canada H3C 3H5;
(bimonthly); ISSN: 0715-9862; OCLC 10008043.
Note: v.1,n.1 Jan 1981 -.
Newsletter from the National Film Board of Canada. Describes
new productions, profiles filmmakers, animators and
technicians working at the Film Board. Published in French
and English.
Dewey: 791.43/02.

Performing Arts Annual (U.S.); Library of Congress; for sale by: Superintendent of Documents, Government Printing Office, Washington, D.C. 20402; (annual); ISSN: 0887-8234; OCLC: 13393337.
Note: v.1, 1986 -.
Compilation of articles written about the performing arts: music, dance, cinema, opera, television and theater, describing the various collections in the Library of Congress. Scholarly treatises, handsomely illustrated with photographs, graphics, posters and frame enlargements taken from the Library's collections.
PN1561.P468; Dewey: 790.2/05.

Perry's Broadcasting and the Law (U.S.). See: **Broadcasting and the Law.**

Persistence of Vision: The Journal of the Film Faculty of the City University of New York (U.S.); The City University of New York c/o Film Dept., Brooklyn College, 0312 Plaza Building, Bedford Ave. & Avenue H, Brooklyn, NY 11210; (3 times/yr); ISSN: OCLC 12043117.
Note: v.1,n.1 Summer 1984 -.
Academic film journal specializing in film theory and criticism. Forum for educators who teach cinema studies to present new theories, or challenge old ones. Reviews current releases; reviews cinema books.

Photographic Trade News (U.S.). See: **Photographic Video Trade News.**

Photographic Video Trade News (U.S.). Formerly: **Photographic Trade News.** PTN Publishing Corp., 210 Crossways Park Dr. West, Woodbury, NY 11797. Tel: 516/496-8000; (biweekly); ISSN: 0031-8779; OCLC 18160068.
Note: v.1-v.51,n.18, 1937-Sep 7, 1987 as **Photographic Trade News**; v.51,n.19, Sep 21, 1987- as **Photographic Video Trade News.** Designed for retailers specializing in photography and video equipment. Reviews media books, cameras and video equipment.

Photoplay (U.S.). Alternate titles: **Photoplay Combined with Movie Mirror; Photoplay with TV Mirror** (0163-5115).
Macfadden Group, 215 Lexington Ave., New York, NY 10016; (monthly); ISSN: 0162-5195.

Note: v.1,n.1-v.18,n.1, Feb 1911-Dec 1940 as **Photoplay**; v.18,
n.2-v.91,n.8, Jan 1941-Aug 1977 as **Photoplay Combined with
Movie Mirror**; v.91,n.9-v.92,n.6, Sep 1977-Jun 1978 as
Photoplay with TV Mirror; v.92,n.7, Jul 1978- as **Photoplay**.
Began as a well written and beautifully illustrated fan
magazine, documenting the golden age of Hollywood. Slowly
gave way to more pulp, less art. Celebrity conscious
magazine focusing on lives and romances of current motion
picture and television stars.
PN1993.P515.

Photoplay Combined with Movie Mirror (U.S.). See: **Photoplay**.

Photoplay Movies & Video (U.K.). See: **Film Monthly**.

Photoplay with TV Mirror (U.S.). See: **Photoplay**.

PhotoVideo (Canada); AVS Publishing, 77 Mowat Ave., No. 209,
    Toronto, Ont. M6K 3E3, Canada; (9 times/yr); ISSN: 0834-227X;
    OCLC 16220893.
    Note: v.1, 1984 -.
    Trade journal for professional video makers and
    photographers. Talks about production, distribution, new
    techniques, cameras, camcorders, suppliers and equipment.
    Published with English and French text.
    TK690; Dewey: 381.45621388332.

Picture House (U.K.); Cinema Theatre Association, Allen Eyles,
    Editor, 44 Warlingham Rd., Thornton Heath, Surrey CR4 7DE,
    England; (2 times/yr); ISSN: 0263-7553.
    Note: [n.1] 1967 -.
    Devoted to the study and appreciation of old movie houses.
    Uses archival photographs and architectural drawings to
    capture the exterior views and interior details of the grand
    old palaces. Subscription to the magazine is part of the
    membership to the association.

Polish Film. Film Polonais (Poland). Formerly: **Film Polski** (0428-
    366X). Film Polski, Export and Import of Films, 00-054
    Warszawa, ul. Mazowiecka 6/8 Poland; (irregular); ISSN: 0015-
    136X; OCLC 5205782.
    Note: n.1-n.[?], 1963-1968 as **Film Polski**; renumbered [n.1],
    1969- as **Polish Film. Film Polonais**.

Bilingual translations in English and French describe the
latest Polish film releases for booking agents and film
importers. Glossy photos accompany the reviews, which list
original Polish title, translation titles, cast, credits,
length and synopsis. Contains short profiles of Polish film
stars.

Positif; Revue de Cinema (France). Alternate titles: **Revue de
Cinema; Revue Periodique de Cinema**. Nouvelles Editions Opta,
1, Quai Conti, 75006 Paris, France. Tel: 43.54.40.96;
(monthly); ISSN: 0048-4911; OCLC 3943070.
Note: n.1, May 1952 -.
Well documented and meticulously researched periodical
containing articles on film history, theory and criticism.
Conducts long interviews with respected international
directors, screenwriters, cinematographers and performers.
Contains intellectual film reviews.
PN1993.P67; Dewey: 791.43/05.

Post Script (U.S.); Post Script, Inc., Jacksonville University,
Jacksonville, FL 32211; (3 times/yr); ISSN: 0277-9897; OCLC
7673970.
Note: v.1,n.1 Fall 1981 -.
"Essays in film and the humanities." Scholarly journal which
seeks to relate cinema studies to the humanities. Individual
issues developed around a theme, covering such topics as
acting styles, set design and costume, film history, music,
cinematic language, adapting literature into movies.
PN1995.P682; Dewey: 791.43/75/05.

Prasen (Denmark); Danske Bornefilmklubber, Niels
Hemmingsensgade 20, bagh. 3-1153, Kobenhavn K Denmark;
(quarterly); ISSN: 0106-7665.
Note: n.1, Jan-Mar 1976 -.
Schedule of film programs presented at the Danish cinema
club. Contains profiles of entertainers and directors with
filmographies. Reports on events, premieres and special
shows.

Pre-Production Newsletter (U.S.); National Film Sources, 10 East
39th St., Suite 1017, New York, NY 10016. Tel: 800/222-3844;
(monthly); ISSN: n/a.
Note: v.1, 1988? -.

Designed as a clearinghouse for information about employment
opportunities for motion picture actors, actresses and technicians.
Researches Screen Actors Guild and non-union films in their
pre-production stages. Lists producers and casting directors
seeking talent and services for future film projects.

Pre Recorded Cassette News (U.S.). See: **P.R.C. News.**

Premiere (Denver); Denver Center for the Performing Arts,
14th and Curtis Sts., Denver, CO 80204. Tel: 303/892-0983;
(bimonthly).
Note: v.1, 1980 -.
Elaborate programming schedule for the Denver Center for the
Performing Arts. Features retrospectives of older sound
classics, works of famous directors and silent masterpieces.
Also presents programs centered around a theme, such as
American musicals, "fascism and film," and the auteur theory.

Premiere (Hollywood). See: **American Premiere.**

Premiere (New York); Premiere Publishing, 2 Park Ave., New
York, NY 10016; (bimonthly); ISSN: 0894-9263; OCLC 16388050.
Note: v.1,n.1 Jul/Aug 1987 -.
Popular, glossy film magazine whose lead story is usually a
biopix article on the current cinematic heartthrob. Looks at
the world behind the screen, featuring stories about film
production. Reviews the latest theatrical releases and new
titles on home video.
PN1993.P72; Dewey: 791.43/05.

Preview; Program Guide to the A.F.I. Theater and Member Events
(U.S.). Alternate title: **A.F.I. Preview.** American Film
Institute, John F. Kennedy Center for the Performing Arts,
Washington, DC 20566. Tel: 202/828-4090; (bimonthly); ISSN:
0194-3847; OCLC 5368458.
Note: v.1, May 1979 -.
Scheduling guide to the film programs at the A.F.I. Theater
in Washington D.C. Includes notices of upcoming events,
special guest appearances, background data on the films to be
shown and ticket information.
PN1993.P74; Dewey: 791.43/05.

Printed Matter (U.S.); Printed Matter c/o The Media Project, PO Box 2008, Portland, OR 97208; (quarterly); ISSN: 0738-9558; OCLC 9697612.
Note: n.1, 1974? -.
A "non-profit media arts organization dedicated to encouraging, promoting and serving the growth and artistic development of the Northwest film and video community." Acts as a clearinghouse for independent film and video makers throughout the Northwest United States.

Prisma; Kino-und Fernseh-Almanach (E.Germany). Alternate title: **Kino-und Fernseh-Almanach.** Henschelverlag Kunst und Gesellschaft, Leinen DDR 15-M, Ausland 20-DM, East Germany; (annual); ISSN: n/a; OCLC 4572514.
Note: v.1, 1971 -.
Compilation of articles by German film scholars. Covers international film history, television production, current East German filmmakers, awards and festivals. Lists contemporary German motion picture and television productions with bibliographic data, such as premiere date, director, screenwriter, cinematographer, music and cast. Indexed by personality and film title; published in German. PN1993.P755.

Pro/Comm (U.S.). See: **The Professional Communicator.**

Pro Film (U.S.). See: **Professional Film Production.**

Producers Guild of America. Journal (U.S.). See: **The Journal of the Producers Guild of America.**

The Producer's Masterguide (U.S.). Formerly: **New York Production Manual** (0163-1276). New York Production Manual, Inc., 330 West 42 St., 16th Floor, New York, NY 10036-6994. 212/465-8889; (annual); ISSN: 0732-6653; OCLC 8412817.
Note: ed.1-ed.2, 1979/80-1981/82 as **New York Production Manual**; ed.3, 1983- as **The Producer's Masterguide.**
Provides a comprehensive listing of names, addresses and telephone numbers for services involved in film and video production throughout the United States, Canada, the Caribbean, Israel, Australia, Great Britain and other countries as well. Contains information on insurance, copyrights, shooting-permits, union and guild contracts,

working conditions, and TV commercials production.
PN1993.5.U77B46a; Dewey: 384.55/025/7.

Production Notes (U.S.); Exhibitor Relations Co., Inc., 116 N.
Robertson Blvd., Suite 708, Los Angeles, CA 90048. Tel: 213/
657-2005; (5 times/yr); ISSN: n/a.
Note: [v.1] 198u -.
For film programmers and theater owners; lists American
features with their projected release dates. Arranged
alphabetically by name of distributor, each entry includes
title, projected release date, producer, director,
screenwriter, cast and synopsis. Companies listed are: Buena
Vista, Columbia, MGM/UA, Orion, Paramount, Tri-Star,
Twentieth Century-Fox, Universal, Warner Bros., Weintraub.

Productions-In-Progress (U.S.); Productions-In-Progress, PO Box
23562, L'Enfant Plaza, Washington, D.C. 20026. Tel: 202/488-0717;
(bimonthly); ISSN: n/a.
Note: v.1,n.1 Jan/Feb 1987 -.
Designed for industry personnel, producers, investors, information
analysts and educators, this trade periodical covers new motion
pictures and television productions currently being made.
Promises "up-to-the minute details on TV and film projects in the
pipeline." Also offers a database subscription package.

The Professional Communicator (U.S.). Formerly: **Matrix**;
Pro/Comm (0279-8255). Women in Communication, 2101 Wilson
Blvd., Suite 417, Arlington, VA 22201. Tel: 703/528-4200; (5
times/yr); ISSN: 0891-1207; OCLC 12958943.
Note: 1915-1980? as **Matrix**; v.1,n.1-v.5,n.7, Feb 1981-Jul
1984 as **Pro/Comm**; v.5,n.8/9 Aug/Sep 1985- as **The Professional
Communicator**.
Magazine for professionals working in communications; covers
print and electronic media, advertising, public relations,
filmmaking, photo journalism and marketing. Profiles women
executives, conducts interviews, reports on topics of
interest to people involved in the mass media.
Dewey: 384 11.

Professional Film Production (U.S.). Alternate titles: **ProFilm**;
Pro Film. PTN Publishing Company, 101 Crossway South Park,
West Woodbury, NY 11797; (bimonthly); ISSN: 0362-5974; OCLC
2303055.

Note: v.1,n.1 Jun 1975 -.
"The business magazine of film and tape." Designed for
professional film and video makers working on features,
sponsored films, TV commercials, industry films, government
and educational films. Articles show how to obtain financing
and distribution; acts as a clearinghouse for professional
opportunities; highlights marketing strategies; covers legal
issues. Interviews professionals working in the industry.
PN1995.9.P7P76; Dewey: 791.43/023/05.

ProFilm (U.S.). See: **Professional Film Production**.

Proletarskoe Kino (U.S.S.R.). See: **Iskusstvo Kino**.

Public Broadcasting Report (U.S.); Television Digest, Inc., 1836
Jefferson Place, NW, Washington, DC 20036. Tel: 202/872-9200;
(biweekly); ISSN: 0193-3663; OCLC 4959753.
Note: [n.1], 1978 -.
"The authoritative news service for public broadcasting and
allied fields." Newsletter reporting on the P.B.S.
television network and its affiliates.
PN1990.9.P82P82; Dewey: 384.54/43.

Public Broadcasting System Video News (U.S.). See: **P.B.S. Video**.

Public Telecommunications Letter (U.S.). See: **Current**.

Public Television Transcripts Index (U.S.); Research
Publications, 12 Lunar Dr., Woodbridge, CT 06525. Tel: 800/732-
2477; 203/397-2600; (quarterly); ISSN: 0897-9642; OCLC
17682657.
Note: v.1, 1987 -.
Published a retrospective cumulative edition covering
programs aired from 1973-1986. Provides access to
transcripts of the following Public Broadcasting System news
shows: *Adam Smith's Money World, Currents, Innovations,
MacNeil/Lehrer News Hour,* and *Metroline.* Programs are
indexed by subject, names of personalities and titles.
Dewey: 791 11.

The Publicists Guild Directory (U.S.). Alternate title: **Directory
of Members. The Publicists Guild of America.** The Publicists
Guild of America, 14724 Ventura Blvd., Penthouse Suite,

Sherman Oaks, CA 91403-3501. Tel: 818/905-1541; (annual);
ISSN: 0742-4000; OCLC 10318943.
Note: v.1, 1983 -.
A directory of members of the Publicists Guild. Members are
responsible for the advertising, promotion and successful
exploitation of motion picture and television productions.
Contains names, addresses, telephone numbers and projects
worked on.
PN1995.9.P79P83a; Dewey: 659.2/93848/02573.

-Q-

Q.R.F.V. (U.S.). See: **Quarterly Review of Film and Video**.

I Quaderni del Cinema Italiano (Italy); Editore ACI, Rome, Italy; (3 times/yr); ISSN: n/a; OCLC 17212149.
Note: v.1,n.1 May/Aug 1982 -.
Scholarly publication studying Italian film and television production. Reviews films and television programs. Published in Italian.

Quaderni di Cinema (Italy); Quaderni di Cinema, Via Benedetto Varchi, 57, 50132, Firenze, Italy; (bimonthly); ISSN: n/a; OCLC 9451962.
Note: v.1,n.1 Apr 1981 -.
Popular journal containing enthusiastic articles on film theory, history and criticism. Studies international filmmaking, with a slight emphasis on Italian productions and directors. Reviews films. Published in Italian.

Quarterly of Film, Radio and Television (U.S.). See: **Film Quarterly**.

Quarterly Review of Film and Video (U.S.). Formerly: **Quarterly Review of Film Studies**; Alternate title: **Q.R.F.V.** Harwood Academic Publishers, Subscription address: S.T.B.S. Marketing Dept., PO Box 786, Cooper Station, New York, NY 10276. Tel: 212/206-8900; (quarterly); ISSN: 0146-0013; OCLC 2601733.
Note: v.1,n.1-v.10,n.4, Feb 1976-Fall 1988 as **Quarterly Review of Film Studies**; v.11,n.1, Spring 1989- as **Quarterly Review of Film and Video**.
Academic film journal publishing in depth articles on film theory and criticism. Tends to analyze motion pictures in the context of literature. Articles cover current feature releases, Hollywood classics, experimental, documentary and independent films. Offers well written reviews of scholarly books on cinema and broadcasting studies. In 1989 added

video studies to its scope.
PN1994.Q34; Dewey: 791.43/05.

Quarterly Review of Film Studies (U.S.). See: **Quarterly Review of Film and Video.**

Quarterly Update (U.S.); National Archives and Records Administration, National Audiovisual Center, 8700 Edgeworth Dr., Capitol Heights, MD 20743-3701; (quarterly); ISSN: n/a; OCLC 6507469.
Note: n.1, Jun 1980 -.
This newsletter publishes a list of audiovisual materials recently produced by federal agencies that are for sale or rent on video and 16mm film. It is a good source for reasonably-priced educational, training and documentary productions. The National Audiovisual Center is the distribution center for audiovisuals produced by the U.S. government. Catalogs are free upon request.
AE1.109.

Qui Fait Quoi (Canada); Revue Qui Fait Quoi, Inc., 3627 St-Denis, Montreal, QC H2X 3L6 Canada; (monthly); ISSN: 0828-6140; OCLC 12045258.
Note: v.1,n.1 Jan 1984 -.
"Professional Guide to Showbiz" in Quebec Province. Keeps current with the latest cultural and entertainment offerings for motion pictures, video, television, animation, theatre, radio, and dance. Acts, in some ways, as a casting directory for Quebec. Published in French.
PN1560; Dewey: 790.2/09714.

Quirk's Reviews (U.S.); Lawrence J. Quirk, 74 Charles St., New York, NY 10014; (irregular); ISSN: n/a.
Note: n.1, 1972 -.
Folksy and opinionated newsletter presenting a historical overview of Hollywood films and stars. Articles capture nostalgic remembrances from a bygone era. Champions celebrities who have fallen into disrepute, such as Joan Crawford, Bette Davis and John Gilbert.

-R-

R.T.M. (W.Germany). See: **Rundfunktechnische Mitteilungen.**

R.T.S. Music Gazette (U.S.); R.T.S. Music Gazette, 711 W. 17th
St., Bldg. G-L, Costa Mesa, CA 92627; (bimonthly); ISSN: OCLC
12691359.
Note: v.1, 1973 -.
A music newsletter that concentrates on film music and
soundtrack recordings. Lists soundtracks for sale with
distribution information.

Radio and Television (Czechoslovakia). Alternate titles: **Radio
and Television International Review; Radio Television.**
International Radio and Television Organization (OIRT),
Skikanska ul. 1, 169 56 Prague 6, Czechoslovakia. Tel: 341
371; (6 times/yr); ISSN: 0033-7676; OCLC 9210016.
Note: v.1, 1950 -.
The International Radio and Television Organization is a
voluntary, non-commercial association not subject to
geographical or political considerations. However, most of
the members represent Eastern European countries. Its aim is
to exchange programs, information and technical development.
The magazine reports on member news, programming, festivals,
and technical advice. Published in English, Russian and
German.
PN1991.I52; Dewey: 384.54/0947.

Radio and Television International Review (Czechoslovakia). See:
Radio and Television.

Radio Star (U.S.). See: **Modern Screen.**

The Radio Supplement (U.K.). See: **Radio Times.**

Radio Televisioni (Albania); Drejtorise se Pergjitheshme te RTV,
Cmimi 2, Leke, Albania; (biweekly); ISSN: n/a.
Note: v.1, 1967 -.

The programming schedule for the state-run radio and
television stations in Albania. Articles on programs,
people, folk culture, and political issues. Published in
Albanian.
PN1991.3.A38R32.

Radio Television (Czechoslovakia). See: **Radio and Television.**

Radio Times (U.K.). Formerly: **The Radio Supplement; World-Radio.**
B.B.C. Magazines, 35 Marylebone High St., London W1M 4AA,
England. Tel: 01 580-5577; (weekly); ISSN: 0033-8060; OCLC
1763373.
Note: [v.1-v.15], 1925-Aug 1939 as **The Radio Supplement**
(later **World-Radio**); [v.16], Sept 1939- as **Radio Times**.
For listeners and viewers of B.B.C. radio and television.
Publishes a complete seven-day guide to programming. Includes
articles on performers, directors, screenwriters, and
musicians; gives background information on new programs,
series, and specials.
TK6540.B78; Dewey: 791.4.

Radio Video Era (U.S.). Prototype issue called **Video Era.** TV
Trade Media, Inc., Dom Serafini, Editor, 211 E. 51st St., New
York, NY 10022. Tel: 212/688-1760; (quarterly); ISSN: 0882-
2646; OCLC 11801034.
Note: v.1,n.1 July 1985 as **Video Era** published in Jul 1985
issue of **Video Age International**; v.1,n.1 Jan/Feb 1986- as
Radio Video Era.
Designed as an international business magazine covering the
communications industry; published in Spanish and Portuguese.
Focuses on satellite networks catering to Latin America.
Dewey: 384 11.

Radio-es Televizio-Ujsag (Hungary). Formerly: **Radio-Ujsag;**
alternate title: **Magyar Radio.** Magyar Radio es a Magyar
Televisio, Budapest VIII, Brody Sandor utca 5-7 (Levelcim:
Budapest 1801) Hungary. Tel: 338-330; (weekly); ISSN: n/a.
Note: v.1,n.1-v.2,n.42, Dec 17, 1956-Oct 21, 1957 as **Radio-
Ujsag**; v.2,n.43, Oct 28, 1957- as **Radio-es Televizio-Ujsag.**
Programming schedule for the Hungarian radio and television
networks. Contains short articles on music and the
performing arts. Offers mostly classical music and cultural
presentations, such as opera, ballet and theater. Published

in Hungarian.
PN1991.3.H93M32.

Radio-Ujsag (Hungary). See: **Radio-es Televizio-Ujsag**.

Recueil des Films (Canada); Office des Communications Sociales,
4005, de Bellechasse, Montreal, Quebec, H1X 1J6 Canada;
(annual); ISSN: 0085-543X; OCLC 2441950.
Note: v.1, 1955/56 -.
Rates and reviews motion pictures based on their humanity and
Christian values. Arranged alphabetically by French release
title, each entry includes original title, production
company, date, director, length, screenwriter, music, editor,
cast, brief plot analysis, a description of the film's
artistic qualities and its appreciation for compassionate
human values: "une appreciation artistique et une
appreciation sur la valeur humaine et chretienne." Published
in French.
PN1995.9.E9035; Dewey: 791.43/7.

The Reel Directory (U.S.); Sunflower Unlimited, PO Box 866,
Cotati, CA 94928. Tel: 707/795-9367; (annual); ISSN: 8755-
786X; OCLC 11323708.
Note: v.1, 1979 -.
A directory of "film, video, multimedia for all of Northern
California." Lists names and addresses for equipment
suppliers, facilities, acting coaches, choreographers,
actors/models, casting directors, talent agents, film and
video distributors, unions, guilds, animators and
advertisers.
PN1993.5.U718R43; Dewey: 384.8/025794.

The Reel Scoop (U.S.); The Reel Scoop, 1410 31st. Ave., Seattle
WA 98122. Tel: 206/329-8034; (monthly); ISSN: n/a.
Note: v.1, 1987? -.
"Assists parents in selecting the best children's and family
videos." Reviews current home video selections, plus classic
films and old favorites. Emphasis is on videos for children,
both fiction and non-fiction, i.e., "Mickey Mantle's
Baseball Tips for Kids of All Ages," although reviews videos
for adults as well, focusing on family themes and
wholesomeness.

The Reel West Film and Video Digest (Canada). See: **Reel West Digest.**

Reel West Digest (Canada). Formerly: **The Reel West Film and Video Digest.** Reel West Productions, Inc., 1106 Boundary Rd., Burnaby, British Columbia, Canada V5K 4T5. Tel: 604/294-4122; (annual); ISSN: 0821-7947; OCLC 9929571.
Note: v.1-v.2, 1981-1982 as **The Reel West Film and Video Digest**; v.3, 1983- as **Reel West Digest.**
"A directory for Western Canada's film, video, graphics, multi-image and music industry." Contains listings for production companies, service industries, equipment manufacturers and independent film and videomakers in Western Canada.
PN1998.A1R39; Dewey: 991.43/02/99.

Reel West Magazine (Canada); Reel West Productions, Inc., 1106 Boundary Rd., Burnaby, British Columbia, Canada V5K 4T5. Tel: 604/294-4122; (bimonthly); ISSN: 0831-5388; OCLC 14121945.
Note: v.1,n.1 Apr/May 1985 -.
Provides publicity and advertising support for the growth of the motion picture and video industries in Western Canada. Covers filming on location; promotes the endeavors of independent Canadian film and videomakers; reports on film festivals and the successful entries from Western Canada.
PN1998.A1; Dewey: 384.8/09712.

Report of the New Zealand Film Commission for the Year (New Zealand). See: **New Zealand Film & Television Directory.**

Reruns (U.S.); Reruns, The Magazine of Television History, PO Box 1057, Safford, AZ 85548-1057. Tel: 602/428-0307; (irregular); ISSN: 0278-6397; OCLC 7842826.
Note: v.1,n.1 Apr 1980 -.
Well written and detailed articles on American prime time television. Documents TV series, giving comprehensive listings of individual episodes. Includes articles on commercials.
PN1992.3.U5R47.

Respondex Movie Guide (U.S.); Video Corporate Research, Inc., PO Box 12208, Fort Wayne, IN 46863-2208; (25 times/yr); ISSN: n/a.

Note: v.1, 1988 -.
"A movie's past is a video's future." Designed for video
retailers and store operators who need to know strengths/
popularity of a film in order to choose their inventory.
Makes use of information released by the film industry and
trade periodicals to assess video titles. Contains a quick
list of recent releases for easy access, "the Video Helper,"
a general catalog of available videos, and the "Respondex Top
100," a rating guide to the most popular titles.

Review of the Arts: Film and Television (U.S.). Alternate titles:
Newsbank. Film and Television; Film and Television. Newsbank,
Inc., 58 Pine St., New Canaan, CT 06840. Tel: 802/875-2910;
(monthly); ISSN: 0737-3988; OCLC 4991071.
Note: v.1, 1975 -.
"An information service providing coverage of the moving
image as reported in newspapers from over 450 U.S. cities."
Reproduces film and television reviews from newspapers around
the country. The reviews are issued on microfiche; the
indexes, containing author, title and subject access, are
issued in print form.

Revista de Cine Y Video (Uruguay). See: **Cinemateca Revista**.

Revista de la Imagen y el Sonido: Eikonos (Spain). See: **Eikonos**.

Revista Lumara de Cultura Cinematografica (Romania). See:
  Cinema.

Revue Belge du Cinema (Belgium). Formerly: **A.P.E.C. Cinema:
  Revue Belge de Cinema**. Association des Professeurs pour la
  Promotion de l'Education Cinematographique, 73, avenue des
  Coccinelles, 1170 Brussels, Belgium; (quarterly); ISSN: n/a;
  OCLC 5244903.
  Note: v.1-v.13, 1963-1976 as **A.P.E.C. Cinema: Revue Belge du
  Cinema**; renumbered n.1, Sep 1976- as **Revue Belge du Cinema**.
  Scholarly journal aimed at university professors of cinema
  studies. Each issue contains a lengthy discussion of one
  particularly good film. The film's analysis includes a
  biographical sketch of the director, a chronology of its
  production from inception to debut, a complete list of cast
  and credits, a detailed plot description, and an analysis of
  cinematic techniques used. Includes a bibliography,

recently published scripts, and an overview of the articles
printed in recent film periodicals, such a **Chaplin, Positiv** and
Cahiers du Cinema. Published in French.
PN1993.5.B4R47; Dewey: 791.43/09493.

Revue de Cinema (France). See: **Positif; Revue de Cinema**.

La Revue de la Cinematheque (Canada). Continues: **Copie Zero**.
Alternate title: **Cinematheque**. Cinematheque Quebecoise, Musee
du Cinema, 355, boulevard de Maisonneuve est, Montreal, QC,
Canada H2X 1K1; (bimonthly); ISSN: 0843-6827.
Note: v.1,n.1 May/Jun 1989 -.
Short articles on current topics of interest to cinephiles
in French-speaking Canada. Contains the schedule of films
showing at the Cinematheque Quebecoise. Reviews current
cinema. Published in French. Replaces the magazine **Copie
Zero**.

La Revue de la Cinematheque (Canada). See also: **Copie Zero**.

La Revue du Cinema (France). See: **Cahiers du Cinema**.

Revue du Cinema/Image et Son/Ecran (France). See: **La Revue du
Cinema/Image et Son**.

La Revue du Cinema/Image et Son (France). Created by a merger
of **Image et Son/Revue du Cinema** (0536-5481) and **Ecran**;
alternate title: **Revue du Cinema/Image et Son/Ecran**. Ligue
Francaise de l'Enseignement, 3, rue Recamier, 75341 Paris Cedex
07, France. Tel: 43.58.96.83; (10 times/yr); ISSN: 0019-2635;
OCLC 1877838.
Note: n.46?-n.352, 1951?-Aug 1980 as **Image et Son/Revue du
Cinema**; n.353, Sep 1980- as **La Revue du Cinema/Image et Son**;
absorbed **Ecran** Jan 1980.
Popular review of international feature films. Each critic
rates the films currently in distribution in France. Reviews
include country of origin, date, length, production company,
distributor, director, screenwriter, cast, still photo and
critique. Includes television productions. Contains
articles on star performers and popular directors with their
filmographies. Published in French.
PN1993.L5215; Dewey: 791.43/05.

Revue International de Filmologie (Italy). See: **Ikon; Cinema, Television, Iconographie.**

Revue Periodique de Cinema (France). See: **Positif; Revue de Cinema.**

Rock Video (U.S.). See: **Hard Rock Video.**

Rock Video Idols Magazine (U.S.). See: **Hard Rock Video.**

Rock Video Magazine (U.S.). See: **Hard Rock Video.**

Rod Serling's The Twilight Zone (U.S.). Alternate title: **The Twilight Zone.** TZ Publications, a Division of Montcalm Publishing Corp., 401 Park Ave. South, New York, NY 10016-8802. Tel: 212/779-8900; (bimonthly); ISSN: 0279-6090; OCLC 7120361.
Note: v.1,n.1 Apr 1981 -.
Well done literary and media review, concentrating on science fiction, horror and fantastic stories, film, and television. Critiques current films and television series, featuring interviews with the directors and cast members. Lists home video releases. Each issue includes a selection of macabre short stories.
PS648.F3R62; Dewey: 813.0876/08.

The Romanian Film (Romania). Alternate title: **Roumanian Film.** Romaniafilm, 25 Julius Fucik St., Bucharest, Romania; (quarterly); ISSN: n/a; OCLC 7213944.
Note: v.1, 1965 -.
Promotes Romanian film productions. Publishes descriptive analyses of latest releases from the state-run film collective. Presents a photo album of actors and actresses; interviews directors and cinematographers. Published in English, French, Russian and Romanian.
PN1993.R65; Dewey: 791.43/09498.

Ross Reports Television (U.S.); Television Index, Inc., 40-29 27th St., Second Floor, Long Island City, NY 11101. Tel: 718/937-3990; (monthly); ISSN: 0035-8355; OCLC 5247997.
Note: v.1, 1949 -.
"Casting, scripts, production" information for television industry personnel, performers, technicians and writers.

Contains listings for New York City and Los Angeles casting directors, literary and talent agencies, TV producers, advertising agencies, producers of TV commercials, unions, network studios and program vendors. Also lists selected programs, such as dramatic and primetime series. PN1992.3.U5R67; Dewey: 384.55/025/73.

Roumanian Film (Romania). See: **The Romanian Film.**

The Royal Television Society Journal (U.K.). See: **Television.**

Rundfunk und Fernsehen (W.Germany); Hans-Bredow-Institute, Heimhuderstrasse 21, 2000 Hamburg 13, West Germany. Tel: 040/ 44 7178; (quarterly); ISSN: 0035-9874; OCLC 1696127.
Note: v.1,n.1 Jan 1953 -.
"Forum der Medienwissenschaft und Medienpraxis." Scholarly journal analyzing communications studies. Looks at international broadcasting, laws and legislation, using video as a teaching device, audience demographics, and the effect of radio and television on society. Reviews educational books on the media. Published in German with summaries in English.
HE8690.R8.

Runkfunk und Fernsehprogramm (E.Germany). See: **Film und Fernsehen.**

Rundfunktechnische Mitteilungen (W.Germany). Alternate title: **R.T.M.** Institut fur Rundfunktechnik, GmbH IRT, Mensing GmbH & Co., KG, Abt. Verlag, 2000 Norderstedt, West Germany. Tel: 040 525 2011; (bimonthly); ISSN: 0035-9890; OCLC 3711416.
Note: v.1,n.1 Feb 1957 -.
Very technical engineering magazine for television, radio and satellite technology. Prints schematics and diagrams of new equipment; publishes new theories of better engineering designs for broadcasting and reception of signals. Complete text in German with summaries in English, French and German.

-S-

S. & V.C.: Sound & Video Contractor (U.S.). See: **Sound & Video Contractor: S. & V.C.**

The S.A.F.T.T.A. Journal (S.Africa). Alternate title: **The South African Film and Television Technicians Association Journal**. South African Film and Television Technicians Association, PO Box 41357, Craighall 2024, Johannesburg, South Africa; (irregular); ISSN: n/a; OCLC 16649000.
Note: v.1-v.6,n.1/2, 1980?-1986.
S.A.F.T.T.A. is a trade union representing members of the film and television industries in South Africa, both full-time and free lance employees. Comments, notes, letters, and stories from the technicians working in South Africa today. Articles cover the cultural boycott, censorship, politics, the stifling of the broadcast industry, and limitations imposed on artistic freedom, as well as new equipment, cinematic techniques, lighting and engineering. Ceased publication.
PN1993.5.S24; Dewey: 384.8/0968.

S.A.G. Hollywood Close-up (U.S.). Alternate titles: **Screen Actors Guild Hollywood Close-up; Hollywood Close-up.** Screen Actors Guild, 7065 Hollywood Blvd., Hollywood, CA 90028-7594. Tel: 213/876-3030; (monthly); ISSN: 0199-7866; 0195-2684; OCLC 6157878.
Note: v.1, Mar 1980 -.
Newsletter for members of the Screen Actors Guild. Keeps members apprised of casting calls, new productions, bylaws, and legislation affecting actors and actresses.

S.C.A.D. Bulletin Radio-TV-Film Supplement (Belgium); Commission of the European Communities, Rue de la Loi 200, Wetstraat, B-1049 Bruxelles, Belgium. Tel: (02) 235.21.22; (irregular); ISSN: 1011-0879.
Note: Began 198u -.
"Publicizes the contents of the audiovisual library which is available to radio and TV networks and any other organizations interested in community activities." Covers

stock-shot, film, photographic and video material. Published in English and French.

S.C.N. Soundtrack Collector's Newsletter (Belgium). See: **Soundtrack!**

S.D. (U.S.). See: **Pacific Coast Studio Directory**.

S.M.A.T.V. News (U.S.). Alternate title: **Satellite Master Antenna T.V. News**. Paul Kagan Associates, Inc., 126 Clock Tower Place, Carmel, CA 93923-8734. Tel: 408/624-1536; (monthly); ISSN: 0734-5399; OCLC 8760846.
Note: n.1, Aug 1982 -.
Newsletter reporting on the economics and marketing issues affecting satellite master antenna television. Covers technical and legal aspects as well.

S.M.P.T.E. Journal (U.S.). Formerly: **Society of Motion Picture Engineers. Transactions; Society of Motion Picture Engineers. Journal** (0097-5834); **Society of Motion Picture and Television Engineers. Journal** (0361-4573); **Journal of the S.M.P.T.E.** (0361-4573). Society of Motion Picture and Television Engineers, 595 W. Hartsdale Ave., White Plains, NY 10607-1824. Tel: 914/761-1100; (monthly); ISSN: 0036-1682; OCLC 2093452.
Note: v.1-v.13, Jul 1916-May 1929 as **Society of Motion Picture Engineers. Transactions**; v.14-v.53, 1930-1949 as **Society of Motion Picture Engineers. Journal**; v.54-v.61,n.6, 1950-Dec 1953 as **Society of Motion Picture and Television Engineers. Journal**; v.62,n.1-v.84,n.12, Jan 1954-Dec 1975 as **Journal of the S.M.P.T.E.**; v.85,n.1, Jan 1976- as **S.M.P.T.E. Journal**.
Premiere trade journal of film and video technology, devoted to the "advancement in theory and practice of motion picture and television engineering, establishing standards, and the dissemination of scientific knowledge." Reports on progress, developments, and activities around the world in television and motion picture technology. Covers cameras, editing equipment, lab techniques, lighting, projection equipment, special effects, high definition TV, transmitter systems, video effects and graphics. Annual issue contains "SMPTE Progress Report" on the latest developments in the industry.
TR845.S6; Dewey: 332.9.

Satellite Age (U.S.). Formerly: **The Satellite Telecommunications Newsletter** (0197-145X). Martin Roberts & Associates, Inc., Box 5254, 270 N. Cannon Dr., Suite 103, Beverly Hills, CA 90210. Tel: 213/273-0381; (quarterly); ISSN: 0738-9698; OCLC 9665103.
Note: v.1-v.5, Oct 1979-Dec 1982 as **The Satellite Telecommunications Newsletter;** v.6,n.1, Jan-Mar 1983- as **Satellite Age.**
Reports on new applications and future usage of satellite communications in business and industry. Written for the layman, in non-technical terms.

Satellite Communications (U.S.); Cardiff Publishing Co., a subsidiary of Argus Press Holdings, Inc., 6300 S. Syracuse Way, Suite 650, Englewood, CO 80111. Tel: 303/220-0600; (monthly); ISSN: 0147-7439; OCLC 3880460.
Note: v.1,n.1 Jan 1977 -.
A business orientated and very technical magazine, focusing on all types of satellite communications, such as microwave, radar, telephone, computer and high speed data transmission, as well as television. It covers broadcasting developments worldwide. Articles analyze frequency protection, pirating signals, interference, European communications satellites, customized software, network design and installation. TK5104.S3636; Dewey: 621.38/0422.

Satellite Dealer (U.S.). See: **Satellite Direct.**

Satellite Direct (U.S.). Formerly: **Satellite Dealer** (0739-876X). CommTek Publishing Co., 9440 Fairview Ave., Boise, ID 83704. Tel: 208/322-2800; (monthly); ISSN: 0892-3329; OCLC 15161170.
Note: v.1,n.1-v.4,n.4 Sep 1983-Dec 1986 as **Satellite Dealer;** v.4,n.5 Jan 1987- as **Satellite Direct.**
Newsletter of the satellite communications industry. Keeps current with new channels, legislation, scrambling information and trade trends. Offers innovative uses for satellite TV, such as in hospitals and universities; or for rural communities and continuing education. Contains a calendar of events listing seminars, conferences, symposia and workshops related to satellite technology.
Dewey: 333 11.

Satellite Dish Magazine (U.S.); Satellite Publications, 460
Tennessee St., PO Box 8, Memphis, TN 38101. Tel: 901/521-1580;
(biweekly); ISSN: 0746-9470; OCLC 10407072.
Note: v.1, Nov 1982 -.
"Your complete satellite TV entertainment guide." A guide to
all programming available through satellite dish reception.
Reviews films to be aired, with recommendations. Contains
information about equipment, installation, maintenance, and
troubleshooting.

Satellite Master Antenna T.V. News (U.S.). See: **S.M.A.T.V. News**.

Satellite News (U.S.); Phillips Publishing, Inc., 7811 Montrose
Rd., Potomac, MD 20854. Tel: 301/340-2100; (weekly); ISSN:
0161-3448; OCLC 3905729.
Note: v.1, May 1978 -.
Newsletter about commercial developments, direct broadcast
satellite business, high definition TV, marketing, and systems
networks. Covers information on ground stations, news from
NASA, and international launches.

Satellite Orbit (U.S.); Satellite Orbit, PO Box 10789, Des
Moines, IA 50347-0789. Tel: 800/792-5541; (monthly); ISSN:
0732-7668; OCLC 8423766.
Note: v.1,n.1 Jul 1982 -.
Monthly programming schedule for over 100 channels carried on
satellite television. Articles examine how to better utilize
dish antennas and related equipment. Keeps up with new
technology, including home computers. Reviews and recommends
programs, home videos, special events.
PN1992.S28; Dewey: 791.45/75/05.

Satellite T.V. Opportunities Magazine (U.S.); Satellite T.V.
Opportunities Magazine, 1733 E. University Ave., Oxford, MS
38655. Tel: 601/236-5510; (monthly); ISSN: 0746-4711; OCLC
10062382.
Note: v.1,n.1 Sep 1983 -.
"Tries to provide dish dealers, distributors and
manufacturers with helpful information designed to enrich
industry marketing and sales skills." A marketing technique
magazine for TVRO professionals. Ceased publication?

Satellite T.V. Week (U.S.); Fortuna Communications Corp., 140 South Fortuna Blvd. (PO Box 308) Fortuna, CA 95540-0308. Tel: 707/725-1185; (weekly); ISSN: 0744-7841; OCLC 8563844.
Note: v.1, 1982 -.
Newspaper format containing accurate and up-to-date lists of satellite television programming. All listings are by date and time. Gives a breakdown of programming by genre; reader can search for programs under general categories, such as movies, children's, educational, music, news, religion, network series, etc. Includes lead stories on special programs, popular entertainers and technical tips.

Satellite T.V. Week T.V.R.O. Dealer (U.S.). See: **T.V.R.O.: Satellite T.V. Week Dealer**.

Satellite Technology (U.K.); Satellite Technology, 12-13 Little Newport St., London WC2H 7PP England. Tel: 441 437-4343; (monthly); ISSN: 0267-6389; OCLC 12357641.
Note: v.1,n.1 Apr 1985 -.
Very technical journal covering all satellite business and government applications: military, scientific and telecommunications. Charts launch dates and descent dates by country, with mission statements. Also covers robotics, space stations, radar and microwave technology.
TL796.A1S33; Dewey: 629.44 19.

The Satellite Telecommunications Newsletter (U.S.). See: **Satellite Age**.

Satellite Times (U.S.); Triple D Publishing Inc., 551 National Press Bldg., Washington, DC 20045. Tel: 202/662-8820; (biweekly); ISSN: 0890-1260; OCLC 14178880.
Note: v.1, 1986 -.
Trade newsletter covering satellite technology and the communications industry. Gives regulatory and technical information, new applications for satellites, marketing data.

Satellite Week (U.S.); Warren Publishing, Inc., 2115 Ward Court, NW, Washington, DC 20037. Tel: 202/872-9200; (weekly); ISSN: 0193-2861; OCLC 5150932.
Note: v.1,n.1 July 30, 1979 -.
"The authoritative news service for satellite communications and allied fields." Covers international satellite news,

such as mergers, meetings, funding, government regulations
and launchings. Covers LandSat, commercial television and
military applications.

Satellite World (U.S.). Formerly: **Satellite Orbit International**
(0741-3734). Satellite World, CommTek Publishing Co., 9440
Fairview Ave., Boise, ID 83704. Tel: 208/322-2800; (monthly);
ISSN: 8756-6184; OCLC 11614789.
Note: v.1,n.1-v.2,n.3, Jan 1984-Feb 1985 as **Satellite Orbit
International**; v.2,n.4, Mar 1985- as **Satellite World**.
Focuses on the international implications of satellite
television. Reports on programming picked up from foreign
satellites. Specializes in the latest technology and
equipment.
Dewey: 384 11.

Scandinavian Film News (Sweden); Nordic Film Authorities, Box 27,
126, S-102 52, Stockholm, Sweden. Tel: 468 65 1127;
(quarterly); ISSN: n/a; OCLC 9545092.
Note: v.1,n.1 Nov 1981 -.
Free newsletter promoting motion pictures made in Denmark,
Norway and Sweden. Designed for film programmers, importers,
distributors and theater owners. Contains reviews of
Scandinavian feature films. Published in English.

De Scenariogids (Belgium). See: **Les Cahiers du Scenario = De
Scenariogids = The Screenwriter's Companion**.

**Schweizer Filmindex = Index Suisse du Cinema = Indice Svizzero
del Cinema** (Switzerland). Formerly: **Jahrbuch der Schweizer
Filmindustrie = Annuaire de la Cinematographie Suisse =
Annuario della Cinematografia Svizzera**. Promoguide S.A., Rue
Bovy-Lysberg 2, 1204 Geneva, Switzerland; (annual); ISSN:
n/a; OCLC 4657021.
Note: 1938/39-1976/77 as **Jahrbuch der Schweizer
Filmindustrie = Annuaire de la Cinematographie Suisse =
Annuario della Cinematografia Svizzera**; renumbered ed.1,
1978- as **Schweizer Filmindex = Index Suisse du Cinema = Indice
Svizzero del Cinema**.
A list of feature films released in Switzerland during the
preceding year. Contains a directory of Swiss motion picture
and television production companies, distributors, archives,
libraries and technical services. The yearbook provides

translations in French, German and Italian.
PN1993.3.S33 for **Schweizer Filmindex;** PN1993.3.J28 for
Jahrbuch der Schweizer Filmindustrie.

Science Books & Films (U.S.). Formerly: **A.A.A.S. Science Books**
(0036-8253); alternate title: **A.A.A.S. Science Books & Films.**
SB & F Subscriptions, PO Box 465, Hanover, PA 17331; (5
times/yr: Sep/Oct, Nov/Dec, Jan/Feb, Mar/Apr, May/Jun);
ISSN: 0098-342X; OCLC 2246677.
Note: v.1-v.11, 1965-Mar 1975 as **A.A.A.S. Science Books;** v.11,
May 1975- as **Science Books & Films.**
Designed for teachers, librarians and acquisitions
specialists. Reviews science books and educational motion
pictures and videos for schools. Predominantly for books,
but contains a special section for audiovisual works. Each
entry gives production and distribution information, date,
length, grade level and synopsis, commenting on its
appropriateness, teaching potential and production quality.
Z7403.S33; Dewey: 016.5.

Scintillation (U.S.). See: **Cinemonkey.**

Screen (U.K.). See: **Screen Incorporating Screen Education.**

Screen Actor (U.S.). Screen Actors Guild, 7065 Hollywood Blvd.,
Hollywood, CA 90028-7594, Tel: 213/876-3030; (quarterly);
ISSN: 0036-956X; OCLC 2062664.
Note: v.1,n.1 Aug 1959 -.
"Official publication of the Screen Actors Guild." Articles
concern actors and actresses: residuals, equal employment
opportunity, safety on the set, taxes, pay scales, health
insurance, pension plans, compensation, minority rights,
plastic surgery. Contains a classified index for employment
and services.
PN1993.S2383.

Screen Actor News (U.S.). Alternate Title: **Screen Actor
Newsletter.** Screen Actors Guild, 7065 Hollywood Blvd.,
Hollywood, CA 90028-7594. Tel: 213/876-3030; (5 times/yr);
ISSN: 0195-2684.
Note: v.1, 1968 -.
Newsletter for members of the Screen Actors Guild. Keeps
current with new productions, casting calls, health and

safety issues, any news and events affecting the careers and livelihood of performers.

Screen Actor Newsletter (U.S.). See: **Screen Actor News**.

Screen Actors Guild Hollywood Close-up (U.S.). See: **S.A.G. Hollywood Close-up**.

Screen Digest (U.K.); Screen Digest, Ltd., 37 Gower St., London WC1E 6HH. Tel: 049-478 3237; (monthly); ISSN: n/a; OCLC 6097086.
Note: unnumbered; [v.1] 1971? -.
Publishes "monthly news, summaries and intelligence on the British communications industry." Short paragraphs outline latest new developments for film, TV, video, cable and satellite. Lists publications and media productions. Covers finance, business, entertainment, products, services, education, advertising and technology. Prints separate annual index.

Screen Education (U.K.). See: **Screen Incorporating Screen Education**.

Screen Finance (U.K.); Financial Times Business Information Limited, Second Floor, Tower House, Southampton St., London WC2E 7HA, England. Tel: 01-240 9391; (biweekly); ISSN: n/a.
Note: v.1,n.1 Jun 1988 -.
Business magazine detailing the financial and marketing aspects of the motion picture and broadcasting industries in Great Britain, Europe and the United States. Charts box office revenues. Keeps current with new executive personnel, buy outs, take overs, mergers and new acquisitions. Gives information on production, distribution and exporting film, television and video.

Screen Incorporating Screen Education (U.K.). Merged with: **Screen Education** (0306-0691); alternate titles: **Screen**; **Screen; the Journal of the Society for Education in Film and Television**. Address: Society for Education in Film and Television (SEFT), Crystal Management Liaison Ltd., 46 Theobalds Rd., London WC1X 8NW, England; (quarterly); ISSN: 0036-9543; OCLC 8731168; 4303646.
Note: n.1-n.46, Oct 1959-Sep/Oct 1968 as **Screen Education**;

renumbered v.10, Jan/Feb 1969- as **Screen Incorporating Screen Education.**
Scholarly journal for academics and students of cinema studies. Each issue is devoted to one topic, such as cybernetics, censorship, semiotics, race issues, or politics and film. Well written articles discuss the theoretical and subjective aspects of film.
PN1993.S2372.

Screen International (U.K.). Formerly: **Kinematograph and Lantern Weekly; Kinematograph Weekly** (0023-155X); **Kine Weekly; Today's Cinema Incorporating Kine Weekly; Cinema TV Today; Screen International & Cinema TV Today.** Address: King Publications, Ltd., Subscriptions Dept. Unit 8, Grove Ash, Bletchley, Milton Keynes, MK1 1BZ England. Tel: 09-087 1981; (weekly); ISSN: 0307-4617.
Note: v.1-v.33, 1907-1919 as **Kinematograph and Lantern Weekly;** v.33-v.511, Sep 1919-Dec 1959 as **Kinematograph Weekly;** v.511-v.651, Dec 1959-Sep 1971 as **Kine Weekly;** merged with **Today's Cinema** in Nov 1971, taking the numbering of the latter, to form **Today's Cinema Incorporating Kine Weekly** n.9953-n.9956, Nov 2, 1971-Nov 20, 1971; n.9957-n.10149, Nov 27, 1971-Aug 30, 1975 as **Cinema TV Today;** renumbered n.1-n.19, Sep 6, 1975-Jan 17, 1976 as **Screen International and Cinema TV Today;** n.20, Jan 24, 1976- as **Screen International.**
"The paper of the entertainment industry" in Great Britain. Trade paper for the motion picture and television industries. Publishes financial news, major developments, mergers, new productions and reviews of latest releases.
PN1993.5G7C5; Dewey: 338.4/7/791430941.

Screen International & Cinema TV Today (U.K.). See: **Screen International.**

Screen International Film and T.V. Yearbook (U.K.). See: **Screen International Film and Television Yearbook.**

Screen International Film and Television Yearbook (U.K.). Formerly: **British Film and Television Year Book; International Film and Television Yearbook;** Alternate titles: **International Film and T.V. Yearbook; Screen International Film and T.V. Yearbook.** Address: King Publications, Ltd. (Yearbook Listings), 6 Great Chapel St., London, W1V 4BR

Great Britain; (annual); ISSN: n/a; OCLC 2679195.
Note: ed.1-ed.30, 1947-1975/76 as **British Film and Television
Year Book**; ed.31-ed.37, 1976/77-1982/83 as **International Film
and Television Yearbook**; ed.38, 1983/84- as **Screen
International Film and Television Yearbook**.
Separated into three parts: the worldwide directory, the
territorial directory (further divided by region: Africa,
Australasia, North and South America, etc.) and "Who's Who."
Directories list agents, broadcasting companies, cable and
satellite operators, distributors, exhibitors and government
agencies by country. Contains biographical data on people in
the film and broadcasting industries.
PN1993.3.B7; Dewey: 791.43/028/0922.

Screen Producers Guild. Journal. See: **The Journal of the
Producers Guild of America**.

Screen Stars (U.S.); Magazine Management Co., Inc., Office of
Publications, 575 Madison Ave., New York, NY 10022;
(monthly); ISSN: n/a; OCLC 1775224.
Note: v.1, Apr 1944 -.
Long running fanzine featuring stories of the month about
screen celebrities. Photo-biographies contain pin ups and
posters of favorite motion picture and television stars, plus
their horoscopes, beauty tips, makeup techniques and diets.
PN1993.S26; Dewey: 791.405.

**Screen; the Journal of the Society for Education in Film and
Television** (U.K.). See: **Screen Incorporating Screen
Education**.

Screen World (U.S.). Formerly: **Daniel Blum's Screen World**. Crown
Publishers, 225 Park Ave. South, New York, NY 10003. Tel:
212/254-1600; (annual); ISSN: n/a; OCLC 5341628.
Note: v.1-v.16, 1949-1965 as **Daniel Blum's Screen World**;
v.17, 1966- as **Screen World**.
Chronological list of international feature films released during
the preceding year. Good at picking up lesser known, more
obscure motion pictures that had limited releases. Each entry
includes distributor, production company, director, detailed cast
and credits list, still photographs, and rating. Publishes
obituaries. Indexed by personality and title.
PN1993.3.D3.

The **Screenwriter's Companion** (Belgium). See: **Les Cahiers du Scenario = De Scenariogids = The Screenwriter's Companion.**

Script (France); L'Association pour la Fondation Internationale du Cinema et de la Communication Audiovisuelle (AFICCA), 50, Av. Marceau, 75008 Paris, France. Tel: (1) 47 23 70 30; (quarterly); ISSN: n/a.
Note: n.1, Summer 1988 -.
Scholarly tribute to scriptwriters, auteurs, and their motion picture and television scripts. Analyzes the works of recent authors, conducts interviews, compiles bibliographies and filmographies. Published in French.

Scriptwriter (U.S.). See: **Scriptwriter News.**

Scriptwriter News (U.S.). Formerly: **Scriptwriter** (0197-9388). Scriptwriter News, Inc., Subscription & Distribution Information, PO Box 956, New York, NY 10023. Tel: 212/582-8463; (bimonthly except Jan, Feb, Jun, Dec); ISSN: 0279-9596; OCLC 7386289.
Note: v.1,n.1-3, Jan-May 1980 as **Scriptwriter**; v.1,n.4 Jun 1980- as **Scriptwriter News**.
"The magazine for entertainment writers." Helpful insights for motion picture and television scriptwriters. Covers contract negotiations, how to acquire rights, copyrighting, and residuals. Articles tell how to acquire an agent, how to write for Broadway, how to write for the Soaps. PN1996.S38.

Segno Cinema (Italy). See: **Segnocinema.**

Segnocinema (Italy). Alternate title: **Segno Cinema.** Cineforum di Vicenza, Segnocinema, via G. Pratti 34, 361000 Vicenza, Italy. Tel: 0444/543749; (quarterly); ISSN: 0393-3865; OCLC 9612583.
Note: v.1,n.1 Autumn 1981 -.
Well researched and quite readable scholarly film magazine. Publishes long reviews of international feature films, giving production company, distributor, director, country of origin, year, scriptwriter, editor, cast, still photograph, and critical analysis. Contains excerpts from scripts of classic films, in their original languages with Italian translations. Articles cover film theory, methodology and criticism.

Published in Italian with excerpts in English, French,
Spanish and German.

Sequence (Pakistan); Bangladesh Better Cinema Front, GPO Box
869, Dacca-2, Bangladesh, Pakistan; (monthly); ISSN: 0586-982X.
Note: v.1, Mar/Apr 1970 -.
Published in English, tries to promote an appreciation for
better quality Pakistani films. Recognizes that cinema can
play a definitive and vital role in the Third World and that
it can be an instrument for social change. Confronts anti-
cinema snobbery and emphasizes film as a cultural art form.
PN1993.S38.

Sequences. Revue de Cinema (Canada); Office des Communications
Sociales, 4005, rue de Bellechasse, Montreal, Quebec, H1X 1J6
Canada. Tel: 514/729-6391; (quarterly); ISSN: 0037-2412; OCLC
2244611.
Note: n.1, 1955 -.
"La revue des cinephiles." Popular French language
publication containing long reviews of current features
giving title, director, screenwriter, editor, music,
photography, country of origin, date and publicity still.
Interviews film personalities. Contains a chart listing
titles with the rating each film received from the magazine's
editors. Reports in depth on the various international film
festivals. Reviews cinema books.
PN1993.S383.

Serial World (U.S.). See: **Favorite Westerns, Serial World**.

Series, Serials & Packages (U.S.) See: **Television Programming
Source Books**.

Shakespeare on Film Newsletter (U.S.); Bernice W. Kliman, Dept.
of English, Nassau Community College, Garden City, NY 11530;
(2 times/yr; Spring & Fall); ISSN: 0739-6570; OCLC 3665688.
Note: v.1,n.1 Dec 1976 -.
Acts as a clearinghouse for films, videos, audio tapes,
books, journal articles, courses and seminars pertaining to
the works of William Shakespeare. Informs secondary school
and college-level teachers about "film and television
treatments of Shakespeare and other figures of early European
literature." Publishes bibliographies and mediagraphies.

Show Business (U.S.). Formerly: **Actors Cues**. Leo Shull
   Publications, 1501 Broadway, New York, NY 10036. Tel: 212/
   354-7600; (weekly); ISSN: 0037-4318; OCLC 1590443.
   Note: v.1-v.8,n.22 1941-Jun 1, 1949 as **Actors Cues**; v.8,n.23,
   Jun 8, 1949- as **Show Business**.
   Trade paper informing actors and actresses about new
   theatrical, film and television productions, casting calls,
   location shooting, employment and classes. Reports on
   industry news, box office statistics, executive changes.

Show Call (U.K.). See: **Showcall**.

Showcall (U.K.). Alternate title: **Show Call**. Carson & Comerford,
   Stage House, 47 Bermondsey St., London, England SE1 3XT. Tel:
   01-403-1818; (annual); ISSN: 0264-4150.
   Note: ed.1, 197u -.
   A directory of stage, TV and motion picture personalities in
   Great Britain. Gives name, agent, telephone number and
   photograph for each performer.

Shows (Spain); Shows, International Edition, Corcega, 546, 5.0-
   08025, Barcelona, Spain. Tel: 347 56 59; ISSN: n/a.
   Note: [n.1] 198u -.
   "Leading Spanish magazine for films, TV, video, discotheques,
   music, theatre and entertainment." Promotional magazine,
   published in English, French and Spanish, giving extensive
   reviews for quality motion pictures made in Spain. Charts
   Spanish films, videos and television programs currently in
   distribution. Interviews Spanish directors.

Side Lights (U.S.); ClearLight, 123 Second Ave., Waltham, MA
   02154. Tel: 800/247-2014; (monthly); ISSN: n/a.
   Note: v.1, 1985 -.
   Newsletter for people who practice the art of multi-image.
   Informs film and video artists about the latest innovations
   in interactive multi-imaging techniques.

Sight and Sound (U.K.). Alternate title: **Sight & Sound**. British
   Film Institute; American subscriptions: Eastern News
   Distributors, Inc., 1671 E. 16th St., Suite 176, Brooklyn, NY
   11229; (quarterly); ISSN: 0037-4806; OCLC 1645027.
   Note: v.1, Spring 1932 -.
   An "independent critical magazine sponsored by and published

by the B.F.I." A literary journal containing well-researched
articles on film history and theory. Reviews films and books
on cinema studies. Publishes in-depth interviews. Reports
on international film festivals.
PN1993.S56; OCLC 791.43/05.

Sightlines (U.S.). Formed by a union of: **The Filmlist, Film Review
Digest** and **E.F.L.A. Bulletin**; absorbed **Film Library Quarterly**
(0015-1327). The American Film & Video Association, Inc., 920
Barnsdale Rd., Suite 152, LaGrange Park, IL 60525. Tel: 312/
482-4000; (quarterly); ISSN: 0037-4830; OCLC 1765552.
Note: v.1, Sep/Oct 1967 -.
An important periodical for educators and librarians,
reviewing educational films and videotapes, as well as books
on cinema studies. Contains scholarly articles on film
history, theory and criticism. Analyzes educational
television and non-fiction programming.
LB1044.Z9S54.

Sinchronos Kinimatografos (Greece). See: **Synchronos
Kinematografos.**

Sinematek (Israel). See: **Cinematheque.**

Six of One (U.K.). See: **Number Six.**

16 MM Film User (U.K.). See: **Audio Visual.**

Skoop (Netherlands). See: **Skoop/Kritisch Filmforum.**

Skoop/Kritisch Filmforum (Netherlands). Formerly: **Skoop** (0586-
6170); merged with **Kritisch Filmforum**. Skoop, Postbus 18277,
1001 ZD Amsterdam, Netherlands; (10 times/yr); ISSN: n/a;
OCLC 8241310.
Note: v.1-v.5, 1962-1969 as **Skoop**; v.6,n.1, Oct 1969- as
Skoop/Kritisch Filmforum.
Popular film journal containing reviews of recent international
features. Prints retrospective nostalgia pieces on film history
from the silent era through the golden age of Hollywood. Lead
articles cover contemporary film directors discussing their most
recent works. Rates the best films of the year. Published in
Dutch.
PN1993.S584.

Skrien (Netherlands); SDU/Openbaar Kunstbezit, De Ruijterkade 41-43, 1012 AA Amsterdam, Postbus 5555, 1007 AN, Amsterdam, The Netherlands. Tel: 020-854511; (8 times/yr); ISSN: 0166-1787.
Note: n.1, 1968? -.
Well photographed popular film magazine which specializes in long reviews of international feature films. Articles study film music, nitrate preservation, politics and film, and new cinematic styles from around the world. Covers television programming and home video in Holland. Interviews creative talents in the motion picture and television industries. Published in Dutch.

Slaughter House Magazine (U.S.); H.C.S. Association, 55 Ave. of the Americas, Suite 309, Box 24, New York, NY 10013. Tel: 212/925-3115; (bimonthly?); ISSN: n/a.
Note: v.1, 1989? -.
Issues are undated in the samples examined. Depicts and reviews contemporary "cut and slash" movies. Specializes in science fiction, horror and fantasy films that cater to gory, bloody and brutal depictions of mayhem and murder. Articles about makeup techniques, special effects, and labs that construct robotic monsters and miniatures.

Small But Enthusiastic Audience (Canada). See: **Spleen**.

Sneak Preview; the Media Digest (U.S.). See: **Media Digest**.

Soap Opera Digest (U.S.); Soap Opera Digest, Box 359036, Palm Coast, FL 32037; (biweekly); ISSN: 0164-3584.
Note: v.1,n.1 Jan 1976 -.
Designed to keep avid soap opera watchers current with all the story lines from both daytime and evening soaps. Keeps up on the gossip, rumors, feuds and invective fueling the stories.

Soap Opera People (U.S.); Tempo Publishing Co., Inc., 475 Park Ave., South, Suite 2201, New York, NY 10016; (bimonthly); ISSN: n/a.
Note: v.1, 1985 -.
A fan magazine which specializes in many exclusive interviews per issue. A photographic panorama of soap opera actors and actresses. Contains stories of happenings on and off the set, reports from prime time, as well as daytime soaps.

Soap Opera Stars (U.S.); Sterling Women's Group, 355 Lexington Ave., New York, NY 10017. Tel: 212/391-1400; (bimonthly); ISSN: 0199-3003; OCLC 5764091.
Note: v.1, 1975 -.
Fan magazine exploring the lifestyles of performers who appear on daytime soap operas. Consists mostly of interviews and photographs of the stars. Contains fan club information, New York and Hollywood gossip, cast lists, and storylines of the shows.

Soap Opera Update (U.S.); Soap Opera Update Magazine, Inc., 158 Linwood Plaza, Fort Lee, NJ 07024; (tri-weekly); ISSN: 0898-1485; OCLC 17735668.
Note: v.1,n.1 Jan 30, 1988 -.
Photographic essays on American soap operas. Summarizes the following shows: *All My Children, Another World, As the World Turns, The Bold and the Beautiful, Days of Our Lives, General Hospital, Guiding Light, Loving, One Life To Live, Santa Barbara, The Young and the Restless, Dallas, Dynasty, Falcon Crest, Knots Landing*.
Dewey: 791 11.

Soap Opera's Greatest Stories & Stars (U.S.); Sterling's Magazines, 355 Lexington Ave., New York, NY 10017. Tel: 212/391-1400; (quarterly); ISSN: 0746-9160; OCLC 10395429.
Note: v.1, 1976 -.
Special retrospective issues encapsulate popular stories from the past and put them in the context of current stories. Readers can learn about the characters' backgrounds and how their personalities have evolved.

Society of Cinematologists. Journal (U.S.). See: **Cinema Journal**.

Society of Motion Picture and Television Engineers. Journal (U.S.). See: **S.M.P.T.E. Journal**.

Society of Motion Picture Engineers. Journal (U.S.). See: **S.M.P.T.E. Journal**.

Society of Motion Picture Engineers. Transactions (U.S.). See: **S.M.P.T.E. Journal**.

Sound & Video Contractor: S. & V.C. (U.S.). Alternate title: **S. & V.C.: Sound & Video Contractor.** Intertec Publishing Corp., Box 12901, 9221 Quivira Rd., Overland Park, KS 66212. Tel: 913/888-4664; (monthly); ISSN: 0741-1715; OCLC 10091393. Note: v.1,n.1 Sep 1983 -.
Trade journal for audio and video retailers, store owners and operators, engineers and support personnel in the media business. Covers new technology, such as HDTV, stereo TV, compact discs, interactive video, computerized video. Discusses applications and uses for the new media technology. Dewey: 729 11.

Soundtrack! The Collector's Quarterly (Belgium). Formerly: **S.C.N. Sound Collector's Newsletter**; alternate title: **Soundtrack Collector's Newsletter.** Belgian Film Music Society, Luc Van de Ven, Astridlaan 171, 2800 Mechelen, Belgium. Tel: (32) 15-41-41-07; (quarterly); ISSN: 0771-6303; OCLC 6741236. Note: v.1-v.5 (n.21), 1975-1980 as **S.N.C. Soundtrack Collector's Newsletter**; v.5-v.7 (n.22-27), Summer 1980-Dec 1981 as **Soundtrack! The Collector's Quarterly.** Renumbered v.1,n.1 Mar 1982- as **Soundtrack! The Collector's Quarterly.**
Forum for buying, selling and trading audio copies of motion picture soundtracks: dialogue, music and sound effects. Interviews film composers; publishes filmographies and discographies. Reviews soundtracks from television series. Lists LP albums of soundtracks by country (Japan, America, Italy, France and Belgium) with title, composer and label produced each year. Published in English.
ML5.S08; Dewey: 782.8/5/05.

Soundtrack Collector's Newsletter (Belgium). See: **Soundtrack!**

The South African Film and Television Technicians Association Journal (S.Africa). See: **The S.A.F.T.T.A. Journal.**

Sovetskii Ekran (U.S.S.R.). See: **Sovetsky Ekran.**

Sovetskoe Kino (U.S.S.R.). See: **Iskusstvo Kino.**

Sovetskoe Radio i Televidenie (U.S.S.R.). See: **Televidenie, Radioveshchanie.**

Sovetsky Ekran (U.S.S.R.). Alternate title: **Sovetskii Ekran;** transliterated title: **Soviet Screen.** Pravda Publishing House, Union of Cinematographists of the U.S.S.R., ul. Chasovaya 5, Moscow, U.S.S.R.; (bimonthly); ISSN: 0038-5123.
Note: n.1, 1957 -.
Describes the achievements of the Soviet cinema, with particular interest in cinematography and camera work. Articles include interviews with successful cameramen explaining how they achieved their effects. Covers the latest productions. Published in Cyrillic.

Soviet Film (U.S.S.R.); Sovexportfilm, 9B. Gnezdnikovsky Pereulok, 103009 Moscow, U.S.S.R. Tel: 229 07 42; (monthly); ISSN: 0038-5395; OCLC 1774122.
Note: n.1, Jun 1957 -.
Glossy, nicely illustrated promotional magazine advertising Soviet film productions for export abroad. Gives a behind-the-scenes description of the latest official productions, interviews directors and contains biographical sketches of popular actors and actresses. Publishes editions in Russian, English, French, German, Spanish and Arabic.
PN1993.5.R9S543; Dewey: 791.43/0947.

Soviet Screen (U.S.S.R.). See: **Sovetsky Ekran.**

Spectator (U.S.); Division of Critical Studies of the School of Cinema-Television, University of Southern California, University Park, Los Angeles, CA 90089-2211; (2 times/yr); ISSN: n/a; OCLC 19842339.
Note: Bound journal began with v.8,n.2, Spring 1988 -.
Prior to the Spring 1988 issue, the periodical was published in a tabloid format and participation was limited to students of the U.S.C. School of Cinema-Television. With the Spring 1988 issue, the format was changed to a bound journal and participation was opened to students, teachers, scholars and filmmakers outside the school. A scholarly journal containing long articles examining new aspects of cinema studies, feminism, film history and criticism.

Spettacolo, Lo (Italy); S.I.A.E., Viale della Letteratura, (E.U.R.) 30 Rome, Italy; (quarterly); ISSN: 0038-738X; OCLC 2268034.
Note: v.1, Jan-Mar 1951 -.

"Rassegna economica e sociale degli spettacoli e delle attivita artistiche e culturali." Covers a wide range of entertainment industries: theater, music, video, cinema and television. Publishes scholarly articles about how the performing arts impact society and how culture influences the performing arts. Reports on film, television, and video in Europe, Australia, Japan and the United States. Published in Italian with summaries in English. GV1.S56.

Spettatore Critico (Italy). See: **Filmcritica.**

Spielfilme im Deutschen Fernsehen A.R.D. (W.Germany). See: **Spielfilme im Ersten Deutschen Fernsehen.**

Spielfilme im Ersten Deutschen Fernsehen (W.Germany). Formerly: **Spielfilme im Deutschen Fernsehen A.R.D.** Rundfunkanstalten der Bundesrepublik Deutschland (ARD), Programmdirektion des Deutschen Fernsehens, Bertramstr. 8, 6000 Frankfurt Am Main, West Germany; (annual); ISSN: n/a; OCLC 11831494.
Note: 1966-1975 published in one register; ed.1-ed.9, 1976-1984 as **Spielfilme im Deutschen Fernsehen A.R.D.**; [ed.10], 1985- as **Spielfilme im Ersten Deutschen Fernsehen.**
A directory of films broadcast on German TV. Each entry gives German title, original title, telecast date, summary and plot. Published in German.
PN1992.8.F5S65; Dewey: 791.43/75/05.

Spiral (U.S.); Spiral Group, Inc., PO Box 5603, Pasadena, CA 91107; (quarterly); ISSN: n/a; OCLC 12302602.
Note: n.1-n.9, Oct 1984-Oct 1986.
Focus was on experimental, independent and avant garde films and videos. Contained interviews and biographical sketches of independent filmmakers. Ceased publication.

Spleen (Canada). Alternate title: **Small But Enthusiastic Audience.** Spleen, 2 Sussex Ave., Toronto, Ont. M5S 1J5 Canada. Tel: 416/588-8940; (2 times/yr); ISSN: n/a.
Note: v.1,n.1 [Spring] 1989 -.
A publication of the Innis Film Society, at Innis College in Toronto, Canada, concentrating on independent, avant-garde and experimental cinema. Presents a forum of debate --"critical essays, personal statements, manifestos and text fragments"--

centering around experimental filmmaking. An academic journal for people teaching and studying film on a college level.

The Stage (U.K.). See: **The Stage and Television Today.**

The Stage and Television Today (U.K.). Formerly: **The Stage.** Carson and Comerford, 47 Bermondsey St., London SE1 3XT England. Tel: 01-403 1818; (weekly); ISSN: 0038-9099; OCLC 14075819.
Note: [n.1]-n.4061, Mar 25, 1881-Feb 12, 1959 as **The Stage**; n.4062, Feb 19, 1959- as **The Stage and Television Today**. Newspaper designed for the acting community and the theatrical and television industries in Great Britain. Gives information about plays, auditions, placements, casting calls and new TV series. Reviews plays in The Stage section; reviews television programs in the "Television Today" section. Contains TV ratings, listing the top thirty shows. PN2001.S8.

Star (U.S.). Alternate titles: **Tiger Beat Star; Tiger Beat Presents Star.** D.S. Magazines, Inc., 1086 Teaneck Rd., Teaneck, NJ 07666. Tel: 201/833-1800; (monthly); ISSN: 0199-1825; OCLC 5243869.
Note: v.1,n.1, Jan 1977 -.
Fan magazine for teenagers. Profiles young motion picture and television stars. Features pin ups and posters that can be cut out. Articles cover biographical data, interviews, gossip, trivia contests and horoscopes.

Star Guide (U.S.). Formerly: **Celebrity Directory.** Axion Information Services, Box 8015, Ann Arbor, MI 48107. Tel: 313/761-4842; (annual); ISSN: n/a; OCLC 17016314.
Note: ed.1-ed.4, 1984-1987 as **Celebrity Directory**; ed.5, 1988/89- as **Star Guide**.
"Featuring over 2,900 names and addresses for movie stars, TV stars, musicians, sports celebrities, politicians, and other famous people." A directory used for contacting celebrities. CT120.S696; Dewey: 920.02 19.

Star Log (U.S.). See: **Starlog.**

Star Trek: The Official Fan Club (U.S.); Star Trek: The Official Fan Club, Inc., 603 Ouray Way, Aurora, CO 80011; (bimonthly);

ISSN: 0883-3125; OCLC 12115065.
Note: n.1, 1979? -.
"Officially licensed by Paramount Pictures Corporation." Fan
magazine for the popular television series, *Star Trek*.
Interviews the cast and crew; reports on works-in-progress,
new *Star Trek* movies and videos. Contains photos, trivia
contests and information on *Star Trek* conventions and
festivals.

Starlog (U.S.). Alternate title: **Star Log**. Starlog
Communications International, Inc., 475 Park Ave. South, New
York, NY 10016; (monthly); ISSN: 0191-4626; OCLC 4601273.
Note: n.1, Aug 1976 -.
"The science fiction universe." Focuses on science fiction
and fantasy adventure films and television. Goes behind the
scenes to show how special effects are achieved. Interviews
the stars, the writers and directors. Shows construction of
models, robots, miniatures, sets. Includes a section for
classified advertising for buying, selling, trading movie
memorabilia.

Stars (Belgium); Grand Angle, rue d'Arschot, 29-6370,
Mariembourg, Belgium. Tel: 060/31.21.68; (quarterly); ISSN:
0776-0698.
Note: v.1,n.1 Sep 1988 -.
"Biofilmographies" of international motion picture stars and
supporting actors and actresses. Information is compiled
through books, magazines, on screen and by interview.
Entries are arranged alphabetically by name and with
biography, filmography and photograph. Concentrates on
European performers. Published in French.

Statistiques de la Culture L'Industrie du Film (Canada). See:
Culture Statistics. Film Industry.

Statistisches Bundesant. Bildung und Kultur (W.Germany); W.
Kihlhammer GmbH, Abt. Veroffentlichungen des Statistischen
Bundesantes, Philipp-Reis-Str.3, 6500 Mainz 42, West Germany.
Tel: 06131/59094-95; (annual); ISSN: n/a.
Note: ed.1, 1974 -.
Very thorough analysis of motion picture statistics in West
Germany. Includes number of theaters, number of screens,
seats and employees. Includes how many films were shown and

attendance. Statistics are divided by region.
PN1993.5.G3G37a.

Stills (U.K.); Stills Magazine, Ltd., 20-22 Wellington St.,
London WC2E 7DD England; (bimonthly); ISSN: n/a; OCLC
10892876.
Note: n.1-n.30, 1980-Mar 1987.
Briefly known as the **Oxford Review of Film and Theatre** when
it began in 1980. Highly regarded film journal with thought
provoking articles that approached cinema studies from a
standpoint of aesthetics combined with craftsmanship. Covered
filmmaking as a business with box office considerations as
well as a craft with artistic considerations. Interviewed
successful directors and other professionals involved with
the motion picture and television industries. Ceased
publication.
PN1992.S8; Dewey: 791.4/05 19.

Studies in Broadcasting (Japan). Japanese title: **Hosogaku Kenkyu**.
Broadcasting Cultural Research Institute, NHK Theoretical
Research Center, 2-1-1, Atago, Minato-ku, Tokyo 105, Japan.
Tel: 03-433-5211; (annual); ISSN: n/a; OCLC 12782496.
Note: v.1, 1961 -.
Surveys the "information environment and related behavior in
Japan." Analyzes the effects of broadcasting and mass media
on the Japanese populace. Some of the topics covered are:
stereotyping of gender images on television, the effects of
exploitation and sensationalism, commercials and advertising, and
the changing demographics of the Japanese audience. Contains
statistical charts for hours watched, broken down by age and
gender. Separate editions published in Japanese and English.
PN1992.S85 (English); PN1992.H67 (Japanese).

Studies in the Humanities (U.S.); Indiana University of
Pennsylvania, 110 Leonard Hall, I.U.P., Indiana, PA 15705; (2
times/yr); ISSN: 0039-3800; OCLC 2002600.
Note: v.1, Mar 1969 -.
For scholars, students, and teachers, a multi-disciplinary
journal incorporating literature, motion pictures, television
and aesthetics. Articles cover the treatment of film and
television in the context of literature and philosophy.
However, cinema studies are not included in every issue.
AS36.I5S78; Dewey: 081.

Studies in Visual Communication (U.S.); Annenberg School of Communications, 3620 Walnut St., Philadelphia, PA 19104-3858; (quarterly); ISSN: 0276-6558; OCLC 6548884.
Note: v.1-v.11,n.4, 1975-Fall 1985.
Excellent scholarly journal with well written and researched articles analyzing all aspects of visual communications--from the theater to photography. Ceased publication in 1985.
BF241.S84; Dewey: 302.2.

Studio Magazin (W.Germany); Studio Presse Verlag Fey & Muller GbR, Beethovenstr. 163/165, 4200 Oberhausen 11, West Germany.
Tel: 0208 60 60 64; (bimonthly); ISSN: n/a.
Note: v.1, 1987 -.
Trade publication for professional audio and video technicians. Covers new equipment, engineering, computer generated graphics, hardware, technical advancements.
Published in German.

Stuffing (Australia); A Stuff Publication, PO Box 222 Northcote Vic. 3070 Australia; (irregular); ISSN: n/a.
Note: [n.1] 1987 -.
Irreverent magazine interested in cult motion pictures and home video fare. Takes in road movies, B westerns, gangster and horror genres.

Swedish Films. Films Suedois (Sweden); The Swedish Film Institute, PO Box 27 126, S-10252, Stockholm, Sweden. Tel: 468/665 1100; (annual); ISSN: n/a; OCLC 6218328.
Note: ed.1, 1973 -.
List of Swedish motion pictures produced during the preceding year. Arranged alphabetically by English (or French) release title, each entry gives a synopsis, profile of the director with filmography, cast, credits and original Swedish title. Includes features and documentaries. Informs about films in production; contains a directory of Swedish production and distribution companies. Publishes English and French editions.

Synchronos Kinimatographos (Greece). See: **Synchronos Kinematografos + Cinema Contemporain.**

Synchronos Kinematografos + Cinema Contemporain (Greece).
Title varies: **Synchronos Kinimatographos; Sinchronos
Kinimatografos.** Subscriptions: Synchronos Kinematografos,
Tzavelle 1, Athens 145, Greece; (3 times/yr); ISSN: n/a; OCLC
13993083.
Note: n.1, Sep 1969 -.
Popular magazine depicting contemporary international cinema.
Covers some business production news; reports on film
festivals. Published in Greek and French.

-T-

T.B.I. Television Business International (U.K.); Telso
Communications, 531-533 Kings Rd., London, England SW10 0TZ.
New York address: c/o Act III Publishing, Television
Division, 401 Park Ave. South, New York, NY 10016. Tel: 212/
302-2680; (monthly, except Aug & Dec); ISSN: 0953-6841; OCLC
19791303.
Note: v.1, 1988 -.
Provides news and analysis of the international broadcasting
communications industry. Reports include global coverage of
over 119 countries on five continents. However, does tend to
emphasize the English speaking markets in the British Isles,
Canada, the U.S. and Australia. Feature articles cover the
European Broadcasting Union, piracy, take overs, buy outs,
new personnel, marketing, commercials and television in the
Third World.

T.B.S. Transponder (U.S.). Alternate titles: **Transponder; Turner
Broadcasting System Transponder.** Turner Cable Network Sales,
Inc., One CNN Center, Box 105366, Atlanta, GA 30348-5366.
Tel: 404/827-2410; (bimonthly); ISSN: n/a.
Note: v.1,n.1 Jan/Feb 1988 -.
Overview of programming and events on the Turner cable
television stations. Highlights special productions,
documentaries and telefeatures made by the Turner company.
Articles cover information about the cable industry, public
relations, affiliate news, ad sales and interviews with
successful broadcasting personnel.

T.D.C. (U.S.). See: **The Discovery Channel: T.D.C.**

T.D.C.: The Discovery Channel (U.S.). See: **The Discovery Channel:
T.D.C.**

T.H.S. Newsletter (U.S.). Alternate title: **Theatre Historical
Society Newsletter.** Theatre Historical Society, Chicago
Center & Archives, 2215 W. North Ave., Chicago, IL 60647.

Tel: 312/252-7200; (quarterly); ISSN: 0735-5734; OCLC
7087813.
Note: Began with v.11,n.1, Jul 1979 issue of **Marquee. The
Journal of the Theatre Historical Society**; numbering corresponds
with that of **Marquee**.
Newsletter reporting on events and happenings of concern to
the members of the Theatre Historical Society. Interested in
the study and preservation of old theaters and movie palaces.
See also entry under **Marquee. The Journal of the Theatre
Historical Society**.

T.I.P.S. Technical Information for Photographic Systems (U.S.).
Alternate title: **Technical Information for Photographic
Systems**. Eastman Kodak Co., 343 State St., Rochester, NY
14650-1123; (quarterly); ISSN: n/a.
Note: v.1, 1970 -.
Technical information fact sheet about camera equipment and
film stock put out by Eastman Kodak. Includes "information
of interest to both professional photographers and processing
labs." Describes new products, lists publications and
pamphlets on how to take care of cameras and film.

T.N.T. Program Guide (U.S.); Turner Broadcasting, T.N.T. Program
Guide, PO Box 105015, Atlanta, GA 30348. Tel: 800/533-1480;
(monthly); ISSN: n/a.
Note: v.1, 1988 -.
Program and movie guide to Ted Turner's cable movie channel.
Contains biographical sketches of Hollywood's greatest
directors, stars, producers and scriptwriters. Descriptions
of the classic MGM, United Artists, pre-1948 Warner Brothers,
and RKO movies broadcast during the month.

T.S. (U.S.). See: **Teen Stars**.

T.V. & Cable Factbook (U.S.). See: **Television & Cable Factbook**.

T.V. and Movie Screen (U.S.). Alternate title: **Television and
Movie Screen**. Sterling's Magazines, 355 Lexington Ave.,
New York, NY 10017. Tel: 212/391-1400; (bimonthly); ISSN:
0041-4492.
Note: v.1,n.1 Nov 1953 -.
Contains mostly photographs, posters and pinups, with short
articles on entertainers. Includes contests, fan club

information and celebrity addresses. Reviews movies and new television shows.
PN1992.T16.

The T.V. Collector (U.S.); Stephen W. & Diane L. Albert, PO Box 188, Needham, MA 02192. Tel: 617/238-1179; (bimonthly); ISSN: 0887-5847; OCLC 13313129.
Note: [n.1], Jun/Jul? 1982 -. Numbering irregular; issues from 1983 are marked volume 2.
Fan magazine for collectors of television shows and memorabilia. Designed as a forum for home video enthusiasts who buy, sell and trade favorite programs. Contains articles on TV series, mediagraphies, biographical sketches, star trivia, marriages, births, and deaths.
Dewey: 791 11.

T.V. Contacts Updates (U.S.); Larimi Communications Associates, Ltd., 246 West 38th St., New York, NY 10018. Tel: 212/819-9310; (monthly); ISSN: n/a.
Note: [v.1], 1977 -.
Monthly newsletter issued as part of the subscription to **Television Contacts**. Contains updates on new television programs, changes, cancellations, personnel, and new editorial requirements.
HE8700.8.T37.

T.V. Digest (U.S.). See: **Television Digest**.

T.V. Dimensions (U.S.). Alternate title: **Television Dimensions**.
Media Dynamics, Inc., 322 East 50th St., New York, NY 10022. Tel: 212/838-1467; (annual); ISSN: 0884-1098; OCLC 11820869.
Note: ed.1, 1983 -.
Designed for broadcasting industry personnel, networks and advertisers, this publication charts audience demographics. Combines Simmons, Nielsen and Arbitron ratings to analyze audience composition, such as hours of television watched by age, gender, economic status and educational level. An important sociological mirror of the American public's viewing habits.
HE8700.8.T917; Dewey: 384.54/43.

T.V. Entertainment Monthly (U.S.). Formerly: **The CableTV Guide**; **Cabletime**. Cable Publications, Inc., 332 Congress St.,

Boston, MA 02210. Tel: 617/574-9400; (monthly); ISSN: n/a.
Note: v.1-v.3?, 1982-1984? as **The CableTV Guide**; v.4?-v.6,
1985?-1988 as **Cabletime**; v.7, 1989- as **T.V. Entertainment
Monthly**.
Publishes specialized program guides for the following cable
companies: ATC Cablevision, American Cablesystems,
Continental Cablevision, District Cablevision, Dimension
Cable Services, Jones Intercable and Viacom. Prepares
listings for the pay channels: Cinemax, The Disney Channel,
HBO, The Movie Channel and Showtime; as well as the basic
package: Arts & Entertainment (A.& E.), American Movie
Classics (AMC), Discovery, The Family Channel, Lifetime,
Nickelodeon, The Nashville Network (TNN), The Shopping
Channels (CVN & QVC), Superstation TBS, Total Sports
Network (ESPN), The Turner Network (TNT), USA Network
and The Weather Channel.

T.V. Facts, Figures & Film (U.S.). Formerly: **Facts, Figures &
Film**; alternate title: **Television Facts, Figures & Film**.
C.C. Publishing, 19 West 44th St., New York, NY. Subscription
address: T.V. Facts, Figures & Film, Subscription Service Dept.,
PO Box 6438, Duluth, MN 55806. Tel: 218/723-9202; (monthly);
ISSN: 0046-3124; OCLC 15479552.
Note: v.1-v.27,n.11, 1955?-Nov 1986 as **Facts, Figures & Film**;
v.28,n.1 Dec 1986- as **T.V. Facts, Figures & Film**.
"The magazine of syndicated programming and promotion."
This trade monthly covers program sales, finance and industry
news, information on the latest shows, plus their viability
ratings. Interviews executive personnel in the broadcasting
industry.

T.V. Feature Film Source Book (U.S.). See: **Television Programming
Source Books**.

T.V. Game $how Magazine (U.S.). Alternate title: **Television Game
$how Magazine**. Serafini Publications, Inc., 211 E. 51st. St.,
New York, NY 10022; (monthly); ISSN: 0884-4992; OCLC
12384905.
Note: v.1, 1986 -.
Profiles the hosts, hostesses, emcees and announcers of past
and present game shows. Gives advice on how to become a
contestant and strategies on how to win.
Dewey: 795 11.

T.V. Game Show Stars (U.S.). Alternate title: **Television Game Show Stars**. Dom Serafini, 211 E. 51st., St., New York, NY 10022; (monthly); ISSN: 0885-646X; OCLC 12708696.
Note: v.1, 1985 -.
A fanzine devoted to television game shows; covers each show with background articles on the hosts and hostesses. Tells how to become a participant.
Dewey: 384 11.

T.V. Guide (U.S.); Triangle Publications, 4 Radnor Corporate Center, Radnor, PA 19088. Subscription address: T.V. Guide, Box 400, Radnor, PA 19088; (weekly); ISSN: 0039-8543; OCLC 1585969.
Note: v.1, Apr 3-9, 1953 -.
The programming guide for television in the United States. Separate editions cover different sections and metropolitan areas of the country. Lists daytime, evening and nighttime programming for all the major networks, plus the independent and public stations. Cable programming is listed in a separate section. Also has cover stories on favorite entertainers and series.

T.V. Horen und Sehen (W.Germany); Heinrich Bauer Verlag, Postfach 100444, 2000 Hamburg 1, West Germany. Tel: 040/30 190; (weekly); ISSN: n/a; OCLC 4686999.
Note: n.1, 1978 -.
Weekly television schedule for West Germany television. Popular, oversized magazine similar in content to the **TV Guide** in the United States. A photomagazine with short articles on performers, many advertisements and cartoons. Contains the radio schedule for each province in West Germany.
PN1992.3.G43T2.

T.V. Host (U.S.). Alternate titles: **T.V. Host Premium & Satellite Monthly; Television Host**. TV Host, 3935 Jamestown Rd., Harrisburg, PA 17109; (monthly); ISSN: 0744-7396; OCLC 8523632.
Note: v.1,n.1 Jul 1981 -.
Publishes comprehensive programming guides to satellite cable channels. Regional editions issued, tailored to local markets. Entries include title, date, time, channel, and network.

T.V. Index (U.S.). See: **Television Index**.

T.V. Network Movies (U.S.). See: **Television Network Movies**.

T.V. News (U.S.); Larimi Communications Associates, Ltd., 246
West 38th St., New York, NY 10018. Tel: 212/819-9310;
(annual); ISSN: n/a; OCLC 11086303.
Note: ed.1, 1977 -.
An annual directory with daily updating service. A guide to
national and local television news programs. Lists news
directors, assignment editors and contact people. Gives
frequency of guest usage, information requirements, and
topics covered.

T.V. News Index and Abstracts (U.S.). See: **Television News Index
and Abstracts**.

T.V. Pro-Log (U.S.). Alternate titles: **T.V. Pro-Log: Television
Programs and Product News; Television Pro-Log**. Television
Index, Inc., 40-29 27th St., Long Island City, NY 11101. Tel:
718/937-3990; (weekly); ISSN: 0739-5574; ISSN 0149-7146; OCLC
3526358.
Note: v.1, 1949 -.
"Television programs and production news." Companion
publication to **Television Index, Network Futures**. Weekly
newsletter relaying updated information about new programs,
telefeatures and specials in production. Designed for
broadcasting industry personnel, it concentrates on the three
major networks: ABC, CBS and NBC.
PN1992.3.U5T2; Dewey: 016.79145/0973.

T.V. Pro-Log: Television Programs and Production News (U.S.).
See: **T.V. Pro-Log**.

T.V. Program Investor (U.S.). Alternate title: **Television
Program Investor**. Paul Kagan Associates, Inc., 126 Clock
Tower Place, Carmel, CA 93923-8734. Tel: 408/624-1536;
(biweekly); ISSN: 0885-2340; OCLC 12603628.
Note: n.1, Sep 13, 1986 -.
Newsletter covering the financial health of public and
private broadcasting companies. Analyzes trends in TV
program distribution and the value of TV series in
syndication. Examines competition among networks, and the

effects of mergers and acquisitions on the industry as a
whole.
Dewey: 332 11.

T.V. Star Annual (U.S.); Ideal Publishing Corp., 2 Park Ave., New
York, NY 10016. Tel: 212/683-4200; (quarterly); ISSN: n/a;
OCLC 7156187.
Note: v.1, 1955 -.
Despite the title, this publication is a quarterly. A fan
magazine with the latest gossip about popular television
entertainers. Contains stories about celebrity feuds,
romances, private and public lives. Tracks new shows, new
stars.
PN1992.4.A2T35.

T.V. Star Parade (U.S.). Alternate title: **Television Star Parade**.
Ideal Publishing Corp., 2 Park Ave, New York, NY 10016. Tel:
212/683-4200; (bimonthly); ISSN: 0041-4530; OCLC 3938423.
Note: v.1,n.1 Fall 1951 -.
Fanzine for avid television watchers. Contains all the
latest news on the celebrity scene. Cover stories feature
biographical sketches and interviews of popular performers.
Reviews new shows.
PN1992.T2.

T.V. Technology (U.S.). Alternate title: **Television Technology**.
Industrial Marketing Advisory Services, 5827 Columbia Pike,
Suite 310, Falls Church, VA 22041. Tel: 703/998-7600;
(monthly); ISSN: 0887-1701; OCLC 13136451.
Note: v.1,n.1 Jan 1983 -.
Designed for professional broadcasters and business managers
of television stations. Articles tell how to protect, fix,
operate broadcasting equipment. Keeps up on changes in the
F.C.C. regulations. Includes a buyers guide to new
equipment.
Dewey: 384 11.

T.V. Times (U.K.); Independent Television Publications, 247
Tottenham Court Rd., London W1P OAU, England. Tel: 01-323
3222; (weekly); ISSN: n/a.
Note: n.1, Sep 22-Oct 1, 1955 -.
Programming guide to independent television in Great Britain;
covers all programming except BBC. Gives date, time and

network for weekly series, news programs, specials,
telefeatures and mini-series. Entries include program title,
cast and synopsis. Topical articles feature background
information on the public's favorite shows.

T.V. Times (U.S.); T.V.S.M. Inc., 309 Lakeside Dr., Horsham, PA
19044. Tel: 215/443-9300; (weekly); ISSN: n/a.
Note: v.1,n.1 Feb 1990 -.
For subscribers to cable satellite networks. A programming
guide to commercial, free and pay TV listings. Customized
editions for each cable franchise area.

T.V. World (U.K.). Alternate title: **Television World**.
International Thompson Business Publishing, 7 Swallow Place,
London W1, England. Tel: 01-491 9484; (10 times/yr); ISSN:
0142-7466; OCLC 6497377.
Note: v.1, 1978 -.
"International business magazine for television and video."
Looks at the broadcasting industry on a global scale.
Feature articles cover how television is being used in
countries around the world; for example, special programs
from Brazil, Germany, Canada and others on the world ecology
movement. Includes ratings, shows in production, and business
trends for the following countries: Brazil, Australia,
Canada, France, Japan, New Zealand, the United Kingdom and
the United States. Charts the market saturation for TV and
video products for all countries, including the third world.
HE8700.T18; Dewey: 384.55/05.

T.V.C. (U.S.). See: **Cable Television Business**.

T.V.R.O.: Satellite T.V. Week Dealer (U.S.). Alternate title:
Satellite T.V. Week T.V.R.O. Dealer. Fortuna Communications
Corp., 140 South Fortuna Blvd. (PO Box 308) Fortuna, CA
95540-0308. Tel: 707/725-1185; (monthly); ISSN: n/a.
Note: v.1, 1986 -.
Trade journal for satellite dish dealers, distributors,
manufacturers and advertisers. Charts market trends, gives
sales per month, estimates number of systems per state,
reports on laws and legislation affecting the industry. Keeps up
on new regulations issued by state and federal governments.

Take One (Canada); Unicorn Publishers, PO Box 1778, Station B,
Montreal, Quebec H3B 3L3 Canada; (bimonthly); ISSN: 0039-
9132; OCLC 1779298.
Note: v.1-v.7,n.9, Sep/Oct 1966-Aug 15, 1979.
Popular journal of general articles on cinema personalities,
criticism, interviews and reviews. Ceased publication.
Dewey: 791.43.

Take One (U.S.); Take One Tradepaper, 14964 Ventura Blvd.,
Sherman Oaks, CA 91403; (8 times/yr); ISSN: 1042-2811; OCLC
16940996.
Note: v.1, 1986 -.
Trade paper for the motion picture and television industries.
Contains information and articles of interest to performers
and behind-the-scenes professionals: editors, cinematographers,
stunt people, electricians, etc., who work in the entertainment
industry.
Dewey: 791 11.

The Talk Show Guest Directory (U.S.). See: **Directory of Experts,
Authorities & Spokespersons.**

Talk Show Guest Directory of Experts, Authorities & Spokespersons
(U.S.). See: **Directory of Experts, Authorities &
Spokespersons.**

Talk Show "Selects" (U.S.); Broadcast Interview Source, 2233
Wisconsin Ave., NW, 406, Washington, DC 20007-4104. Tel: 202/
333-4904; (2 times/yr); ISSN: 1045-9553; OCLC 20293088.
Note: ed.1, 198u -.
A directory to over 640 of the most influential talk show
hosts, producers and programming executives in the radio and
television industries. Provides contact name, program title,
call letters or network, programming format, telephone,
address and Fax number. Available in book format and on
computer floppy disk.
Dewey: 791 11.

Teaching Aids News (U.S.). See: **Educational Technology.**

Teatro e Cinema (Italy); Silva Editore, via Fieschi 3/22, Genoa,
Italy; (quarterly); ISSN: n/a.
Note: n.1, Jan-Mar 1967 -.

Long scholarly articles addressing the creativity of Italian theater and cinema. Published in Italian. PN1560.T36.

Tech Photo Pro Imaging Systems (U.S.). Created by a union of: **Technical Photography** (0040-0971) and **Functional Photography** (0360-7216); absorbed by: **Industrial Photography**. See: **Industrial Photography**.

Technical Information for Photographic Systems (U.S.). See: **T.I.P.S. Technical Information for Photographic Systems**.

Teen Beat All-Stars (U.S.); MacFadden Holdings, Inc., 215 Lexington Ave., New York, NY 10016. Tel: 212/340-7500; (quarterly); ISSN: n/a.
Note: v.1, 1976? -.
Fanzine for young readers. Photos, pinups, gossip, and interviews track the lives and loves of adolescent celebrities.

Teen Set (U.S.). See: **TeenSet**.

Teen Stars (U.S.). Alternate title: **T.S.** Starlog Theater Merchandising Corp., 475 Park Ave. South, New York, NY 10016; (quarterly); ISSN: 8756-3312; 8755-3104; OCLC 11542232.
Note: n.1, Spring 1985 -.
Fan magazine for young readers. Light hearted articles about teenagers working in the film and television industries. Contains contests, games, horoscopes, pictures, pinups, question and answer columns.

TeenSet (U.S.). Alternate title: **Teen Set**. L.F.P., Inc., Subscriptions: Teen Set, PO Box 16507, North Hollywood, CA 91615-9955; (monthly except Mar, Jun, Nov); ISSN: n/a.
Note: v.1,n.1 Jan 1984 -.
"Hollywood's Teen Magazine!" Fan magazine featuring adolescent motion picture and television celebrities. Contains biographical sketches, interviews and numerous photographs to illustrate the lifestyles and careers of the youthful stars.

Tele-media (France); Tele-media, 10, rue Louis-Philippe, 92-Neuilly, France; (monthly); ISSN: n/a.

Note: n.1, Sep 5, 1969 -.
"Le magazine de la communication," published in French. A
trade journal for motion picture and television industry
personnel. Covers industry news, audiovisual equipment, new
technology. Reviews new hardware and broadcasting equipment.
PN1992.T38.

Tele-Satellit (W.Germany); TELE-audiovision Mediengesellschaft,
MbH, 80 1965, 8000 Munchen, West Germany. Tel: 0894-47 04 43;
(monthly); ISSN: n/a.
Note: v.1, 1987 -.
Central Europe's satellite magazine. Carries programming
information, reports on new series and interviews performers.
Articles inform about reception, transmission and equipment.
Published in German.

Telecommunications Product Review (U.S.); Marketing Programs &
Services Group, Inc., PO Box 217, Gathersburg, MD 20877. Tel:
301/840-0800; (monthly); ISSN: 0736-4156; OCLC 9121279.
Note: [v.1], 1973 -.
Trade journal specializing in reviewing and reporting on new
electronic media products and equipment. For station
operators, managers, engineers and home enthusiasts.

Telemedia (U.S.); National Association of Broadcasters, 1771 N.
St., NW, Washington, DC 20036. Tel: 202/429-5376;
(bimonthly); ISSN: 0746-0902; OCLC 9735231.
Note: v.1,n.1 Jul/Aug 1983 -.
"The television magazine of the National Association of
Broadcasters." Contains information on the broadcasting
industry, news about conferences, and events of interest to
members. Reports on new legislation, recent books, and
periodicals pertaining to the industry.
Dewey: 384 11.

Telespan's Business TV (U.S.). See: **Business TV**.

Telespan's Business Television (U.S.). See: **Business TV**.

Televidenie, Radioveshchanie (U.S.S.R.). Formerly: **Sovetskoe
Radio i Televidenie**; alternate title: **Televideniye i
Radioveshchaniye**; transliterated title: **Television and Radio
Broadcasting**. State Committee for Television and Radio,

Pyatnitskaya ul.25, Moscow 113326, U.S.S.R. Tel: 292-8268; (monthly); ISSN: 0131-694X; OCLC 13735841.
Note: v.1,n.1-[v.14],n.10, 1957-Oct 1970 as **Sovetskoe Radio i Televidenie**; renumbered v.1,n.11, Nov 1970- as **Televidenie Radioveshchanie**.
Organ of the U.S.S.R. State Committee for Television and Radio. Popular format with many photographs illustrating all state sponsored and directed radio and television broadcasts. Lists programs. Contains additional articles on major events such as the Olympics, other important games and sporting events, news coverage, musical/variety shows and documentaries.
PN1991.3.R8S6.

Televideniye i Radioveshchaniye (U.S.S.R.). See: **Televidenie, Radioveshchanie**.

Television (U.K.). Formerly: **The Royal Television Society Journal**; alternate title: **Television: Journal of the Royal Television Society**. Royal Television Society, Tavistock House East, Tavistock Square, London, WC1H 9HR England. Tel: 01-387 1970/1332; (6 times/yr); ISSN: 0308-454X; OCLC 2386325.
Note: v.1-v.15,n.12, 1961?-Nov/Dec 1975 as **The Royal Television Society Journal**; v.16,n.1 Jan/Feb 1976- as **Television**.
A technical journal for members, containing long articles on broadcast standards, European television, cable and satellite hookups, the B.B.C. and the independent networks in Great Britain. Rather argumentative, containing articles for and against controversial topics.
TK6630.A1T425; Dewey: 621.388/005.

Television: Journal of the Royal Television Society (U.K.). See: **Television**.

Television Action Update (U.S.). Alternate title: **Weekly Television Action Update**. Warren Publishing, 2115 Ward Court NW, Washington, DC 20037. Tel: 202/872-9200; (weekly); ISSN: n/a; OCLC 8899749.
Note: n.1, Feb 1, 1982 -.
"The authoritative news service of F.C.C. actions" regarding television stations. Contains weekly updates on new licenses approved, pending and revoked. Lists number of stations

operating, commercial and non commercial, VHF and UHF; includes information on low power TV, TV translators, and instructional television stations. Companion newsletter to **Cable Action Update**.
TK6675.W43; Dewey: 384.55/47/0973.

Television & Cable Factbook (U.S.). Alternate titles: **T.V. & Cable Factbook; Television and Cable Factbook**. Warren Publishing, Inc., 2115 Ward Court, NW, Washington, DC 20037. Tel: 202/872-9200; (annual); ISSN: 0732-8648; 0741-188X; OCLC 8456262.
Note: v.1, 1945 -.
Publishes two volumes: "Stations" and "Cable & Services." The "Stations" volume includes all network affiliates and independent stations state-by-state. Lists call numbers, addresses, personnel, ownership and a map of the transmitting area for each station. Contains a buyers guide for antennas, towers, equipment, and services, such as labs, storage facilities, producers and set designers. The "Cable & Services" volume includes a directory of all cable systems on a state-by-state basis. Gives names and addresses for pay-TV and satellite services, cable construction and installation services and a buyers guide for equipment.
TK6540.T453; Dewey: 384.55/025/73.

Television and Cable Factbook (U.S.). See: **Television & Cable Factbook**.

Television & Children (U.S.). See: **Television & Families**.

Television & Families (U.S.). Formerly: **Television & Children** (0276-7309); alternate title: **Television and Families**.
National Council for Families & TV, 3801 Barham Blvd., Ste. 300, Los Angeles, CA 90068. Tel: 213/876-5959; (quarterly); ISSN: 0894-6248; OCLC 12225031.
Note: v.1,n.1-v.7,n.3&4, Spring 1978-Summer/Fall 1984 as **Television & Children**; v.8,n.1 Winter 1985- as **Television & Families**.
"A non-profit, non-adversarial, educational organization whose goal is to enhance the quality of family life in the United States by positively affecting the creation and uses of prime time entertainment T.V." Articles promote quality prime time television that is appropriate viewing for young audiences.

Reviews new series and specials.
HQ784.T4N35A; Dewey: 305.2/3.

Television and Families (U.S.). See: **Television & Families**.

Television and Movie Screen (U.S.). See: **T.V. and Movie Screen**.

Television and Radio Broadcasting (U.S.S.R.). See: **Televidenie, Radioveshchanie**.

Television Broadcast (U.S.); P.S.N. Publications, Paul G. Gallo, Publisher, 2 Park Ave., New York, NY 10016. Tel: 212/779-1919; (monthly); ISSN: 0898-767X; OCLC 13141802.
Note: v.1, 1978 -.
"Covering television equipment, news, applications and technology." Oversized trade journal designed for broadcast industry personnel. Speaks about international cable systems, broadcast standards, computer graphics, legislation affecting the industry, impact of satellite technology, video recorders and playback.
TK6540.B8432; Dewey: 621 11.

Television Business International (U.K.). See: **T.B.I. Television Business International**.

The Television Collector (U.S.). See: **The T.V. Collector**.

Television Contacts (U.S.); Larimi Communications Associates, 246 West 38th St., New York, NY 10018. Tel: 212/819-9310; (annual); ISSN: 0147-3352; OCLC 3144223.
Note: v.1, 1977 -.
An annual directory with a daily updating service and a monthly newsletter, **T.V. Contacts Updates**. Concerned with programming; lists national, syndicated and local programs' guests, product and information requirements. Entries for local listings include address, personnel, network affiliation, and program titles.
HE8700.8.T37.

Television Digest (U.S.). See: **Television Digest with Consumer Electronics**.

Television Digest with Consumer Electronics (U.S.). Alternate
titles: **Television Digest; T.V. Digest.** Warren Publishing,
Inc., 2115 Ward Court, NW, Washington, DC 20037. Tel: 202/
872-9200; (weekly); ISSN: 0497-1515; ISSN 0897-4632; OCLC
2451044.
Note: Began 1945; published weekly, renumbered v.1, 1961 -.
"The authoritative service for broadcasting, cable, consumer
electronics and allied fields." Business oriented magazine
concerned with sales, export and import data on television
sets and parts, video games, and other products related to
telecommunications. Contains weekly financial reports by
company giving revenues and net earnings.
Dewey: 384 11.

Television Digest's Cable & Station Coverage Atlas (U.S.). See:
Cable & Station Coverage Atlas and Zone Maps.

Television Dimensions (U.S.). See: **T.V. Dimensions.**

Television Facts, Figures & Film (U.S.). See: **T.V. Facts, Figures
& Film.**

Television Feature Film Source Book (U.S.). See: **Television
Programming Source Books.**

Television Game $how Magazine (U.S.). See: **T.V. Game $how
Magazine.**

Television Game Show Stars (U.S.). See: **T.V. Game Show Stars.**

Television Index (U.S.). Alternate title: **T.V. Index.** Television
Index, Inc., 40-29 27th St., Long Island City, NY 11101. Tel:
718/937-3990; (weekly); ISSN: 0149-7367; OCLC 3526331.
Note: v.1, 1949 -.
Designed for the broadcasting industry, this loose-leaf
service gives detailed show-by-show listings of programs
aired on ABC, CBS and NBC. Covers debuts, reruns, specials,
news, public affairs, and sports programs. Gives network
changes, additions, and cancellations. Contains a separate
listing for regularly scheduled programs during prime time.
Indexed twice a year. Issued with two companion newsletters:
Television Index Network Futures and **T.V. Pro-Log,** which are

published separately.
PN1992.T43; Dewey: 791.45/7.

Television Index Network Futures (U.S.); Television Index, Inc.,
40-29 27th St., Long Island City, NY 11101. Tel: 718/937-
3990; (weekly); ISSN: 0149-7375; OCLC 3526206.
Note: v.1, 1949 -.
For broadcasting industry personnel. Issued with its
companion newsletter: **T.V. Pro-Log.** A newsletter giving
weekly updates on television program listings for the three
major networks. Chronicles "program debuts, returns,
specials and changes" in the program schedules for ABC, CBS
and NBC.
PN1992.3.U5T39; Dewey: 016.79145/0973.

Television International (U.S.); Television International
Publications, Subscriptions, PO Box 94754, Pasadena, CA
91109-4754. Tel: 213/462-1099; (bimonthly); ISSN: n/a; OCLC
13014388.
Note: v.1,n.1 Jul 1956 -.
Reports on the broadcasting industry--programming debuts,
children's television, competition among networks and
sponsors. Short articles cover marketing, impact of cable,
use of computer graphics and T.V. festivals.

Television Network Movies (U.S.). Alternate title: **T.V. Network
Movies.** Television Index, Inc., 40-29 27th St., Long Island
City, NY 11101. Tel: 718/937-3990; (annual); ISSN: 0149-7359;
OCLC 3526404.
Note: v.1, 1973/74 -.
Trade publication in looseleaf format. An alphabetical
listing by title of theatrical movies, telefeatures,
miniseries and individually scheduled pilots broadcast on
ABC, CBS and NBC. Does not cover cable networks. Gives
network, telecast dates, producer, distributor, major cast
members, director and writer. For TV season running from
September to August of the following year.
PN1992.T44; Dewey: 791.43/7.

Television News Index and Abstracts (U.S.). Alternate title: **T.V.
News Index and Abstracts.** Vanderbilt Television News
Archive, Jean and Alexander Heard Library, Vanderbilt
University, Nashville, TN 37240-0007. Tel: 615/322-2927;

(monthly); ISSN: 0085-7157; OCLC 1795244.
Note: v.1,n.1 Aug 1968 -.
A detailed index chronicling the evening news programs on the
ABC, CBS and NBC television networks. Designed for
researchers, educators, librarians, and students, it is
invaluable for finding out when certain events aired on the
nightly news. Presented by network and arranged chronologically
by date and air time, the index gives short descriptions of the
news segments. From August 1968 to December 1971, issued only
on microfilm. Printed version available starting January 1972.
Publishes an annual index.
AI3.T44; Dewey: 011.

Television Pro-Log (U.S.). See: **T.V. Pro-Log**.

Television Program Investor (U.S.). See: **T.V. Program Investor**.

Television Programming Source Books (U.S.). Created by a merge
between: **T.V. Feature Film Source Book** and **Series, Serials &
Packages**. BIB/Channels, a Division of ACT III Publishing,
401 Park Ave. South, New York, NY 10036. Subscription address:
BIB/Channels, Order Dept., 19 W. 44th St., Suite 812, New
York, NY 10036. Tel: 212/545-5187; (annual, with monthly
updates); ISSN: 0739-2400; OCLC 9718603.
Note: v.1-29, 1949-1988 as **T.V. Feature Film Source Book**;
[v.30], 1989- as **Television Programming Source Books**.
A three volume edition; volume one comprises an alphabetical
listing by title of all feature films and telefeatures
available in distribution. Each entry includes title, date,
original production company, cast, synopsis and current TV
distributor. Volume two contains program packages, listing
titles under general subject categories, such as "westerns,"
"horror/science fiction," and "holiday" packages. The
distributors' index is also in volume two, giving the
complete addresses and telephone numbers for all the
distributors listed with program titles. Volume three
contains all the titles of TV series in syndication. The
volume is divided into sections: long form (over 60
minutes), hour long series, half-hour series, half-hour
sitcoms, Spanish language, and holiday series. It also has a
comprehensive title index. An important reference for
television station managers and programmers.
PN1992.8.F5T18.

Television Quarterly (U.S.); National Academy of Television Arts and Sciences, 291 S. La Cienega Blvd., Beverly Hills, CA 90211. Subscription address: Television Quarterly, 111 W. 57th St., New York, NY 10019. Tel: 212/586-8424; (quarterly); ISSN: 0040-2796; OCLC 1696403.
Note: v.1,n.1 Feb 1962 -.
Scholarly journal with long articles analyzing television history, theory and criticism. Studies the impact of television on culture, viewing trends in the United States, international broadcasting, competition from cable, censorship, and legislation affecting the industry. PN1992.T45.

Television/Radio Age (U.S.). Absorbed: **Cableage**; Television Editorial Corp., Editorial, Circulation and Publication Offices, 1270 Ave. of the Americas, Rockefeller Center, Suite 502, New York, NY 10020. Tel: 212/757-8400; (biweekly); ISSN: 0040-277X; OCLC 2246124.
Note: v.1, 1953 -. Absorbed **Cableage** Nov 21, 1983.
Trade journal for broadcasting industry personnel. Charts television and radio corporations' growth, revenues, profits and annual earnings. Reports on international meetings and conventions. Gives statistics of commercial sales, advertising volume, syndicated programming and markets. Publishes **Cableage** in separate section within the magazine. HE8690.T42; Dewey: 384.54/05.

Television Star Parade (U.S.). See: **T.V. Star Parade**.

Television Technology (U.S.). See: **T.V. Technology**.

Television Weekly (U.K.). See: **Broadcast**.

Television World (U.S.). See: **T.V. World**.

Televisions (U.S.). Formerly: **Community Video Report**. Washington Community Video Center, Inc., PO Box 21068, Washington, DC 20009. Tel: 202/462-6700; (quarterly); ISSN: n/a; OCLC 2254317.
Note: v.1, 1983? -.
Concerned with the theory and practice of media journalism. Follows technological developments, programming events and

regulations affecting the broadcast industry. Monitors cable and public access television in the Washington, DC metropolitan area.

Televisual (U.K.). Formerly: **Corporate Video.** Circulation Dept., Televisual, St. Giles House, 50 Poland St., London, W1V 4AX England. Tel: 01-439 4222; (monthly); ISSN: n/a; OCLC 17851616.
Note: [v.1], Sep 1983 as **Televisual.**
"The business magazine for independent producers, facilities and the broadcast industry." Interviews independent TV producers and broadcast personnel. Articles cover interactive video, HDTV, commercials, animation, audience measurement systems, audio technology, future trends and American influences on worldwide television.
PN1992.T47; Dewey: 384.55/4/05.

Theatre Historical Society Newsletter (U.S.). See: **T.H.S. Newsletter.**

The Third Channel (Korea); International Broadcasting Society, 18 Yoido-dong, Youngdungpo-gu, Seoul, Korea. Tel: 781-2423; (2 times/yr); ISSN: n/a; OCLC 14373359.
Note: v.1, 1985 -.
"IBS journal of international communication." Scholarly journal concerned with broadcasting in the Third World. Articles concentrate on economics, policy planning and progress towards an international communications network. Published in English.

13 Program Guide (U.S.). Formerly: **Dial. WNET/Thirteen.** WNET/13, 356 W. 58th St., New York, NY 10019. Tel: 212/560-2000; (monthly); ISSN: 0884-2078; OCLC 11275666.
Note: v.1-v.7, 1980-1987 as **Dial. WNET/Thirteen**; renumbered v.1,n.1 Jan 1987- as **13 Program Guide.**
Schedule of programs aired on the PBS television station WNET, serving the New York City area. Contains background articles on current programs and upcoming series and specials.
PN1992.8; Dewey: 791.44/0973.

Three Sixty (U.K.). Alternate title: **ThreeSixty.** British Film Institute, 21 Stephen St., London, England W1P 1PL;

(irregular); ISSN: n/a.
Note: [n.1] 1985? -.
Newsletter describing events, restoration projects,
fund raising, festivals and conferences hosted by the British
Film Institute. Contains editorials, book reviews and
details of films funded by the B.F.I.

ThreeSixty (U.K.) See: **Three Sixty**.

Tiger Beat (U.S.); D.S. Magazines, Inc., 1086 Teaneck Rd.,
  Teaneck, NJ 07666. Tel: 201/833-1800; (monthly); ISSN: 0040-
  7380; OCLC 2250584.
  Note: v.1, 1965 -.
  A fan magazine geared towards the young adult reader.
  Biographical sketches, interviews and photographs of teenage
  film and television performers. Includes information on pop
  music and rock stars.

Tiger Beat Presents Star (U.S.). See: **Star**.

Tiger Beat Special, FantaZone (U.S.). See: **FantaZone**.

Tiger Beat Star (U.S.). See: **Star**.

Time & Tide (India). Alternate title: **Time and Tide**. Time & Tide,
  1, Ansari Rd., Daryaganj, New Delhi 110002, India. Tel:
  272046; 592383; (monthly); ISSN: 0040-7836; OCLC 1797739.
  Note: n.1, 1952 -.
  "Indian journal of film and television," published in
  English. Tabloid format magazine reporting on the state of
  Indian filmmaking. Includes reprints from older English-
  language periodicals. Editorializes on the quality of Indian
  films and television, the increasing popularity of video, the
  management of Indian film studios. Reports on international film
  festivals. Reviews films and television programs.
  PN1993.T55; Dewey: 791.43/05.

Time and Tide (India). See: **Time & Tide**.

Today's Cinema (U.K.). See: **Screen International**.

Today's Cinema Incorporating Kine Weekly (U.K.). See: **Screen
  International**.

Ton Magazin (W.Germany). See: **Fotomagazin.**

Toni Holt's Movie Life (U.S.). See: **Movie Life.**

Top Secret (U.S.); Caruba Enterprises, PO Box 1146, Maplewood, NJ
   07040. Tel: 201/992-5600; (quarterly); ISSN: 0887-2317; OCLC
   13146558.
   Note: v.1,n.1-v.1,n.4, Oct 1985-Jul 1986.
   Fan magazine written for people interested in motion pictures
   and television series about spies and mysteries. Ceased
   publication.

Topicator (U.S.); Topicator, Inc., Box 1009, Clackmas, OR 97015-
   1009. Tel: 503/653-1007; (bimonthly); ISSN: 0040-9340; OCLC
   1781584.
   Note: v.1, 1965 -.
   "Classified article guide to the advertising/communications/
   marketing periodical press." A current index to articles
   published in selective broadcasting, advertising and
   communications magazines. Indexes the following magazines:
   **Advertising Age, Broadcasting, Channels, Columbia Journalism
   Review, Direct Marketing, Educational Communications and
   Technology, Editor & Publisher, E. & I.T.V.,** Folio, **Graphic
   Arts Monthly, Journal of Advertising, Journal of Broadcasting
   & Electronic Media, Journal of Communication, Marketing &
   Media Decisions, Packaging, Sales & Marketing Management,
   Television/Radio Age, T.V. Guide,** and **Variety.**

Toronto Film Society Newsletter (Canada); Toronto Film Society,
   77 Quebec Ave., No. 1928, Toronto, Ont. M6P 2T4 Canada;
   (quarterly); ISSN: n/a.
   Note: v.1, Jun 1949 -.
   Part of membership to the film society, the newsletter
   informs members of events, programs and special exhibitions
   concerned with motion pictures. Conducts interviews with
   people in the entertainment industry, prints editorials on
   the state of the art, compiles statistics on the film
   showings and the audiences' responses. Membership also
   includes prolific film notes on every program.

Trade News North (Canada). See: **Cinema Canada.**

The Trainer's Resource (U.S.); Human Resource Development Press,
22 Amherst Rd., Amherst, MA 01002. Tel: 413/253-3488;
(annual); ISSN: n/a; OCLC 13550596.
Note: ed.1, 1981 -.
"A comprehensive guide to packaged training programs." A
directory to packaged audiovisual programs in the fields of
career development, interpersonal communications,
interviewing skills, management development, negotiation
performance appraisal, problem solving, time management,
sales training, supervisory skills and other related topics.
Each package includes at least two different media in order
to be listed.
HD30.412.T73; Dewey: 658.3/124/0973.

Transponder (U.S.). See: **T.B.S. Transponder.**

Turner Broadcasting System Transponder (U.S.). See: **T.B.S.
Transponder.**

The Twilight Zone Magazine (U.S.). See: **Rod Serling's The
Twilight Zone Magazine.**

Tygodniowy Magazyn Filmowo-Telewizyjny (Poland). See: **Ekran;
Kino TV Video.**

-U-

U.F.O.C.E.L. Informations (France). See: **Image et Son/Revue du Cinema.**

Under Western Skies (U.S.); World of Yesterday Publications, Route 3, Box 263-H, Waynesville, NC 28786. Tel: 704/648-5647; (irregular); ISSN: 0279-6244; OCLC 7120292.
Note: n.1, Jan 1978 -.
Magazine for fans and collectors of old American westerns on film, radio, television and comic books. Includes long biographical articles, with extensive filmographies on western stars, such as Hoot Gibson, William S. Hart, Tom Mix and William Boyd.

Undercut (U.K.). London Filmmakers' Co-operative: 42 Gloucester Ave., London, NW1, England; (quarterly); ISSN: 0267-8497; OCLC 10987818.
Note: n.1, Mar/Apr 1981 -.
Serious journal underwritten by the London Filmmakers' Coop. Interested in independent, experimental and avant-garde cinema. Each issue contains several articles which center around a theme, such as exploring the context of film in society, or tracing cultural identities in film. Interviews successful filmmakers.

Unir Cinema (Senegal). Alternate title: **Unir, L'echo de Saint-Louis.** Office Catholique du Cinema du Senegal, 1, rue Neuville, B.P. 160, Saint-Louis, Senegal. Tel: 61.10.27; (irregular); ISSN: 0253-195X; OCLC 12281561.
Note: n.1, 1973 -.
"Revue du Cinema Africain." Tracks new African cinema, reviewing films and interviewing filmmakers. Recommends titles not found objectionable. Covers film festivals and film clubs in Senegal. Published in French.

University Art Museum. Calendar. Pacific Film Archive (U.S.). See: **Calendar / University Art Museum.**

-V-

V Magazine (U.S.); Fairfield Publishing co., Inc., 104 Fifth
Ave., New York, NY 10011. Tel: 800/634-8478; (bimonthly);
ISSN: 1041-1402; OCLC 18375918.
Note: v.1, 1987 -.
"The mail order magazine of videocassettes." A magazine
informing subscribers about what is available on home video.
Covers both entertainment and non fiction. Articles include
interviews, profiles, notes on best sellers, reviews and
distribution centers.
Dewey: 791 11.

The V.C.R. Letter (U.S.). See: **Video Investor**.

V.Q.T.: Viewers for Quality Television (U.S.). Alternate title:
Viewers for Quality Television: V.T.Q. Viewers for Quality
Television, PO Box 195 Fairfax Station, VA 22039. Tel: 703/
425-0075; (bimonthly); ISSN: n/a.
Note: n.1, 1985 -.
Specializes in articles for promoting quality television
programming. Lobbies against cancellation of good shows.
Offers alternate broadcasting, such as cable, syndication and
pay-TV, to save good series. Conducts viewer surveys of the
new Fall shows. Interviews performers, writers, directors
and producers of quality programs.

Variety (U.S.). Alternate title: **Weekly Variety**. A Cahners
Publication, 475 Park Ave. South, New York, NY 10016;
(weekly); ISSN: 0042-2738; OCLC 1768958.
Note: v.1, Dec 16, 1905 -.
The trade newspaper for the motion picture, theater and
television industries. Reports on financial and business
news concerning the major film studios, independent
producers, television networks, foreign production and
distribution companies, and the American theater. Contains
comprehensive reviews for both foreign and domestic films and
television shows. Publishes special editions covering

international film competitions. Each year in January, it publishes an annual index which lists the top 50 motion pictures that made the most money during the preceding year. The index gives the citations for the previous year's film and TV reviews.
PN2000.V3; Dewey: 790.2/05.

Variety's Complete Home Video Directory (U.S.). See: **Bowker's Complete Video Directory.**

Variety's Complete Home Video Directory. Adult Video Supplement (U.S.). See: **Bowker's Complete Video Directory.**

The Velvet Light Trap (U.S.); Wisconsin Center for Film & Theater Research, PO Box 9240, Madison, WI 53715. Subscription address: University of Texas Press, Box 7819, Austin, TX 78713-7819. Tel: 512/471-4032; (irregular); ISSN: 0149-1830; OCLC 2587297.
Note: n.1, Jun 1971 -.
Scholarly journal of film history, theory and criticism. Usually, issues center around a theme with several articles studying various aspects of it. The issues cover such topics as widescreen aesthetics, alternative methodologies, the MGM studio, and Warner Brothers films of the 1930s. Tries to offer articles and new theories that provoke debate.
PN1993.V44; Dewey: 791.43/05.

Versus (Netherlands); Department of Cinema & Theater of the University of Nijmegen, Bijlevddsingel 9, 6521 AP Nijmegen, The Netherlands; (quarterly); ISSN: n/a.
Note: n.1, Winter 1984 -.
Scholarly journal discussing film theory, history and criticism. Each issue is built around a theme, such as motion picture music, film narration, methodology, aesthetics, semiotics or special effects technology.
Published in Dutch.

Vertigo (France); Avancees Cinematographiques-Vertigo, 99, rue Notre-Dame des Champs, 75006 Paris, France; (2 times/yr); ISSN: 0985-1402; OCLC 20073232.
Note: v.1, 1988 -.
Scholarly and artistic journal combining history and cinema studies. Each issue has a distinctive title, and is a

collection of essays concerned with how film has treated
historical events, such as the French Revolution. Also
concerned with how history is presented and romanticized by
the arts. Published in French.

Via Satellite (U.S.); Phillips Magazines, Inc., 7811 Montrose
Rd., Potomac, MD 20854. Tel: 301/340-2100; (monthly); ISSN:
1041-0643; OCLC 18619276.
Note: v.1, 1986 -.
"The magazine of satellite broadcasting." Focuses on
communications delivery in the satellite age, covering
television, radio, telephone, advertising, news releases and
religious broadcasting. Prints a yearly "transmission
services miniguide" listing all satellite equipment,
manufacturers, sales representatives, and attendant services
in the U.S. and Canada.
Dewey: 384 11.

Video (New York); Reese Communications, Inc., 460 W. 34th St.,
New York, NY 10001. Tel: 212/947-6500; (monthly); ISSN: 0147-
8907; OCLC 3428421.
Note: v.1, Winter 1978 -.
Comprehensively reviews home videos released in the United
States. Tests equipment and recommends products based on
quality control results. Keeps readers apprised of latest
technological innovations, answers technical questions,
profiles people in video production.
TK6630.A1V49; Dewey: 778.59/9/05.

Video (San Francisco). See: **Video and the Arts**.

Video (W.Germany); Vereinight Motor-Verlage-GmbH & Co. K.G.,
Postfach 106036, 7000 Stuttgart 10, West Germany. Tel: 07 11/
20 43-481; (monthly); ISSN: n/a; OCLC 11537593.
Note: v.1, Oct 1980 -.
Slick, popular magazine surveying the video scene in West
Germany. Reviews TV programs and new videos; profiles
German entertainers. Conducts tests on television monitors,
video cameras, playback equipment and recorders, recommending
the better products for consumers. Published in German.

Video Age International (U.S.). Alternate title: **VideoAge
International**. TV Trade Media, Inc., Dom Serafini, Editor,

211 E. 51 St., New York, NY 10022. Tel: 212/688-1760; (6 times/yr: Feb/Mar, Apr/May, Jun/Jul, Sep/Oct, Nov/Dec); ISSN: 0278-5013; 0279-4020; OCLC 7817679.
Note: v.1,n.1 Sep 1981 -.
International outlook on broadcasting communications. Examines satellite networks in Europe and America. Keeps current with English speaking productions from Australia, Canada, and Great Britain. Publishes updates on international law, marketing, new products, and financing affecting the communications industry.
PN1992.V53; Dewey: 384.55/4/05.

Video Age International Newsletter (U.S.). Alternate title: **VideoAge International Newsletter**. TV Trade Media, Inc., Dom Serafini, Editor, 211 E. 51 St., New York, NY 10022. Tel: 212/688-1760; (biweekly); ISSN: 0733-8341; OCLC 8645776.
Note: v.1,n.1 Sep 1982 -.
Newsletter reporting on latest events, conferences, seminars and festivals concerned with the communications industry. Contains information on new technology, products and services.

Video Aktiv (W. Germany). See: **VIDEOaktiv**.

Video & Sound (U.S.). Alternate title: **Video and Sound**. ABC Consumer Magazines, Inc. Circulation Dir/N., 825 7th Ave., 8th floor, New York, NY 10019. Tel: 212/265-8360; (quarterly); ISSN: 0893-0422; OCLC 15244630.
Note: v.1,n.1 Winter 1981 -.
Concentrates on high fidelity sound systems and home video. Feature articles address new technologies and future equipment for home systems. Conducts field and lab tests on new equipment, publishing buyer's guides recommending or rejecting certain products. Reviews pop and jazz music videos and compact discs.
Dewey: 789 11.

Video and Sound (U.S.). See: **Video & Sound**.

Video and the Arts (U.S.). Formerly: **Video**. San Francisco International Video Festival (SFIVF), 650 Missouri St., San Francisco, CA 94107. Tel: 415/863-8434; (quarterly); ISSN: 0276-0835; OCLC 7313610.

Note: v.1-v.4?, 1980-1983? as **Video**; renumbered n.1, Summer 1984 - as **Video and the Arts**.
Quarterly journal for members of the SFIVF. Interested in promulgating video as an art form. Interviews artists working in the medium. Promotes independent and experimental works through reviews and exhibitions.

Video Business (U.S.); International Thompson Retail Press, Inc., 345 Park Ave. South, New York, NY 10010. Subscription address: Video Business, Box 2019, Langhorne, PA 19047-9956. Tel: 212/686-7744; (monthly); ISSN: 0297-571X; OCLC 7102477.
Note: v.1,n.1 Jan 1981 -.
Designed for the video store retailer. Gives marketing tips, financial outlook, promotional advice. Charts best sellers and predicts what box office hits will be popular on home video.
HD9697.V543U546; Dewey: 621.388/33.

Video Choice (U.S.); Connell Communications, Inc., 331 Jaffrey Rd., Peterborough, NH 03458. Subscription address: Video Choice, PO Box 696, Holmes, PA 19043-9966. Tel: 800/356-8849; (monthly); ISSN: 0896-2871; OCLC 16978456.
Note: v.1,n.1 Mar 1988 -.
Extensive lists of new releases on video in all categories, including children's, documentary, exercise, hobby, music, sports and travel, with prices and distributors. Gives longer reviews and rates entertainment features. Articles written by experts offer insights into the industry with recommendations on hardware, price information, evolving technology.
Dewey: 384 11.

Video Digest (U.S.); Video Digest, Inc., 1046 Hypoluxo Rd., Hypoluxo, FL 33462; (monthly); ISSN: n/a.
Note: [v.1-v.2?], 1987-1988?
Modeled after **TV Guide**, this magazine was devoted to home video enthusiasts. Discontinued publication.

Video Era (U.S.). See: **Radio Video Era**.

Video Games (U.S.); Pumpkin Press, Inc., Empire State Building, 350 Fifth Ave., Suite 6204-05, New York, NY 10118; (bimonthly); ISSN: 0733-6780; OCLC 8664905.

Note: v.1,n.1 Aug 1982 -.
Popular magazine for people involved with video games. Gives
software reviews, strategies for winning, business news and
sales statistics.

Video Games & Computer Entertainment (U.S.). See: **VideoGames
& Computer Entertainment.**

Video Games Player (U.S.). See: **Computer Games.**

Video Games Today (U.S.); Phillips Publishing, Inc., 7811
Montrose Rd., Potomac, MD 20854. Tel: 301/340-2100;
(monthly); ISSN: 0733-6632; OCLC 8636366.
Note: v.1,n.1-v.2, Aug 1982-1983; ceased in 1983?
Publication describing the latest video and computer games.
Dewey: 794 11.

Video Insider (U.S.); Video Insider, 1920 Chestnut St., Suite
200, Philadelphia, PA 19103. Tel: 215/496-0200; (biweekly);
ISSN: n/a.
Note: v.1, 1983 -.
"A biweekly confidential marketing newsletter for the video
retailer and manufacturer." Charts data on video titles:
rental potential, weeks on the "best seller" list, and
indication of upward movement in popularity. Carries news
about state legislation, obscenity laws and adult videos.
Lists the latest releases, giving title, date, director,
cast, MPAA rating, synopsis and price. Advises retailers how
many copies to buy.

Video Investor (U.S.). Formerly: **The V.C.R. Letter** (8755-9927).
Paul Kagan Associates, Inc., 126 Clock Tower Place, Carmel,
CA 93923-8734. Tel: 408/624-1536; (monthly); ISSN: 1042-7694;
OCLC 19212288.
Note: n.1-n.53?, Nov 26, 1984-Dec 1988 as **The V.C.R. Letter**;
n.54, Jan 31, 1989- as **Video Investor.**
Newsletter devoted to the videocassette recording industry.
Reports on the economic viability of the home video industry
and its relationship to pay TV. Examines hardware, software
and retail developments.
Dewey: 384 11.

The Video Librarian (U.S.); Randy Pitman, Publisher, PO Box 2725, Bremerton, WA 98310. Tel: 206/377-2231; (monthly); ISSN: 0887-6851; OCLC 13306621.
Note: v.1,n.1 Mar 1986 -.
Newsletter for public and school librarians, teachers, audiovisual specialists and parents. Reviews and recommends videotapes for children, concentrating on kindergarten through high school. Includes educational, training and motivational, as well as fiction and animation. Rates video vendors and offers tips on how to buy video wholesale.
Dewey: 025 11.

Video Life (U.S.). See: **Video Shopper.**

Video Magazin (W.Germany). See: **VideoMagazin.**

Video Magazine (Italy); Publimedia Editrice, C. So Venezia, 18, 20121 Milano, Italy. Tel: 02/77521; (monthly); ISSN: n/a; OCLC 9594974.
Note: v.1,n.1 Sep 1981 -.
Slick, glossy magazine covering the latest international features and non-theatrical releases on home video in Italy. Profiles popular stars such as Dan Aykroyd, Sean Connery and Sophia Loren, listing their videographies. Tests video equipment and reports findings to consumers. To a lesser extent covers theater on video, computer graphics and satellite technology. Published in Italian.
TK9960.V536; Dewey: 621.388/332/05.

Video Maker Magazine (U.S.). See: **Videomaker Magazine.**

Video Manager (U.S.). Formerly: **Video User** (0273-7817).
Knowledge Industry Publications, 701 Westchester Ave., White Plains, NY 10604. Tel: 914/328-9157; (monthly); ISSN: 0747-3745; OCLC 10676047.
Note: v.1-v.7, 1978-1984 as **Video User**; v.7,n.4, Apr 1984- as **Video Manager**.
Reports on the latest in technology, industry events and equipment. Covers management objectives, marketing, growth potential and applications of video systems.

Video Marketing Newsletter (U.S.). Formerly: **VideoNews** (0145-9023). Phillips Publishing, Inc., 7811 Montrose Rd., Suite

100, Potomac, MD 20854. Tel: 301/340-2100; 800/722-9120;
(biweekly); ISSN: 0196-4429; OCLC 5842820.
Note: v.1, 1979?-.
A timely newsletter which tracks home video. Analyzes the
financial health of the consumer video retailing business.
Covers the telecommunications, broadcasting and entertainment
industries with international marketing research.
Dewey: 384 11.

Video Marketing Surveys and Forecasts (U.S.); Vidmar, a
subsidiary of Phillips Publishing, Inc., 1680 Vine St., Suite
820, Hollywood, CA 90028. Tel: 213/462-6350; (monthly); ISSN:
0740-4247; OCLC 9934512.
Note: v.1,n.1 Sep 1983 -.
A looseleaf reference service compiling statistics on the
electronic media industry. Covers sales, growth,
predictions, stock analysis, new technology and international
competition.
HD9696.T463U695; Dewey: 381.45621388332.

Video Marketplace (U.S.); World Publishing Co., 990 Grove St.,
Evanston, IL 60201-4370. Subscription address: Video
Marketplace, Box 3764, Escondido, CA 92025-0964. Tel: 800/
666-3376; (bimonthly); ISSN: 0895-2892; OCLC 16534891.
Note: v.1,n.1 Sep/Oct 1987 -.
"Your shop-at-home buying source for 1000's of video
subjects." Detailed listings of movies and non-fiction
videos available to the home consumer, either from the
private distributor or through the magazine. Arranged by
genre: action/adventure, children/family, comedy, drama,
travel, music, sports, health/fitness, etc., with synopses
and prices.
PN1992.95.V4945; Dewey: 016.79143/75.

Video Master Guide (U.S.). See: **Bowker's Complete Video Directory**.

Video Monitor (U.S.). See: **Media Relations/Video Monitor**.

Video Movies (U.S.). See: **Video Times**.

The Video Programs Retailer (U.S.). See: **The Video Retailer**.

Video Rating Guide for Libraries (U.S.); ABC-CLIO, 130 Cremona Dr., PO Box 1911, Santa Barbara, CA 93116-1911. Tel: 800/422-2546, ext. 141; (quarterly); ISSN: 1045-3393; OCLC 20074892.
Note: v.1,n.1 Jan 1990 -.
A directory of videos available for public, school and university library acquisitions. Applicable for home and business video acquisitions. Gives the title, date, producer, distributor, length, price, audience level, rating and detailed review. Concentrates on special interest, educational, training and children's videos.

The Video Register & Teleconferencing Resources Directory (U.S.). Formed by a union of: **Teleconferencing Resources Directory** (0739-2966) and **Video Register** (0190-3705). Knowledge Industry Publications, 701 Westchester Ave., White Plains, New York 10604; (annual); ISSN: 0887-3836; OCLC 13205052.
Note: ed.1-ed.8, 1979-1986 as **Teleconferencing Resources Directory**; ed.9, 1987- as **The Video Register & Teleconferencing Resources Directory**.
A directory listing users and suppliers involved in professional video communications. Gives the name, address, telephone number and personnel of the company. Sections include manufacturers of audio and video equipment, video lab facilities and services, dealers that rent or sell video products, companies that do post-production work, cable access systems and program distributors.
TK6655.V5V5374; Dewey: 338.4/7/77859.

The Video Retailer (U.S.). Formerly: **The Video Programs Retailer** (0199-9745). National Video Clearinghouse, Inc., 100 Lafayette Dr., Syosset, NY 11791. Tel: 516/364-3686; (6 times/yr; Jan, Feb/Mar, Apr/May, Jun/Jul, Sep/Oct, Nov/Dec); ISSN: 0730-3505; OCLC 7993268.
Note: v.1,n.1-v.3,n.1, Summer 1980-Jan 1982 as **The Video Programs Retailer**; v.3,n.2-v.7, Feb 1982-1986 as **The Video Retailer**.
Used for the distribution of new video products. Listed the latest releases by companies, including music videos.
Discontinued publication.
HD9697.V543U547; Dewey: 381.4562138833.

Video Review (U.S.); Viare Publishing, 902 Broadway, New York, NY 10010. Tel: 212/477-2200; (monthly); ISSN: 0196-8793; OCLC

5914050.
Note: v.1,n.1 Apr 1980 -.
Comprehensively reviews new titles available on 1/2-inch
videocassette for the home video market. Critiques new
products and equipment. Interviews and profiles movie and TV
personalities. Previews and recommends "watchables and
tapeables". Publishes articles on popular television series,
old classics and music videos.

Video Shopper (U.S.). Absorbed: **Video Life; Video Swapper.** Arena
Publishing Co., PO Box 309, Fraser, MI 48026; (monthly);
ISSN: n/a.
Note: v.1,n.1-v.4,n.9 Jul? 1985-Sep 1988; v.3,n.1 Jan 1987-
absorbed **Video Life** and **Video Swapper**; merged with **Movie
Collector's World,** Oct 1988 taking the name and numbering of
the latter.
A collector's magazine for buying, selling and trading
videotapes of motion pictures and television programs.

Video Software Dealer (U.S.); V.S.D. Publications, Inc., 5519 S.
Centinela Ave., Los Angeles, CA 90066-6945. Tel: 213/306-
2907; (monthly); ISSN: 0894-3001; OCLC: 13448343.
Note: v.1,n.1 Sep 1985-.
"The magazine of the home video industry." Designed for
video store owners and operators, this magazine contains
product information, market trends, profit strategies,
production notes, and pre-ordering. Charts popularity of
video titles in different sectors of the U.S.: Northeast,
South Central, North Central and West.
HD9697.V543U549; Dewey: 791.43/05.

The Video Source Book (U.S.); Gale Research, Inc., Book Tower,
Detroit, MI 48226; (annual); ISSN: 0748-0881; OCLC 5998038.
Note: ed.1, 1979 -.
A directory to all the videocassettes for sale or rent in the
United States. Includes entertainment as well as non-fiction
and educational tapes. Arranged alphabetically by title,
each entry includes format, date, production company,
distribution company, length, cast and synopsis. Indexed by
personality and subject. Includes a separate index to the
video distributors listed in the main entry giving the name,
address and telephone number for each.
PN1992.95.V52.

Video Store (U.S.); Edgell Communications, 1700 E. Dyer Rd.,
    Suite 250, Santa Ana, CA 92705, Subscriptions address: 1 East
    First St., Duluth, MN 55802. Tel: 714/250-8060; 800/854-3112;
    (monthly); ISSN: 0195-1750; OCLC 5331939.
    Note: v.1, 1979 -.
    Glossy magazine designed for video retailers and owners of
    video stores. Keeps current with all 1/2-inch videocassettes
    available in the United States, video games, and video
    hardware and accessories. Offers promotional tips and
    marketing strategies for selling and renting videotapes.
    HD9697.V543U56; Dewey: 381.4562138833.

Video Swapper (U.S.). See: **Video Shopper**.

Video Systems (U.S.); Intertec Publishing Corp., 9221 Quivira
    Rd., PO Box 12901, Overland Park, KS 66212. Tel: 913/888-
    4664; (monthly); ISSN: 0361-0942; OCLC 2245120.
    Note: v.1, Nov/Dec 1975 -.
    For electronics professionals engaged in various applications
    of video and audio production and communications research.
    Issues cover electronic graphics, state of the art video
    equipment, projected new technology, software, utilizing
    computers and video monitors for presentations, commercials
    and special effects.
    TK6680.V53; Dewey: 384.55/5/05.

The Video Tape & Disc Guide to Home Entertainment (U.S.);
    National Video Clearinghouse, 100 Lafayette Dr., Syosset, NY
    11791. Tel: 516/364-3686; (annual); ISSN: n/a; ISBN 0-935478-
    36-1.
    Note: ed.1, 1980 -.
    A comprehensive list of all entertainment videotapes and
    videodiscs available for sale or rent in the United States.
    Designed for owners of videocassette players who need a quick
    index to entertainment tapes. Entry is listed alphabetically
    under title with date, length, price, rating, cast and
    synopsis. Contains subject indexing by broad genre
    categories, such as westerns, science fiction, adventure,
    martial arts, etc.
    PN1992.95.V54; Dewey: 016.79143/75.

Video Technology Newsletter (U.S.); Phillips Publishing, Inc.,
    7811 Montrose Rd., Suite 100, Potomac, MD 20854. Tel: 301/

340-2100; 800/722-9120; (biweekly); ISSN: 1040-2772; OCLC 18367367.
Note: v.1,n.1 Sep 26, 1988 -.
A business oriented newsletter covering all types of video uses: broadcasting, computers, consumer electronics, education, fiber optics and news media satellites. Analyzes market trends and profitability of new products and equipment.
Dewey: 384 11.

Video Times (U.S.). Formerly: **Video Movies.** Publications International, 3841 W. Oakton St., Skokie, IL 60076; (monthly); ISSN: 0742-8111; OCLC 11854134.
Note: v.1,n.1-10, Mar-Dec 1984 as **Video Movies**; v.1,n.1-v.4, n.4, Jan 1985-Apr 1987 as **Video Times**.
Well done magazine with reviews of all the latest home videos. Contained lead articles about the film, television and video industries. Ceased publication in 1987.
PN1992.95.V495; Dewey: 791.45/05.

Video Trade News (U.S.); Charles Tepfer, Publisher, Circulation Dept: Video Trade News, 56 Branchville Rd., Ridgefield, CT 06877; (bimonthly); ISSN: 0164-8551; OCLC 4309190.
Note: v.1, 1975 -.
Thin, tabloid-size newspaper reporting on international meetings of video companies, product-development seminars, committee meetings. Reports on American companies, buy outs, transfers of personnel, and competition from the Japanese video industry.

Video User (U.S.). See: **Video Manager.**

Video Week (U.S.); Warren Publishing, Inc., 2115 Ward Court, NW, Washington, DC 20037. Tel: 202/872-9200; (weekly); ISSN: 0196-5905.
Note: v.1, 1980 -.
"Devoted to the business of program sales and distribution for videocassettes, disc, pay TV, and allied new media." Business news for industry executives as well as video retailers. Contains sales and rental statistics.

VideoAge International (U.S.). See: **Video Age International.**

VideoAge International Newsletter (U.S.). See: **Video Age International Newsletter.**

VIDEOaktiv (W.Germany). Alternate title: **Video Aktiv.**
VIDEOaktiv, Heinrich-Vogl-Strasse 22, 8000 Munich, 71, West Germany. Tel: 089 79 7091; (bimonthly); ISSN: 0724-4399.
Note: [n.1] Jan/Feb 1986 -.
Slick, professional magazine published in German. Covers all aspects of the video industry: television, communications, computers, videocassette recorders and playback equipment, camcorders, music videos, professional and home technology and films on video.

Videodisc and Optical Disk (U.S.). See: **Optical Information Systems.**

Videodisc and Optical Disk Update (U.S.). See: **Optical Information Systems Update.**

The Videodisc Monitor (U.S.); Future Systems, Inc., PO Box 26, Falls Church, VA 22046. Tel: 703/241-1799; (monthly); ISSN: 0739-7089; OCLC 9797951.
Note: v.1,n.1 Sep 1983 -.
Covers "applications, innovation and technology within interactive video, compact disc and related fields." Keeps readers apprised of new video software and hardware. Compiles statistics on business growth, gives an analysis of the stock market for video companies and related businesses. HD9696.V52V52.

Videodisc Update (U.S.). See: **Optical Information Systems Update.**

Videodisc, Videotex (U.S.). See: **Optical Information Systems.**

Videofax (U.S.); Videofax, Ltd., PO Box 481248, Los Angeles, CA 90048-9743; (quarterly); ISSN: 0896-0321; OCLC 16891994.
Note: v.1, 1985 -.
Technical magazine promoting the use of video for information storage and retrieval. Describes the film-to-tape mastering process, gives product reports on laser and videodiscs, and evaluates new equipment.
Dewey: 384 11.

VideoGames & Computer Entertainment (U.S.). Alternate title: **Video Games & Computer Entertainment**. L.F.P., Inc., 9171 Wilshire Blvd., Suite 300, Beverly Hills, CA 90210. Tel: 818/ 760-8983; (monthly); ISSN: n/a.
Note: v.1 Dec 1988 -.
Handsomely illustrated magazine designed for video players of all ages. Reviews new packages, gives strategies for winning and game plans. Reports on technical advances and computer software. Tries to keep up with videogaming abroad in countries such as Japan and Great Britain.

Videogaming & Computergaming Illustrated (U.S.). Formerly: **Videogaming Illustrated**. Ion International, Inc., 45 W. 34th St., Room 407, New York, NY 10001; (monthly); ISSN: 0739-4373; OCLC 9752913.
Note: v.1,n.1-v.1,n.5, Jan-May 1983 as **Videogaming Illustrated**; v.1,n.6, Jun 1983- as **Videogaming & Computergaming Illustrated**.
Designed for youthful enthusiasts of video arcade games. Plots strategies for winning, gives breakdown and diagnosis for individual games.

Videogaming Illustrated (U.S.). See: **Videogaming & Computergaming Illustrated**.

Videography (U.S.); P.S.N. Publications, 2 Park Ave., Suite 1820, New York, NY 10016; (monthly); ISSN: 0363-1001; OCLC 2409346.
Note: v.1,n.1 Apr 1976 -.
Business orientated magazine with articles on the latest equipment, technical innovations, research and development. Covers computer and video applications in business and industry, such as computer graphics, television commercials, animation, interactive video, medical uses, information storage and retrieval.
TK6630.A1V53; Dewey: 621.388/005.

Videolog (U.S.); Trade Service Corp., 10996 Torreyana Rd., San Diego, CA 92121. Tel: 619/457-5920; (weekly); ISSN: 0746-7680; ISSN 0746-7699; OCLC 9629829.
Note: v.1, 1981 -.
A loose leaf service, updated weekly, listing all the videocassettes and videodiscs available for sale or rent in

the United States. It is divided into 15 separate genre
categories, such as adventure, science fiction/horror,
westerns, sports/recreation, adult, etc. The entries are
arranged alphabetically by title within each section and
include date, length, format, cast, production company, video
distributor and brief synopsis. There are overall indexes by
title, director, star and distributor.

VideoMagazin (W.Germany). Alternate title: **Video Magazin**. S.Z.V.
Spezial-Zeitschriften-Verlag, GmbH & Co., K.G. Schellingstr.
39-43, 8000 Munchen, 40 West Germany. Tel: 089/237 260;
(monthly); ISSN: n/a.
Note: [v.1], 1986? -.
Popular magazine listing the latest home video releases, for
both entertainment and non fiction videos. Offers articles
on new technical achievements in the field, biographical
portraits of stars, and a separate section for adult fare.
Published in German.

Videomaker (U.S.). Formerly: **Videomaker Newsletter**. Videomaker,
Inc., Box 4591, Chico, CA 95927. Tel: 916/891-8410;
(bimonthly); ISSN: 0889-4973; OCLC 13992449.
Note: 1985-1986 as **Videomaker Newsletter**; v.1,n.1 Jun/Jul
1986- as **Videomaker**.
Geared exclusively to people producing videos. Covers all
aspects of video production, from the amateur hobbyist to the
business professional. Gives information on techniques, new
equipment, editing basics, use of computers, incorporating
graphics and animation. Includes directions, tips and tools
for successful productions.
Dewey: 384 11.

Videomaker Newsletter (U.S.). See: **Videomaker**.

Videomania Magazine (U.S.). Formerly: **Bob's Videomania**.
Videomania, PO Box 47, Princeton, WI 54968; (bimonthly);
ISSN: n/a.
Note: v.1-v.3, 1983-1985 as **Bob's Videomania**; v.3,n.29 Nov
1985- as **Videomania**.
"The newspaper for videonuts." Designed for video
collectors; forum for buying, selling, trading home video
products. Articles review the latest technical advances.

The Videophile (U.S.); Small Potatoes Publishing Co., 2003
  Apalachee Parkway, Tallahassee, FL 32301; (bimonthly); ISSN:
  0164-5862; OCLC 4513037.
  Note: v.1,n.1 Nov/Dec 1977 -.
  A collectors' magazine for video enthusiasts. A forum for
  buying, selling and trading home videos. Reviews new
  releases on video.

Videotex Now (U.S.). Chronicle Information Services, Inc.: 275
  5th St., San Francisco, CA 94103, Tel: 415/989-3611;
  (irregular); ISSN: 0749-5358; OCLC 11145927.
  Note: v.1,n.1 Jul 9, 1984 -.
  Newsletter promoting the use of video for two-way
  telecommunications. Reports on interactive video
  applications, such as electronic shopping, real estate
  listings and store guides.

Vidiot (U.S.); Creem Magazine, Inc., 210 S. Woodward, Suite 209,
  Birmingham, MI 48011. Tel: 313/642-8833; (bimonthly); ISSN:
  n/a.
  Note: v.1,n.1 Jan 1983 -.
  "The magazine of video lunacy." Popular magazine for
  youthful readers. Contains the latest information on video
  games, music videos, video art and software. Reviews and
  rates video arcade games, such as Pacman, Timepilot, Q*Bert.

Viewers for Quality Television: V.T.Q. (U.S.). See: **V.T.Q.:
Viewers for Quality Television**.

24 Images (Canada). Alternate title: **Vingt-Quatre Images**.
  24 Images, 3781 rue Laval, Montreal, Quebec H2W 2H8
  Canada. Tel: 514/286-1688; (quarterly); ISSN: 0707-9389;
  OCLC 5841389.
  Note: n.1, Feb 1979 -.
  "La revue Quebecoise du cinema." Reviews the latest feature
  films and noteworthy cinema books. Each film review contains
  detailed cast and credits as well as a long critique. Also
  contains a rating chart whereby new films are evaluated by
  several critics. Articles cover state of the cinematic arts
  in Quebec Province, Canadian filmmaking and long interviews
  with film personalities.
  Dewey: 791.43/05.

Vision. A Journal of Film Comment (U.S.). See: **Film Comment**.

Visions (Belgium); Centre Culturel d'Animation Cinematographique
ASBL, 9 rue Traversiere, 1030 Bruxelles, Belgium. Tel: (02)
513.95.10; (monthly); ISSN: n/a.
Note: n.1-n.41, 1982-Sep 1986.
Popular magazine concentrating on the latest international
feature films. Published in French; discontinued in 1986.

Visions (Canada); Federation Professionnelle des Realisateurs et
Realisatrices de Television et de Cinema, C.P. 870,
Succursale N., Montreal, Quebec, Canada H2L 4L6; (quarterly);
ISSN: 0838-293X; OCLC 19461531.
Note: v.1,n.1 Apr 1988 -.
Newsletter for members of the professional guild. Reports on
the state of Canadian film and television production.
Published in French.
PN1992.75; Dewey: 791.406 0714.

Visor (Venezuela); Creativos M.A.G.A., Visor, C.A., Apartado de
Correos 60844, Chacao, Caracas, Venezuela; (annual); ISSN: n/
a; OCLC 5239166.
Note: ed.1, 1974/75 -.
"Guia Venezolana de medios audiovisuales." A directory of
companies specializing in motion picture and television
products and services in Venezuela. A guide to professionals
working in the entertainment industry, distributors,
importers and cine clubs. Contains alphabetical lists of
feature and short films made in Venezuela during the
preceding year, giving title, cast, credits, synopsis and
still. Published in Spanish.
PN1993.5.V4V57; Dewey: 791.025/87.

Visual Anthropology (U.S.); Center for Visual Communication, PO
Box 128, Mifflintown, PA 17059, Subscription address: Harwood
Academic Publishers GmbH, c/o STBS Ltd., One Bedford St.,
London WC2E 9PP England; (quarterly); ISSN: 0894-9468; OCLC
16318487.
Note: v.1,n.1 Nov 1987 -.
Scholarly journal concerned with the study of anthropology
through the aid of visual media. Interested in the "study,
use and production of anthropological and ethnographic films,
videos and photographs for research and teaching." Analyzes

the imaging process in ethnographic inquiry.
GN347.V57; Dewey: 306.0208.

Visual Media = Medias Visuels (Canada). Formerly: **A Newsletter Called Fred** (0315-6923). Ontario Film Association, Inc., PO Box 366, Station Q, Ontario, M4T2M5 Canada. Tel: 416/575-2076; (bimonthly); ISSN: 0840-4313; OCLC 19491680.
Note: v.1-16?, 1972-1988 as **A Newsletter Called Fred**; renumbered v.1,n.1 Sep/Oct 1988- as **Visual Media = Medias Visuels**.
Bilingual English/French publication designed for audiovisual specialists who buy films and videocassettes for school and industry. Reviews educational 16mm films, some feature films and home video.
PN1993; Dewey: 791.43/75/05.

-W-

W.E.T.A. Magazine (U.S.). Formerly: **The Dial from W.E.T.A.**
Greater Washington Educational Telecommunications Assoc., Box
2626, Washington, DC 20013. Tel: 703/998-2800; (monthly);
ISSN: 0273-4044; OCLC 7009311.
Note: v.1,n.1-v.8,n.9, Sep 1980-Sep 1987 as **The Dial from
W.E.T.A.**; renumbered v.1,n.1 Oct 1987- as **W.E.T.A. Magazine.**
Program guide to the public broadcasting station WETA,
Channel 26, in the Washington, D.C. metropolitan area. Gives
background reports on the new shows, specials and series
being aired. News of upcoming events, plus profiles of
performers.
PN1992.D5; Dewey: 384.55/4.

W.G.A. West Newsletter (U.S.). See: **The Writers Guild of America,
West Journal.**

W.G.A.W. Newsletter (U.S.). See: **The Writers Guild of America,
West Journal.**

W.J.R. Washington Journalism Review (U.S.). Alternate title:
Washington Journalism Review. College of Journalism of the
University of Maryland at College Park, W.J.R., 2233
Wisconsin Ave., NW, Washington, DC 20007. Tel: 800/525-0643;
(monthly; except Jan/Feb & Jul/Aug); ISSN: 0741-8876; 0743-
9881; OCLC 10218965.
Note: v.1,n.1 Jan/Feb 1979 -.
Despite the name, this magazine covers television
broadcasting as much as, if not more than, print journalism.
Analyzes media coverage of major news events, examining how
the story is treated, government interference, foreign
reports, and denouement. Keeps current with laws and
legislation concerning the media and business trends in
broadcasting. Reviews scholarly books on journalism.

W.R.T.H. Downlink (U.S.); Billboard Publications, Inc., 1515
Broadway, 39th Floor, New York, NY 10036; (quarterly); ISSN:

n/a.
Note: v.1,n.1 Mar 1989 -.
This is an update of the **World Radio TV Handbook**. Contains the latest schedules of international broadcasters, news from collaborators and monitors, a shortwave frequency list and pertinent articles. Published in English, German and Spanish.

W.R.T.H. Handbook (U.S.). See: **World Radio TV Handbook**.

W.T.N. Worldwide Television News (U.K.); Worldwide Television News London, 31-36 Foley St, London W1P 7LB England. Tel: 01-323-3255; (quarterly); ISSN: n/a.
Note: [n.1] 1986 -.
Newsletter for subscribers to Worldwide Television News, a stock video library for international news. Articles include how news events are covered from around the world. Latest updates on satellite broadcasts, news and events.

Weekly Cable Action Update (U.S.). See: **Cable Action Update**.

Weekly Television Action Update (U.S.). See: **Television Action Update**.

Weekly Variety (U.S.). See: **Variety**.

The Western Film (U.S.); Grady Franklin, Editor, 1943 Jasmine Dr., Indianapolis, IN 46219. Tel: 317/897-3069; (bimonthly); ISSN: n/a.
Note: [n.1] 1981 -.
A newsletter for fans and collectors of American westerns. Articles, notices, reviews and editorials of interest to western fans, focusing on theatrical features and serials, but including information on new TV series and cable presentations.

What's On Video and Cinema (Australia). Formerly: **Australian Video and Cinema** (0185-628X); merged with **Australian Video and Communications, incorporating Australian Video Review** (0706-6902). General Magazine Company (Australia) Pty Ltd, 9 Paran Place, PO Box 186, Glen Iris, Victoria 3146, Australia. Tel: (03) 25 6456; (monthly); ISSN: 0185-628X; OCLC 13563080.
Note: v.1-v.5,n.50, 1982-Jan 1986 as **Australian Video and**

Cinema; v.5,n.51 Mar 1986- as **What's On Video and Cinema.**
Merged with **Australian Video and Communications,**
incorporating Australian Video Review in Sep 1984.
Popular magazine reviewing the latest international films as
well as new releases on video. Profiles performers,
interviews stars, comments on music videos and Australian
television programs.
PN1992.95.A9; Dewey: 791.43/05.

Who's Who in Entertainment (U.S.); Marquis Who's Who,
Macmillan Directory Division, 3002 Glenview Rd., Wilmette, IL
60091; (annual); ISSN: 1044-0887; OCLC 19003710.
Note: ed.1, 1989/1990 -.
A directory to professionals working in the motion picture,
broadcasting and theater industries. Includes directors,
producers, managers, as well as performers. Each entry gives
date of birth, education, credits, contact address and short
biographical sketch.
PN1583.W47; Dewey: 791.092/2.

Who's Who in Television (U.S.); Packard Publishing Co., PO Box
2187, Beverly Hills, CA 90213; (annual); ISSN: n/a; OCLC
17995503.
Note: ed.1, 1987 -.
Business directory of television producers, directors,
writers, networks, production companies, studios, and pay/
cable services. Gives one or more contact addresses and
phone numbers, plus a list of credits. Indexed by individual
names, company names, agents and agencies.

Who's Who in the Motion Picture Industry (U.S.); Packard
Publishing Co., PO Box 2187, Beverly Hills, CA 90213;
(annual); ISSN: 0278-6516; OCLC 7845742.
Note: ed.1, 1981 -.
A directory of producers, writers, directors, special effects
supervisors, cinematographers, major studios, and production
and distribution companies in the United States. The entry for
individuals gives name, business manager or agent, address,
telephone number and list of credits. For companies, gives
addresses for East and West coast offices and chiefs of staff.
PN1998.A2W624; Dewey: 791.43/023/02573.

Wide Angle (U.S.); Ohio University, Athens Center for Film & Video, Box 388, Athens, OH 45701; (quarterly); ISSN: 0160-6840; OCLC 2757185.
Note: v.1,n.1 Spring 1976 -.
"A film quarterly of theory, criticism and practice." A scholarly journal where each issue is devoted to one or two special topics which are then analyzed from several different angles. Covers all aspects of cinema and broadcasting studies, from semiotics to music videos.
PN1993.W48; Dewey: 791.43/05.

Wide Screen (U.S.). See: **American Widescreener**.

Wind Rose (U.S.); Mystic Seaport Museum, Mystic, CT 06355-0990. Tel: 203/572-0711; (bimonthly); ISSN: 0049-7567; 0049-7657.
Note: v.1, 1970? -.
A newsletter for members of the museum. In addition to preserving the heritage of New England seafaring and sailing, the museum acts as a stock film library for historic maritime film and video footage.

The World of Bela Lugosi (U.S.); The Bela Lugosi Society, c/o Garydon Rhodes, 330 G St., SW, Ardmore, OK 73401; (quarterly); ISSN: n/a.
Note: [n.1] 1987 -.
A tribute to Bela Lugosi and his films. A newsletter for fans of the most famous movie Dracula.

The World of Yesterday (U.S.); The World of Yesterday Publications, Route 3, Box 263-H, Waynesville, NC 28786. Tel: 704/648-5647; (irregular); ISSN: 0273-5679; OCLC 5193606.
Note: n.1, Feb 1976 -.
Fanzine for collectors of motion pictures, radio serials and television programs covering the years 1935-1955.

World-Radio. See: **Radio Times**.

World Radio TV Handbook (U.S.). Alternate title: **W.R.T.H. Handbook**. Billboard Publications, Inc., 1515 Broadway, New York, NY 10036; (annual); ISSN: 0144-7750; OCLC 4244995.
Note: v.1, 1947 -.
"A complete directory of international radio and television." Although mostly radio, it has a section for television,

covering the development of TV services around the world.
Lists high power stations, systems used, antenna polarization,
number of channels, sound and vision modulation for Europe,
Africa, the Near and Middle East, Asia, the Pacific, North
America, Central America and the Caribbean, and South
America. Has numerous supplements; published in English,
Spanish, German.
TK6540.W67.

The Writers Guild of America, West Journal (U.S.). Formerly:
W.G.A. West Newsletter; alternate title: **W.G.A.W. Newsletter**.
Address: Writers Guild of America, 8955 Beverly Blvd., West
Hollywood, CA 90048-2456. Tel: 213/550-1000; (11 times/yr);
ISSN: n/a; OCLC 20140910.
Note: [v.1-v.24], Oct 1965-Oct 1988 as **W.G.A. West Newsletter**;
[v.25], Nov 1988- as **The Writers Guild of America, West
Journal**.
For members of the Writers Guild, the trade organization for
motion picture and television screenwriters. Informs members
of news and events affecting their profession. Gives
marketing lists, featuring contact submission information on
current writing projects.

-Y-

Yeonghwa (Korea). Alternate titles: **Cinema; Film**. Motion Picture Promotion Corporation, 34-5, 3-ka, Namsan-dong, Chung-ku, Seoul, Republic of Korea; (bimonthly); ISSN: n/a.
Note: [v.1] 1967? -.
Well illustrated, popular film journal containing articles on Korean filmmaking, history of the cinema, and film theory. Interviews and profiles Korean stars. Reviews international feature films released in Korea. Published in Korean.

Young Cinema (Czechoslovakia). See: **Young/Jeune Cinema & Theatre**.

Young Cinema & Theatre (Czechoslovakia). See: **Young/Jeune Cinema & Theatre**.

Young/Jeune Cinema & Theatre (Czechoslovakia). Formerly: **Young Cinema**; alternate titles: **Young Cinema & Theatre**; **Jeune Cinema & Theatre**; **Joven Cine & Teatro**. Address: International Union of Students, 17 November St., P.O.B. 58, 11001, Prague 01, Czechoslovakia; (quarterly); ISSN: 0513-5958; OCLC 4120000.
Note: [1957-1966] as **Young Cinema**; n.1, 1967- as **Young/Jeune Cinema & Theatre**.
An international magazine for precocious students interested in cinema and theater, published in English and French. Interested in avant garde, revolutionary and controversial topics as related to and interpreted by the performing arts. Reports on film festivals world wide.
PN1993.Y59; Dewey: 791.

Young Viewers (U.S.); Media Center Children, 451 West Broadway, New York, NY 10012-3156; (quarterly); ISSN: 0886-4802; OCLC 5315066.
Note: v.1,n.1-v.10,n.2-3 Fall 1977-Spring 1988.
Promoted the development of media for children as an art form. Reviewed films and videos intended for children and tried to encourage quality productions. Discontinued

publication.
P94.5.C55Y68.

The Yugoslav Film (Yugoslavia). See: **Jugoslavia Film News**.

-Z-

Z: Filmtidsskrift (Norway); Norsk Filmklubbforbund, Wesselsgt. 4, 0165, Oslo, Norway. Tel: (02) 11 42; (5 times/yr); ISSN: 0800-1464; OCLC 11608417.
Note: n.1, 1983? -.
Scholarly, well illustrated magazine of film criticism. Articles analyze the work of popular, although diverse directors, such as Wim Wenders, Francois Truffaut and Robert Flaherty. Publishes extensive filmographies; reviews films and cinema books; interviews famous film personalities. Written in Norse, with English summaries.
PN1993.Z2.

Zeitschrift fur Filmkultur und Filmwissenschaft (Austria). See: **Filmkunst: Zeitschrift fur Filmkultur und Filmwissenschaft.**

Zelluloid (W.Germany); Anschrift der Redaktion Zelluloid, c/o Kolner Filmhaus, Luxemburgerstr. 72, 5000 Koln 1, West Germany. Tel: 02 21/ 41 77 68; (quarterly); ISSN: 0724-7656.
Note: n.1, 1981 -.
Scholarly journal interested in the study of early film history in Germany and Europe. Each issue is devoted to the work of one particular film pioneer. Published in German.

Zve do Kina (Czechoslovakia). See: **Kino; Obrazkovy Filmovy Crtnactidenik.**

GEOGRAPHICAL INDEX

Albania

Radio Televisioni (1967-)

Algeria

Les Deux Ecrans (1978-1983)

Argentina

Anuario del Cine (1977-)
Cine Argentino (1968-)

Australia

Australian Films (1959-)
The Australian Journal of Screen Theory (1976-1984)
Australian Video and Cinema (1982-1986)
Australian Video and Communications (1982-1984)
Cantrill's Filmnotes (1971-)
Cinema Papers (1974-)
The Cinema Papers Australian Production Yearbook: Film, Television, Video (1980-)
Communications Law and Policy in Australia (1988-)
Continuum: An Australian Journal of the Media (1987/88-)
Encore (198u-)
Federation News (1956?-1979)

Filmviews (1980-1988)
Media Information Australia (1976-)
Media Watch (1988-)
Metro: Media and Education Magazine (1960?-)
National Film & Sound Archive Newsletter (1985-)
Stuffing (1987-)
What's on Video and Cinema (1986-)

Austria

Blimp (1986?-)
Film Logbuch (198u-1989)
Filmkunst: Zeitschrift fur Filmkultur und
    Filmwissenschaft (1949/50-)
Mitteilungen des Osterreichischen Filmmuseums (1962?-)
Mitteilungen: Osterreichische Gesellschaft fur Filmwissenschaft
    Kommunikations- und Medienforschung (1952-)

Bangladesh

Sequence (1970-)

Belgium

A.P.E.C. Cinema: Revue Belge de Cinema (1963-1976)
A.S.I.F.A. News (1974?-)
Andere Sinema (1978-)
Annuaire du Film Belge = Jaarboek van de Belgische Film (1958-)
Les Cahiers du Scenario = De Scenariogids = The Screenwriter's
Companion
    (1988-)
Cine-Revue (1919?-1987)
Cine-Tele-Revue (1987-)
F.I.A.F. Bulletin (1971?-)
Film en Televisie + Video (1956?-)
Grand Angle (1978?-)
Media Magazine (1985-)
Mediafilm (19uu-)
Le Moniteur du Film (1981?-)
Revue Belge du Cinema (1976-)

S.C.A.D. Bulletin Radio-TV-Film Supplement (198u-)
S.N.C. Soundtrack Collector's Newsletter (1975-1980)
Soundtrack! The Collector's Quarterly (1980-)
Stars (1988-)
Visions (1982-1986)

Brazil

Boletim Informativo S.I.P. (1974-)
Cinejournal (198u-)
Cinema em Close-up (1977?-)
Filme Cultura (1966-)
Moviola (1984-)

Bulgaria

Bulgarian Films (1959?-)
Fil'movi Novini (1955-)
Kino i Vreme (1972-)
Kinoizkustvo (1935-)
Kinorabotnik (1968-)

Canada

A.S.I.F.A. Bulletin de l'Association Internationale du Film
    d'Animation, Canada (1974?-)
A.V. Business Communications (1977?-1986)
Action (1986-)
Bibliography: F.I.A.F. Members Publications = Bibliographie:
    Publications des Membres de la F.I.A.F.
Broadcast Technology (1975-)
Broadcaster (1942-)
C.F.F.S. Newsletter (1980-)
Cable Communications Magazine (193u-)
Canadian Cinematography (1961-1967)
Canadian Communications Network Letter (1981-)
Canadian Film Digest Yearbook (1973/74-1985)
Canadian Journal of Communication (1974-)
Cine Bulles (1980-)
Cine-Tracks (1977-1982)

Cineaction! (1985-)
Cinema (19uu-)
Cinema Canada (1967-)
Cinemag (1977-1981)
Copie Zero (1979-1988)
Culture Statistics. Film Industry = Statistiques de la Culture
    L'Industrie du Film (1978/79-)
Domitor (1986?-)
Ecrits Sur le Cinema (1982-)
Film & T.V. World (1977-1983)
Film Canada Yearbook (1986-)
Film Canadiana (1969-1983/84)
Film/Video Canadiana (1985/86-)
Infocus: Academy of Canadian Cinema & Television (1982-)
Media Magazine (1980-)
MediaWatch Bulletin. Evaluation-Medias (1987-)
A Newsletter Called Fred (1972-1988)
Opsis (1984-)
Perforations (1981-)
PhotoVideo (1984-)
Qui Fait Quoi (1984-)
Recueil des Films (1955/56-)
Reel West Film and Video Digest (1981-1982)
Reel West Digest (1983-)
Reel West Magazine (1985-)
La Revue de la Cinematheque (1989-)
Sequences. Revue de Cinema (1955-)
Spleen (1989-)
Take One (1966-1979)
Toronto Film Society Newsletter (1949-)
24 Images (1979-)
Visions (1988-)
Visual Media = Medias Visuels (1988-)

Chile

Enfoque (1984?-)

Colombia

Cine (1981?-)

Cine: Publicacion de la Compania de Fomento Cinematografico
   (1980-)
Cinemateca (1977-)

Cuba

Cine Cubano (1960-)

Czechoslovakia

The Czechoslovak Film (1948-)
Film a Divadlo (1957-)
Film A Doba; Mesicnik pro Filmovou Kulturu (1955-)
Kino; Obrazkovy Filmovy Crtnactidenik (1946?-)
Panorama (1960-)
Radio and Television (1950-)
Young Cinema (1957-1966)
Young/Jeune Cinema & Theatre (1967-)

Denmark

Danish Films (1966-)
Filmmuseet (1969-)
Filmsaesonen Dansk (1979/80-)
Kosmorama (1954-)
Levende Billeder (1975-)
Macguffin (1973-1987)
Prasen (1976-)

East Germany

Beitrage zur Film- und Fernsehwissenschaft (1982-)
Deutsche Filmkunst (1953-1962)
Film und Fernsehen (1959-)
Filmo-Bibliografischer Jahresbericht (1965?-)
Filmspiegel (1963-)
Filmwissenschaftliche Beitrage (1960-1981)
Prisma; Kino-und Fernseh-Almanach (1971-)
Rundfunk und Fernsehprogramm (1955-1959)

Finland

Facts About Film Finland (1971-1977)
Finland-Filmland: Facts About Film in Finland (1978-)
Finnish Films = Films Finlandais (1980-)
Filmihullu (1968-)
Kaitafilmi (1954-)

France

L'Activite Cinematographique Francaise en C.N.C., Centre National
    de la Cinematographie (1977?-)
Animatographe (1987-)
L'Annee du Cinema (1977-)
Annuaire du Cinema Francais (1977-1982)
Annuaire du Cinema Francais et de L'Audiovisuel (1983/84-)
Annuaire du Cinema et Television (1964-1985)
Annuaire du Cinema, Television, Video (1986-)
Anthologie du Cinema (1965-)
Archives (1986-)
Archives/Cahiers de la Cinematheque (1971-1976)
L'Avant-Scene Cinema (1961-)
Ca: Cinema (1973-)
Les Cahiers de la Cinematheque (1977?-)
Cahiers du Cinema (1951-)
Camera/Stylo (1985-)
Catalogue de la Production Cinematographique Francaise (1975-)
Cinema (1954-)
Cinema Francais (1976-)
Le Cinema Francais (1945-1976)
Cinema Francais, Production (1977-)
CinemAction (1978-)
Cinematheque (196u-)
Cinematographe (1973-1987)
CineMotion (1988-)
Cinethique (1969-1985)
Conseil International du Cinema de la Television et de la
    Communication Audiovisuelle (1979-)
Ecran (1958-1980)
L'Ecran Fantastique (1976?-)
1895: Bulletin de L'Association Francaise de Recherche sur
    L'Histoire du Cinema (1987-)

Etudes Cinematographiques (1960-)
Film Echange (1978-)
Le Film Francais (1944-)
Films et Documents (1946-)
Grand Maghreb (1981-)
Hors Cadre (1983-)
I.F.T.C. Newsletter (1973-1979)
Image et Son/Revue du Cinema (1951?-1980)
Informations C.N.C. (1947-)
Iris (1983-)
Jeune Cinema (1964-)
Positif; Revue de Cinema (1952-)
La Revue du Cinema/Image et Son (1980-)
Script (1988-)
Tele-media (1969-)
U.F.O.C.E.L. Informations (1947?-1951?)
Vertigo (1988-)

Ghana

G.B.C. Radio and TV Times (1976-)
Ghana Radio & Television Times (1965-1976)
Ghana Radio Review and TV Times (1960-1965)

Greece

Cine 7 (198u-)
Synchronos Kinematografos + Cinema Contemporain (1969-)

Hong Kong

Chia Ho Tien Ying (1972?-)
Chung Wai Ying Hua (1979?-)

Hungary

Audio-vizualis Kozlemenyek (1964-)
Film Szinhaz Muzsika (1957-)
Filmkultura (1970-)

Filmmuveszeti Konyvtar (1961-)
Filmvilag (1958-)
Hungarofilm Bulletin (1965?-1988)
Radio-es Televizio-Ujsag (1957-)
Radio-Ujsag (1956-1957)

India

Bulletin on Film (1955?-)
C.F.S. Review (1983-)
Chitrabikshan (1968-)
Cinema In India (1987-)
Cinema India-International (1984-)
Cinema Vision India (1980-1983)
Cinemaya (1988-)
Cinewave (1981-)
Close-Up (1968-)
Filmindia (1935-1960)
Filmworld (1964-)
Indian Cinema (1965?-)
Indian Film Culture (1979?-)
Media Monitor (1986-)
Mother India (1960-)
Movement (1968-)
Time & Tide (1952-)

Indonesia

Bulletin K.F.T.: Media Karyawan Film dan Televisi Indonesia
   (1980?-)

International

Celebrity Bulletin (1952-)
F.I.A.T./I.F.T.A. Bulletin (1980?-)

Israel

Cinematheque (Jerusalem, 198u-)

Cinematheque (Tel Aviv, 1981-)
Kolnoa (1974-1981)

Italy

Animafilm. The Journal of Animated Film (1984-)
Artibus et Historiae (1980-)
Attualita Cinematografiche (1963-)
Bianco e Nero (1937-)
Bulletin, Calendar of International Film and Television Events =
    Bulletin, Calendrier des Evenements Internationaux du Cinema et
    de la Television (1977/1978-)
Il Castoro Cinema (1974-)
Ciak si Gira (1985-)
Ciennepi (1981?-)
Cineforum (1961-)
Cinegrafie (1989-)
Cinema (1977-)
Cinema D'Oggi (194u-)
Cinema e Cinema (1974-)
Cinema Nuovo (1952-)
Cinema Societa (1966-)
Cinemasessanta (1960-)
Cinemasud (1958?-)
La Cosa Vista (1985-)
Cult Movie (1980-)
Film Tutti i Film Della Stagione (1983-)
Filmcritica (1950-)
Giornale Dello Spettacolo (19uu-)
Griffithiana (1978-)
Ikon; Cinema, Television, Iconografia (1962-1977)
Ikon: Ricerche Sulla Comunicazione (1978-)
Immagine (1985-)
M.N.C. Museo Nazionale del Cinema (1989-)
Patalogo (1978-1984)
Patalogo. Cinema + Televisione (1985-1986)
Patalogo. Cinema + Televisione + Video (1987-)
I Quaderni del Cinema Italiano (1982-)
Quaderni di Cinema (1981-)
Revue Internationale de Filmologie (1947-1961)
Segnocinema (1981-)
Spettacolo, Lo (1951-)

Teatro e Cinema (1967-)
Video Magazine (1981-)

Japan

A.B.U. Technical Review (196u-)
Eiga Mokuroku (1980?-)
Eiga Gijutsu (1948-1965)
Eiga Terebi Gijutsu (1965-)
Eigakan Meibo (1978?-)
Eigashi Kenkyu (1973-)
Far East Film News (1953-1961)
Movie Marketing (1961-1966)
Movie/TV Marketing (1966-)
Nihon Eiga Kaigai Fukyu Kyokai (1958-)
Nihon No Yushu Eiga (1974-)
Studies in Broadcasting (1961-)

Korea

Korea Cinema (1967-)
The Third Channel (1985-)
Yeonghwa (1967?-)

Malaysia

Bullentin Finas (1986-)

Mexico

Cineteca Nacional (1979?-)
Cineteca Nacional Mexico (1976-)

The Netherlands

Cinematheek Journal (1978?-)
Dutch Film (1986-)
I.A.M.H.I.S.T. Newsletter (1977?-)

Interfilm Reports (1976-)
N.F.M. Programma (19uu-)
Skoop (1962-1969)
Skoop/Kritisch Filmforum (1969-)
Skrien (1968?-)
Versus (1984-)

New Zealand

Illusions (1986-)
New Zealand Film (1982-)
New Zealand Film & Television Directory (1984-)
New Zealand Film Archive Newsletter (1982-)
OnFilm (1983-)
Report of the New Zealand Film Commission for the Year (1983)

Northern Ireland

Film Directions (1977-)

Norway

Film og Kino (1965-)
Norsk Filmblad (1930-1964)
Z: Filmtidsskrift (1983?-)

Pakistan

Cinema the World Over (1975-)
Sequence (1970-)

Panama

Formato Dieciseis (1977?-)

People's Republic of China (P.R.C.)

China Screen (1964?-)
Chung-kuo Tien Ying Nien Chien (1981-)

Philippines

Filipino Film Review (1983-)

Poland

Ekran; Kino TV Video (1957-)
Film (1946-)
Film Polski (1963-1968)
Filmowy Serwis Prasowy (1955-)
Iluzjon (1981-)
Kino (1966-)
Polish Film. Film Polonais (1969-)

Portugal

Celuloide (1958?-1986)
Cinema (1982-)

Puerto Rico

Imagenes (1985-)

Republic of China

Chung-hua Nein Kuo Tien Ying Nien Chien (1984-)

Romania

Cinema (1963-)
The Romanian Film (1965-)

Senegal

Unir Cinema (1973-)

Singapore

Asian Mass Communication Bulletin (A.M.C.B.) (1974-)
Media Asia (1974-)

Spain

Casablanca (1981-1984)
Cine Para Leer (1972-)
Cinema 2002 (1975-)
Contracampo (1979-)
Dirigido Por... (1973?-)
Eikonos (1976-)
Filmoteca Espanola (unnumbered)
Shows (198u-)

South Africa

Critical Arts (1980-)
The S.A.F.T.T.A. Journal (1980?-1986)

Sweden

Audio Video (1985?-)
Chaplin (1959-)
Filmarsboken (1961-)
Filmhaftet (1973-)
Filmrutan (1958-)
Scandinavian Film News (1981-)
Swedish Films. Films Suedois (1973-)

Switzerland

Filmklub-Cineclub (1955-1961)

Cinema (1961-)
La Cinematheque Suisse (1954-)
E.B.U. Review (1950?-)
Filmbulletin (1959?-)
Jahrbuch der Schweizer Filmindustrie = Annuaire de la
    Cinematographie Suisse = Annuario della Cinematografia Svizzera
    (1938/39-1976/77)
Schweizer Filmindex = Index Suisse du Cinema = Indice Svizzero
    del Cinema (1978-)

Togo

Cine Qua Non (1972-)

Turkey

Denk Ajans (1989-)

Union of Soviet Socialist Republics

Aktery Zarubezhnogo Kino (1965-)
Iskusstvo Kino (1936-)
Kino (194u-)
Kino i Vremia (1977-)
Mnenya (1989-)
Na Ekranakh Mira (1966-)
Novyny Kinoekrana (1983-)
Novyny Kinoekranu (1961?-1983)
Proletarskoe Kino (1931-1932)
Sovetskoe Kino (1933-1935)
Sovetskoe Radio i Televidenie (1957-1970)
Sovetsky Ekran (1957-)
Soviet Film (1957-)
Televidenie, Radioveshchanie (1970-)

United Kingdom

Afterimage (1970-)
Airwaves (1984/85-)

International Film and Television Yearbook (1976/77-1982/83)
International Film Guide (1964-)
International Index to Film Periodicals (1972-)
International Index to Television Periodicals (1979/1980-)
International Journal of Micrographics and Video Technology
    (1982-)
International T.V. & Video Guide (1983-1987)
Invision (1986-)
Kemp's Film and Television Yearbook (International) (1970-1977/78)
Kemp's International Film & Television Directory (1956-1969)
Kemp's International Film & Television Year Book (1978/1979-)
Kine Weekly (1959-1971)
Kinematograph and Lantern Weekly (1907-1919)
Kinematograph Weekly (1919-1959)
The Listener (1929-)
Making Better Movies (1985-)
Media, Culture & Society (1979-)
Media in Education and Development (1968?-)
Microdoc (1962-1982)
Monthly Film Bulletin (1934-)
Movie (1962-)
Movie Maker (1967-1984)
N.F.T. National Film Theatre (1956-)
The New Magic Lantern Journal (1978-)
New Media Markets (1983-)
Number Six (1985-)
Photoplay Movies & Video (1982-1989)
Picture House (1967-)
The Radio Supplement (1925-1939)
Radio Times (1939-)
The Royal Television Society Journal (1961?-1975)
Satellite Technology (1985-)
Screen Digest (1971?-)
Screen Education (1959-1968)
Screen Finance (1988-)
Screen Incorporating Screen Education (1969-)
Screen International (1976-)
Screen International Film and Television Yearbook (1983/84-)
Showcall (197u-)
Sight and Sound (1932-)
Six of One (1967/68-1985)
16 MM Film User (1946-1947)
The Stage (1881-1959)

The State and Television Today (1959-)
Stills (1980-1987)
T.B.I. Television Business International (1988-)
T.V. Times (1955-)
T.V. World (1978-)
Television (1976-)
Televisual (1983-)
Three Sixty (1985?-)
Today's Cinema Incorporating Kine Weekly (1971)
Undercut (1981-)
W.T.N. Worldwide Television News (1986-)

United States

A. & E. Cable Network Program Guide (1984-)
A.A.A.S. Science Books (1965-1975)
A.B.C. News Index (1986-)
A.E.J.M.C. News (1983-)
A.E.J.M.C. Newsletter (1968?-1983)
A.F.I. Close-up (1982-1986?)
A.F.I. Education Newsletter (1978-1982)
A.F.T. & T. (1985-)
A.F.V.A. Bulletin (1988-)
A.I.T. Newsletter (1973-)
A.V. Video (1984-)
Aamplitude (1985-)
Academy Players Directory (1937-)
Access (1975-)
Action! (1966-)
Actors Cues (1941-1949)
Adam Film World Guide (1984-)
Adult Cinema Review (1981-)
Adult Video News (1985?-)
Advertising in Movies (1985-)
Afterimage (1972-)
American Cinematheque Newsletter (1984-1989)
American Cinematographer (1920-)
American Cinemeditor (1971-)
American Classic Screen (1976-1984)
American Film (1975-)
American Movie Classics Magazine (1988-)
American Museum of the Moving Image Newsletter (1988?-)

American Premiere (1981-)
The American Screenwriter (1984-1988)
American Widescreener (1982-)
Animation Magazine (1987-)
Animato! (1983?-)
The Animator (1972-)
Annual Index to Motion Picture Credits (1978-)
Arbitron Television Audience Estimates (1949-)
Art & Cinema (1973-)
Art Murphy's Box Office Register (1982-)
ArtsAmerica Fine Art Film and Video Source Book (1987-)
Asian Cinema (1988-)
Asian Cinema Studies Society Newsletter (1985-1988)
Association of Independent Video and Filmmakers Newsletter
    (1976-1978)
Audience (1982-)
Audio Video Market Place: A.V.M.P. (1969-)
Audio/Video Interiors (1989-)
Audio-Visual Communications (1967-)
Audio Visual Directions (1980-1984)
The Audio-visual Equipment Directory (1953-1983)
Audio Visual Product News (1978-1980)
AudioVideo International (1973-)
AudioVideo Review Digest (1989-)

B.M./E.: The Magazine of Broadcast Management/Engineering
    (1965-1988)
B.M.E. for Technical and Engineering Management (1988-)
B Westerns in Perspective (1983-)
Back Stage (1960-)
Back Stage TV Film & Tape Directory (1982-1984)
Back Stage TV Film & Tape Production Directory (1985-)
Backstage: TV Film, Tape & Syndication Directory (1974-1981)
Bertha Landers Film Reviews (1956-1959)
Better Radio & Television (1960-)
Bibliography on Cable Television: B.C.T.V. (1975-)
The Big Reel (1974-)
The Big Trail (1984-)
Billboard (1894-)
Billboard International Talent Directory (1979/80-1980/81)
Black Camera (1985-)
Black Film Review (1984-)
The Black Video Guide (1985/86-)

Cable T.V. Advertising (1980-)
The Cable T.V. Financial Databook (1982-)
Cable T.V. Franchising (1981-)
Cable T.V. Investor (1969-)
Cable T.V. Investor Charts (1982-)
Cable T.V. Law & Finance (1983-)
Cable T.V. Law Reporter (1984-)
Cable T.V. Programming (1981-)
Cable T.V. Regulation (1975-1981)
Cable T.V. Technology (1981-)
Cable Television Business (1982-)
Cable Update (1989-)
Cableage (1981-)
Cablenet Cableguide (1982-1985)
The CableTV Guide (1982-1984?)
Cabletime (1985?-1988)
Cableview (1981-)
CableVision (1976?-)
Calendar / University Art Museum (1978?-)
Camera Obscura (1976-)
Canyon Cinema News (1963-1976)
Captioned Films/Videos for the Deaf (1988/1989-)
Carnegie Institute Travel Sheet (1974-1987)
Catalog of Educational Captioned Films for the Deaf (1980/81-
    1984/85)
Catalog of Educational Captioned Films/Videos for the Deaf
    (1985/86-1987/88)
Catholic Film Newsletter (1935-1975)
Celebrity Directory (1984-1987)
Celebrity Focus (1987-1988)
Celebrity Plus (1988-)
Channel Guide (1978-)
Channels (1986-)
Channels of Communications (1981-1986)
Children's Video Report (1985-)
Children's Video Review Newsletter (1987-)
Christian Film & Video (1984-)
Cineaste (1967-)
Cinefan (1974-)
Cinefantastique (1970-)
Cinefex (1980-)
Cinegram (1976-)
The Cinegram (1989-)

The Dial from W.E.T.A. (1980-1987)
The Dial from W.T.T.W./Eleven (1980-1987)
Dial/W.G.B.H. (1980-1986)
Directory of Experts, Authorities & Spokespersons (1987/88-)
Directory of Members. Directors Guild of America (1967/68-)
The Directory of Religious Broadcasting (1974?-)
Disc Deals (1985-)
Discourse (1978-)
The Discovery Channel: T.D.C. (1985-)
Discovery In Focus (1987-)
The Disney Channel Magazine (1983-)
Downlink Directory (1986-)

E.F.L.A. Bulletin (1977-1987)
E.-I.T.V. Magazine (1983-1988)
East-West Film Journal (1986-)
Educational & Industrial Television (1969?-1983)
Educational Technology (1966-)
Educators Guide to Free Audio and Video Materials (1954-)
Educators Guide to Free Films (1941-)
Educators Guide to Free Filmstrips and Slides (1949-)
Educators Guide to Free Guidance Materials (1962-)
Educators Guide to Free Health, Physical Educational and
    Recreation Materials (1968-)
Educators Guide to Free Home Economics Materials (1984-)
Educators Guide to Free Science Materials (1960-)
Educators Guide to Free Social Studies Materials (1961-)
Educators Guide to Media & Methods (1964-1969)
8 MM Collector (1962-1966)
Electronic Fun with Computers & Games (1982-)
Electronic Games (1982-1985)
The Eleven Magazine (1987-)
Emmy (1979-)
The Entertainment and Sports Lawyer (1982-)
Entertainment Law & Finance (1985-)
Entertainment Law Journal (1981)
Entertainment Law Reporter (1979-)
Entertainment Legal News (1983-1985)
Entertainment Weekly (1990-)
The Equipment Directory of Audio-visual, Computer and Video
    Products (1984-)

F./T.A.A.C. Newsletter (1988-)
Facets Features (1975-)
Facts, Figures & Film (1955?-1986)
Famous Monsters of Filmland (1958-)
Fandom Directory (1979-)
Fangoria (1979-)
Fantastic Films (1977-1984?)
FantaZone (1989-)
Favorite Westerns (1980?-1984)
Favorite Westerns, Serial World (1984-)
Fiber Optics Weekly Update (1981?-)
Field of Vision (1977-)
Filament (1981-)
Film (197u-)
Film & Broadcasting Review (1976-1980)
Film & History (1971-)
Film & Video Finder (1987-)
Film & Video News (1984-)
Film & Video Production (1983-)
Film Bulletin (1933-)
Film Collector's World (1978-1983)
Film Comment (1962-)
Film Criticism (1976-)
Film Culture (1955-)
Film File: Media Referral Service (1981/1982-1984/1985)
Film Heritage (1965-1977)
Film History (1987-)
Film in the Cities (197u-)
The Film Journal (1979-)
Film Library Quarterly (1967/68-1984)
Film Literature Index (1973-)
Film News (1939-1981)
Film News-International (1982-)
Film Producers, Studios & Agents Guide (1988-)
Film Quarterly (1958-)
Film Reader (1975-)
Film Review Annual (1981-)
Film Review Digest (1953-1967)
Film Society Newsletter (1955-1965)
Film Society Review (1965-1972)
Film Technology News (1986-)
Film Threat (1985-)
Film Writers Guide (1988-)

Filmfax (1986-)
The Filmlist (1965-1967)
Filmmakers (1978-1982)
Filmmakers Newsletter (1968-1978)
Films in Review (1950-)
Films of Yesteryear (1977-)
Flicker Film Journal (198u-)
Focus! (1967-1977?; 1990-)

'G.B.H. (1987-)
G.P.N. Newsletter (1974-)
Galaxy One Magazine (198u-)
Gambit (1970-1980)
Game Player's (1989-)
Gamepro (1989-)
Get Animated! Review (1989-)
Get Animated! Update (1986?-)
The Golden Years of Radio & T.V. (1987?-)
GoreZone (1988-)
Graffiti (1979-)
Great TV Entertainment (1980-l982)
Greater Amusements; America's Foremost Motion Picture Regional
    Trade Journal (1914-1965)
Greater Amusements and International Projectionist (1965-)
Guide to Free Computer Materials (1983-)

H.D.T.V. Review (1990-)
Hard Rock Video (1985-)
The Health Science Video Directory (1977-)
Hollywood Close-up (1958-)
Hollywood Quarterly (1945-1951)
The Hollywood Reporter (1930-)
Hollywood Reporter Studio Blu-Book Directory (1978-)
Hollywood Scriptwriter (1980-)
Hollywood Studio Magazine (1966-)
Home Satellite T.V. (1985-)
Home Shopping Investor (1986-)
Home Video Publisher: H.V.P. (1984-)
Home Viewer. The Monthly Video Program Guide (1981-)
Home Viewer's Official Video Software Directory Annual (1985-)
Hope Reports Briefing (1986-)
Hope Reports Industry Quarterly (1972-)
How-to Video (1987)

I.D.A. Directory (1984-)
I.E.E.E. Journal on Selected Areas in Communications (1983-)
I.E.E.E. Transactions on Broadcasting (1955-)
I.E.E.E. Transactions on Communications (1953-)
I.F.P. Newsletter (1979?-)
I.F.P.A. Communicator (1973-)
I.F.P.A. Newsletter (19uu-1972)
I.N.T.V. Journal (1987-)
I.N.T.V. Quarterly (1985-1986)
Image (1952-)
In Cinema (1980-)
In Focus (1989-)
In Motion (1982-)
In Plant (198u-)
The Independent (1979-)
The Independent (1937-1946)
The Independent Feature Project (1981-)
The Independent Film Journal (1946-1979)
Industrial Photography (1988-)
The Informer (198u-1986)
International Buyer's Guide (1970/71-)
International Communications Industries Association. Membership
    Directory (1984-)
International Documentary: The Newsletter of the International
    Documentary Association (1982-)
International Journal of Instructional Media (1973-)
International Motion Picture Almanac (1929-)
International Museum of Photography at George Eastman House
    Newsletter (1979-)
International Talent & Touring Directory (1981/82-)
International Television (1983-1986)
International Television Almanac (1956-1986)
International Television & Video Almanac (1987-)

Jewish Media Roundup (1977-1987)
Journal of Broadcasting & Electronic Media (1956/1957-)
Journal of Communication (1951-)
Journal of Educational Technology Systems (1972-)
Journal of Film and Video (1984-)
Journal of Mass Media Ethics (1985/1986-)
Journal of Popular Film (1972-1978)
Journal of Popular Film and Television (1978-)

The Journal of the Producers Guild of America (1967-)
Journal of the S.M.P.T.E. (1954-1975)
The Journal of the Screen Producers Guild (1952-1966)
Journal of the University Film and Video Association (1982-1983)
Journal of the University Film Association (1968-1981)
Journal of the University Film Producers Association (1949-1967)
JoyStik (1982-1988)
Jump Cut (1974-)

K.C.E.T. Magazine (1988-)
K.C.T.S. Magazine (1987-)
The Kagan Media Index (1987-)

The L.P.T.V. Report (1986-)
Lamp (1984-1986)
Landers Film Reviews (1960-)
The Laser Disc Newsletter (1984-)
Latest Composite Feature Release Schedule (1974-)
Legal Video Review (1985-)
Librarian's Video Review (1986/87-)
Lighting Dimensions (1977-)
Lightwave: The Journal of Fiber Optics (1984-)
Literature/Film Quarterly (1973-)
Loyola Entertainment Law Journal (1982-)

M.B. News (1977-)
Mad World Update (1985-)
Magill's Cinema Annual (1982-)
Marketing New Media (1984-)
Marquee (1969-)
The Mass Communication Bibliographers' Newsletter (1986-)
Matrix (1915-1980?)
The Mayberry Gazette (1985-)
Media & Methods (1969-)
Media & Values (1977-)
Media Arts (1982?-)
Media Business News (1987-)
Media Business Review (1987-)
Media Digest (1972-1985?)
Media Ethics Update (1988-)
Media History Digest (1980-)
Media Matters (1984?-)
Media Mergers & Acquisitions (1987-)

Nielsen National T.V. Ratings (1982-)
Nielsen Newscast (1961?-)
Nielsen Report on Television (1956-)
Nosotros Reporter (1970-)

The Off-Hollywood Report (1986-)
Official Video Directory & Buyers Guide (1987-)
On Cable (1980-)
On Film (1976-)
On Line at the Movies (1989-)
On Location (1977-1987)
On Location. The National Film & Videotape Production Directory
    (1977-1986/87)
Optical Information Systems (1986-)
Optical Information. Systems Update (1986-)
Orbit Video (1989-)

P.B.S. Video News (1986-)
P.R.C. News (1988-)
Pacific Coast Studio Directory (1920-)
Panorama (1980-)
The Pay TV Movie Log (198u-)
The Pay TV Newsletter (1971-)
The Perfect Vision (1986-)
Performing Arts Annual (1986-)
Perry's Broadcasting and the Law (1971-1984)
Persistence of Vision: The Journal of the Film Faculty of the
    City University of New York (1984-)
Photographic Trade News (1937-1987)
Photographic Video Trade News (1987-)
Photoplay (1911-1940; 1978-)
Photoplay Combined with Movie Mirror (1941-1977)
Photoplay With TV Mirror (1977-1978)
Post Script (1981-)
Pre-Production Newsletter (1988?-)
Premiere (Denver; 1980-)
Premiere (Hollywood; 1980-1981)
Premiere (New York; 1987-)
Preview; Program Guide to the A.F.I. Theater and Member Events
    (1979-)
Printed Matter (1974?-)
Pro/Comm (1981-1984)
The Producer's Masterguide (1983-)

Production Notes (198u-)
Productions-In-Progress (1987-)
The Professional Communicator (1985-)
Professional Film Production (1975-)
Public Broadcasting Report (1978-)
Public Telecommunications Letter (19uu-1980)
Public Television Transcripts Index (1987-)
The Publicists Guild Directory (1983-)

Quarterly of Film, Radio and Television (1951-1957)
Quarterly Review of Film and Video (1989-)
Quarterly Review of Film Studies (1976-1988)
Quarterly Update (1980-)
Quirk's Reviews (1972-)

R.T.S. Music Gazette (1973-)
Radio Video Era (1986-)
The Reel Directory (1979-)
The Reel Scoop (1987?-)
Reruns (1980-)
Respondex Movie Guide (1988-)
Review of the Arts: Film and Television (1975-)
Rock Video (1984-1985)
Rock Video Idols Magazine (1985)
Rod Serling's The Twilight Zone (1981-)
Ross Reports Television (1949-)

S.A.G. Hollywood Close-up (1980-)
S.M.A.T.V. News (1982-)
S.M.P.T.E. Journal (1976-)
Satellite Age (1983-)
Satellite Communications (1977-)
Satellite Dealer (1983-1986)
Satellite Direct (1987-)
Satellite Dish Magazine (1982-)
Satellite News (1978-)
Satellite Orbit (1982-)
Satellite Orbit International (1984-1985)
Satellite T.V. Opportunities Magazine (1983-)
Satellite T.V. Week (1982-)
The Satellite Telecommunications Newsletter (1979-1982)
Satellite Times (1986-)
Satellite Week (1979-)

Satellite World (1985-)
Science Books & Films (1975-)
Screen Achievement Records Bulletin (1976-1977)
Screen Actor (1959-)
Screen Actor News (1968-)
Screen Stars (1944-)
Screen World (1949-)
Scriptwriter (1980)
Scriptwriter News (1980-)
Serial World (1976?-1984)
Series, Serials & Packages (1949-1988)
Shakespeare on Film Newsletter (1976-)
Show Business (1949-)
Side Lights (1985-)
Sightlines (1967-)
Slaughter House Magazine (1989?-)
Soap Opera Digest (1976-)
Soap Opera People (1985-)
Soap Opera Stars (1975-)
Soap Opera Update (1988-)
Soap Opera's Greatest Stories & Stars (1976-)
Society of Cinematologists. Journal (1961/62-1964/65)
Society of Motion Picture and Television Engineers. Journal
    (1950-1953)
Society of Motion Picture Engineers. Journal (1930-1949)
Society of Motion Picture Engineers. Transactions (1916-1929)
Sound & Video Contractor: S. & V.C. (1983-)
Spectator (1988-)
Spiral (1984-1986)
Star (1977-)
Star Guide (1988/89-)
Star Trek: The Official Fan Club (1979?-)
Starlog (1976-)
Studies in the Humanities (1969-)
Studies in Visual Communication (1975-1985)

T.B.S. Transponder (1988-)
T.H.S. Newsletter (1979-)
T.I.P.S. Technical Information for Photographic Systems (1970-)
T.N.T. Program Guide (1988-)
T.V. and Movie Screen (1953-)
The T.V. Collector (1982-)
T.V. Contacts Updates (1977-)

T.V. Dimensions (1983-)
T.V. Entertainment Monthly (1989-)
T.V. Facts, Figures & Film (1986-)
T.V. Feature Film Source Book (1949-1988)
T.V. Game $how Magazine (1986-)
T.V. Game Show Stars (1985-)
T.V. Guide (1953-)
T.V. Host (1981-)
T.V. News (1977-)
T.V. Pro-Log (1949-)
T.V. Program Investor (1986-)
T.V. Star Annual (1955-)
T.V. Star Parade (1951-)
T.V. Technology (1983-)
T.V. Times (1990-)
T.V.R.O.: Satellite T.V. Week Dealer (1986-)
Take One (1986-)
The Talk Show Guest Directory (1985-1986)
Talk Show Guest Directory of Experts, Authorities & Spokespersons
    (1986/87)
Talk Show "Selects" (198u-)
Tech Photo Pro Imaging Systems (1988)
Technical Photography (1968-1988)
Teen Beat All-Stars (1976?-)
Teen Stars (1985-)
TeenSet (1984-)
Telecommunications Product Review (1973-)
Teleconferencing Resources Directory (1979-1986)
Telemedia (1983-)
Television Action Update (1982-)
Television & Cable Factbook (1945-)
Television & Children (1978-1984)
Television & Families (1985-)
Television Broadcast (1978-)
Television Contacts (1977-)
Television Digest with Consumer Electronics (1945-)
Television Index (1949-)
Television Index Network Futures (1949-)
Television International (1956-)
Television Network Movies (1973/74-)
Television News Index and Abstracts (1968-)
Television Programming Source Books (1989-)
Television Quarterly (1962-)

Television/Radio Age (1953-)
Televisions (1983?-)
13. Program Guide (1987-)
Tiger Beat (1965-)
Top Secret (1985-1986)
Topicator (1965-)
The Trainer's Resource (1981-)

Under Western Skies (1978-)

V Magazine (1987-)
The V.C.R. Letter (1984-1988)
V.Q.T.: Viewers for Quality Television (1985-)
Variety (1905-)
Variety's Complete Home Video Directory (1988-1989)
Variety's Complete Home Video Directory. Adult Video Supplement
    (1988-1989)
The Velvet Light Trap (1971-)
Via Satellite (1986-)
Video (1978-)
Video & Sound (1981-)
Video Age International (1981-)
Video Age International Newsletter (1982-)
Video and the Arts (1980-)
Video Business (1981-)
Video Choice (1988-)
Video Digest (1987-1988?)
Video Games (1982-)
Video Games Today (1982-1983?)
Video Insider (1983-)
Video Investor (1989-)
The Video Librarian (1986-)
Video Manager (1984-)
Video Marketplace (1987-)
Video Marketing Newsletter (1979?-)
Video Marketing Surveys and Forecasts (1983-)
Video Marketplace (1987-)
Video Monitor (1983-1988)
Video Movies (1984)
Video Rating Guide for Libraries (1990-)
The Video Register & Teleconferencing Resources Directory
    (1987-)
The Video Programs Retailer (1980-1982)

Wind Rose (1970?-)
The World of Bela Lugosi (1987-)
The World of Yesterday (1976-)
World Radio TV Handbook (1947-)
The Writers Guild of America, West Journal (1988-)

Young Viewers (1977-1988)

Uruguay

Cinemateca (1977-)
Cinemateca Revista (1977-)

Venezuela

Cine al Dia (1967-)
Visor (1974/75-)

West Germany

A.R.D. Fernsehspiel (195u-)
A.V. Praxis (1972-)
C.I.C.I.M.: Revue pour le Cinema Francais (1983?-)
Deutschen Institut fur Filmkunde. Information aus dem Deutschen
    Institut fur Filmkunde (1973-)
E.P.D. Film (1984-)
Fernseh- und Kino-Technik (1969-)
Das Fernsehspiel im Z.D.F. (1973?-)
Deutsche Kameramann (1952-1977)
Diskurs Film (1987-)
Film, Bild, Ton (1951-1971)
Film-Echo (1947-1962)
Film-Echo/Filmwoche (1962-)
Film Theory: Bibliographic Information and Newsletter (1983-)
Film & [i.e. und] Fakten (198u-)
Film & [i.e. und] T.V. Kameramann (1978-)
Film + [i.e. und] Ton-Magazin (1966-1981)
Filmfaust (1977-)
Der Film Kreis (1955-1965)
Filmkritik (1957-1984)

Jugoslavija Film News (1963-)
Katalog Jugoslovenskog Dokumentarnog I Kratkometraznog Filma
    (1960-)
The Yugoslav Film (1961-1963)

FILM PERIODICALS INDEX

A.F.I. Close-up
A.F.I. Education Newsletter
A.F.T. & T.
A.F.V.A. Bulletin / American Film and Video Association
A.S.I.F.A. Bulletin de l'Association Internationale du Film
   d'Animation, Canada
A.S.I.F.A. News
A.V. Business Communications
A.V. Praxis
Aamplitude
Academy Players Directory
Action (Canada)
Action! (U.S.)
L'Activite Cinematographique Francaise en C.N.C., Centre National
   de la Cinematographie
Adam Film World Guide
Adult Cinema Review
Advertising in Movies
Afterimage (U.K.)
Afterimage (U.S.)
Aktery Zarubezhnogo Kino
American Cinematographer
American Cinemeditor
American Classic Screen
American Film
American Movie Classics Magazine
American Museum of the Moving Image Newsletter
American Premiere
The American Screenwriter
American Widescreener

Andere Sinema
Animafilm. The Journal of Animated Film
Animation Magazine
Animato!
Animatographe
Animator (U.K.)
The Animator (U.S.)
L'Annee du Cinema
Annuaire du Cinema Francais et de L'Audiovisuel = Directory of
     the French Film and Audiovisual Industries
Annuaire du Cinema, Television, Video
Annuaire du Film Belge = Jaarboek van de Belgische Film
Annual Index to Motion Picture Credits
Anthologie du Cinema
Anuario del Cine
Archives
Art & Cinema
Art Murphy's Box Office Register
Artibus et Historiae
ArtsAmerica Fine Art Film and Video Source Book
Asian Cinema
Attualita Cinematografiche
Audience
Audio Video Market Place: A.V.M.P.
Audio Visual
Audio-Visual Communications
Audio-vizualis Kozlemenyek
AudioVideo Review Digest
Australian Films
The Australian Journal of Screen Theory
Australian Video and Communications
L'Avant-Scene Cinema

B.U.F.V.C. Catalogue
B Westerns in Perspective
Back Stage
Back Stage TV Film & Tape Production Directory
Beitrage zur Film- und Fernsehwissenschaft
Bianco e Nero
Bibliography: F.I.A.F. Members Publications = Bibliographie:
     Publications des Membres de la F.I.A.F.
The Big Reel
The Big Trail

Black Camera
Black Film Review
The Black Video Guide
Blimp. Zeitschrift fur Film
Boletim Informativo S.I.P.
Boxoffice
Bright Lights
British National Film & Video Catalogue
Bulgarian Films
Bullentin Finas
Bulletin, Calendar of International Film and Television Events =
    Bulletin, Calendrier des Evenements Internationaux du Cinema
    et de la Television
Bulletin for Film and Video Information
Bulletin K.F.T.: Media Karyawan Film dan Televisi Indonesia
The Bulletin of the Academy of Motion Picture Arts and Sciences
Bulletin of the Center for Soviet & East-European Studies
Bulletin on Film

C.F.F.S. Newsletter
C.F.S. Review
C.I.C.I.M. Revue pour le Cinema Francais
C.T.V.D. Cinema, TV Digest
Ca: Cinema
Les Cahiers de la Cinematheque
Cahiers du Cinema
Les Cahiers du Scenario = De Scenariogids = The Screenwriter's
    Companion
Calendar / University Art Museum
Camera Obscura
Camera/Stylo
Canadian Communications Network Letter
Canadian Film Digest Yearbook
Canadian Journal of Communication
Cantrill's Filmnotes
Captioned Films/Videos for the Deaf
Casablanca
Castoro Cinema, Il
Catalogue de la Production Cinematographique Francaise
Celebrity Bulletin
Celebrity Plus
Celuloide

Chaplin
Chia Ho Tien Ying
China Screen
Chitrabikshan
Christian Film & Video
Chung-hua Nein Kuo Tien Ying Nien Chien
Chung-kuo Tien Ying Nien Chien
Chung Wai Ying Hua
Ciak si Gira
Ciennepi
Cine
Cine al Dia
Cine Argentino
Cine Bulles
Cine Cubano
Cine Para Leer
Cine: Publicacion de la Compania de Fomento Cinematografico
Cine Qua Non
Cine 7
Cine-Tele-Revue
Cine-tracks
Cineaction!
Cineaste
Cinefan
Cinefantastique
Cinefex
Cineforum
Cinegrafie
Cinegram (Ann Arbor)
The Cinegram (Hollywood)
Cinejournal
Cinema (Canada)
Cinema (France)
Cinema (Italy)
Cinema (Portugal)
Cinema (Romania)
Cinema (Switzerland)
Cinema Canada
Cinema D'Oggi
Cinema e Cinema
Cinema em Close-up
Cinema Francais
Cinema Francais, Production

Cinewave
Classic Images
Cliffhanger
Close-Up (India)
Columbia Film View
Communications Booknotes
Communications Research
Comparative Literature and Film Studies
Conseil International du Cinema de la Television et de la
    Communication Audiovisuelle
Continuum: An Australian Journal of the Media
Contracampo
Copie Zero
La Cosa Vista
Critic
Critical Arts
The Cue Sheet
Cult Movie
Culture Statistics. Film Industry = Statistiques de la Culture
    L'Industrie du Film
Current Research in Film
The Czechoslovak Film

Daily Variety
Danish Films
Deep Focus
Deep Red
Denk Ajans
Deutschen Institut fur Filmkunde. Information aus dem Deutschen
    Institut fur Filmkunde
Les Deux Ecrans
Directory of Members. Directors Guild of America
Dirigido Por...
Discourse
Domitor
Dutch Film

E.P.D. Film
East-West Film Journal
L'Ecran Fantastique
Ecrits Sur le Cinema
Educational Technology
Educators Guide to Free Films

Film & Fakten
Film & History
Film & T.V. Kameramann
Film & T.V. World
Film and Television Yearbook
Film & Video Finder
Film & Video News
Film & Video Production
Film Bulletin
Film Canada Yearbook
Film Comment
Film Criticism
Film Culture
Film Directions
Film Dope
Film Echange
Film-Echo/Filmwoche
Film en Televisie + Video
Film File: Media Referral Service
Le Film Francais
Film Heritage
Film History
Film in the Cities
The Film Journal
Film Library Quarterly
Film Literature Index
Film Logbuch
Film Making
Film Monthly
Film News-International
Film og Kino
Film Producers, Studios & Agents Guide
Film Quarterly
Film Reader
Film Review Annual
Film Review Digest
Film Szinhaz Muzsika
Film Technology News
Film Theory: Bibliographic Information and Newsletter
Film Threat
Film Tutti i Film Della Stagione
Film und Fernsehen
Film/Video Canadiana

Framework
Frauen und Film

Get Animated! Update
Get Animated! Review
Giornale Dello Spettacolo
GoreZone
Graffiti
Grand Angle
Grand Maghreb
Greater Amusements and International Projectionist
Griffithiana
Guide to Wildlife, Science and Research Film-makers

Historical Journal of Film, Radio and Television
Hollywood Close-up
Hollywood Reporter Studio Blu-Book Directory
The Hollywood Reporter
Hollywood Scriptwriter
Hollywood Studio Magazine
Hors Cadre
Hungarofilm Bulletin

I.A.M.H.I.S.T. Newsletter
I.D.A. Directory
I.F.P. Newsletter
I.F.P.A. Communicator
Ikon: Ricerche Sulla Comunicazione
Illusions
Iluzjon
Image
Image Technology
Imagenes
Immagine
In Cinema
In Focus
In Motion
The Independent
The Independent Feature Project
Indian Cinema
Indian Film Culture
Industrial Photography

Kosmorama
Kultur Chronik

Lamp
Landers Film Reviews
Latest Composite Feature Release Schedule
Levende Billeder
Lighting Dimensions
Literature/Film Quarterly
Loyola Entertainment Law Journal

M.N.C. Museo Nazionale del Cinema
Macguffin
Mad World Update
Magill's Cinema Annual
Making Better Movies
Mannheimer Analytika = Mannheim Analytiques
Marquee. The Journal of the Theatre Historical Society
Media & Methods
Media Asia
Media Digest
Media Ethics Update
Media History Digest
Media in Education and Development
Media Magazine (Belgium)
Media Perspektiven
Media Review Digest
Mediactive
Mediafilm
MediaWatch Bulletin
Medien und Erziehung
Medien-Wissenschaft: Rezensionen
Medienforschung, Kommunikationspolitik und
    Kommunikationswissenschaft
Medium (W.Germany)
Medium (U.S.)
Membership Directory. Costume Designers Guild
Memories
Metro: Media and Education Magazine
Midnight Marquee
Millennium Film Journal
Millimeter
Mitteilungen des Osterreichischen Filmmuseums

Mitteilungen: Osterreichische Gesellschaft fur Filmwissenschaft
  Kommunikations- Und Medienforschung
Mnenya
Modern Screen
Le Moniteur du Film
Monthly Film Bulletin
Mother India
Motion Picture (Collective for Living Cinema; New York)
Motion Picture (Macfadden; New York)
The Motion Picture Guide Annual
Motion Picture Investor
Motion Picture Product Digest
Motion Picture, TV and Theatre Directory
Movement
Movie
Movie Collector's World
Movie Life
Movie Mirror
Movie/TV Marketing
Moviegoer
Movieline
Movies U.S.A.
Moving Image Review
Moviola

N.F.T. National Film Theatre
N.F.M. Programma
N.Y. Film Bulletin
Na Ekranakh Mira
National Film & Sound Archive Newsletter
National Gallery of Art Film Calendar
The New Magic Lantern Journal
The New York Center for Visual History Newsletter
New Zealand Film. New Zealand Film Commission
New Zealand Film & Television Directory
New Zealand Film Archive Newsletter
News From Women Make Movies
Nihon Eiga Kaigai Fukyu Kyokai
Nihon No Yushu Eiga
Nosotros Reporter
Novyny Kinoekrana

The Off-Hollywood Report
On Film
On Line at the Movies
On Location
On Location. The National Film & Videotape Production Directory
OnFilm
Opsis

Pacific Coast Studio Directory
Panorama (Czechoslovakia)
Patalogo. Cinema + Televisione + Video
The Pay TV Movie Log
The Perfect Vision
Perforations
Performing Arts Annual
Persistence of Vision: The Journal of the Film Faculty of the
    City University of New York
Photoplay
Picture House
Polish Film. Film Polonais
Positif; Revue de Cinema
Post Script
Prasen
Pre-Production Newsletter
Premiere (Denver)
Premiere (New York)
Preview; Program Guide to the A.F.I. Theater and Member Events
Printed Matter
Prisma; Kino-und Fernseh-Almanach
The Producer's Masterguide
Production Notes
Productions-In-Progress
The Professional Communicator
Professional Film Production
The Publicists Guild Directory

Quaderni del Cinema Italiano, I
Quaderni di Cinema
Quarterly Review of Film and Video
Quarterly Update
Qui Fait Quoi
Quirk's Reviews

Soundtrack! The Collector's Quarterly
Sovetsky Ekran
Soviet Film
Spectator
Spettacolo, Lo
Spielfilme im Ersten Deutschen Fernsehen
Spiral
Spleen
Star
Star Guide
Starlog
Stars
Statistisches Bundesant. Bildung und Kulture
Stills
Studies in the Humanities
Studies in Visual Communication
Stuffing
Swedish Films
Synchronos Kinematografos + Cinema Contemporain

T.H.S. Newsletter
T.I.P.S. Technical Information for Photographic Systems
Take One (Canada)
Take One (U.S.)
Teatro e Cinema
Teen Beat All-Stars
Teen Stars
TeenSet
Tele-media
Three Sixty
Tiger Beat
Time & Tide
Top Secret
Toronto Film Society Newsletter
The Trainer's Resource

Under Western Skies
Undercut
Unir Cinema

Variety
The Velvet Light Trap
Versus

TELEVISION PERIODICALS INDEX

A. & E. Cable Network Program Guide
A.B.C. News Index
A.B.U. Technical Review
A.E.J.M.C. News
A.F.T. & T.
A.I.T. Newsletter
A.R.D. Fernsehspiel
Academy Players Directory
Access
Action (Canada)
Action! (U.S.)
Airwaves
American Cinemeditor
American Movie Classics Magazine
American Museum of the Moving Image Newsletter
American Premiere
The American Screenwriter
Andere Sinema
Animator (U.K.)
Annuaire du Cinema Francais et de L'Audiovisuel = Directory of
    the French Film and Audiovisual Industries
Annuaire du Cinema, Television, Video
Annuaire du Film Belge = Jaarboek van de Belgische Film
Arbitron Television Audience Estimates
Asian Mass Communication Bulletin (A.M.C.B.)
Audience
Audio Video
Audio/Video Interiors
Audio-Visual Communications
Audio-vizualis Kozlemenyek

B.M.E. for Technical and Engineering Management
Back Stage
Back Stage TV Film & Tape Production Directory
Better Radio & Television
Bianco e Nero
Bibliography on Cable Television: B.C.T.V.
The Black Video Guide
Broadcast
Broadcast Banker/Broker
Broadcast Engineering
Broadcast Investor
Broadcast Investor Charts
Broadcast Pioneers Library Reports
Broadcast Programming & Production
Broadcast Stats
Broadcast Technology
Broadcaster
Broadcasting
Broadcasting and the Law
Broadcasting/Cable Yearbook
Bulletin, Calendar of International Film and Television Events =
    Bulletin, Calendrier des Evenements Internationaux du Cinema
    et de la Television
Bulletin K.F.T.: Media Karyawan Film dan Televisi Indonesia
Bulletin of the Center for Soviet & East-European Studies
Burrelle's Media Directory. TV Clips
Business Media Week
Business TV

C.B.S. News Index
C.P.B. Report
C.T.I.C. Cable Reports
C.T.V.D. Cinema, TV Digest
C-SPAN Update
Cable Action Update
Cable and Station Coverage Atlas and Zone Maps
Cable Communications Magazine
Cable Contacts Yearbook
Cable File
The Cable Guide
Cable Hotline
Cable Libraries
Cable Marketing

Continuum: An Australian Journal of the Media
Corporate Television
La Cosa Vista
Critic
Critical Arts
Current

Daily Variety
Daytime T.V.
Daytime T.V. Presents
Daytime T.V.'s Greatest Stories
Denk Ajans
Development Communication Report
Directory of Experts, Authorities & Spokespersons
Directory of International Broadcasting
Directory of Members. Directors Guild of America
The Directory of Religious Broadcasting
Discourse
The Discovery Channel: T.D.C.
Discovery In Focus
The Disney Channel Magazine
Downlink Directory

E.B.U. Review
E.-I.T.V. Magazine
Eiga Terebi Gijutsu
Eikonos
Ekran
Ekran; Kino TV Video
The Eleven Magazine
Emmy
Encore
The Entertainment and Sports Lawyer
Entertainment Law & Finance
Entertainment Law Reporter
Entertainment Weekly
Eyepiece

F.I.A.T./I.F.T.A. Bulletin
F./T.A.A.C. Newsletter
Famous Monsters of Filmland
Fantastic Films
FantaZone

H.D.T.V. Review
Historical Journal of Film, Radio and Television
The Hollywood Reporter
Hollywood Reporter Studio Blu-Book Directory
Hollywood Scriptwriter
Home Satellite T.V.
Horfunk und Fernsehen

I.A.M.H.I.S.T. Newsletter
I.E.E.E. Journal on Selected Areas in Communications
I.E.E.E. Transactions on Broadcasting
I.E.E.E. Transactions on Communications
I.N.T.V. Journal
Ikon: Ricerche Sulla Comunicazione
Illusions
Imagenes
In Motion
Infocus: Academy of Canadian Cinema & Television
Interfilm Reports
InterMedia
International Index to Television Periodicals
International T.V. & Video Guide
International Television & Video Almanac
Invision

Journal of Broadcasting & Electronic Media
Journal of Communication
Journal of Mass Media Ethics
Journal of Popular Film and Television
The Journal of the Producers Guild of America

K.C.E.T. Magazine
K.C.T.S. Magazine
Kemp's International Film & Television Year Book
Kino (Poland)
Kino; Obrazkovy Filmovy Crtnactidenik
Kultur Chronik

The L.P.T.V. Report
Levende Billeder
Lighting Dimensions
Lightwave: The Journal of Fiber Optics

The Listener
Loyola Entertainment Law Journal

M.B. News
Mannheimer Analytika = Mannheim Analytiques
The Mass Communication Bibliographers' Newsletter
The Mayberry Gazette
Media & Values
Media Asia
Media Business News
Media Business Review
Media, Culture & Society
Media Digest
Media Ethics Update
Media History Digest
Media in Education and Development
Media Information Australia
Media Magazine (Belgium)
Media Magazine (Canada)
Media Matters
Media Mergers & Acquisitions
Media Monitor
Media Perspektiven
Media Relations/Video Monitor
Media Sports Business
Media Watch
Mediafilm
MediaWatch
MediaWatch Bulletin. Evaluation-Medias
Medien Bulletin
Medien-Wissenschaft: Rezensionen
Medienforschung, Kommunikationspolitik und
    Kommunikationswissenschaft
Medium
Medium. Jewish Uses of the Media
Membership Directory. Costume Designers Guild
Millimeter
Modern Screen
Le Moniteur du Film
Mother India
Motion Picture, TV and Theatre Directory
Movie Collector's World
Movie Life

Movie Mirror
Movie/TV Marketing
Multicast
Multichannel News

N.B.C. Television Network Advance Program Schedule &
    Supplement
Neue Medien
New Media Markets
New Zealand Film & Television Directory
New Zealand Film Archive Newsletter
Nielsen National T.V. Ratings
Nielsen Newscast
Nielsen Report on Television
Nosotros Reporter
Number Six

On Cable
On Location
On Location. The National Film & Videotape Production
    Directory
OnFilm

P.B.S. Video News
Pacific Coast Studio Directory
Panorama
Patalogo. Cinema + Televisione + Video
The Pay TV Movie Log
The Pay TV Newsletter
The Perfect Vision
Performing Arts Annual
Pre-Production Newsletter
Prisma; Kino-und Fernseh-Almanach
Productions-In-Progress
The Professional Communicator
Professional Film Production
Public Broadcasting Report
Public Television Transcripts Index
The Publicists Guild Directory

Quaderni del Cinema Italiano, I
Qui Fait Quoi

Sightlines
Skrien
Soap Opera Digest
Soap Opera People
Soap Opera Stars
Soap Opera Update
Soap Opera's Greatest Stories & Stars
Sound & Video Contractor: S. & V.C.
Soundtrack! The Collector's Quarterly
Spectator
Spettacolo, Lo
Spielfilme im Ersten Deutschen Fernsehen
The Stage and Television Today
Star
Star Guide
Star Trek: The Official Fan Club
Starlog
Stills
Studies in Broadcasting
Studies in the Humanities
Studies in Visual Communication

T.B.I. Television Business International
T.B.S. Transponder
T.N.T. Program Guide
T.V. and Movie Screen
The T.V. Collector
T.V. Contacts Updates
T.V. Dimensions
T.V. Entertainment Monthly
T.V. Facts, Figures & Film
T.V. Game $how Magazine
T.V. Game Show Stars
T.V. Guide
T.V. Horen und Sehen
T.V. Host
T.V. News
T.V. Pro-Log
T.V. Program Investor
T.V. Star Annual
T.V. Star Parade
T.V. Technology
T.V. Times (U.K.)

Video Age International Newsletter
Video Choice
Video Investor
Video Review
Video Shopper
Visor

W.E.T.A. Magazine
W.J.R. Washington Journalism Review
W.R.T.H. Downlink
W.T.N. Worldwide Television News
The Western Film
What's On Video and Cinema
Who's Who in Entertainment
Who's Who in Television
Wide Angle
The World of Yesterday
World Radio TV Handbook
The Writers Guild of America, West Journal

Young Viewers

VIDEO PERIODICALS INDEX

A.F.V.A. Bulletin
A.S.I.F.A. Bulletin de l'Association Internationale du Film
  d'Animation, Canada
A.S.I.F.A. News
A.V. Business Communications
A.V. Praxis
A.V. Video
Aamplitude
Adam Film World Guide
Adult Cinema Review
Adult Video News
Afterimage (U.S)
American Museum of the Moving Image Newsletter
Andere Sinema
Animafilm. The Journal of Animated Film
Animation Magazine
Animato!
Animatographe
The Animator
Annuaire du Cinema Francais et de L'Audiovisuel = Directory of
  the French Film and Audiovisual Industries
Annuaire du Cinema, Television, Video
Art & Cinema
ArtsAmerica Fine Art Film and Video Source Book
Asian Cinema
Audio Video Market Place: A.V.M.P.
Audio Video
Audio/Video Interiors
Audio Visual
Audio-vizualis Kozlemenyek
AudioVideo International

AudioVideo Review Digest
Australian Films

B.U.F.V.C. Catalogue
The Big Reel
Billboard
Black Camera
The Black Video Guide
Bowker's Complete Video Directory
British National Film & Video Catalogue
Broadcast Engineering
Bulletin, Calendar of International Film and Television Events =
    Bulletin, Calendrier des Evenements Internationaux du
    Cinema et de la Television
Bulletin for Film and Video Information
Business Media Week

C.D.-1 News
C.D. Data Report
C.D.-ROM Librarian
Canadian Film Digest Yearbook
Canadian Journal of Communication
Captioned Films/Videos for the Deaf
CD-ROM Enduser
Children's Video Report
Children's Video Review Newsletter
Christian Film & Video
Cine 7
Cinefex
Cinegram
Cinejournal
The Cinema Papers Australian Production Yearbook: Film,
    Television, Video
Cinema Technology
Cinemacabre
Cinemagic
Cinematograph
Cinemateca Revista
CineVue
Classic Images
Communications and the Law
Communications Daily
Communications Research

G.P.N. Newsletter
Game Player's
Gamepro
Get Animated! Update
Get Animated! Review
GoreZone
Graffiti
Guide to Wildlife, Science and Research Film-makers

Hard Rock Video
The Health Science Video Directory
Home Video Publisher: H.V.P.
Home Viewer. The Monthly Video Program Guide
Home Viewer's Official Video Software Directory Annual
Hope Reports Industry Quarterly
Hope Reports Briefing
How-to Video

I.D.A. Directory
I.F.P.A. Communicator
Image Technology
In Motion
In Plant
The Independent
Industrial Photography
Informations C.N.C.
Interfilm Reports
International Buyer's Guide
International Communications Industries Association. Membership
    Directory
International Documentary: The Newsletter of the International
    Documentary Association
International Journal of Micrographics and Video Technology
International Journal of Instructional Media
International T.V. & Video Guide
International Talent & Touring Directory
International Television & Video Almanac

Jeune Cinema
Journal of Film and Video
Journal of Broadcasting & Electronic Media
Journal of Educational Technology Systems
JoyStik

Optical Information: Systems Update
Orbit Video

P.R.C. News
Patalogo. Cinema + Televisione + Video
The Perfect Vision
Perforations
Photographic Video Trade News
PhotoVideo
Premiere (New York)
Printed Matter
The Producer's Masterguide
Professional Film Production

Quarterly Review of Film and Video
Quarterly Update. National Archives and Records Administration
Qui Fait Quoi

Radio Video Era
The Reel Directory
The Reel Scoop
Reel West Digest
Reel West Magazine
Respondex Movie Guide
Rundfunk und Fernsehen

S.C.A.D. Bulletin Radio-TV-Film Supplement
Satellite Week
Science Books & Films
Screen Finance
Shakespeare on Film Newsletter
Side Lights
Sightlines
Skrien
Sound & Video Contractor: S. & V.C.
Spettacolo, Lo
Spiral
Studio Magazin
Stuffing

T.V. World
Telecommunications Product Review
Topicator

Videogaming & Computergaming Illustrated
Videography
Videolog
VideoMagazin
Videomaker
Videomania Magazine
The Videophile
Videotex Now
Vidiot
Visual Anthropology
Visual Media = Medias Visuels

W.T.N. Worldwide Television News
What's On Video and Cinema
Wind Rose

Young Viewers

POPULAR / COLLECTOR / FAN PERIODICALS INDEX

A. & E. Cable Network Program Guide
A.R.D. Fernsehspiel
Adult Cinema Review
Adult Video News
Aktery Zarubezhnogo Kino
American Classic Screen
American Film
American Movie Classics Magazine
American Premiere
Andere Sinema
Animato!
Australian Video and Communications

B Westerns in Perspective
The Big Reel
The Big Trail
Bright Lights
Bulgarian Films

The Cable Guide
Cahiers du Cinema
Casablanca
Celebrity Plus
Celuloide
Channel Guide
Chaplin
Chia Ho Tien Ying
China Screen
Chung Wai Ying Hua
Ciak si Gira
Cine al Dia

Cine Cubano
Cine: Publicacion de la Compania de Fomento Cinematografico
Cine 7
Cine-Tele-Revue
Cinefan
Cinefantastique
Cinegram (Ann Arbor)
Cinema (France)
Cinema (Romania)
Cinema Canada
Cinema em Close-up
Cinema India-International
Cinema News
Cinema Papers
Cinema the World Over
Cinema 2002
Cinemacabre
Cinemagic
Cinemasessanta
Cinemascore
Cinemateca (Colombia)
Cinemateca (Uruguay)
Cinemateca Revista
Cinematheque (Jerusalem)
Cinematheque (Tel Aviv)
La Cinematheque Suisse
Cinematographe
Cinemaya
CineMotion
Classic Images
Classic T.V.
Cliffhanger
Computer Entertainment
Computer Games
Contracampo
The Czechoslovak Film

Daytime T.V.
Daytime T.V. Presents
Daytime T.V.'s Greatest Stories
Deep Red
Denk Ajans
Les Deux Ecrans

Films of Yesteryear
Films On Screen and Video
Filmski Svet
Filmspiegel
Filmviews
Filmwoche
Filmworld
Flicker Film Journal
Formato Dieciseis

G.B.C. Radio and TV Times
Galaxy One Magazine
Game Player's
Gamepro
Get Animated! Review
The Golden Years of Radio & T.V.
GoreZone
Grand Angle

Hard Rock Video
Hollywood Close-up
Hollywood Studio Magazine
Home Viewer. The Monthly Video Program Guide
Hungarofilm Bulletin

In Cinema
The Informer

Journal of Popular Film and Television
Jugoslavija Film News

Kino (Poland)
Kino (U.S.S.R.)
Kino: Filme der Bundesrepublik Deutschland
Kino; German Film
Kino; Obrazkovy Filmovy Crtnactidenik
Kinorabotnik
Kolnoa
Kosmorama

The Laser Disc Newsletter
Levende Billeder
The Listener

La Revue du Cinema/Image et Son
Rod Serling's The Twilight Zone
The Romanian Film

Satellite Dish Magazine
Satellite T.V. Week
Scandinavian Film News
Screen Stars
Sequences
Skoop/Kritisch Filmforum
Skrien
Slaughter House Magazine
Soap Opera Digest
Soap Opera People
Soap Opera Stars
Soap Opera Update
Soap Opera's Greatest Stories & Stars
Soundtrack! The Collector's Quarterly
Soviet Film
Star
Star Trek: The Official Fan Club
Starlog
Stuffing
Synchronos Kinematografos + Cinema Contemporain

T.N.T. Program Guide
T.V. and Movie Screen
The T.V. Collector
T.V. Entertainment Monthly
T.V. Game $how Magazine
T.V. Game Show Stars
T.V. Guide
T.V. Horen und Sehen
T.V. Host
T.V. Star Annual
T.V. Star Parade
T.V. Times (U.K.)
T.V. Times (U.S.)
Take One (Canada)
Teen Beat All-Stars
Teen Stars
TeenSet
Televidenie, Radioveshchanie

SCHOLARLY / EDUCATIONAL PERIODICALS INDEX

A.B.C. News Index
A.E.J.M.C. News
A.F.I. Education Newsletter
A.F.V.A. Bulletin
A.I.T. Newsletter
A.V. Praxis
Aamplitude
Afterimage (U.K.)
American Film
Animatographe
Animator
Annual Index to Motion Picture Credits
Anthologie du Cinema
Archives
Art & Cinema
Artibus et Historiae
ArtsAmerica Fine Art Film and Video Source Book
Asian Cinema
Asian Mass Communication Bulletin (A.M.C.B.)
Audience
Audio Visual
Audio-vizualis Kozlemenyek
AudioVideo Review Digest
The Australian Journal of Screen Theory
L'Avant-Scene Cinema

B.U.F.V.C. Catalogue
Beitrage zur Film- und Fernsehwissenschaft
Better Radio & Television
Bianco e Nero
Bibliography on Cable Television: B.C.T.V.

Bianco e Nero
Bibliography on Cable Television: B.C.T.V.
Black Camera
Black Film Review
Blimp. Zeitschrift fur Film
Bowker's Complete Video Directory
British National Film & Video Catalogue
Broadcasting and the Law
Bulletin of the Center for Soviet & East-European Studies

C.B.S. News Index
C.F.S. Review
C.I.C.I.M. Revue pour le Cinema Francais
C.T.V.D. Cinema, TV Digest
C-SPAN Update
Ca: Cinema
Cable Libraries
Cable T.V. Advertising
Cable T.V. Law Reporter
Les Cahiers de la Cinematheque
Cahiers du Cinema
Les Cahiers du Scenario = De Scenariogids = The Screenwriter's
    Companion
Camera Obscura
Camera/Stylo
Canadian Journal of Communication
Cantrill's Filmnotes
Captioned Films/Videos for the Deaf
Carnegie Institute Travel Sheet
Castoro Cinema, Il
Chaplin
Children's Video Report
Children's Video Review Newsletter
Chitrabikshan
Ciennepi
Cine
Cine Qua Non
Cine-tracks
Cineaction!
Cineaste
Cineforum
Cinegrafie
Cinejournal

Educators Guide to Free Filmstrips and Slides
Educators Guide to Free Guidance Materials
Educators Guide to Free Health, Physical Educational and
    Recreation Materials
Educators Guide to Free Home Economics Materials
Educators Guide to Free Science Materials
Educators Guide to Free Social Studies Materials
Eigashi Kenkyu
1895: Bulletin de L'Association Francaise de Recherche sur
    L'Histoire du Cinema
The Entertainment and Sports Lawyer
Entertainment Law Reporter
Etudes Cinematographiques

Field of Vision
Filament
Film A Doba; Mesicnik pro Filmovou Kulturu
Film & History
Film & Video Finder
Film & Video News
Film Comment
Film Criticism
Film Culture
Film Directions
Film Dope
Film Echange
Film-Echo/Filmwoche
Film Heritage
Film History
Film Library Quarterly
Film Literature Index
Film Quarterly
Film Reader
Film Review Annual
Film Review Digest
Film Theory: Bibliographic Information and Newsletter
Film Tutti i Film Della Stagione
Filmbulletin
Filmcritica
Filme Cultura
Filmhaftet
Filmkritik
Filmkultura

Jeune Cinema
Journal of Broadcasting & Electronic Media
Journal of Communication
Journal of Educational Technology Systems
Journal of Film and Video
Journal of Mass Media Ethics
Journal of Popular Film and Television
Jump Cut

Kinematograph
Kino i Vreme
Kino i Vremia
Kinoizkustvo
Kosmorama

Lamp
Landers Film Reviews
Legal Video Review
Levende Billeder
Librarian's Video Review
Literature/Film Quarterly
Loyola Entertainment Law Journal

Macguffin
Magill's Cinema Annual
Mannheimer Analytika = Mannheim Analytiques
Marquee. The Journal of the Theatre Historical Society
The Mass Communication Bibliographers' Newsletter
Media & Methods
Media & Values
Media Arts
Media Asia
Media, Culture & Society
Media Ethics Update
Media History Digest
Media in Education and Development
Media Information Australia
Media Monitor
Media Perspektiven
Media Review Digest
Mediafilm
Medien und Erziehung
Medien-Wissenschaft: Rezensionen

Science Books & Films
Screen Incorporating Screen Education
Script
Segnocinema
Sequence
Sequences. Revue de Cinema
Shakespeare on Film Newsletter
Sight and Sound
Sightlines
Skoop/Kritisch Filmforum
Skrien
Soundtrack! The Collector's Quarterly
Spectator
Spettacolo, Lo
Spleen
Stars
Stills
Studies in Broadcasting
Studies in the Humanities
Studies in Visual Communication
Synchronos Kinematografos + Cinema Contemporain

T.H.S. Newsletter
T.V. World
Teatro e Cinema
Television & Families
Television News Index and Abstracts
Television Quarterly
The Third Channel
Topicator
The Trainer's Resource

Undercut

The Velvet Light Trap
Versus
Vertigo
Video and the Arts
The Video Librarian
Video Rating Guide for Libraries
Video Review
24 Images (Spelled as Vingt-Quatre Images)
Visual Anthropology

Visual Media = Medias Visuels

W.J.R. Washington Journalism Review
Wide Angle

Young/Jeune Cinema & Theatre
Young Viewers

Z: Filmtidsskrift
Zelluloid

TECHNICAL / PROFESSIONAL PERIODICALS INDEX

A.B.U. Technical Review
A.S.I.F.A. Bulletin de l'Association Internationale du Film
d'Animation, Canada
A.S.I.F.A. News
A.V. Business Communications
A.V. Video
Academy Players Directory
Access
Action (Canada)
Action! (U.S.)
L'Activite Cinematographique Francaise en C.N.C., Centre
National de la Cinematographie
Advertising in Movies
Afterimage (U.S.)
Airwaves
American Cinematographer
American Cinemeditor
The American Screenwriter
American Widescreener
Animafilm. The Journal of Animated Film
Animation Magazine
L'Annee du Cinema
Annuaire du Cinema Francais et de L'Audiovisuel = Directory of
the French Film and Audiovisual Industries
Annuaire du Cinema, Television, Video
Annuaire du Film Belge = Jaarboek van de Belgische Film
Anuario del Cine
Arbitron Television Audience Estimates
Art Murphy's Box Office Register
Attualita Cinematografiche
Audio Video

Audio/Video Interiors
Audio Video Market Place: A.V.M.P.
Audio-Visual Communications
AudioVideo International
Australian Films

B.M.E. for Technical and Engineering Management
Back Stage
Back Stage TV Film & Tape Production Directory
Bibliography: F.I.A.F. Members Publications = Bibliographie:
    Publications des Membres de la F.I.A.F.
Billboard
The Black Video Guide
Boletim Informativo S.I.P.
Boxoffice
Broadcast
Broadcast Banker/Broker
Broadcast Engineering
Broadcast Investor
Broadcast Investor Charts
Broadcast Pioneers Library Reports
Broadcast Programming & Production
Broadcast Stats
Broadcast Technology
Broadcaster
Broadcasting
Broadcasting/Cable Yearbook
Bullentin Finas
Bulletin, Calendar of International Film and Television Events =
    Bulletin, Calendrier des Evenements Internationaux du Cinema
    et de la Television
Bulletin K.F.T.: Media Karyawan Film dan Televisi Indonesia
The Bulletin of the Academy of Motion Picture Arts and Sciences
Burrelle's Media Directory. TV Clips
Business Media Week
Business TV

C.D. Data Report
C.D.-1 News
C.D.-ROM Enduser
C.D.-ROM Librarian
C.P.B. Report
C.T.I.C. Cable Reports

Combroad
Communications and the Law
Communications Daily
COMSAT Technical Review
Conseil International du Cinema de la Television et de la
    Communication Audiovisuelle
Corporate Television
Corporate Video Decisions
Culture Statistics. Film Industry = Statistiques de la Culture
    L'Industrie du Film
Current

Daily Variety
Danish Films
Deutschen Institut fur Filmkunde. Information aus dem Deutschen
    Institut fur Filmkunde
Directory of Experts, Authorities & Spokespersons
Directory of International Broadcasting
Directory of Members. Directors Guild of America
The Directory of Religious Broadcasting
Downlink Directory
Dutch Film

E.B.U. Review
E.-I.T.V. Magazine
Eiga Mokuroku
Eiga Terebi Gijutsu
Eigakan Meibo
Emmy
Encore
Entertainment Law & Finance
The Equipment Directory of Audio-visual, Computer and Video
    Products
Eyepiece

F.I.A.F. Bulletin
F.I.A.T./I.F.T.A. Bulletin
F./T.A.A.C. Newsletter
Fernseh- und Kino-Technik
Fiber Optics Weekly Update
Film & T.V. Kameramann
Film & T.V. World
Film and Television Yearbook

I.E.E.E. Transactions on Communications
I.F.P. Newsletter
I.F.P.A. Communicator
I.N.T.V. Journal
Image
Image Technology
In Motion
In Plant
The Independent Feature Project
Industrial Photography
Industrial Screen
Infocus: Academy of Canadian Cinema & Television
Informations C.N.C.
International Buyer's Guide
International Communications Industries Association. Membership
    Directory
International Documentary: The Newsletter of the International
    Documentary Association
International Film Guide
International Journal of Micrographics and Video Technology
International Motion Picture Almanac
International T.V. & Video Guide
International Talent & Touring Directory
International Television & Video Almanac
Invision
Iskusstvo Kino

The Journal of the Producers Guild of America

Kabel & Satellit
The Kagan Media Index
Katalog Jugoslovenskog Dokumentarnog I Kratkometraznog Filma
Kemp's International Film & Television Year Book
Kino: Filme der Bundesrepublik Deutschland
Korea Cinema

The L.P.T.V. Report
Latest Composite Feature Release Schedule
Lighting Dimensions
Lightwave: The Journal of Fiber Optics

Making Better Movies
Marketing New Media

Photographic Video Trade News
PhotoVideo
Polish Film. Film Polonais
Pre-Production Newsletter
Prisma; Kino-und Fernseh-Almanach
The Producer's Masterguide
Production Notes
Productions-In-Progress
The Professional Communicator
Professional Film Production
Public Broadcasting Report
The Publicists Guild Directory

Qui Fait Quoi

Radio Video Era
Reel West Digest
Respondex Movie Guide
Ross Reports Television
Rundfunktechnische Mitteilungen

The S.A.F.T.T.A. Journal
S.A.G. Hollywood Close-up
S.C.A.D. Bulletin Radio-TV-Film Supplement
S.M.A.T.V. News
S.M.P.T.E. Journal
Satellite Age
Satellite Communications
Satellite Direct
Satellite News
Satellite Orbit
Satellite TV Opportunities Magazine
Satellite Technology
Satellite Times
Satellite Week
Satellite World
Schweizer Filmindex = Index Suisse du Cinema = Indice Svizzero
    del Cinema
Screen Actor
Screen Actor News
Screen Digest
Screen Finance
Screen International

Televisual

Variety
Via Satellite
Video Age International
Video Age International Newsletter
Video & Sound
Video Business
Video Insider
Video Investor
Video Manager
Video Marketing Newsletter
Video Marketing Surveys and Forecasts
The Video Register & Teleconferencing Resources Directory
The Video Retailer
Video Software Dealer
The Video Source Book
Video Store
Video Systems
Video Technology Newsletter
Video Trade News
Video Week
VIDEOaktiv
The Videodisc Monitor
Videofax
Videography
Videolog
Videomaker
Videotex Now
Visions (Canada)
Visor

W.R.T.H. Downlink
Who's Who in Entertainment
Who's Who in Television
Who's Who in the Motion Picture Industry
World Radio TV Handbook
The Writers Guild of America, West Journal

ANNUALS INDEX

A.B.C. News Index
Academy Players Directory
L'Activite Cinematographique Francaise en C.N.C., Centre
    National de la Cinematographie
Adam Film World Guide. Adam Film World Directory of Adult
    Films
L'Annee du Cinema
Annuaire du Cinema Francais et de L'Audiovisuel = Directory of
    the French Film and Audiovisual Industries
Annuaire du Cinema, Television, Video
Annuaire du Film Belge = Jaarboek van de Belgische Film
Annual Index to Motion Picture Credits
Anuario del Cine
Art Murphy's Box Office Register
ArtsAmerica Fine Art Film and Video Source Book
Attualita Cinematografiche
Audio Video Market Place: A.V.M.P.
Australian Films

B.U.F.V.C. Catalogue
Back Stage TV Film & Tape Production Directory
Bibliography: F.I.A.F. Members Publications = Bibliographie:
    Publications des Membres de la F.I.A.F.
Bibliography on Cable Television: B.C.T.V.
The Black Video Guide
Boletim Informativo S.I.P.
Bowker's Complete Video Directory
Broadcasting/Cable Yearbook
Bulletin, Calendar of International Film and Television Events =
    Bulletin, Calendrier des Evenements Internationaux du Cinema
    et de la Television

C.B.S. News Index
Cable and Station Coverage Atlas and Zone Maps
Cable Contacts Yearbook
Cable File
The Cable T.V. Financial Databook
Canadian Film Digest Yearbook
Captioned Films/Videos for the Deaf
Catalogue de la Production Cinematographique Francaise
Chung-hua Nein Kuo Tien Ying Nien Chien
Chung-kuo Tien Ying Nien Chien
Cine Argentino
Cine Para Leer
Cinema (Italy)
Cinema (Switzerland)
Cinema Francais, Production
The Cinema Papers Australian Production Yearbook: Film,
    Television, Video
Cinemas
Cinematographers, Production Designers, Costume Designers &
    Film Editors Guide
Cineteca Nacional Mexico
Comparative Literature and Film Studies
Culture Statistics. Film Industry = Statistiques de la Culture
    L'Industrie du Film
Current Research in Film

Danish Films
Directory of Experts, Authorities & Spokespersons
Directory of International Broadcasting
Directory of Members. Directors Guild of America
The Directory of Religious Broadcasting
Diskurs Film
Downlink Directory
Dutch Film

Educators Guide to Free Audio and Video Materials
Educators Guide to Free Films
Educators Guide to Free Filmstrips and Slides
Educators Guide to Free Guidance Materials
Educators Guide to Free Health, Physical Educational and
    Recreation Materials
Educators Guide to Free Home Economics Materials
Educators Guide to Free Science Materials

Katalog Jugoslovenskog Dokumentarnog I Kratkometraznog Filma
Kemp's International Film & Television Year Book
Kino i Vremia
Korea Cinema

Landers Film Reviews

Magill's Cinema Annual
Media Review Digest
Membership Directory. Costume Designers Guild
The Motion Picture Guide Annual

Na Ekranakh Mira
New Zealand Film & Television Directory
Nielsen Report on Television
Nihon No Yushu Eiga

Official Video Directory & Buyers Guide
On Location. The National Film & Videotape Production
    Directory

Patalogo. Cinema + Televisione + Video
Performing Arts Annual
Prisma; Kino-und Fernseh-Almanach
The Producer's Masterguide
Public Television Transcripts Index
The Publicists Guild Directory

Recueil des Films
The Reel Directory
Reel West Digest

Schweizer Filmindex = Index Suisse du Cinema = Indice Svizzero
    del Cinema
Screen International Film and Television Yearbook
Screen World
Showcall
Spielfilme im Ersten Deutschen Fernsehen
Star Guide
Statistisches Bundesant
Studies in Broadcasting
Swedish Films

Television & Cable Factbook
Television Contacts
Television Network Movies
Television Programming Source Books
The Trainer's Resource

The Video Register & Teleconferencing Resources Directory
The Video Source Book
The Video Tape & Disc Guide to Home Entertainment
Visor

Who's Who in Entertainment
Who's Who in Television
Who's Who in the Motion Picture Industry
World Radio TV Handbook